SELF-GUIDED
Italy

SELF-GUIDED
Italy

With 75 illustrations and photographs;
61 maps in color and black and white

LANGENSCHEIDT PUBLISHERS, NEW YORK

Publisher:	Langenscheidt Publishers, Inc.
Managing Editor:	Lisa Checchi Ross
U.S. Editorial Adaptation:	John Albright, Stephen Brewer, Gertrude Buchman, Tad Gast, Barbara Hults, Lenore Malen, Donald S. Olson, Janet Piroco
U.S. Editorial Staff:	Maria Caliandro, Dana Schwartz
Cartography:	Franz Huber, Gert Oberländer; Adaptations by Polyglott-Redaktion
Illustrations:	Vera Solymosi-Thurzó
Cover Design:	Diane Wagner
Cover Photograph:	Image Bank, Munich, W. Germany
Text Design:	Irving Perkins Associates
Production:	Ripinsky & Company
Photographs:	No. 1, Image Bank, Munich, W. Germany (Gordon); No. 2, No. 3, Heidi Weidner; No. 4, Eugen-Egon Hüsler; No. 5, No. 6, Heidi Weidner; No. 7, No. 8, No. 9, No. 10, Bavaria, Munich, W. Germany (Picture Finders), No. 11, Bavaria (Mu. H.), No. 12, Bavaria (Barone); No. 13, Marlis Kappelhoff
Translation:	Translation Company of America
Original German Text:	Dr. Hans Lajta (author); Polyglott-Redaktion (editorial)
Letters:	We welcome your comments and suggestions. Our address: Langenscheidt Publishers, Inc., 46–35 54th Rd., Maspeth, N.Y. 11378.

Contents

PRACTICAL INFORMATION   329

Foreword

Twenty-five hundred years of art and architecture cast a potent spell on modern travellers to Italy; the debt owed by Western civilization to ancient Rome and the Italian Renaissance is apparent at almost every footstep. Yet this unparalleled cultural treasury merely forms a backdrop to the charm and vibrancy of an exciting modern nation—equally known for the warmth of its people, ingenuity of its modern designs, and distinctive flavors of its regional cuisines.

Langenscheidt's *Self-Guided Italy* lets you explore this wondrous country at your own pace, be it whirlwind or leisurely. Pick and choose from the best of Classical, Renaissance, and contemporary Italy along our 24 Travel Routes, crisscrossing the countryside, and our Walking Tours of major cities. Whether your road leads to Rome or from Rome— or ignores Rome altogether—*Self-Guided Italy* will help you enjoy the country at its fullest.

Self-Guided Tours

The heart of this book is its self-guided tours, written especially for seasoned travellers by writers who specialize in the areas they cover. Walking tours of each major city describe all important sites and put them in historical perspective. Travel routes connect major cities and other areas of interest, covering many fascinating and beautiful areas of the countryside. Detailed maps outline every route.

Because many travellers begin in Rome, we begin our tours with a selective guide to Rome and sights outside the city. In addition, there are walking tours of Milan, Florence, Venice, and Naples. Our 24 Travel Routes cover the most scenic and interesting areas between major cities; taking in regions such as Calabria, Tuscany, Liguria, Campania, and more. The Travel Routes intersect in various cities, allowing you the flexibility to create your own itinerary and pursue your own interests.

Using This Guide

This travel guide helps you plan, organize, and enjoy your holiday in Italy. In "Getting Your Bearings," a brief rundown of Italy's different regions will help choose the areas in which you'd like to spend the most time. It also offers insights into Italian culture and regional cuisine. An historical chronology and essays on art, literature, and architecture provide helpful background and perspective on the sights you'll be seeing. Walking tours of Rome and Italy's other major cities precede the 24 Travel Routes that take visitors to the country's major points of interest.

Langenscheidt's writers also offer a subjective guide to the most appealing sights. Our unique three-star system appears throughout the guide:

*** Worth a special trip—don't miss it!
  ** The most important sights on the tour
    * Highlights

Other sights along the way are also worth seeing, but are not necessarily as important as the starred sights.

Total distance is provided in kilometers and miles from the departure point of each tour. Major towns and sights appear in boldface for easy reference, while other notable places appear in italics. Numbers in parentheses correspond to locations on the maps.

The guide concludes with a Practical Information chapter divided into two parts. The first is General Trip Planning, to help you gather information you'll need before you depart for Italy. The second part is specific information—such as local tourist information offices and hotels—listed town-by-town.

Notes and Observations

Travel information, like fruit, is perishable. We've made every effort to double-check information in this guide. But hotels do close and museums do shut down for renovation, so check ahead wherever possible.

We welcome your comments and updates of our information. Please write us at:

Langenscheidt Publishers, Inc.
46-35 54th Road
Maspeth, N.Y. 11378

Getting Your Bearings

Italy has a major problem—there is simply far too much to see, too much to do, too many marvelous new tastes to sample on lovely outdoor terraces.

What is a traveller to do? The joy of choosing can be painful. And then when you've finally chosen one itinerary out of hundreds of possibilities, you discover the Italians—a people so unashamedly endowed with appetite for life that you want to stay longer, in hopes that the condition is contagious. To prove the point, let's take a look at the pleasures you have in store, from the north to the south, the top of the boot to the tip, and the splendid islands offshore.

The Regions of Italy

To the northwest, at the French border, lies the region of *Piedmont,* still under the spell of the Alps, but giving way to farms and castles, the broad, misty valley of the Po, and the elegant city of Turin, whose regal 18th-century architecture, fine museums, old-world cafés and parks come as a happy surprise to those who mistakenly assume that the industry it's famous for is located in the city proper. As for cheese and wine, Piedmont admits few peers.

At Piedmont's northern edge, tiny *Valle d'Aosta* is bordered by the southern slopes of Mont Blanc and other Alpine ranges. It is here that skiers and hikers will find the hills they seek and après-sport resorts in which to unwind.

In the north-central part of Italy, handsome *Lombardy* is the region of Milan, whose designs in clothes and furnishings lead the world in practical high fashion; and where grand opera has an historic home at La Scala.

The lakes of Lombardy are an enchanted world of stillness encircled with subtropical plants and flowers, owing to a quirk of climate. Thinking about Lake Como evokes visions of romantic castles rising from a crystalline lake—and then there is still Lake Maggiore and Lake Garda to explore. With their Romanesque cathedrals and splendid views, the Lombardian cities of Pavia, Brescia, and Cremona inevitably reward the traveller.

Heading east, the *Trentino–Alto Adige,* with its majestic Dolomites, mountain lakes, and alpine towns, castles, and cathedrals, combines a northern European outlook with a liberal dash of Italian charm. This is an area beloved by Europeans, but little known to North American travellers.

At the eastern coast, Venice remains a miracle of fantasy that time and tide threaten but don't overcome. (Proposals to save Venice from the sea are as numerous as the 117 islands that make up the city and the 400 bridges that connect them.) But apart from the Queen of the Adriatic, the *Veneto* has much to offer visitors. Palladio's villas, from which Georgian and Federal architectural styles were derived, dot the countryside. The lovely hill town of Asolo preserves a timeless charm. On the arm of land that reaches to the Yugoslav border, Trieste has lured exiles such as James Joyce to its shores.

Along the western coast, curving south from the French Riviera is the holiday region of *Liguria,* known mainly for its beaches and its flower market—the largest in Italy. Genoa, the birthplace of Christopher Columbus, is now getting into gear for the 1992 celebration of the 500th anniversary of his discovery of America.

East of Liguria, often Medieval in appearance, but modern in outlook, is the region of *Emilia-Romagna*. Extending to the Adriatic, this is a land of castles and cuisine, the latter so famous that Bologna has long been considered a culinary capital of Italy. Parma and Modena run a good race for that title, however. Bologna, with Italy's oldest university; Parma, with art treasures, elegant streets and memories of Verdi (whose birthplace and villa are nearby); Ravenna, with its brilliant Byzantine mosaics; Faenza, whose perfection of ceramic work (faïence) make it internationally known; Ferrara, of moated castles and luxurious Ferraris—the roster of prominent cities is perhaps the most impressive of any region.

Golden *Tuscany,* at the heart of the country, is famous not only for the Renaissance splendor of Florence but also for the hills of grain and olive trees and cypress that form the background of so many Renaissance paintings, and for its bountiful vineyards. Siena, one of Italy's most beautiful small cities, the many-towered San Gimiginano, and Pisa, with its tilting tower, enrich an overflowing cornucopia of treasures.

The gentle hills, valleys, and towns of *Umbria,* especially Assisi, attract the traveller in search of tranquillity, but Perugia's exuberance and intellectual energy keep the region in touch with the world. Orvieto's magnificent cathedral is as intricate as an altarpiece, and Gubbio's ancient streets and buildings remain amazingly Medieval. The good wines of Umbria—like the landscape itself—give rise to reverie.

The wooded and hilly *Marche* follow the Adriatic on the eastern side mellow tranquillity in winter. Pescara and Urbino, both delightful, may reflect the grand days of the province, but they do so with a contemporary flair, and Ancona is today a lively commercial center.

Rome's region of *Latium* (Lazio) is dominated by the Eternal City, but its small towns and back roads provide Romans with many happy Sunday drives. The Castelli Romani (hills, not castles) are filled with spirited harvest feasts and the fragrant wines and tender pork alone are worth the trip.

At Tarquinia, Cerveteri, and Viterbo, the ancient birth of central Italy can be glimpsed in the beautiful and mysterious tombs and artifacts of the Etruscans. Research continues to enrich our knowledge of this vanished race whose customs and laws formed one of the bases of Roman society, thereby directly influencing the West.

Abruzzo's wild mountains, to the east of Latium, are popular with mountain-climbers and skiers—and to those who love good country meals. The beautiful city of L'Aquila is not as well known as its rich architectural and historical heritage would suggest, a fact that will delight those who do make the discovery.

Molise, which together with Abruzzo to its north make up "the Abruzzi," also has a scenic, mountainous landscape—with castles of Frederick II Hohenstaufen, ski resorts, and culinary specialties adding to the list of enjoyments.

Campania's Amalfi Coast and the islands of Capri and Ischia have some of the world's most beautiful shorelines and landscapes. Naples, with Vesuvius across its bay, and the archaeological sites of Paestum, Pompeii, and Herculaneum endow the region with pleasures for all tastes.

The heel of the boot is *Apulia,* well-known to vacationing Europeans, but relatively unknown to English-speaking travellers. The spur above the heel—called the *Gargano peninsula*—is a mountainous land of monasteries and rocky coves. The flatter land to the south finally leads to the conical dry-stone *trulli,* small whitewashed houses of Paleolithic origin. They dot a countryside at its loveliest in spring when the almond trees open their pink and white blossoms. The Baroque city of Lecce and the beaches of the Gulf of Taranto are special treats, as is the inventive cuisine.

Basilicata, at the south center, or the instep, has an austere beauty that few tourists have seen. At ancient Metaponto, the archaeological treasures of Magna Graecia reveal the former grandeur of Greek civilization on the Italian peninsula. The beaches here are numerous, and the regional cooking shows that simple fare can be not only delicious, but healthier than richer, more sophisticated cuisines.

At the toe of the boot, white beaches flanked by mountains, and towns with traces of Greek civilization, characterize *Calabria.* Handcrafts, excellent seafood, and the resort facilities along the coast make the region a favorite with vacationers.

Just across the Strait of Messina from Calabria, *Sicily* is an island of Greek temples silhouetted against the sea, with extraordinary towns like Taormina, founded by the Greeks and with superb views of the Ionian Sea and Mount Etna. Palermo's brilliant Arab-Norman heritage is reflected in its buildings and museum collection, while the mountain towns of the island's center impart the rugged simplicity of traditional Sicilian life.

Sardinia—easily reached from Sicily to its south or from Civitavecchia, near Rome—is known for its beaches, considered by many to be the most beautiful in Europe. Its prehistoric cone-shaped buildings, the *nuraghi*, can be seen throughout the island. Traditional foods and handcrafts evoke Sardinian life.

North of Sardinia, the island of *Elba*—the place of Napoleon's exile—makes for a fascinating day trip from Sardinia—or the mainland.

Size, Geographic Location, Population

The democratic republic of Italy (Repubblica Italiana), which includes the major islands of Sicily and Sardinia, as well as several smaller islands, has a total land surface of 301,260 sq. km. (116,300 sq. miles)

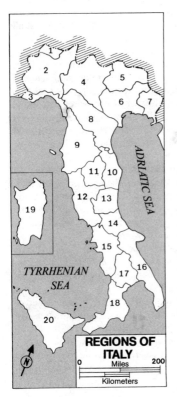

Regions, Major Cities and Towns

1. Valle d'Aosta: Aosta
2. Piedmont: Turin
3. Liguria: Genoa
4. Lombardy: Bergamo, Cremona, Mantua, Milan
5. Trentino–Alto Adige: Bolzano, Trento
6. Venetia: Padua, Venice, Verona, Vicenza
7. Friuli-Venezia Giulia: Trieste
8. Emilia-Romagna: Bologna, Ferrara, Modena, Parma, Piacenza, Ravenna
9. Tuscany: Florence, Leghorn, Pisa, Siena
10. The Marches: Ancona, Urbino
11. Umbria: Perugia
12. Latium: Rome, Viterbo
13. Abruzzi: L'Aquila
14. Molise: Campobasso
15. Campania: Naples, Salerno
16. Apulia: Bari, Brindisi, Lecce, Tarento
17. Basilicata: Potenza
18. Calabria: Catanzaro, Reggio di Calabria
19. Sardinia: Cagliari, Nuovo, Cristano, Sassari
20. Sicily: Agrigento, Catania, Messina, Palermo, Ragusa, Syracuse, Taormina, Trapani

REGIONS OF ITALY

ADRIATIC SEA

TYRRHENIAN SEA

0 Miles 200

Kilometers

and a population of 58 million. Its peninsular shape is generally compared to a boot. From its northern border, bounded by the Alps and, from west to east, by France, Switzerland, Austria and Yugoslavia, Italy extends south into the Mediterranean for 1,200 km. (745 miles). The peninsula is surrounded by four inland seas—the Ligurian and Tyrrhenian to the west, the Ionian to the south, and the Adriatic to the east. The Adriatic separates Italy from its eastern neighbors, Yugoslavia and Albania, while the Ionian separates it from Greece to the southeast.

Sicily (Sicilia), triangular in shape, with an area of 25,709 sq. km. (10,027 sq. miles) and a population of five million, is the largest island in the Mediterranean and is geologically the continuation of the Italian peninsula. Separated from the southernmost tip of the mainland by the narrow Strait of Messina—only 3 km. (1.8 miles) wide at its narrowest point—Sicily is only 93 miles from the coast of Tunisia in Africa. The second largest Mediterranean island, Sardinia (Sardegna), has an area of 24,089 sq. km. (9,300 sq. miles) and a population exceeding 1.6 million; it lies just south of the French island of Corsica. Elba, part of the Tuscan archipelago that includes Gorgona, Pianosa, Capraia, Giglio, Giannutri, and Monte Cristo, is a small island (27 km.; 16 miles long, and 18.5 km.; 11 miles at its widest; population 30,000) between the north Italian coast and Corsica in the Tyrrhenian Sea; the Pontine Islands (Isole Ponziane) are farther south, off the coast of Latium, and the famous resort islands of Capri and Ischia lie off the tip of the Sorrento peninsula on the south side of the Bay of Naples. The Aeolian Islands (also known as the Lipari Islands, or Isole Lipari) and Egadi Islands (Isole Egadi) are located off the northern and western coasts of Sicily, respectively. The Tremeti Islands (Isole Tremeti) form an archipelago in the Adriatic just north of the Monte Gargano promontory.

Topography

Italy is a land of great and continual contrasts—dizzying, snow-covered mountain peaks; sweltering plains; dazzling blue seas; charming, verdant hills; flat, humid lagoons; sheltered lakes; and balmy islands. Although you can find an endless variety of landscapes and climates within its borders, the country is generally divided into only three major geographic regions: the Alps, the Po valley, and the Apennine chain.

Forming a magnificent natural border to the north, the Alps help to shield Italy from the climate of northern Europe, and contain some of the continent's most famous peaks, including Mont Blanc (4,810 meters; 15,780 feet), the Matterhorn (4,807 meters; 15,766 feet), Cervino (4,480 meters; 14,692 feet), Mount Rosa (4,634 meters; 15,200 feet) and in the Brenta Dolomites in northeast Italy, Marmolada (3,342 meters; 10,960 feet). The Alps are primarily shale, while the Dolomites are limestone. Passes at the heads of the valleys allow year-round access to and from France, Switzerland and Austria.

A limestone fringe of the Alps, the Pre-Alps, forms the background to three major lakes in the northwestern part of the Lombardy region: Lago Maggiore, Lago di Lugano, and Lago di Como; all three are highly picturesque, with palm trees, azaleas and cypresses along their sheltered shores. Lago di Garda, the largest of Italy's lakes (390 sq. km.; 234 sq. miles) and the much smaller Lago Iseo, lie farther to the east, and are equally favored as resorts.

Covering some 15 percent of Italy between the Alps and the Apennine mountains, and descending east toward the Adriatic, is the Po valley, made up of parts of Piedmont, Lombardy, Veneto and the eastern section of Emilia-Romagna. The most densely populated area of the country, it is both the agricultural and industrial heartland of the country, with Milan its chief center of industry. The Po River—at 682 km. (410 miles) the longest in Italy—gives the valley its name, and, as it reaches the Adriatic, creates a flat, sandy delta with numerous lagoons, the most famous being that of Venice. The volcanic Euganean Hills rise from the plain west of Venice. Other rivers in the Po valley include the Adige, the Brenta, the Ticino, the Mincio, and the Trebbia.

Generally called the backbone of Italy, the Apennine mountains run north to south, from the Gulf of Genoa in Liguria to Aspromonte in Calabria, and continue on into Sicily. The Apennines, far older than the Alps, are also much lower, with slopes that are often bare, wild and eroded as in the Abruzzi, east of Rome, although some are gently weathered and covered with chestnut forests. The Gran Sasso d'Italia in the Abruzzi is, at 2,914 meters (9,560 feet), the highest peak in the Apennines. The Sabine and Alban Hills (the Castelli Romani)—both volcanic massifs with numerous small crater lakes—are embedded in the chain, as is the active volcano, Mt. Vesuvius, in the district of Naples.

Mt. Etna (3,340 meters; 10,967 feet), another active volcano (the highest in Europe), dramatically dominates the Ionic coast of the mountainous island of Sicily, which is a geographical continuation of the Apennines on the mainland. The bare, treeless, broken mountains of the Gennargenta range characterize the island of Sardinia.

Florence's Arno, and the Tiber, which flows through Rome, are the most important of the Apennine rivers; both have flooded over the centuries, the most recent instance being in 1966, when the waters of the Arno caused extensive damage in Florence. The Salso River in Sicily separates the western and eastern halves of the island.

Italy is a country with 7,500 km. (4,500 miles) of coastline. Liguria, curving along the Gulf of Genoa, has a rocky, indented coastline with several small, deep-water ports. South of Leghorn, the coast of Tuscany is sometimes rocky, but it becomes the sandy and flat *Maremma* to the south—a formerly marshy area that has now been reclaimed. Lying along the Tyrrhenian Sea, Latium's coast is generally sandy, and its once-great seaports, such as Ostia, have long been silted up. With its rugged coastline and clear waters, whose colors range from deep purple to turquoise, Campania, with its capital of Naples, has perhaps the most admired and well-known of Italy's maritime landscapes. The Gulf of Naples, with the offshore islands of Capri and Ischia, is highly picturesque, as is the lush Amalfi coast, with its white cliffside villages. Farther to the south, separating the Tyrrhenian from the Ionic Sea, is Calabria; a corniche road runs along the most scenic stretch of the Calabrian Riviera, between Gioia Tauro and Reggio. A prosperous coastal plain stretches along the Gulf of Taranto, where grapes, citrus and olive trees are cultivated. The coastal landscape on the Adriatic side of the peninsula is basically flat and sandy, with the peaks of the Apennines rising up behind. Sicily's coastline can be rugged and sublime; Sardinia's is considered by many to be the most beautiful in Italy, and steps are being taken to preserve some of its most spectacular stretches.

Constitution and Representation

At the end of the Second World War, Italy became a parliamentary republic (Repubblica Italiana) by popular referendum. The monarchy ended in 1946, and the country has been governed since then by three branches of government: the executive, the legislative, and the judiciary. By the terms of the Constitution (1 January 1948), the President, whose duties are primarily representative, is elected for a seven-year term by both houses of Parliament, together with three additional delegates from each region. The two Houses of Parliament consist of the Camera dei Deputati (Chamber of Deputies), with 630 members who are elected every five years in a general election, and the 320-seat Senato (Senate), whose members, elected on a regional basis, also serve for five years. The Presidente del Consiglio, or Prime Minister, appointed by the President, is by far the more important governmental figure, and depends upon a coalition between himself and the other ministers to maintain power. Together they form the Consiglio dei Ministri (Cabinet). A Corte Costituzionale (Supreme Court) is responsible for ensuring that the requirements of the constitution are carried out. Although the governments in Italy change with almost incomprehensible rapidity, the cast of characters—the leaders of the principle parties—changes only slightly, giving the country a stability that defies any easy explanation.

Italy is divided into 20 *regioni* (regions), each of which has some legislative, administrative and financial powers. Within the 20 regions there are 94 *province* (provinces). Municipal councillors elect a Sindaco to head each district. Under a special statute, certain regions (Sicily, Sardinia, Alto Adige, Friuli, Venetia and the Valle d'Aosta) retain some administrative autonomy.

Italy is a member of the European Economic Council (EEC) and the North Atlantic Treaty Organization (NATO).

Customs and Manners

Few nations have been so loved for their friendliness to foreigners as Italy. Although tourists pour into Italy in record numbers, most Italians seem to regard them as people with needs to be met with care, comfort and hospitality, rather than as part of the country's prime industry.

The Italian way of life, however, for all of its apparent charm, liveliness, and grace, can sometimes bewilder and frustrate visitors who are accustomed to a more "efficient" and regulated existence. This is more true in southern Italy than it is in the north.

Northern Italy, because of its Austrian and French past, reflects more the character of the rest of Europe and is slightly formal—although always with a *brio* that is quintessentially Italian. Southern Italy, on the other hand, has been influenced by its Greek-Spanish-Arab past, which has helped to imbue it with a kind of characteristic emotionalism and drama. The simplest exchange in Rome or Naples can sound and appear almost operatic in intensity, replete with eloquent and elaborate hand gestures and vocal inflections. A passionate love for and involvement with the family, and especially children, is common to both northern and southern Italy.

Though the residents of the northern regions are apt to lead a more orderly existence, forming lines at ticket windows and bus stops, the south seems to regard queues as unnaturally lifeless ways to spend precious moments of one's life. Jockeying for position, especially at the last minute, gives the moment its bit of drama. Most tourists rarely appreciate this age-old "tradition," and should be prepared to exercise patience and good humor when travelling south from Rome. If you're standing in a long line at a post office or bank, and can't fathom why every exchange seems to take forever and involves the filling out of countless forms, all of which must be stamped, remember that bureaucracy was invented in Rome, and has been an Italian way of life for centuries.

Italians of all regions and economic groups are proud people, and they dress accordingly. Entering a public place without appropriate attire is considered the result of a poor upbringing. Women cannot enter churches wearing shorts, sleeveless dresses or tops, or resort wear, and must have their arms and head covered. In Rome, men and women place great emphasis on creating *la bella figura*, that is, making oneself a well-coiffed, well-groomed, beautifully attired work of art. A sense of style is always appreciated in Italy.

The majority of Italians nominally belong to the Roman Catholic church, although this is no longer the state religion. For many, churches are part of the daily fabric of life—places to stop for mass, prayers or devotions, not necessarily lengthy, or to light a candle in a favorite chapel; in this sense, the church acts almost as a public square, and is often filled with worshippers moving about freely. Italian churches are, of course, great repositories of art, and are visited by countless tourists; this is generally acceptable, even when a mass is being said, provided you are dressed appropriately and remain unobtrusive. Remember that most churches close during the afternoon, and reopen around 4 P.M.

This leads us to another Italian tradition, again more prominent in the south than in the north: the afternoon siesta. Visitors eager to see the sights from dawn to dusk are forced to reckon with the fact that everything—churches, offices, palaces, museums, monuments, stores—closes at about 1:30 or 2:00 P.M., and does not reopen until 4:00 or 5:00 P.M. In large northern cities like Milan, business hours are generally "non-stop," that is, they remain open all afternoon; but in Rome, Florence, Naples and dozens of other cities, siestas are still the norm. Many Italians travel home from their jobs to take lunch as a family, after which, during the hottest part of the afternoon, it used to be customary to have a quiet period of rest. Nowadays, however, this afternoon lull in the day's public activities does not necessarily mean that Italians are sleeping—this is their time for taking care of family and business matters. The siesta has unfortunate consequences, however, in that it creates two additional peak traffic hours as people travel home for lunch and then back to their work.

In many of Italy's smaller cities (and, to a lesser extent, in places like Rome), the evening stroll or *passeggiata,* is a daily part of life. Before dinner, well-dressed couples and individuals promenade in the main square or main streets, greeting friends and acquaintances, window-shopping, or perhaps stopping for an espresso or aperitivo. Watching the show from a café terrace is fascinating and fun.

Italians, passionate about their cars, can be extremely aggressive on the road. Play it safe if you are driving in Italy, and don't be flustered by the constant use Italians make of their horns, or lose your temper if you are passed. The Italians remove all valuables, including radios, from their cars when they leave them—a practice you would be wise to follow.

Travellers with children, older travellers or the handicapped will find few specific accommodations, but most of the country is perfectly happy to make the necessary arrangements on the spot, if possible. Except in formal restaurants, children are treated as delightful additions to the scene and are apt to receive more attention than their parents.

Food and Drink

Italian cooking has long been enjoyed throughout the world, even in less well-prepared versions. But now the Mediterranean diet has also been recognized for its healthy balance of excellent basic ingredients, simply cooked to retain original nutrients and freshness. The rich variety of pasta sauces and meat and fish preparations is astonishing, with each regional variation creating entirely new tastes out of similar ingredients. The cuisines of the northern regions have a buttery base, and cream sauces are an important part of the menu, but olive oil reigns in the south, the luxuriant product of trees brought to Italy more than two millennia ago from Greece. Since olive oil contains no cholesterol, even the cream-loving north has begun to use what once was thought of as butter's poor relation. Dining out of doors (*al fresco*) is part of the fun, and large cities and small towns respond to the demand by creating leafy pergolas and flowery terraces to take advantage of the good weather.

Although some foods are nearly ubiquitous, there are many regional specialties.

In Piedmont, *fonduta,* made with melted cheese, milk, egg yolks and truffles, is worth the trip to many; *agnolotti* (stuffed pasta); *bagna cauda* is a hot sauce of butter, oil, anchovies, garlic, and white truffles into which you dip vegetables. Desserts include toffees, chocolates, and marrons glacés. Piedmont's wines are among the best in the country: Barolo, Barbera, Barbaresco, and Freisa are all worthy of a thoughtful taste. This is also the home of the sparkling wines of Asti and fine vermouths. Lombardy's rice fields supply the *riso* that created *risotto alla milanese,* saffron rice, which encircles a fragrant *osso bucco,* the meaty veal bone whose marrow is prized. Soup lovers will delight in *minestrone*—a hearty vegetable soup. Lombardy's gorgonzola cheese makes a surprisingly delicious pasta sauce—surprising for those who thought they hated blue cheeses. Bel Paese and stracchino are especially satisfying cheeses when accompanied by Lake Garda's rosé wines.

The Veneto is Venice's province, appreciative of its neighboring sea as a source of shellfish and salt-water fish. *Polenta,* a cornmeal dish often served with sausages, and *fegato alla veneziana*—the dish that can make liver-haters repent (the liver is cut in julienne strips, liberally accompanied with onions, seasoned with sage)—are two delicious specialties. Fine wines such as Soave and Valpolicella come from the Verona area. Liguria, another region abutted by sea, has added a delicious non-seafood dish to the repertoire—*pesto alla genovese,* in which crushed basil leaves are flavored with pine nuts, garlic, oil and Parmesan. Cinqueterre wine is the local favorite.

Emilia-Romagna is famous for the excellence of its cuisine, with the cities of Bologna, Modena, and Parma all vying for the culinary laurels. *Tortellini alla Bolognese* must be tasted—pasta stuffed with meat and cheese, so light it entices the faintest of appetites. *Zamponi* are Modena's treat, stuffed pig's trotters that taste far more interesting than their name suggests; balsamic vinegar is another prize from Modena, aged ten years. From Parma come Parmesan cheese and prosciutto. Tuscany's famous *bistecca alla fiorentina* is a T-bone steak cooked over aromatic charcoal, and its roast meats and game are also delicious. *Cacciucco*, a tasty fish soup, and *triglie alla livornese*, red mullet cooked with tomatoes and oil, are delicious products of the Tuscan coast. Along with Piedmont, Tuscany is one of the country's most famous wine regions. Chianti is Tuscany's magnificent wine, centered on the area between Florence and Siena. A rich dessert much enjoyed is *castagnaccio*, a chestnut cake of distinction. Siena's *panforte*, rather like a hard fruitcake full of almonds, is a favorite Christmas gift.

Umbria is the place for game birds and roast suckling pig. Truffles and various nuts are used in many dishes. Orvieto and Verdicchio, Torgiano and Montefalco, are wines to look for.

Rome's region of Latium glorifies the simple foods. Artichokes and beans, pork and roast lamb are much appreciated, and zucchini flowers with a dash of anchovy paste inside are delicacies of the summer. *Saltimbocca,* slices of veal topped with prosciutto, *spaghetti alla carbonara,* with finely chopped bacon, eggs, and cheese, are Roman specialties, and pasta *all' arrabbiata* (angry-style) is as hot as the name implies. Wines from the Colli Albani, Cesanese, Frascati and the rest of the Castelli Romani are excellent accompaniments.

In Campania, where Naples and Capri are located, seafood is king, especially *vongole veraci*—the tiniest, tastiest clams in the world, many contend. But Naples's pasta, usually called *maccheroni* rather than pasta, is superb. Simple *spaghetti al pomodoro,* with tomato sauce, is here brought to perfection. Pizza, which originated here, is baked in a brick oven, often over a wood fire, and is rarely duplicated anywhere. Buffalo mozzarella from farms near Naples is a prized treat, and the provolone comes as a wonderful surprise to those who know it only as a supermarket processed cheese. Capri produces some good wines, and everyone tries Lacryma Christi del Vesuvio (Christ's Tear, from Mt. Vesuvius) perhaps initially intrigued by its name. Ischia's wines and Ravello's Episcopio are always light and pleasant.

Apulia is another region that has elevated the humble *cucina povera* (poor people's cooking) to noble heights. Puréed fava beans with braised chicory in olive oil, a regional specialty, are a delicious introduction. Pasta with cauliflower (*cavolfiore*), *cima di rape* (turnip tops) or broccoli will delight vegetable lovers and those who think they aren't. Grilled lamb and kid are specialties here. Sheep-milk ricotta is superb, and the wines—Locorotondo, Castel del Monte, and San Severo—complement the unusual tastes of the food.

Sicily's cuisine is an exciting experience, with traces of the Arabs, Greeks, Normans and Spanish who colonized the island. In the west, *pasta con sarde* (a blend of fresh sardines, fennel, raisins, pine nuts and other flavors) and couscous on Trapani's coast are typical dishes. Seafood of a thousand descriptions (best appreciated in Palermo's Vucciria market) provides a paradise for the lovers of this bounty. *Caponata*, an antipasto of olives, eggplant and capers in the west, but more given to red peppers (*pepperoni*) in the east, is a delicious taste to try. In Catania, *spaghetti alla Norma,* with an eggplant-and-cheese sauce, delights the palate and the opera lover (it was named for Bellini's opera *Norma*), and *falsomagro,* a stuffed meat roll, balances the sea-oriented menus. Cacciocavallo cheese is a favorite, and Sicilian wines are excellent. Try Regaleali, Etna, Corvo, and sweet Marsala. The sweetest tooth is enchanted by the almond pastries—and rich half-frozen *cassata*. Sicily is also known for its ices and ice creams, part of its Arab-Muslim heritage.

Sardinia is fond of game and wild boar—in sausages, chops, or ham. Suckling pig, snails, and fish stews enliven the menu. Breads and cheeses are exceptional, especially with a glass of Malvasia, Nasco, or Moscato.

Chronology

Prehistory

Long before advanced cultures built their cities throughout present-day Italy, prehistoric peoples were living on the islands of Sicily and Sardinia and in southern Italy. Remains of their settlements can be seen near Taranto, where there are megalithic chamber tombs; on the rugged hillsides of Sardinia, where Stone Age inhabitants built round fortress houses known as *nuraghi;* and in Apulia, where the Grotta Romanelli is decorated with Paleolithic incised drawings. In northern Italy, copper daggers dating from ca. 1800–1600 B.C. (Early Metal Age) have been found in Brescia, and excavations have revealed traces of the Bronze Age Terramare culture (1600–1200 B.C.), whose simple pile dwellings were clustered into fortified villages. After 1200 B.C. the Italian peninsula was invaded from the north by migrating Indo-European tribes. The Iron Age (1000–500 B.C.) Villanovan culture, which formed small villages and cremated its dead, placing the ashes in tall clay or bronze urns, developed around present-day Bologna and spread south.

The Etruscans

Between the eighth and fifth centuries B.C., central Italy was colonized by the Etruscans and southern Italy by the Greeks. The Etruscans, settling on the west coast of present-day Tuscany, were said by the Greek historian Herodotus to come from Asia Minor. This has remained a generally accepted theory until recently, when new archaeological evidence began to suggest that the Etruscans could, in fact, have been native to Italy, and their culture the result of Phoenician influence. Whatever the origin of these mysterious people, they were highly civilized, and their art suggests a joyous spirit. Forming a loose confederation of 12 cities, the Etruscans developed overland trade routes to reach the Greek cities in the south, and, according to generally accepted accounts, chose a Latin village called Rome as a trading post. A succession of Etruscan kings ruled Rome for 300 years, from the late eighth century B.C. onward, and were responsible for its early period of growth. Once they were overthrown by the Romans, their history was deliberately destroyed, and new myths were employed in the service of the new Roman state.

The Greeks

In the early eighth century B.C. the other great force that was to shape the culture and civilization of Italy arrived. Greek settlers founded more than 40 colonies on the coasts of Sicily and southern Italy up to near Naples. Each of these cities was linked to a parent city on the Greek mainland, and together they formed Magna Graecia. Some of the famous Greek residents include Aeschylus, Archimedes, and Pythagoras. As farmers, the Greeks were the first to cultivate the vine and the olive, those staples of Italian agriculture, both of which had formerly grown only in a wild state. Trade flourished, as the bronze and ceramic wares of the Greeks were sought eagerly throughout the peninsula and provided models that the native peoples imitated. Greek sculpture, architecture, and religious mythology also provided important models for the native Italians. The Greek alphabet, which was adapted by tribes throughout the peninsula, developed into the Latin alphabet. The powerful and wealthy Greek colonies were engaged in warfare more often than not, however; this prevented them from uniting Italy under their leadership and also provided valuable military information to the Italian natives, who would eventually become the new conquerors of the known world.

Foundations of the Roman Empire

There are two early Romes, one based on myth and one based on archaeological evidence. According to later, official legend, Rome was never ruled by Etruscan kings but had only fallen temporarily under their power. The most recent archaeological evidence suggests that the Romans may, in fact, have been less influenced by the Greeks and Etruscans than has been generally supposed. In one mythical story, the son of the last Etruscan king, Tarquinius Superbus, rapes Lucretia, a Roman noblewoman, and provides the impetus for a Roman revolt against the Etruscan masters and the establishment of a republic. In Virgil's nationalistic epic the *Aeneid,* the origins and rise of legendary Rome are traced from heroic Troy in Asia Minor to the newly established principate of Octavius Caesar (later Augustus). The famous lines spoken by Anchises to his son, Aeneas, illustrate the approved ideal of Roman character: "Roman, remember that you shall rule the nations by your authority, for this is to be your skill, to make peace the custom, to spare the conquered, and to wage war until the haughty are brought low." State-approved myths and legends often were superimposed on real or imagined events in Roman history.

753 B.C.: According to the Roman author Varro, Rome was founded by Romulus, a descendent of Aeneas, on April 21. The date is speculative.

600 B.C.: The Etruscan Tarquinii rule Rome. Sardinia is occupied by Carthaginians, who war with the Greeks and eventually occupy large sections of Sicily.

510 B.C.: Rome is transformed from a kingdom into a republic based on the Greek model. The Senate, comprising Rome's leading citizens, takes legislative control of the city; two consuls, elected for one-year terms, head the state. Rome's supremacy is established after numerous battles against the Etruscans, the Greeks, and the Carthaginians. During the next 200 years, Rome conquers most of the Italian peninsula, builds military roads and founds military colonies to ensure control.

390–378 B.C.: The Gauls (Celts) invade northern Italy, take Rome, and defeat the Romans in the battle of the Allia River. Rome is rebuilt after its destruction, and walls are erected around its seven hills.

312 B.C.: Construction of the Via Appia, a military road that eventually stretches from Rome to Brindisi.

264–241 B.C.: First Punic War. Carthage, a North African city founded by the Phoenicians, controls the western Mediterranean. In order to extend its borders south, Rome must defeat Carthage. The two powers begin a battle for the Greek city of Messina, in Sicily, and the Carthaginians are finally driven out of Sicily, which becomes Rome's first province.

238 B.C.: Rome annexes Sardinia and Corsica and soon conquers Cisalpine Gaul (northern Italy), extending its borders to the Alps.

219–201 B.C.: Second Punic War. Greek Syracuse, in Sicily, allies with Carthage and is conquered by Rome. The Carthaginian general Hannibal crosses the Alps and defeats Rome at Lake Trasimeno and Cannae. Rome counterattacks Carthage and defeats Hannibal. Carthage is stripped of its overseas possessions.

209 B.C.: Taranto, the last Greek city-state in Italy, is subjugated by Rome.

149–146 B.C.: Third Punic War. Carthage, once again an important commercial power, indirectly challenges Rome. Rome completely destroys Carthage and sells the Carthaginians into slavery. Macedonia and Greece become Roman provinces.

136–71 B.C.: Increasing impoverishment and exploitation of the peasants, and increasing power and luxury of the upper classes causes numerous slave revolts, including one led by Spartacus, and protracted, bitter civil wars. Conditions in lower Italy and Sicily deteriorate, and many cities are abandoned. Roman assimilation of Greek and Oriental culture. Sicily becomes the "granary of Rome."

133 B.C.: Roman occupation of Spain. Tiberius Gracchus elected tribune and tries to check the growing power and abuses of the Senate by proposing agrarian land reforms; the Senate blocks his plan and has him murdered.

122–79 B.C.: Gaius Gracchus, younger brother of the reformer Tiberius, is elected tribune and again calls for sweeping land reform and redistribution. The Senate incites the Roman people to riot and Gaius is blamed; he is killed and his followers imprisoned. Roman politics now becomes dominated by army commanders. The general Gaius Marius and his supporters murder leaders of the Senate and other aristocratic Romans. The Senate turns to Sulla, a rival general, who becomes dictator and institutes a two-year bloodbath. The Roman Republic is dead.

70 B.C.: Pompey and Crassus are appointed consuls. Reinstitution of some suspended Republican liberties.

60 B.C.: The first Triumvirate is formed by Pompey, Crassus, and Caesar. When Crassus dies, Caesar and Pompey quarrel.

58–51 B.C.: Caesar conquers Gaul.

49 B.C.: Against the orders of the Senate, Caesar and his army cross the Rubicon River, the border between Cisalpine Gaul and Italy, and head toward Rome, beginning a civil war. Pompey, with his own army and most of the Senate, flees to Greece.

49–45 B.C.: Caesar defeats Pompey and his allies in Spain and Greece. Pompey flees to Egypt, where he is killed. Caesar writes his history of the Gallic War.

44 B.C.: Returning to Rome in triumph, Caesar has himself appointed dictator for life. A conspiracy forms against him, and he is assassinated on March 15.

43 B.C.: A brief second Triumvirate is formed by Octavian, Caesar's nephew; Mark Antony, Caesar's co-consul; and Lepidus, an army leader. Antony falls in love with the Egyptian queen, Cleopatra, but later is forced to marry Octavian's sister.

37–30 B.C.: Octavian turns the Senate against Antony and defeats him at Actium. Antony and Cleopatra kill themselves.

The Early Empire

27 B.C.– A.D. 14: Octavian receives the title of Augustus Caesar and reigns for 41 years. A period of peace and prosperity for Rome. Augustus, careful to allow the Republic to function as it had, rules behind the scenes, creating a personal civil service to help run the Empire. Rome sees a flourishing of art and literature under his reign; Virgil writes the *Aeneid* to deify the emperor's family; Horace and Ovid are active. Augustus rebuilds the capital and claims, according to Suetonius, that he found Rome a city of brick and left it a city of marble.

14–68: Reigns of Tiberius, Caligula, Claudius, Nero. Under Claudius, the Empire expands to include Britain. Rome burns in A.D. 64. Nero begins the first persecutions of the Christians.

69: "The Year of the Three Emperors": Galba, Otho, Vitellius.

70–96: Reign of the Flavian dynasty. Vespasian reunifies the Empire and brings an end to civil strife. Titus, Vespasian's son, rules briefly. Domitian, Vespasian's second son, becomes a hated tyrant.

79: Eruption of Vesuvius and destruction of Pompeii and Herculaneum.

98–180: The century of the Antonines: Nerva, Trajan, Hadrian, Antoninus Pius, Marcus Aurelius. Under Trajan, the Roman Empire reaches its greatest geographical extent, extending from Scotland to the Sahara and from the Spain to Mesopotamia.

180–270: Troubled period of military anarchy. Threatened in the east and west by barbarian tribes, the Empire doubles the size of its army, draining manpower and causing an economic crisis. The army places "barracks emperors" on the throne.

212: Caracalla gives Roman citizenship to every freeborn subject in the Empire.

270–275: Aurelian, *restitutor orbis*, reestablishes the unity of the Empire.

The Later Empire

284–305: Diocletian initiates drastic reforms in government and the social order. The Roman Empire is partitioned into western and eastern political sections with two emperors (augusti) assisted by two caesars, or "vice emperors." Persecution of the Christians under Diocletian: "the age of martyrs."

306–337: Reign of Constantine. The Edict of Milan (A.D. 313) grants religious liberty to Christians and others, and Christianity is gradually established as the state religion. Constantine moves the capital of the Roman Empire east to Byzantium (renamed Constantinople).

379–395: Reign of Theodosius. At his death, the Empire is divided into the Western Roman Empire, with its capital at Ravenna, and the Eastern Roman Empire, with its capital at Constantinople.

5th c.: The Roman Empire is attacked repeatedly by barbarian tribes.

410: Rome is captured by the Visigoths under Alaric.

455: Capture and sack of Rome by the Vandals under Genseric.

476: The last Western Roman Emperor, Romulus Augustulus, is deposed by the Germanic general Odoacer, bringing an end to the Western Empire.

Italy in the Early Middle Ages

493–526: Theodoric the Great founds an Ostrogothic kingdom in Italy, with capitals in Ravenna, Pavia and Verona.

535–553: The Byzantine Emperor Justinian succeeds in reimposing the rule of Constantinople by making Italy a province of the Eastern Roman Empire.

568–774: Lombard invasion under Alboin, who drives the Byzantines out of upper Italy, Tuscany, and Umbria and founds a Lombard kingdom in northern and central Italy. The pope appeals to Pepin the Short, king of the Franks, who defeats the Lombards and forces them to recognize Frankish suzerainty.

774: Charlemagne, Pepin's son, conquers the Lombard kingdom and unites it with the Frankish kingdom.

Italy under the German Emperors

800: Charlemagne is crowned first Holy Roman Emperor in Rome by Pope Leo III (the new Empire of the West, as opposed to the Byzantine or Eastern Empire). Only Friuli remains independent under a Lombard duke. In southern Italy, the sea republics of Amalfi and Naples and the Duchy of Gaeta seek protection from Byzantium.

827–901: The Magyars move into the Po plain and plunder northern Italy. The Saracens conquer Sicily, which becomes an emirate with its capital at Palermo.

950: Marquis Berengar II of Friuli and his son Adalbert are crowned kings of Italy.

951: Otto I, king of Saxony, becomes king of the Franks and Lombards through marriage and gains control of northern Italy.

NORTH AND CENTRAL ITALY
CIRCA A.D. 1000

962: Otto I is crowned emperor in Rome and founds the Holy Roman Empire of the German Nation, restoring Roman imperial status. His attempts to conquer southern Italy fail.

951–1268: Northern and central Italy is ruled by the German emperors. Conflicts with the popes. Formation of two parties: the Ghibellines, who support the emperor, and the Guelphs, who support the pope.

1000–1200: The Normans combine southern Italy and Sicily into a new kingdom. Byzantine and Arab cultural influences continue. Independent city-states and the sea republics of Genoa, Pisa and Venice emerge.

1027: Under the leadership of Robert Guiscard, the Normans conquer the Byzantine territories in Calabria.

1059: The pope invests Guiscard with southern Italy and Sicily, which has not yet been conquered.

1076–1122: Investiture conflict: confrontation between the empire and the papacy over emperor's right to appoint archbishops.

1077: The excommunicated Emperor Henry IV humbles himself before the pope at Canossa.

1091: The Normans conquer Sicily and Malta.

1110: Foundation of a medical school in Salerno.

1119: First university in Europe founded at Bologna.

1130–1137: Roger II founds the Norman kingdom in Italy and is crowned king of Naples and Sicily.

1194–1268: Southern Italy and Sicily come under Hohenstaufen rule. Emperor Frederick II moves the court from Palermo to Naples. Under the Hohenstaufens, numerous fortresses are built in southern Italy. Resumption of struggles between pope and emperor.

1222–1224: Establishment of universities in Padua and Naples.

Humanism and the Renaissance in Italy

From 1250: Rise of city-states and kingdoms within a politically fragmented Italy. Republican constitutions of Italian towns end with the rule of powerful local families such as the Viscontis (Milan), Della Scalas (Verona), and Gonzagas (Mantua). Increased wealth leads to patronage of the arts. Humanists such as Dante, Petrarch and Boccaccio rediscover ancient texts, which stimulates literature and learning. The Renaissance, a period of unprecedented artistic and intellectual achievement, spreads to all the great cities in Europe from the end of the 15th century onward and sees the work of great artists and architects, such as Giotto, Raphael, Michelangelo, Leonardo da Vinci, Brunelleschi and Palladio.

1265: Pope Clement IV gives Sicily and southern Italy to Count Charles I of Anjou as a fief. In 1268, the last of the Hohenstaufens, Conradin, is beheaded in Naples.

1282: A revolt against the despotic French reign breaks out in Palermo and ends with the massacre of all the French (Sicilian Vespers). The kingdom of Charles of Anjou is reduced to Naples. Sicily comes under the rule of the Spanish House of Aragon.

14th century: Almost all of Italy is controlled by the Papal States. The sea republic of Venice is at the height of its power, and the city-states of Florence and Milan establish their reigns over a large section of northern and central Italy. Italians consider themselves citizens of individual cities, not members of a larger national entity.

1347: The Black Death, or bubonic plague, decimates Europe; the death rate is as high as 60% in some Italian cities.

1378–1381: War of Chioggia, naval conflict between Genoa and Venice for supremacy in the Mediterranean, in which Venice is the victor.

1442: Alfonso V, King of Aragon, conquers Naples and becomes king of the Two Sicilies.

1469: Under Lorenzo il Magnifico, the Medici of Florence are at the height of their power.

1472: Dante's *Divine Comedy*, written in Tuscan Italian before 1321, first printed at Foligno.

1481: Botticelli, Ghirlandaio, Perugino, Pinturricchio, and Signorelli paint frescoes in the Sistine Chapel, Rome.

1500: The end of the early Renaissance and the beginning of the high Renaissance.

Italy from the 16th Century to the Napoleonic Era

16th century: The Austrian House of Hapsburg and the French kings begin their struggle for northern Italy, which is divided into numerous small states. All the ruling houses of Italy eventually are subjugated by either the Austrian or the Spanish line of the House of Hapsburg.

1505: Pope Julius II calls Michelangelo to Rome. Bramante begins to rebuild St. Peter's in Rome in 1506. In 1508, Michelangelo begins his work on the Sistine Chapel; he will not finish until 1512.

1527: Capture and sack of Rome by the troops of Charles V.

Legend

PR — Principality
MG — Margravate
GP — Grand Principality
Rep — Republic
DY — Duchy
GD — Grand Duchy
KG — Kingdom

NORTH AND CENTRAL ITALY
15TH AND 16TH CENTURY

0 — Miles — 200
Kilometers

1540: Philip II, son of Charles V, is given the Duchy of Milan, which remains in Spanish hands until 1700. Milan, together with the Kingdom of Naples and Sicily, exerts Spanish influence in Italy.

1546: Michelangelo designs the dome and undertakes the completion of St. Peter's, Rome.

1560: Foundation of the Uffizi in Florence.

1569: The duke of Florence, Cosimo de' Medici, becomes grand duke of Tuscany.

17th century: The popes join the French in the battle against the Spanish-Austrian rulers. Savoy becomes the strongest state in northern Italy.

1633: Galileo is forced by the Roman Inquisition to recant the theories of Copernicus.

1706: As a result of the victory of Prince Eugene near Turin, Austria controls all of Lombardy.

1713: Following the Spanish War of Succession, Austria receives the Kingdom of Naples and the island of Sardinia. Austria is now the major power in Italy.

1718: Venice loses its possessions in the Turkish War (1714–1718) and no longer occupies a commanding trade position with the East.

1718–1720: Victor Amadeus II, duke of Savoy, receives Sardinia and the title of king.

1719: Herculaneum, buried in A.D. 79 by the eruption of Vesuvius, is rediscovered. Excavations begin in 1737 in Herculaneum, 1748 in Pompeii.

1738: With the Peace of Vienna, Austria receives large sections of central Italy but must yield Naples and Sicily to the Spanish Bourbons in return. With the demise of the last Medici in Florence, the Grand Duchy of Tuscany also becomes part of Austria. The Bourbons remain in Naples and Sicily until 1806.

1796–1798: Napoleon begins his Italian campaign. He defeats the Austrians at Lodi, enters Milan, and establishes the Lombard and Cispadane Republic. In 1797 he founds the Ligurian Republic in Genoa and unites the Cisalpine with the Cispadane Republic. The French capture Rome in 1798 and proclaim the Roman Republic. The pope flees Rome.

1799: French defeat at Cassano ends Cisalpine Republic. The Russians enter Turin.

1800: The French under Napoleon defeat the Austrians at Marengo. Austria retains Venice and land south of the Adige. Eventually Napoleon dissolves the Papal States and incorporates them into Italy.

1801: Peace of Luneville between Austria and France marks the actual end of the Holy Roman Empire.

1802: Napoleon becomes president of Italian (formerly Cispadane) Republic, annexes Piedmont, Parma, and Piacenza.

1805: Napoleon is crowned king of Italy in Milan Cathedral.

1806: Joseph Bonaparte, Napoleon's brother, named king of Naples.

1809: Papal States are annexed to the French Empire. Pope Pius VII is imprisoned in France.

1814: Demise of the Napoleonic regime. The pope returns to Rome.

1814–1815: Congress of Vienna reaffirms supremacy of Austria in Italy. Lombardy and Veneto become Austrian provinces. Tuscany is ruled at a distance by Austria, and Austrian troops invade Naples and Sicily. The Papal States are reestablished.

The Risorgimento

1831: Following several popular revolts against the Austrians, Giuseppi Mazzini founds Young Italy, a secret movement for independence. The growth of Italian nationalistic feelings and plans to throw off Austrian rule in order to liberate and unify Italy is called the *Risorgimento*.

1837–1848: Popular revolts in Naples, Palermo, and parts of northern Italy are crushed. The Kingdom of Sardinia declares war on Austria and is defeated.

1849: Victor Emmanuel II of the House of Savoy becomes king of Sardinia. The French conquer Rome. Cavour's government reorganizes the state of Piedmont.

1858: Cavour and Napoleon III create an alliance at Plombières.

1859: Austria declares war against France and Piedmont. Victor Emmanuel II places his army under the command of Garibaldi. Franco-Piedmontese victories result in Piedmont obtaining Lombardy.

1860–1861: Garibaldi conquers and unifies southern Italy. Including Sardinia, this region constitutes the Kingdom of Italy, under Victor Emmanuel II, with its capital at Florence.

1866: Italy declares war on Austria but is defeated. Austria sinks the entire Italian fleet. The Prussians join Italy and defeat the Austrians near Königgrätz (Hradec Králové, Czechoslovakia), forcing them to retreat from Italy. Mazzini puts forward Italian claims to Istria, Friuli, and South Tirol.

1870: Rome finally is occupied by Italian troops and becomes the capital of Italy. Italian unification is complete. France withdraws its troops from the Papal States, and the pope retains sovereignty over Vatican City.

1882: Italy makes peace with Austria. Under Umberto I, Italy forms the Triple Alliance with Germany and Austria-Hungary. Foundation of the Italian Socialist Party.

1887–1889: In the war with Abyssinia (Ethiopia), Italy gains the colonies of Eritrea and Italian Somaliland.

Italy in the 20th Century

1900: King Umberto I is assassinated by an anarchist, and Victor Emmanuel III ascends the throne.

1911–1912: As a result of the Turkish-Italian war, Italy annexes Cyrenaica, Tripoli, and the Dodecanese.

1912: Introduction of universal suffrage.

1915: Although initially neutral, with territorial guarantees from Britain and France, Italy breaks the Triple Alliance treaty and declares war on Germany and Austria-Hungary.

1919: Under the Peace Treaty of Saint-Germain-en-Laye, Austria-Hungary relinquishes the South Tirol up to the Brenner Pass, Istria, and a number of Dalmatian islands.

1922: After his march on Rome, Benito Mussolini is granted dictatorial powers by Parliament. He establishes a Fascist state and becomes Il Duce (leader).

1929: The conflict between church and state is settled with the Lateran Treaty, which makes Vatican City a sovereign state.

1931: Measures of state control to deal with the Depression.

1935–1936: Italy invades and annexes Abyssinia.

1936: Germany and Italy enter into the Rome-Berlin Axis. Italian troops fight for Franco in Spain.

1937: Italy, a founding member since 1919, leaves the League of Nations.

1939: Occupation of Albania and military alliance with Germany.

1940: Italy sides with Nazi Germany and declares war on France and Britain. Italian-French armistice signed in Rome. Three-power pact with Germany and Japan.

1941: After military failures in North Africa, Italy loses Abyssinia.

1943: Allied troops land in southern Italy and conquer Sicily. The Italian forces surrender; fall of the Fascist regime and arrest of Mussolini. Formation of a new government under Badoglio, who signs an armistice with the Allies and declares war on Germany. A rival government is formed by Mussolini, who is freed by German commando troops.

1945: Surrender of the Germany army. While fleeing, Mussolini is executed by partisans. The Christian Democratic Party forms a government led by de Gasperi.

1946: King Victor Emmanuel III abdicates, and Umberto II is proclaimed king of Italy. However, a popular referendum reveals that a majority favors a republic, and a democratic government is established. Umberto II abdicates.

1947: In the Treaty of Paris, Italy renounces its colonies, ceding Istria to Yugoslavia and the Dodecanese to Greece. Italy is allowed to keep South Tirol. Trieste becomes a free state.

1948: Italy joins the Western powers, becoming a founding member of NATO. Beginning of economic resurgence after harsh difficulties of the postwar period.

1953: The Christian Democratic Party loses political control; constant creation of new governments becomes the norm.

1954: The city of Trieste is attached to Italy.

1957: The European Economic Community (EEC) is founded in Rome. Reconstruction of the country moves quickly. Migration from the south to industrial regions in the north and to other countries.

1960: Summer Olympic games are held in Rome.

1963: Aldo Moro forms the first Center-Left government.

1966: The worst flooding in the history of the country destroys irreplaceable works of art in Florence, Venice, and other cities.

1970: Following widespread strikes and labor unrest, the Statuto del Lavoratore (statute of the worker) provides job security.

From 1974: Economic recession results in unemployment, high inflation, foreign debts. A new economic program is frustrated by domestic political crises, party strife, strikes, corruption scandals and terrorist kidnappings.

1975: Communist Party makes inroads in regional, provincial, and municipal elections.

1976: Earthquakes in Friuli and the province of Udine cause widespread damage.

1978: Aldo Moro, chairman of the Christian Democratic party, is kidnapped by the Red Brigades and found murdered 54 days later.

1980: Earthquakes severely damage southern Italy.

1981: Pope John Paul II is injured in an assassination attempt.

1983: Benito Craxi is the first Social Democrat to become head of the Italian government.

1984: The Holy See and the Republic of Italy reach an agreement determining that Catholicism is no longer the state religion of Italy. Rome ceases to be the Holy City.

1988: Archaeologists working on the lower slopes of the Palatine Hill in Rome announce discovery of the remains of a wall, possibly confirming the traditional founding of Rome in the eighth century B.C.

Art and Culture

Prehistory

The Italian peninsula is so rich a repository of ancient art and culture that reminders of the past have seeped into the very fabric of modern life. The earliest evidence of human habitation has been found in southern Italy, Sicily, and Sardinia. Remains of megalithic culture were discovered in the chambered tombs near Taranto. On the hillsides of Sardinia, Stone Age inhabitants built round fortress houses known as *nuraghi;* in Apulia, the Grotta Romanelli is decorated with Paleolithic incised drawings. The Museo Preistorico ed Etnografico Luigi Pigorini in Rome houses an excellent collection of prehistoric artifacts.

Etruscan Art

By the beginning of the eighth century B.C. the Etruscans had settled in central Italy. A mysterious non–Indo-European people from the East, the Etruscans were strongly influenced by Greek and oriental culture. Little is known about their architecture, but their art suggests a joyous spirit. In wall paintings found in their elaborate tombs, they enjoy feasting, dancing, sports, hunting, and music. Their sculpture attests to a pronounced realism, and their decorated sarcophagi indicate a belief in an afterlife. Ancient Rome was deeply influenced by Etruscan culture, but by the mid-third century B.C., all of Etruria was dominated by Rome. Especially fine examples of Etruscan art are on exhibit in the Archaeological Museum in Florence, the Villa Giulia in Rome, and in the city museums of Chiusi, Tarquinia, Veii, and Volterra.

Greek Art

Beginning in the early eighth century B.C., the Greeks founded more than 40 colonies on the coasts of Sicily and southern Italy, which they called Magna Graecia. The Greek Doric temples in Sicily are more numerous and better preserved than those in Greece; by the fifth century B.C., the Sicilian city of Syracuse rivaled Athens in splendor and power. Extensive remains of the Greek civilization, conquered by the Romans by the third century B.C., are to be found throughout Italy. Among the best collections of Greek art and artifacts are in the National Archaeological Museum in Naples and in the National Museum in Reggio di Calabria and Taranto.

Roman Art

The eruption of Mount Vesuvius in A.D. 79, which tragically buried the towns of Pompeii and Herculaneum, preserved streets and houses in layers of ash and mud, giving us an accurate view of Roman art and culture and a fascinating glimpse of daily life in ancient times. The major architectural contribution of Rome was the refinement of the arch— which allowed them to create vast interior spaces—and the use of concrete. The high quality of Roman engineering is evidenced in the construction of roads, baths, amphitheaters, palaces, aqueducts, and triumphal arches. All forms of art flourished under the Romans. During the Republican period (500–27 B.C.), portrait sculpture gradually became less idealized and more realistic. In the Empire, the equestrian image of the emperor became an established tradition, as was evidenced in the famous bronze statue of Marcus Aurelius (165 A.D.) which stood on the Capitoline Hill in Rome before being removed because of pollution damage. Painting reached its highest peak during the first century B.C. and the first century A.D. Still lives, portraits, and landscapes— often incorporating architectural details—were depicted on wall frescoes with an exquisite eye for naturalistic detail, using an early form of perspective. These paintings of bucolic scenes and classical Greek themes often make use of *trompe-l'oeil* techniques. The extraordinary artistic achievements of ancient Rome ended before the demise of the Empire; forgotten, their art and the knowledge that made it possible did not resurface until the late Middle Ages and the Renaissance.

Byzantine Art

When Emperor Constantine moved the capital from Rome to Byzantium in A.D. 330, the Roman Empire was already in decline. From that time until the 13th century, Early Christian and Byzantine art dominated the Italian peninsula. The most significant monuments of the Early Christian era are the catacombs constructed from the second to fourth centuries A.D. These served as secret meeting places for the Christians and as mortuaries, and were adorned with symbolic paintings and frescoes. When Constantine established Christianity as the official religion of the Roman Empire, the first basilicas were built, modeled on the Roman courts of law.

The best examples of Byzantine art in Italy are to be found in Venice and Ravenna. Under the Emperor Justinian (527–565), Ravenna became the Byzantine capital in Italy, and its basilicas of Sant'Apollinare and San Vitale (built around polygon-domed structures) became the prototypes for religious structures in Rome, Venice, Sicily, and Lombardy well into the 13th century. Most of these structures are decorated with lavish mosaics in which formal images are depicted on a gold background without perspective.

Romanesque Art

Romanesque art, which developed in the 11th century, was in part a revival of Roman and Early Christian styles. Romanesque cathedrals, the first stone edifices constructed since antiquity, are characterized by round arches, semicircular barrel vaults or domelike groin vaults, heavy stone walls, and large, simple, geometric masses. The Italian Romanesque style flourished in Lombardy. One of the best-known Romanesque churches is the basilica of St. Ambrogio in Milan, known for its unusual atrium and octagonal tower over the crossing. The Tuscan-Romanesque style is best preserved in the cathedral in Pisa. This magnificent building is an amalgam of an Early Christian basilica with a Latin-cross plan. It has a wooden roof, a dome at the crossing, and Classical columns supporting the nave. The marble striping produced by alternating black (or dark green) and cream-colored marble is a hallmark of the Tuscan style. The figurative sculpture, paintings, and mosaics of this period show a strong Byzantine influence.

Gothic and Trecento Art

The Gothic style was first introduced to Italy in the 13th century by the French Cistercians, whose abbeys in central and northern Italy influenced the Franciscans (in Assisi) and the Dominicans (in Florence). Typical Gothic features—ribbed vaulting, pointed arches, flying buttresses, tracery windows—are most visible in the gigantic 15th-century cathedral in Milan, the only structure in Italy built in a true northern Gothic style. Italian church architects otherwise continued to use Romanesque elements, stressing a more austere horizontal mass. The double church at Assisi, consecrated by the Franciscans in 1253, had walls designed for frescoes rather than for stained-glass windows, as would have been used in France. In Florence, the impressive three-aisled Duomo, begun in 1296, has a marble exterior with geometric designs and corresponds to the 11th-century baptistry nearby. The Italian blend of Romanesque and Gothic features is also apparent in the Hohenstaufen castles in southern Italy. Only in Venice did the Gothic style in civil and domestic architecture find a congenial home. Venetian Gothic, characterized by triple-arched windows, loggias and internal courts, can most readily be seen in the Doge's Palace and the Ca d'Oro palazzo, both of which show a measure of Eastern influence as well.

The earliest Italian Gothic sculpture was produced in southern Italy, but little of it remains. The great Gothic sculptor Nicola Pisano (c. 1220–1278), who designed the marble pulpits for the Duomo in Siena and the baptistry in Siena, worked in that tradition. His son Giovanni Pisano (c. 1250–1320) employed a more purely Gothic style. The end of the 14th century witnessed a trend toward greater realism, embodied in the work of Lorenzo Ghiberti (1378–1455), who won a competition to design the bronze doors of the baptistry in Florence.

In the 14th century, often called the *Trecento* (meaning 1300s), painting saw an explosion of creativity. Byzantine, Gothic, and ancient Roman murals (in the form of mosaics and frescoes) were the primary influence on Cimabue (c. 1240–1302), Duccio di Buoninsegna (c. 1260–1319), and Giotto, but their work has a monumentality, simplicity, humanity, and naturalism that makes it the forerunner of the Renaissance.

Early Renaissance

The Renaissance had its roots in classical antiquity and reached its zenith in Florence in the 15th century, or *Quattrocento*. The architects of this period adopted a new style modeled on Classical architectural forms. In Florence, Filippo Brunelleschi (1377–1446) used dramatic new techniques in building the dome of the Duomo, the churches of San Lorenzo and Santo Spirito, and the Pazzi Chapel. The subject matter of sculpture, heavily influenced by Classical art, now included secular, mythological, and historical themes. Portrait sculptures emphasized greater realism. Donatello (Donato de' Bardi, 1386–1466) was regarded as the leader of the early Renaissance. His works included the equestrian statue of Gattamelata in Padua, statues of Saint George and Saint Mark at Orsanmichele in Florence, and the *Judith and Holofernes* which stood in front of the Palazzo Vecchio in Florence (these were the first free-standing sculptures of modern times). Among the early Renaissance painters are Masaccio (Tommaso Guidi, 1401–1428), who created a style of monumental grandeur using the new technique of scientific perspective; Fra Angelico (1387–1455), whose paintings have a lyrical tenderness; Botticelli (1444–1510); Fra Filippo Lippi (1406–1469); Andrea Mantegna (1431–1506); Piero della Francesca (c. 1420–1492); Paolo Ucello (1397–1475); and Andrea del Castagno (c. 1423–1457).

High Renaissance

The High Renaissance occurred in the first half of the *Cinquecento*, or 16th century. Early in this period, Donato Bramante (1444–1514) designed the new St. Peter's in Rome. After Bramante's death, Michelangelo Buonarroti (1475–1564), the leading master of the High Renaissance, took over the project. Michelangelo's works in Florence include the famous statue of *David* and the mausoleum of the Medici in the church of San Lorenzo. In Rome, he painted the magnificent cycle of frescoes in the Sistine Chapel. The transcendent power of his work set the stage for Baroque art. Leonardo da Vinci (1452–1519) was the other great genius of the High Renaissance. The quintessential Renaissance man, da Vinci was a sculptor, architect, painter, scientist, and builder. He worked in Florence, Rome, France, and at the Sforza court in Milan. His most celebrated works are the *Gioconda* (*Mona Lisa*), now in the Louvre in Paris, and *The Last Supper,* at the monastery of Santa Maria delle Grazie in Milan. Other masters of the High Renaissance include Raphael (Raffaello Santi, 1483–1520), Giovanni Bellini (1430–1516), and Giorgione (Giorgio da Castelfranco, 1478–1510).

Late Renaissance

The Neoclassical architecture of Andrea Palladio (1508–1580) evoked the splendor of ancient Rome and provided a model for all of Europe. His principal works are the Basilica and the Villa Rotonda in Vicenza, and the church of San Giorgio Maggiore in Venice. Titian (Tiziano Vecellio, 1477–1576) was a great master of Venetian painting whose works presaged the development of the Baroque style.

Mannerism and the Baroque

The art of the Counter-Reformation (mid-16th century–mid-17th century) was designated Mannerism because it emphasized the study of attitudes and expressions. It delighted in the unusual and bizarre, in allegory and metaphor, in ornateness and artificiality. The foremost painters of this style were Jacopo da Pontormo (1494–1556); Rosso Fiorentino (1494–1541); Parmigianino (1503–1540); and Bronzino (1503–1572). The greatest sculptor was Benvenuto Cellini (1500–1571), also known for his autobiography.

The Baroque style developed out of Mannerism in the 17th century and the early part of the 18th century. The painters, sculptors, and architects of the Baroque, foremost among them Caravaggio (1573–1610), Gianlorenzo Bernini (1598–1680), and Francesco Borromini (1599–1677), delighted in the theatrical and emphasized the effects of movement, perspective, and *trompe-l'oeil*. The architecture and sculpture of the period are distinguished by the use of the curve, countercurve, and scrollwork. Lecce, in Apulia, is considered to be the most beautiful Baroque city in Italy. Rome and Naples owe much of their outstanding architecture to this period. In northern Italy, Baroque art flourished in Genoa and Turin.

Neoclassicism

In the middle of the 18th century, the ornateness of the Baroque style gave way to the simpler lines of Classicism (or Neoclassicism), which was modeled after Greek and Roman art forms. The foremost sculptor of the style was Antonio Canova (1757–1822), most famous for his reclining figure of Pauline Borghese.

The Twentieth Century

When the Fascists gained power in 1922, all branches of art were directed to reflect the monumental style of antiquity. Since the Second World War, however, Italian artists and architects have made many unique and highly celebrated achievements. Among the 20th-century Italian artists who have received international recognition are: Giorgio de Chirico (1888–1978), the painter whose works were influenced by Cézanne and the Cubists; the painter Giorgio Morandi (1890–1964); Amedeo Modigliani (1884–1920), regarded by many as one of Italy's leading early-20th-century painters; Marino Marini (1901–1980), famous for his depiction of horses and riders; and Giacomo Manzù (b. 1908), who returned to an older Italian theme with his bronze door reliefs.

Opera and Music in Italy

No form of music is more Italian by nature than opera, and no country is as passionate about opera as modern Italy. Monteverdi (1567–1643) was the first composer to make opera available to a wider audience, and the operatic music of Scarlatti (1660–1725) and Pergolesi (1710–1736) set the stage for the flowering of Italian opera in the next century. Verdi (1813–1901), an amazingly prolific artist whose works include *Rigoletto, Il Trovatore, La Traviata, Otello* and *Falstaff*, escalated opera to an extraordinarily popular music form. Puccini (1858–1924) carried on the now famous Italian operatic tradition with *La Bohème, Tosca, Madama Butterfly, Gianni Schicchi* and *Turandot*.

Italy's most famous opera house is Milan's La Scala, where it's difficult and often impossible to obtain a spur-of-the-moment ticket—but there is an official December-to-April opera season in all major Italian cities. The Teatro San Carlo in Naples with its perfect acoustics, La Fenice in Venice, and the Teatro dell'Opera in Rome often feature internationally known singers and conductors; "second string" houses, such as those in Palermo, Turin, Parma, Trieste and Genoa, can also provide a memorable evening of entertainment. Audiences can be noisy, rude and enthusiastic by turns. In the summer, spectacular outdoor opera performances are held in Verona's magnificent Roman amphitheater and in the Baths of Caracalla in Rome. Florence hosts a famous music festival, the Maggio Musicale Fiorentino, every May and June, and the Festival of Two Worlds, held in Spoleto in June and July, features opera, dance and theatre performances.

Music-lovers should also check with city or regional tourist offices upon arrival for information on orchestral and chamber music concerts, and dance programs.

***Rome

You might say that Rome is excessive. There seems to be, especially at first sight, too much of everything—history, art, churches, palaces, traffic, noise, and people. It is bewildering; it is exciting; it is awe inspiring, fascinating, inexhaustible, and irresistible. You need strength for the city, because there is so much to do and see. Its mixture of pre- and Early Christian, Classical, Medieval, Baroque, and modern is like a cat's cradle of cultural elements. All these interwoven strands demand and warrant response.

Because concentrated exposure can be very wearing to body and spirit, it is advisable, even during a short stay, to deal with Rome a little at a time, with frequent interludes of rest. There are many delightful places—quite apart from restaurants or cafés—in which to renew your energies for sightseeing. Fortunately for visitors, Rome is built on seven hills—the Palatine, Capitoline, Aventine, Quirinal, Caelian, Esquiline, and Viminal—all of which afford thrilling views over this great city. The views not only allow some respite from the clamor in the streets but underline a sense of the city's 2,500-year history. Hardly the center of the world today, Rome was once the hub of a vast empire and remains the cradle of the Catholic world. A very graphic depiction of the expansion of the Roman Empire is displayed in the series of map plaques on the walls along the Via dei Fori Imperiali.

History

(Readers should refer to the Chronology chapter on page 13, especially the sections "Foundations of the Roman Empire," "The Early Empire," and "The Later Empire" for more detailed information on the early history of Rome.)

According to tradition, Rome was founded on the Palatine hill by Romulus, its first king, in 753 B.C., at the meeting point of Latin, Sabine and Etruscan territories. The site was important for Rome's later growth in military dominance and power—it was close to the sea, in a central position on the Italian peninsula, and at an easy crossing point of the Tiber. In this earliest period, seven legendary kings ruled and waged war against neighboring tribes.

The kingdom was abolished and Rome became a republic in 510 B.C. By this time, Rome was strong enough to conquer the Etruscans (474 B.C.) and the Samnites, and by the third century B.C. it had declared war on Magna Graecia and Sicily and began to challenge Carthage, its mightiest rival. The three Punic Wars ended with Rome's victory over

Carthage in 146 B.C. Through an unending series of ambitious military campaigns, and despite rampant internal strife between the aristocracy (patricians) and underclasses (plebs), Rome took control over all of Italy as well as more distant territories: Greece, Illyria and Macedonia all came under Roman domination as did, eventually, Asia Minor, Gaul, Syria, Palestine and Britain. Under the reign of Trajan (A.D. 98–117), the Roman Empire reached its maximum expansion, and included all of the then known world.

The city of Rome, headquarters of the Empire, grew steadily in size and importance, incorporating foreign cults and customs. Roman architects, after the conquest of Greece, began to use Greek models for their own buildings.

The foundation of the Empire under Octavian (later Augustus) inaugurated a period of peace and prosperity for Rome. Augustus, in a vigorous building program, had many beautiful monuments erected and older buildings restored. Divided by Augustus into 14 Regiones, Rome attained under his reign the size it was to maintain for centuries. After a fire in A.D. 64, Nero began to rebuild Rome on a regular plan. Later emperors also left their mark on the city. The Colosseum was begun in 72 by Vespasian and completed eight years later by his son, Titus; Hadrian was responsible for the erection of the Pantheon and his Mausoleum, which later became Castel Sant'Angelo; Caracalla's magnificent Baths were constructed in 217. Imperial Rome was undoubtedly a place of great splendor, filled with temples, monuments, fora, markets, palaces and sumptuous villas; and equally great squalor, for the enormous underclass of Romans and slaves had to make do as best they could. The city had a population of over a million by the second century A.D.

Rome's decline as ruler of the temporal world began when Diocletian (284) divided the empire into two administrative units: the Western Empire and Eastern Empire. Under Constantine, the seat of government was moved from Rome to Byzantium (330) and Rome began to change from a pagan city to a Christian one. The old temples were closed, pagan gods renounced, and in 334 Christianity became the official state religion. The first basilica of St. Peter was consecrated in 326, and the building of other great basilicas and countless churches began.

Barbarian tribes repeatedly sacked Rome in the fifth century, and the Byzantines and the Goths disputed over its possession. Early in the seventh century, through the intercession of Pepin the Frank, Rome came under the protection of the popes. In 800 it was the pope, Leo III, who crowned Pepin's son, Charlemagne, Emperor of the "Holy Roman Empire." Despite constant upheavals, war and intrigue, the Holy Roman Empire was to last for over a thousand years.

A Norman, Robert Guiscard, devastated the city in 1084, but Rome continued to grow as an administrative center of the Church, and by the

13th century it had become capital of the Christian world. Pilgrims flocked to the Holy City for the Christian jubilee declared in the year 1300; only nine years later, however, began the "Babylonian Captivity," when the popes moved from Rome to Avignon in France. Rome during this period was torn apart by rival factions of the various aristocratic families. The popes returned to Rome in 1378, choosing now to live on the Vatican hill rather than the Lateran palace, but it was not until some 40 years later that the city began to be restored.

A humanistic revival of the arts—the Renaissance—began in Florence, but soon reached Rome. During the next 250 years, beginning with Pope Julius II (1503–1513), who utilized the talents of Bramante, Michelangelo, and Raphael, Rome was virtually transformed. The new St. Peter's was begun, countless magnificent palaces and churches were built, buildings were restored, and town planning was carried out on a major scale.

The Renaissance style in Rome was generally austere and sober, and the period came to an end with the sack of the city by the army of Charles V. Pope Sixtus V (1585–1590) built new monumental streets and used ancient obelisks to close their vistas. (There are more Egyptian obelisks in Rome than there are in Egypt.) Much of the Rome a visitor sees today is a product of 16th century Baroque. Stylistic austerity in architecture was replaced by a theatrical sweep and flow of design and inspiration. The genius of Bernini was put to full use under Pope Urban VIII (1623–1644). Besides designing magnificent churches and palaces, Bernini was responsible for the splendid colonnade in front of St. Peter's and the elaborate fountains in Piazza Navona. The amazing work of these and other great artists, who seemed to be equally adept at architecture, painting and sculpture, is found throughout the city.

In 1798 the French entered Rome, proclaimed it a republic, and took Pope Pius VI as a prisoner to France. Napoleon annexed the States of the Church to the French Empire and in 1811 conferred the title of King of Rome on his son. Rome, the second capital of Napoleon's French Empire, began to lose many of its art treasures to the French, who removed them to Paris. Most of them were returned after the fall of Napoleon. The new pope returned to the Vatican in 1814.

Rome took an active part in Italy's next period of political turmoil, the nationalistic Risorgimento. When Pius IX, refusing to relinquish control of the Papal States, went into exile, a republic was declared in Rome. The pope called on the French for military aid and, after bitter fighting around the city walls and gates, the triumphant French army entered Rome in 1849. Pius IX returned the following year. The unification of Italy continued, however, and papal forces were defeated in 1860; King Victor Emmanuel II of Sardinia was declared King of Italy, and Rome, although it was still in the hands of the pope, was declared the capital of the new kingdom. It took another ten years before French troops left the city; the Italian army of the king entered Rome in 1870 by the Porta Pia. The following year the king established his court at the Quirinal and the pope retired to the Vatican. The great families of Rome, as they had done for centuries, again took to feuding amongst themselves, some declaring allegiance to the pope, others to the king. A great speculative building boom changed whole sections of the city, which now became a bureaucratic center of government.

The First World War had little direct effect on Rome, but immediately afterwards the Fascismo movement, under Benito Mussolini, grew in popularity. Mussolini's "March on Rome" took place in 1922, and King Victor Emmanuel III was forced to invite Mussolini to form a government. The Lateran Treaty, signed in 1929, made Vatican City an independent sovereign state. Roman buildings from this Fascist period are generally coldly grandiose attempts to restore and regain imperial grandeur. The Via della Conciliazione leading up to St. Peter's is one example (1937) as is the district called E.U.R. with its Foro Italico.

Italy entered the Second World War on the side of the Axis in 1940. The American 5th Army entered Rome in 1944, Mussolini was killed in 1945, while trying to escape, and Victor Emmanuel III abdicated a year later. A general election approved the establishment of a republic and in 1946 the first of Italy's many Presidents was elected.

Rome today faces the same international problems of terrorism, crime, congestion and pollution that are encountered in all great cities. It has dealt with these problems, in varying degrees, for centuries. It has been the greatest city in the western world, and a forgotten, malarial backwater. With nearly 3,000 years of history behind (and under) it, Rome still manages to be vibrant, exciting, and Eternal.

Attractions

Since Rome is hardly to be "done" and crossed off a list with a sense of virtuous accomplishment, serious visitors will make no bones about excluding points of no special interest from a personal itinerary. Of course it is literally impossible to take any walk or ride without seeing famous sights long familiar from photographs and paintings, nor would you want to. So much the better, since even passing glances stimulate both the senses and the imagination. Even images of what has not been explored may linger vividly in the memory.

If you are a casual visitor, take Rome's pleasures without feeling guilty about what you miss. One of life's simplest pleasures, people watching, can be indulged in easily here, since the Italians, with their dramatic expressions, gestures, and tones of voice, can enliven even mundane daily activities. The Romans' relaxed and familiar way with their city's marvels could make even the most dedicated sightseer lighten up and, in the true spirit of *la dolce vita,* take life as it comes and just enjoy *being there,* savoring the pasta and ice cream as well as the monuments.

Begin by arming yourself with a good city map and bus map and with information from the Tourist Office about entrance times and fees, shopping hours, and where to buy tickets for local and out-of-town buses. (Note that tickets must be purchased *before* you board the bus.) Orientation tours on city buses or with commercial agencies are available. If you plunge into the streets on your own, make sure you're wearing comfortable walking shoes, preferably the kind with thick, nonslip soles. Keep your valuables close to your chest and walk close to the buildings, especially on narrow streets where the term *sidewalk* becomes something of a joke. You'll be less vulnerable to both mad drivers and purse-snatching motorcyclists.

Our suggested routes for walks take in the major features of each area in the most convenient way.

WALK 1: *Piazza Venezia–***Forum Romanum– ***Colosseum

See map on pages 40–41.

This walk starts at the city's geographical center and offers both entry into the greatest of Rome's ruins and a rather daunting introduction to the challenge of Rome's traffic, most of which seems to swirl around Piazza Venezia.

In the center of the fray stands a white-gloved policeman on a little podium. The theatrical aplomb with which he directs the flow may give the scene the quality of a production number in a musical, but the fumes and the problems of crossing safely are something different. Get used to it you must, because there is a major bus stop just off the piazza where you later may want to board buses to other parts of the city.

As you enter ***Piazza Venezia** (1), you'll see the **Victor Emmanuel II monument** (2)—a huge, elaborate marble structure that has been called both a "wedding cake" and a "typewriter." Although it has Classical elements, it is hardly ancient, having been completed in 1911 to commemorate the unification of Italy and Italy's first king. Many antiquities, however, were removed from the site to make way for this monument. It isn't all show, for it serves several functions and contains the Tomb of Italy's Unknown Soldier. (Soldiers stand guard at all times.) The monument is anything but harmonious with old Rome, but it is useful as a rendezvous and as a starting point for other ventures.

Across the piazza is the 15th-century ***Palazzo Venezia,** which has been the home of popes and the Venetian embassy; it also served as Mussolini's official residence during the Fascist period.

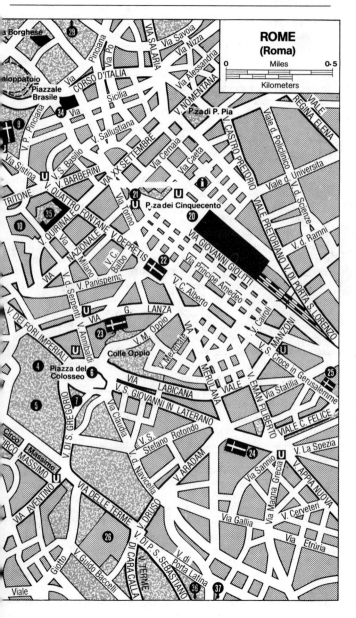

Old newsreels show Il Duce addressing thousands of people from its central balcony. With the adjoining *Palazzetto Venezia,* it now houses an art museum. Immediately adjacent is the ***basilica of San Marco,** which has stood on this spot through successive rebuildings since the fourth century. Although its interior decoration now dates mostly from the 17th–18th centuries, its splendid ceiling and portico are from the 15th century.

One of the great sights of Rome is on the slope of the *Capitoline hill* just to the left and behind the Victor Emmanuel monument—the long, broad flight of 14th-century steps leading to the austerely beautiful façade of the **church of Santa Maria d'Aracoeli.* Inside this Romanesque-Gothic church is an altar dedicated to the Madonna by the Emperor Augustus after he had a vision of the Virgin. The interior is filled with treasures and architectural elements assembled from Classical buildings and palaces; the many tombs and chapels, the fine ceiling, and the works of art serve as a kind of illustrated history of Rome. Anyone lucky enough to be in the city on Christmas Eve should try to attend midnight mass here. Inside all is gorgeous and solemn; outside crowds gather to hear the Abruzzi mountain shepherds who roam the city in that season. They play old tunes on their bagpipes in honor of the Santo Bambino, the Holy Infant, actually a bejeweled figure in a case, which is firmly believed to work miracles.

Beside this church is a shallow-stepped ramp leading to the ****Campidoglio** (3), on the Capitoline hill. This wonderful complex is made up of three palaces that form three sides of a piazza; the piazza stairs and building façades were all designed by Michelangelo. The central building is the *Palazzo Senatorio,* Rome's city hall. The flanking two are museums of sculpture and painting—the ***Museo Capitolino** on the left, the **Museo del Palazzo dei Conservatori** on the right. (One ticket admits you to both.) In the Conservatori courtyard, note the startling fragments of the colossal statue of Constantine the Great, and climb the steps of the Senatorio to view the geometrically designed mosaic paving of the piazza. Until 1981 one of the world's most famous equestrian statues, that of Emperor Marcus Aurelius, stood on the center of the piazza. Alas, not only the gold that covered it but the very fabric of the bronze statue itself had so suffered from pollution that it had to be removed for restoration. Before you leave, explore the paths off the piazza for some very special views over the city and the Forum.

Behind the Palazzo Senatorio walk down the hill and turn left to Via dei Fori Imperiali, where you enter the *****Forum Romanum** (4), that unique conglomeration of Classical ruins that has always been the goal of everyone who visits Rome. This was the site of all aspects of the ancient city's public life—social, religious, administrative, judicial, and commercial. The impressive remains are partial, broken, scattered, overgrown—and intensely evocative to anyone with the least imagination.

You can wander happily and randomly among these ruins, from columns to arches to temples to basilicas to palaces, or you can get a map that identifies the various remains. Three Corinthian columns show where the fifth-century B.C. *Temple of Castor and Pollux* (the Dioscuri) stood; the arching roof of the *basilica of Maxentius* is unmistakable; the circular *Temple of Vesta* stands next to the *House of the Vestal Virgins.* There is the *Triumphal Arch of Septimus Severus,* second century A.D.; the *Temple of Saturn,* dating from nearly 500 B.C.; and the first-century *Arch of Titus;* the second-century A.D. *Temple of Antoninus and Faustina;* and many other remains that transport the mind back into ancient history.

The Forum lies below the **Palatine Hill** (5), which has been inhabited since the Iron Age. The hill itself is intensely picturesque, with the remains of imperial palaces, *Domitian's Stadium,* the enchanting frescoes in the lovely *House of Livia,* and the beautiful *Farnese Gardens.*

Apart from the views that its height offers, the natural setting is varied and delightful, with rocks, trees, shrubbery, and paths—a perfect place for a discreet picnic—although never in the middle of a summer day, given Rome's temperatures.

**Trajan's Forum* is across the Via dei Fori Imperiali and to the left. The column that marks the Emperor's grave is covered with spiraling reliefs illustrating his military victories. There are also the remains of a semicircular **market* and the open spaces of the double forum.

From Trajan's Forum, proceed to the ***Colosseum** (6)—unmissable and unmistakable. An imposing structure of columned arcades rising high into the air, the Colosseum curves around an immense amphitheater used for gladiatorial combats, both man to man and man to beast. It was begun in the first century; after the decline of the Roman Empire, it was much vandalized until an 18th-century pope declared it sacred, in memory of the Christians martyred there. Fittingly, just outside the Colosseum is the handsome fourth-century **Arch of Constantine** (7). He was the first emperor to accept Christianity.

WALK 2: **Piazza di Spagna–**Spanish Steps– **Fontana di Trevi–**Pantheon–**Piazza Navona

See map on pages 40–41.

This walk takes in some of Rome's extraordinary Renaissance, Baroque, and late-Baroque monuments—lively piazzas, cascading stairways, colossal fountains, all of them incorporated into the rich daily fabric of the city. You begin just below the famous Spanish Steps at the Piazza di Spagna. Rome's smartest clothing and furniture shops are located on the streets leading off the piazza, and you'll see the Italian art of creating "la bella figura" (looking as beautiful as possible) being practiced with great aplomb. The walk takes you to one of Rome's (and the world's) greatest ancient monuments, the Pantheon, and ends in Piazza Navona, the most beautiful square in the city.

The ****Piazza di Spagna** (8), named for the Spanish Embassy here, is a universally favorite spot, always a crowded mecca for foreign visitors. In the spring the ****Spanish Steps** are banked with azaleas; usually there are informal art exhibitions, and there is always someone selling flowers. Because of the troops of young world-wanderers, it is often difficult to appreciate the architectural beauty of the stairs that lead up to the 15th–16th-century ***church of Trinità dei Monti** (9). (Its three levels allude to the Trinity.) At the base of the double staircase is the **Barcaccia Fountain,* shaped like a boat and usually attributed to Bernini, and the house where Keats died. On all sides of the piazza are distinguished 17th- and 18th-century buildings, and the streets leading from it contain Rome's most elegant and distinctive shopping areas. The famous Caffé Greco, on the Via dei Condotti, has been serving celebrated visitors and residents for more than two centuries, and restaurants, specialty shops, and food and wine stores abound.

From the Piazza di Spagna, Via Due Macelli leads to the *church of Sant'Andrea delle Fratte,* with its unusual brick cupola by Borromini. Just past the church is Via del Tritone, a broad, busy avenue filled with shops. From there it is a short walk to Via della Stamperia, which will bring you to the ****Fontana di Trevi** (10), Rome's grandest fountain, featured in such films as *Three Coins in the Fountain* and *La Dolce Vita*. It is extravagantly Baroque and expansive, with its lively sculptured landscape, animals, deities, and gushing water. According to old custom, visitors who throw a coin into the basin ensure a return to Rome. (The money that accumulates is used for charity.)

Backtrack to Via del Tritone, then turn left into the ***Piazza Colonna** (11) where the *Column of Marcus Aurelius* is located. It is similar to Trajan's column and in its spiraling sculptures celebrates imperial triumphs. Just beyond is the *Piazza di Montecitorio* with Bernini's 17th-century palace, now Italian government offices. The majestic obelisk at its center, topped by a sundial, was brought to Rome from Heliopolis by Augustus. It was restored from its derelict condition in the 18th century.

A short walk south brings you to Via dei Pastini. Turn left to the **Piazza di Pietra** (12), where a former customs house, now the Borsa, or Stock Exchange, has 11 tall Corinthian columns embedded in the façade. Originally they were part of a Temple of Neptune, erected by Hadrian; some of the statues from it have been moved to the Conservatori Museum on the Campidoglio.

In the neighboring *Piazza Sant'Ignazio,* the entrancing 18th-century architectural setting so cunningly suggests a stage set that you'll expect characters from some lighthearted opera to emerge from the several "wings." Here you'll find the *church of Sant'Ignazio,* erected to honor Saint Ignatius of Loyola's canonization. The ceiling of the church has a fascinating example of illusionist perspective painting, executed by Andrea Pozzo. The best spot from which to view it is marked on the floor of the church.

From Sant'Ignazio it is a moment's walk along Via del Seminario to the *Piazza della Rotonda* and one of Rome's most beautiful buildings, the ****Pantheon** (13). It has had a checkered history. Although fervently admired for almost 2,000 years, it has undergone fire and rebuilding. The inscription on the façade announces proudly that Agrippa built it: He did build the first Pantheon, at the beginning of the first century A.D. The building was enterprising and imaginative but was destroyed by fire. It is thanks to Hadrian, who rebuilt it begin-

ning in A.D. 119, and two other emperors who restored it, that we can see this glorious structure intact today. It was converted to a church early in the seventh century. Its very simple, subtle plan, its astonishing entry and door, its circular interior with a coffered dome through which Rome's rain as well as sunlight falls, its royal tombs and its artists' tombs (especially Raphael's), are its main features. The piazza itself has a Renaissance fountain, surmounted by a Rameses obelisk, and plenty of café and restaurant tables from which to feast your eyes on this very special Roman gem.

A walk around the left side of the Pantheon brings you to *Piazza della Minerva,* dominated by the Renaissance ***church of Santa Maria sopra Minerva,* with some lovely frescoes by Filippino Lippi

San Agnese and Bernini's Fountain

within. This piazza has an obelisk charmingly supported by a Bernini elephant.

If you return to the Piazza della Rotonda and then go left, angling through the small streets and crossing the Corso del Rinascimento, you will find yourself in the city's most famous and ravishing space, the ****Piazza Navona** (14)—a long oval where the Emperor Domitian's stadium once stood. It is ringed by lovely buildings in characteristic warm colors. The piazza is home to the Baroque **church of Sant'Agnese in Agone*

and the picturesque ***fountain* by Bernini, with its four symbolic representations of the Nile, the Ganges, the Danube, and the Plate rivers. Smaller fountains adorn each end of the piazza. Among the palaces at the south end of the piazza is the *Palazzo Braschi,* which houses a modern art gallery and the *Museo di Roma,* for those interested in the visual and documentary history of the city. The piazza is a popular meeting place thronged with Romans and visitors day and night.

WALK 3: **Castel Sant'Angelo–***St. Peter's Basilica–***Vatican Museums–*Gianicolo

See map on pages 40–41.

This walk begins on the west bank of the Tiber at Castel Sant'Angelo, a massive edifice that began life in pagan antiquity as a royal mausoleum and successively became a residence, fortress, and prison. From here, the walk takes you to St. Peter's Basilica, the largest church in Christendom and the home of the Roman Catholic Church. (If heights are no problem for you, be sure to go up to the roof.) An incredible (and sometimes overwhelming) wealth and variety of art treasures are found in the collections of the Vatican Museums, next on the itinerary. The Gianicolo hill, last stop on this walk, provides greenery, magnificent views of the city, and is a perfect place to sit and reflect on the glories that were and are Rome.

The ****Castel Sant'Angelo** (15) was built by Hadrian as a mausoleum for himself and his successors, but it has since been used as a residence by kings and popes, as a fortress, and as a prison. (In the latter role it is the setting for the opera *Tosca.*) Its position on the bank of the River Tiber is stunning, as are the views from its ram-

parts. Its collections of arms and furnishings and its dungeons and courtyards are of singular historical interest.

From the Castel Sant'Angelo walk toward the ****Piazza di San Pietro** (16) on the broad, modern Via della Conciliazione, to Bernini's spectacular curving colonnade in front of the basilica. The piazza embraced by the colonnade also has fountains and an Egyptian obelisk.

***San Pietro (St. Peter's) (17) (*see map on page 59*) was erected on the site of Constantine's fourth-century basilica marking the spot of Saint Peter's martyrdom (his tomb is here). Consecrated in the early 17th century, it incorporates the work of several architects, among them Michelangelo and Bramante. The interior is grandiose, with a glittering impressiveness that can hardly be denied. It is no small task to look at the many statues, monuments, mosaics, chapels, and tombs in the basilica and its grottoes. Michelangelo's *Pietà* can be seen in the first chapel on the right as you enter. The *Porta Santa* (Holy Door), opened and closed only to mark the beginning and end of a Holy Year, is the first door on the right before you enter the basilica; the balcony from which the Pope addresses the populace is above. Notice the Swiss Guards at doorways, dressed in colorful costumes designed by Michelangelo.

The *****Vatican Museums** (18), which are part of the largest palace in the world, contain immense and valuable collections of art and scholarly works. The public entrance to the museums is around to the left from St. Peter's, along the wall of Vatican City. There is so much to see here that one can choose timed routes offered at the entrance. There are endless salons and passages, but inevitably it is Michelangelo's *****Sistine Chapel** to which every visitor turns. It is the Pope's private chapel, and there is a treasury of Renaissance art on every wall, as well as the amazing ceiling that Michelangelo worked on, flat on his back, for four years. His great wall fresco of the *Last Judgment* dominates one end of the chapel (the recent and on-going cleaning and restoration work has revealed the vivid, lively colors of the original work) and there are wonderful paintings by Pinturicchio, Botticelli, Signorelli, and others on the side walls. Do bring along a pair of opera glasses or binoculars for better viewing of the works in this chapel, as well as for other places, both inside and out.

You can get to the ***Gianicolo** (Janiculum) (19), the highest point in Rome, from the *Piazza della Rovere*, downriver from St. Peter's by Ponte Principe Amedeo. Whether you walk up, passing lovely buildings as you climb, or

St. Peter's Basilica

take a bus, you will be rewarded at the top by a superb view of the city. There is a monument to Garibaldi, his wife, and his colleagues in their bitter struggle against the French, in defense of the republic. On the way up is the lovely 15th-century *church* and *cloister of Sant'Onofrio,* where you can see the tomb of the Renaissance poet Tasso, as well as frescoes in the interior and in the portico connecting the church to the monastery. Just beyond is the oak tree, now propped up with iron supports, under which Tasso sat.

Going along the Passeggiata del Gianicolo, past the *Porta San Pancrazio,* take a bus downhill to the river—and into Trastevere (Trans-Tiber area). Below the hill, almost parallel with the river, is Via della Lungara, on which is the elegant *Palazzo Corsini,* today a museum of ancient art. The 18th-century building replaced the palace where Queen Christina of Sweden lived amid her art collection and where she maintained a salon for intellectuals. Opposite this palace is the **Villa Farnesina,* with its gardens and its important collection of prints. In the 16th century it was a center of fashion and cultural life; now it is an occasional venue for receptions held by learned societies.

WALK 4: Stazione Termini–***Santa Maria Maggiore– ***San Giovanni in Laterano–**Baths of Caracalla– **San Paolo fuori le Mura

See map on pages 40–41.

Beginning in the eternally busy squares around Rome's main train station, this itinerary takes you to three of the city's four great basilicas (St. Peter's being the fourth): Santa Maria Maggiore, San Giovanni in Laterano, and San Paolo fuori le Mura. Huge and imposing, all three are important repositories of Christian history and art. The Baths of Caracalla, where important Roman men met, did business, exercised, and relaxed some 18 centuries ago, is also on this tour.

Stazione Termini (20), Rome's main railway station and one of the largest and most up to date in Europe, immediately provides one of the city's piquant contrasts: right in front of it is a fragment of the ancient *Servian Wall.* The station fronts on two squares, the *Piazza dei Cinquecento* and beyond the *Piazza della Repubblica,* with its sparkling **Naiad fountain.* On this piazza is the entrance to the ***church of Santa Maria degli Angeli** (21), created from part of ****Diocletian's Baths** (or *Terme*) by Michelangelo on papal commission.

The ***Terme Museum* (officially *Museo Nazionale Romano delle Terme*) contains many ancient works of art and archaeological finds, and the structure itself is a remarkable antiquity. In recent years it has often been closed for restoration, but it may be more accessible now; it's well worth an inquiry.

From the Piazza della Repubblica proceed along the busy commercial avenue Via Nazionale, then turn left into Via Torino (the Rome Opera is located here) until you come to ***Santa Maria Maggiore** (22), one of Rome's four great basilicas, dedicated to the Virgin. The first church on this site was built privately in the fourth century by an aristocratic Roman who had been so instructed by the Virgin in a vision. Since then it has undergone many alterations that have incorporated extremely interesting features. Among them are the wonderful Cosmati mosaic floors, the 14th-century columns, and the gilded ceiling. The campanile was added by Pope Julius II. The rich interior has work of every description by many notable hands, and several of its chapels are world famous: the *Cappella Paolina* for

Santa Maria Maggiore

its Byzantine image of the Virgin, and the *Cappella Sistina* for its treasured Christmas manger scene of half-life-size figures by Arnolfo di Cambio.

From Piazza Santa Maria Maggiore take Via del Olmata to the **church of Santa Prassede,** another architectural palimpsest from the 9th–19th centuries. The markedly Byzantine mosaics, especially in the delightful little **Cappella di San Zeno* on the right, are brilliantly colorful and have caused the church to be called the "Paradise Garden."

Next, turn right and right again to *Piazza San Martino,* then right on Via G. Lanza to the Largo Venosta and up to **San Pietro in Vincoli** (23) a fifth-century church rebuilt in the eighth and 15th centuries. The chains that are said to have bound Saint Peter are kept here in a reliquary. What brings most visitors here, however, is Michelangelo's majestic statue of **Moses*. It is only one item in the sculptor's original, and frustrated, plan for the **tomb of Pope Julius II,* meant to be installed in St. Peter's; Michelangelo intended it to consist of 40 figures, several of which are now in museums elsewhere in Europe.

The church abuts the *Esquiline hill* and the **Parco Oppio,** noted for the location of Nero's *Domus Aurea* (Golden House). What was once a luxurious palace and baths is for the most part still buried, though in process of excavation, so that its undoubted glories may be brought once more to light from beneath what became the Baths of

Michelangelo's Moses

Trajan. From here cross the park, taking Viale dei Domus Aurea towards the Colosseum, and then turn left on Via San Giovanni in Laterano, which leads to the *****basilica of San Giovanni in Laterano** (24), the cathedral of Rome and the world. The first basilica in Rome stood here, built by Constantine in the fourth century A.D., but it was replaced in the fifth century. Traces of the first one, as well as of palace baths, can still be seen. The basilica complex contains several noteworthy items among its many superb works, including the oldest bell in Rome, the tallest and oldest obelisk in Rome, bronze doors to the Chapel of St. John the Baptist that give off a musical tone when moved, and one of the most exquisite **cloisters in the city.

Beside the church, in the southwest corner of the piazza, is ***San Giovanni in Fonte,* also known as the Baptistry of Saint John, built by Constantine in A.D. 315–324. The design of this octagonal building was subsequently used as a model for other baptistries.

A red granite obelisk, Rome's oldest and tallest, stands in the *Piazza San Giovanni Laterano.* Dating from the reign of the Egyptian pharaoh Thothmes IV (15th century B.C.), it was brought to Rome by Constantinius II in A.D. 357 and formerly stood in the Circus Maximus.

The adjacent *Palazzo Laterano,* the Popes' residence and ecclesiastical center before the exile to Avignon, now houses several museums, one of them devoted to missionary documentation. Opposite the palazzo is a 16th-century building designed by Domenico Fontana to house the ***Scala Santa** (Holy Staircase) that leads up to the *chapel of San Lorenzo,* or the *Sanctum Sanctorum,* once the Pope's private palace chapel. The wood-covered staircase is one that devout Catholics ascend on their knees, although the beauty of the chapel may be seen only through a grille. The staircase is traditionally iden-

Scala Santa

tified as the one on which Christ's blood was shed when he mounted into Pontius Pilate's presence.

A walk of about 15 minutes through the *Piazza di Porta San Giovanni* along Viale Carlo Felice past a ruined amphitheater (the Aurelian Wall runs parallel) brings you to the ***church of Santa Croce in Gerusalemme** (25). Its central structure is an early Roman palace that was taken over by Constantine's mother, Helena, who is said to have brought a fragment of the True Cross from Jerusalem in about A.D. 320 to be a relic for her church. Despite earlier elements, the church today is Baroque, even Rococo in style.

From the piazza in front of the church, follow Via Eleniana to the *Porta Maggiore,* the junction point for two Roman aqueducts dating from A.D. 52, which Aurelius utilized as a gate in his city wall and which later became part of a fortification. Outside the gate is a picturesquely decorated tomb that a first-century Roman baker, Eurysaces, erected for himself and his wife. Just past the gate on the Via Prenestina is another unusual feature, the underground ****Basilica di Porta Maggiore,** a first-century relic belonging perhaps to an ancient sect. Its interior is covered with well-preserved stuccos, some on mythological subjects, some representing daily activities or symbolic appurtenances. The building now lies practically under railway tracks and was unearthed only in 1916.

To complete this walk, you can take Via Porta Maggiore to the *Piazza Vittorio Emanuele II* (an interesting market square) then go on to Via Carlo Alberto and Santa Maria Maggiore and next Via Cavour back to *Stazione Termini.* Or, given time and energy, you can continue the tour, going by bus or taxi from Piazza San Giovanni in Laterano through Via di San Stefano Rotondo. On the small hill of *Monte Celio* there is a fifth-century church, **San Stefano Rotonda,* which is one of the largest and oldest circular churches in existence, but generally closed because of excavation and restoration work. The interior frescoes, showing scenes of martyrdom, are particularly gruesome.

Cross Monte Celio on Via della Navicella to come to the ****Terme,** or **Baths of Caracalla** (26), dating from the third–fifth centuries. The largest, most luxurious of Roman baths, they are now impressive, vast ruins in the midst of which operas are staged in the summer. From here go along Via di Porta San Sebastiano (which leads directly to the Via Appia Antica) to the **Sepolcro degli Scipioni* (tomb of the Scipio family) and several underground *columbaria;* the word may mean "dovecote," but these were cineraria, for the burial urns of cremated Romans.

From the Baths of Caracalla, Viale Giotto leads west to ***Porta San Paolo** in the Aurelian Wall (27), with its fortified towers. There the impressive white stone **pyramid of Gaius Cestius,* who died in 12 B.C., rises well above the wall. Farther on is the so-called *Protestant Cemetery* (it is in fact reserved for all non-Catholics), where Keats's body and Shelley's heart are buried.

From the *Piazzale Ostiense,* just outside the Porta San Paolo, go about 2 km. (1 mile) south to the ***basilica of San Paolo fuori le Mura** (28) one of the most important churches of the Christian world. It was erected by Constantine on the site of the Apostle Paul's burial but was replaced with a larger basilica by later emperors and was completed in the year 400. It was added to, decorated, and restored over several centuries. It stood strong through a number of earthquakes but was brought down by a fire in 1825 and then was almost completely rebuilt. Fortunately, many of its treasures were saved and needed only restoration. Both architecturally and horticulturally, the *cloisters* are among Rome's finest and most beautiful.

WALK 5: **Villa Borghese–*Pincio–*Piazza del Popolo–*Piazza del Quirinale

See map on pages 40–41.

The park of the Villa Borghese, where this walk begins, is a green oasis set amongst the roar and tumult of modern Rome. Equally refreshing is the adjoining park called the Pincio, which provides a camera-ready panoramic view out over the palaces, churches, domes, roof gardens, and spires of the Eternal City—with St. Peter's gleaming in the distance across the Tiber. The Piazza del Quirinale, on the highest of Rome's seven hills, is the last major attraction on this walk. It is the site of the Quirinal Palace, which was the summer residence of the popes before it became the residence of the Italian royal family, and is now the home of the President of the Italian Republic.

Villa Borghese is Rome's largest park, created for Cardinal Scipione Borghese's private use in the early 17th century. The "villa" itself is more a palace; it houses the **Museo Borghese** (29) collections of antiquities and masterpieces by most of the greatest Italian masters. Because of restoration, access to it has been difficult in recent years, so check with the authorities about entrance. The park is a lovely place, green and flowering, varied in character from area to area, crisscrossed by footpaths, and furnished with benches. You go from formal gardens to natural landscapes, from race track (Galoppatoio) to zoo to charming lake with a Classical temple, to tree-covered slopes, and groves of Rome's umbrella pines. The *Piazza di Siena* and its amphitheater are the scene of an annual international horse show.

Other museums are on the north side of the park, on the Viale della Belle Arti—the *Galleria Nazionale d'Arte Moderna (30), and down the road from it the ****Museo Nazionale di Villa Giulia** (31), filled with an enormous and important collection of Etruscan works of art and artifacts. This is housed in a 16th-century palace built for Pope Julius III but never really lived in, only used as a refuge and for entertainment in its once extensive and beautifully planted gardens.

The ***Pincio** (32) is a public park laid out in the early 19th century in the style of the 17th and 18th centuries. This has always been a hill of gardens, and these formal gardens are complete with dozens of busts of famous Italians. The Pincio adjoins the *Borghese gardens;* one need only cross a path from one to the other. It contains a rather expensive restaurant, the *Casina Valadier,* some snack bars, a diverting and unusual water clock, and a bandstand where brass bands play operatic arias. It is a good place to sit and watch Roman families at play. Most of all, it is famous for its terrace (*Piazzale Napoleone I*), which overlooks the Piazza del Popolo as well as most of Rome; it is a view not to be missed.

At the foot of the Pincio is the ***Piazza del Popolo** (33) with its *Porta del Popolo;* this arch has Michelangelo's designs on the outside and Bernini's inside. It was decorated by Bernini to honor Queen Christina's entry into Rome. The arch is flanked by the twin churches of *Santa Maria di Monte Santo* and *Santa Maria dei Miracoli*. Opposite them is **Santa*

Maria del Popolo (the one closest to the Pincio wall). Small as it is, it contains works by Pinturicchio, Sansovino, Raphael, and Caravaggio, among others. The piazza, with its churches and palaces, is one of the city's liveliest areas as well as one of the most attractive. A large café faces a very popular restaurant across a space that features the second oldest obelisk in Rome, also brought by Augustus from Heliopolis. Three streets fan out toward the center of the city. The central one, Via del Corso, leads to *Piazza Venezia;* the left one, Via del Babuino to the *Piazza di Spagna,* and farther along to the *Quirinal Palace.* You can also leave Villa Borghese by the wide, tree-lined Via Vittorio Veneto (34).

Palazzo del Quirinale (35), the late-16th-century palace on the **Piazza Quirinale* was once the summer residence of the popes, then of the kings of Italy, and is now the presidential palace. To reach it, follow Via Babuino

Piazza del Quirinale

from Piazza del Popolo to Piazza di Spagna, where you take Via Due Macelli to Via di Traforo. On its elevated position, the Palazzo Quirinale is especially impressive. It has an austere Renaissance façade, a great courtyard, and a magnificent interior with a hall of mirrors and a superb staircase.

The two huge marble sculptures of Castor and Pollux with their horses, flanking the entrance to the courtyard, are particularly arresting. Opposite the palace is the 18th-century *Palazzo della Consulta,* once the seat of a court concerned with papal matters and now a ministry.

WALK 6: **Via Appia Antica

See map on pages 40–41.

The Old Appian Way, which is covered in this walk, was opened in 312 B.C. to link Rome with southern Italy. It is one of the most picturesque, moving, and historically rich areas of the city, for here you will find the great early Christian catacombs of Saint Callistus, Saint Sebastian, and Domitilla. The modern imagination cannot help but be stirred by these ancient burial sites, some of them dating back to the very beginnings of Christianity, and the scattered reminders of ancient Rome—tomb markers and paving stones—beside the road.

From the **Baths of Caracalla,* the Via di Porta San Sebastiano leads toward the *Arch of Drusus* (second century B.C.), once a support for the aqueducts bringing water to the baths, and the *Porta San Sebastiano* (36). This gateway in the Aurelian Wall is particularly fine, with its two towers housing the *Museo delle Mura Romane,* especially interesting for those who are curious about the history of the city walls. The 20-km.- (12-mile-) stretch of the **Via Appia Antica,** which you enter through this gate, served long ago as a passageway for funeral processions, since the dead were not permitted burial inside the walls. As a result, there are a number of catacombs along the ancient road, together with the

ruins of the fortified, circular *tomb of Cecelia Metella,* familiar from any pictorial representation of the road with its pines and cypresses, and other evocative remains. A short distance from the gateway is the chapel erected in the ninth century, *Domine quo vadis?* (37) on the spot where Saint Peter, fleeing from Roman persecution, had a vision of Jesus coming toward the city and asked "Domine, quo vadis?" "(Lord, where are you going?") At Christ's answer, "I go to be crucified anew," Peter, ashamed, changed course and returned to the city and his own martyrdom.

Less than a mile beyond the church is the entrance to the **Catacombe di San Callisto,**

Tusculum, Cato's birthplace, which includes a theater, amphitheater, reservoir, and forum, as well as Cicero's villa, which is mentioned along with others in Latin literature.

Some 3 km. (2 miles) beyond Frascati on the Via Vittorio Veneto is the town of *Grottaferrata,* set among vineyards. Its main feature is an 11th-century Greek *abbey* that later became the property of Pope Julius II. Shortly beyond Frascati and Marino on a picturesque corniche is the *Via dei Laghi,* which first skirts the dark, very deep crater lake, *Lago di Albano,* in its wonderful setting. Just beyond and higher up is *Monte Cabo;* the town on its slopes is *Rocca di Papa,* the highest spot in the Castelli Romani and the site of a 12th-century papal castle. Go on to *Nemi* and its lovely lake, *Lago di Nemi,* another deep crater whose slopes are covered with vineyards. The name derives from the grove sacred to the goddess Diana (Nemus Dianae), of which only substructures have been found.

From Nemi a road leads upward to *Genzano,* known for its wine as well as for its view of the lake. On the shore of the lake is the *Museo delle Navi Romani,* which has replicas of two Roman imperial ships. A few kilometers along the Via Appia Nuova is *Ariccia,* with some buildings by Bernini, including the *Palazzo Chigi,* with a wooded park, and the domed *church of Santa Maria dell' Assunzione.* Ariccia is connected with Albano by a viaduct built by Pope Pius IX in the 19th century.

*Albano, the largest town in these hills, has associations with Pompey and Domitian and was a bishop's seat, becoming a papal property in the late 17th century. Among the ruins of its ancient buildings are the *Porta Praetoria*—gateway to a fort built by Septimius Severus—an amphitheater, monasteries and tombs, and a cistern built into the rock. The *church of Santa Maria della*

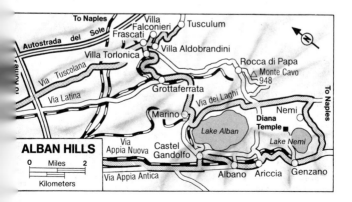

Rotonda, with interesting frescoes, was erected above an ancient circular temple.

It is another 2 km. (about 1 mile) to **Castel Gandolfo* on Lago di Albano. Since the 17th century, popes have maintained their summer residence here in a palazzo designed by Maderna. The *church of San Tommaso da Villanova*, on the piazza, was built by Bernini.

From Castel Gandolfo the Via Appia Nuova (Route S 7) leads back to Rome.

ST. PETER'S BASILICA

Façade by Maderna (1)
Navicella by Giotto (2)
Entrance hall by Maderna (3)
Bronze door by Filarete)4)
Porta Santa (5)
Cappella della Pietà (6)
Pietà by Michelangelo (7)
Ancient sarcophagus (8)
Cappella del Crocifisso (9)
Statue of Leo XII (10)
Monument to Queen Christina of Sweden (11)
Cappella di San Sebastiano (12)
Monument to Innocent XII (13)
Monument to Countess Mathilde of Tuscany by Bernini (14)
Cappella del Santissimo Sacramento by Borromini (15)
Altar of the Cappella del Santissimo Sacramento, ciborium by Bernini, The Trinity by Pietro da Cortona (16)
Stairway to the Scala Regia (17)
Staircase to organ (18)
Monument to Gregory XIII (19)
Tomb of Gregory XIV (20)
Communion of St. Jerome (21)
Tomb of Gregory XVI (22)
Chapel of the Madonna del Soccorso (23)
Altar of Saint Basil (24)
Tomb of Benedict XIV (25)
Mosaic of Saint Wenceslas (26)
Martyrdom of Saints Processus and Martinian (27)
Martyrdom of Saint Erasmus (28)
Altar of the Navicella (29)
Monument to Clement XIII by Canova (30)
Mosaic of Saint Michael (31)
Mosaic of Saint Petronilla (32)
Mosaic of Saint Peter raising Tabitha (33)
Monument to Clement X (34)

Monument to Urban VIII by Bernini (35)
Chair of Saint Peter by Bernini (36)
Monument to Paul III (37)
Monument to Alexander VIII (38)
Mosaic of Saint Peter healing the paralytic (39)
Tomb of Saint Leo the Great (40)
Madonna della Colonna (41)
Monument of Alexander VII (42)
Apparition of the Sacred Heart (43)
Mosaic of Saint Thomas (44)
Mosaic of the Crucifixion of Saint Peter (45)
Mosaic of Saint Joseph (46)
Monument to Pius VIII; entrance to sacristy and treasury (47)
Pier of Saints Andrew, Ananias, and Sapphira (48)
Tomb of Saint Gregory the Great (49)
Monument to Pius VII by Thorvaldsen (50)
Transfiguration (51)
Monuments of Leo XI (52)
Monument to Saint Innocent XI (53)
Altar with mosaic of the Immaculate Conception (54)
Cappella del Coro (55)
Monument to Saint Pius X (56)
Monument to Innocent VIII (57)
Cappella della Presentazione (58)
Monument to Clementina Sobieski; entrance to the cupola (59)
Monument to the Last Stuarts by Canova (60)
Baptistry (61)
Holy water font (62)
Statue of Saint Peter (63)
Statue of Saint Longinus by Bernini (64
Statue of Saint Helena (65)
Statue of Saint Veronica (66)
Statue of Saint Andrew (67)
High altar with Confessione (68)
Baldacchino by Bernini (69)

ST. PETER'S BASILICA

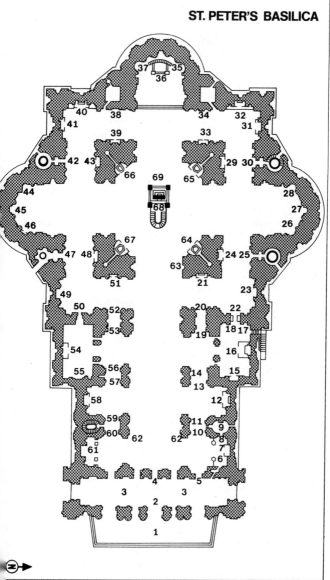

***Florence

Florence (Firenze) gave birth to the Renaissance in the 14th century. More than 600 years later, thanks to legislative limits on building and traffic in the center of the city, the Medieval and Renaissance aspects still dominate it. Marble-clad churches, stately palazzi, and red-roofed buildings spread gently across the city's site on a small basin along the Arno River, all overlooked by the graceful red dome that Filippo Brunelleschi designed for the cathedral in 1420. The city's stark architecture provides quite a contrast to the throngs of tourists who flock here year-round for its renowned artistic tradition as well as for its contemporary crafts and leather goods.

History

Though the site of Florence was inhabited as early as the tenth century B.C., it was overshadowed for centuries by the larger and more important Fiesole, a nearby Etruscan city which, like Florence, later became Roman. Under Julius Caesar, Florentia ("the flourishing one") was made a veterans' colony; it began to live up to its name only when it became the Roman administrative capital of Tuscany and Umbria around the third century A.D. Subsequently overrun by Ostrogoths, Byzantines, Lombards, and Franks, Florence became an autonomous commune in 1115. The city lost no time in destroying Fiesole (1125), establishing itself as the leading power in Tuscany, and beginning the Guelph (pro-pope) and Ghibelline (pro-emperor) conflicts that—along with plagues and famines—tore the city apart over the next few centuries. The Medici family came to power in 1421. The prosperity and relative political stability associated with their reign set the stage for an increased interest in the Classical age of Rome and Greece and in secular humanism, which later spread throughout Europe and became known as the Renaissance. Despite brief interruptions brought about by three banishments and the rise of the ascetic reformer Girolamo Savonarola, the Medici ruled until 1737, when Florence passed to the Austrian House of Lorraine. Following the unification of Italy, Florence enjoyed a brief period as the national capital (1865–1871), after which its importance shifted from politics to art history and tourism. Today it serves as the regional capital of Tuscany.

Attractions

The historical center is closed to almost all automobile traffic from 8 A.M. to 8 P.M., and in any case, walking is the best way to see Florence. You can park your car in lots near the *Fortezza da Basso* and the train station, or in front of the *Palazzo Pitti* across the river.

WALK 1: Stazione di Santa Maria Novella–***Duomo– ***Galleria degli Uffizi–*Santa Croce

See map on pages 62–63.

This walk is designed to introduce you to the main ("must-see") sights of Florence, a city of almost inexhaustible treasures. The Duomo, with its famous landmark dome by Brunelleschi, is only one part of a breathtaking complex of religious buildings that includes the baptistry, one of the city's oldest structures, and the 14th-century campanile designed by Giotto. The Piazza della Signoria, on the other hand, is Florence's greatest urban square. One masterpiece after another lines the gallery walls of the Uffizi, where you can view the world's greatest collection of Florentine Renaissance art. Two of the city's most important churches—Santa Maria Novella and Santa Croce—are also on this itinerary.

Designed in 1934 by Giovanni Michelucci using golden stone, the main train station, *Stazione di Santa Maria Novella* (1), reflects the color and crisp lines of the surrounding buildings. The back of the church for which the station was named, ***Santa Maria Novella*** (2), is across the piazza, and its entrance is around the corner on its own piazza. Originally part of a Dominican monastery, the present complex was begun in the 13th century. The lower part of the church's façade is Romanesque, using green and white marble similar to that of the Battistero, and dates from the mid-14th century, while its portal and upper portion were completed in a compatible Classical style by Leon Battista Alberti in 1470, the date inscribed to the architect's patron, Giovanni di Paolo Rucellai, in Roman numerals under the pediment. Santa Maria Novella is generally considered to be the most important Gothic church in Tuscany. Among the works of art in the triple-naved interior of the church, restored to its present state by Giorgio Vasari in the mid-16th century, are the *Cappella Rucellai,* with a marble statue of the *Madonna and Child* signed by Nino Pisano; the *Cappella di Filippo Strozzi,* with frescoes depicting the lives of Saint Philip and Saint John the Evangelist by Filippino Lippi; the main altar, with a bronze crucifix by Giambologna and, in the sanctuary behind it, frescoes by Domenico Ghirlandaio; the *Cappella Gondi,* with a wooden crucifix by Brunelleschi; the *Cappella Strozzi* with frescoes by Nardo di Cione and an altarpiece by his brother Andrea (more commonly known as Orcagna); the sacristy with a crucifix by Giotto; and in the third bay of the left aisle, the fresco of the *Holy Trinity with the Virgin, Saint John the Evangelist, and Donors*

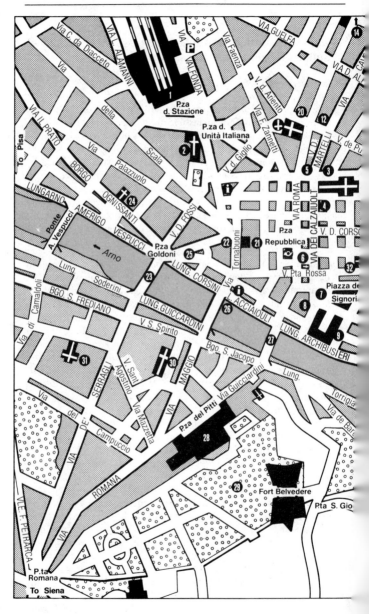

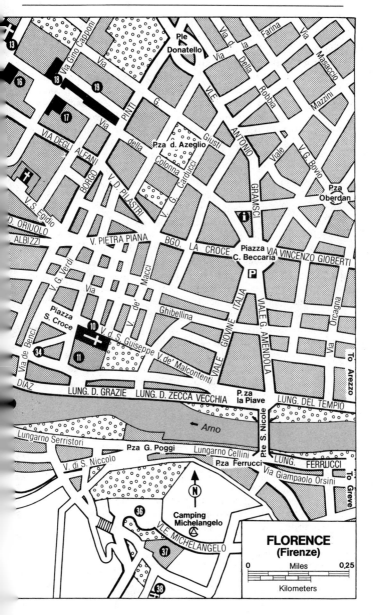

FLORENCE
(Firenze)

0   Miles   0.25

Kilometers

by Masaccio. Next door in the *Chiostro Verde* are the frescoes considered to be Paolo Uccello's masterpieces; their green tint give the cloister its name. North of the cloister is the *Cappellone degli Spagnoli*, used as a place of worship by the courtiers of Spanish-born Eleonora di Toledo, wife of Cosimo I de' Medici (or di Buonaiuto).

Leaving the complex by way of Via de' Banchi and continuing east on Via de' Cerretani with its splendid palazzi, you will come to the ***Duomo** (3) of Santa Maria del Fiore ("Fiore" is an allusion to Florence). Dominated by Brunelleschi's dome, which in turn dominates all of Florence, the cathedral was begun in 1294 by Arnolfo di Cambio. Its façade (made of white marble from Carrara, green marble from Prato, and red marble from the Maremma), was finished only in 1887. The stark interior contains 15th-century stained glass by Lorenzo Ghiberti in the nave, frescoes by Vasari and Federico Zuccari in the dome, and such monumental works as Tino da Camaino's *Tomb of Antonio d'Orso* dating from about 1321, and the 15th-century frescoes of Uccello and Andrea del Castagno, both of which commemorate *condottieri* on horseback. The 463-step ascent to the dome provides views of the inside of the church, the construction of the dome, and the city outside.

More works of art relating to the Duomo may be found at the nearby *Museo dell'Opera del Duomo,* which houses Michelangelo's ****Pietà**, and works by Donatello. Rising beside the Duomo is the ***Campanile** (4), or bell tower, made of the same three marbles as the cathedral. It was begun by Giotto in 1334 and finished by Francesco Talenti in 1359; you can climb its 414 steps for views of the Duomo and the rest of Florence.

In front of the cathedral is the ***Battistero di San Giovanni** (5), or baptistry. One of Florence's oldest structures, the octagonal building was once believed to have been a Roman temple of Mars. It was probably built in the sixth or seventh century, and in the 12th century it was given the green-and-white marble facing which so influenced Tuscan Romanesque architecture. The 14th-century bronze doors by Andrea Pisano, on the baptistry's south side, were the first such portals cast since antiquity. Ghiberti continued the tradition in the 15th century by casting the north doors and then the east doors, his most famous work. Called the "Gates of Paradise" by Michelangelo, the latter set depicts scenes from the Old Testament. Inside are 13th-century ceiling mosaics, some of them designed by Giovanni Cimabue, and a 15th-century tomb by Donatello and Michelozzo.

From the *Piazza San Giovanni* in front of the cathedral, lively Via de' Calzaiuoli leads south toward the Arno River. On the right, a few blocks from the Duomo, is ***Orsanmichele** (6), a 14th-century Gothic building that originally was a market with a granary above and later was converted to a church. Statues in its exterior niches are by Andrea del Verrocchio, Ghiberti, and Donatello. The interior contains a tabernacle by Orcagna that frames a *Madonna* painted by Bernardo Daddi.

A few steps farther is the *Piazza della Signoria,* a spacious square where excavations are under way to uncover an extensive area of Medieval residences. The ***Palazzo Vecchio** (7), also known as the *Palazzo della Signoria,* was begun at the end of the 13th century to designs attributed to Arnolfo di Cambio. It housed the original Signoria, the elected ministers of the Florentine Republic, and even today is used as the city hall. Between 1540 and 1550 it was the residence of the Medici family, who entrusted Vasari with extensive decoration. The courtyard contains a copy of a 15th-century bronze fountain of a putto

with a dolphin by Verrocchio (the original is in the Cancelleria upstairs). Upstairs is the *Salone dei Cinquecento,* with Michelangelo's *Victory,* and another room called the *Studiolo di Francesco I,* decorated by Vasari. Another flight up is the *Quartiere di Eleonora di Toledo,* containing frescoes by Bronzino, a Donatello statue of *Judith and Holofernes,* and Verrocchio's original bronze putto from the fountain.

In front of the palace, in the *Piazza della Signoria,* there is a copy of Michelangelo's *David* (the original is in the Galleria dell'Accademia). Many of the other statues that once adorned the piazza are in the Museo del Bargello. However, an *equestrian statue* of Cosimo I de' Medici, by Giambologna, and the *Neptune fountain* by Bartolomeo Ammannati, still remain.

On one side of the square is the ****Loggia dei Lanzi** (8), an arcaded gallery built in the 14th century for public gatherings and festivities. Since the 18th century, such celebrated 16th-century works as Benvenuto Cellini's *Perseus* and Giambologna's *Rape of the Sabine* have been displayed here.

The *Palazzo degli Uffizi* extends off Piazza della Signoria. Built by Vasari as government offices (*uffici* or *uffizi*) in the mid-16th century, it is now home of the *****Galleria degli Uffizi** (9), which contains the most important collection of Florentine Renaissance art in the world. The

Florence: Palazzo Vecchio

tour begins with a room displaying three painters' versions of the *Maestà:* Duccio di Buoninsegna's surface-oriented depiction, Cimabue's late Byzantine panel, and Giotto's spatially sophisticated later vision. The Sienese painter Simone Martini's *Annunciation* is in the next room, followed by Gentile da Fabriano's *Adoration of the Magi* and Paolo Uccello's *Battle of San Romano.* Further on, Sandro Botticelli has several famous works, including the *Primavera* and the *Birth of Venus.* Leonardo da Vinci's *Adoration of the Magi* and *Annunciation* lead to the octagonal room called the Tribuna, which houses the *Medici Venus,* a Roman copy of a Greek original, the most famous work of Classical art in Florence. In the museum's west corridor are Michelangelo's *Doni Tondo,* Raphael's *Portrait of Leo X,* Titian's *Venus of Urbino,* and Parmigianino's *Madonna of the Long Neck.*

From the Piazza della Signoria, follow Via della Ninna, a typically Medieval Florentine street, east as it becomes Via de' Neri. Turn left on Via de' Benci to *Piazza Santa Croce,* the location of the church of ***Santa Croce** (10). Rebuilt in the 13th century, it has a 19th-century façade like the Duomo. Its interior contains over 200 *tombs,* including those of Galileo, Michelangelo, Machiavelli, Foscolo, Alfieri, and Rossini. Among its treasures are a 15th-century marble pulpit by Benedetto da Maiano to the right of the nave, a relief of the *Annunciation* by Donatello in the right aisle, and 14th-century frescoes by Giotto in the first two chapels to the right of the choir. Reached by a separate entrance south of the church portal is a cloister with the *Cappella dei Pazzi,* a masterpiece of architecture by Brunelleschi with terracotta roundels by Luca della Robbia. Off the same cloister is the *Museo dell'Opera di Santa Croce,* which contains the Cimabue *Crucifix,* restored after the 1966 flood caused extensive damage to the museum and the adjacent *Biblioteca Nazionale* (11). On the left side of the church, Via delle Pinzochere leads to Via Ghibellina, where at No. 70 is *Casa Buonarroti,* a house bought by Michelangelo for his nephew Leonardo, where two early bas-reliefs by the artist, as well as various models and drawings, are on display.

WALK 2: ***Duomo–*San Marco–*Santissima Annunziata–*Museo Archeologico

See map on pages 62–63.

Three important museums are featured in Walk 2. A former Dominican monastery next to the church of San Marco contains unsurpassed examples of Fra Angelico's fresco work; Michaelangelo's famous statue of David is housed in the Galleria dell'Accademia; and superb Etruscan and

Egyptian works are displayed in the Museo Archeologico. Also on the itinerary is the 15th-century Spedale degli Innocenti, a foundling hospital considered to be one of the first true buildings of the Renaissance, and the Palazzo Medici-Riccardi, once the home of the Medici family.

From *Piazza San Giovanni* in front of the Duomo, follow Via de' Martelli north until it becomes *Via Cavour;* on the left is the ***Palazzo Medici-Riccardi** (12). Constructed in the mid-15th century by Michelozzo for Cosimo de' Medici, it served as the family's residence until they moved into the Palazzo Vecchio and contains a chapel decorated with frescoes by Benozzo Gozzoli of the *Procession of the Magi into Bethlehem,* actually portraits of the Medici family. In 1670 the palazzo passed into the hands of the Riccardi family, who nonetheless allowed the Medici family's glorification to be continued with the Luca Giordano fresco in the gallery, depicting the *Apotheosis of the Medici,* painted in 1683.

Farther along Via Cavour is the ***church of San Marco** (13),

Palazzo Medici-Riccardi

started during the Romanesque period, renovated during the Renaissance by Michelozzo, and given a Baroque façade in 1780. At the end of the 15th century, Savonarola, the prior of San Marco, led Florentines in a puritanical heresy against the wealth and excesses of the church. (In 1498, the city turned against him and burned him at the stake in the Piazza della Signoria.) The adjacent Dominican monastery built by Michelozzo, now houses the **Museo dell'Angelico* or *di San Marco,* a collection of the 15th-century works of Fra Angelico, many gathered from former locations in Florence. In addition, there are frescoes painted by Fra Angelico and his assistants in the corridors and monks' cells, as well as a *Last Supper* by Domenico Ghirlandaio in the refectory.

Taking Via degli Arazzieri off *Piazza San Marco* and continuing to where it becomes Via XXVII Aprile, at No. 1 you will come to the **Cenacolo di Sant' Apollonia** (14), where Andrea del Castagno's fresco of *The Last Supper,* second in importance only to Leonardo da Vinci's depiction of the subject in Milan, is on display in the refectory. Above it are three more frescoes by Castagno.

Farther down Via Cavour is the *Casino Mediceo* at No. 57, built by Buontalenti for Francesco I de' Medici. It once housed a sculpture garden assembled by Lorenzo de' Medici, but today holds law courts. Continuing along Via Cavour, you will come to the ***Chiostro dello Scalzo** (15), at No. 69, which has a beautiful colonnade and 16th-century frescoes by Andrea del Sarto, depicting scenes from the life of Saint John the Baptist.

On the opposite side of Piazza San Marco at Via Ricasoli No. 60 is the ***Galleria dell'Accademia** (16), best known as the location of Michelangelo's original *David* but also containing other examples of the artist's work. The Galleria also has numerous paintings of the Florentine school, from the Middle Ages to the Renaissance.

Around the corner to the right, off Piazza San Marco, Via Cesare Battisti leads to the *Piazza della Santissima Annunziata,* dominated by an *equestrian statue* of Grand Duke Ferdinand I, begun by Giambologna and finished by his pupil Pietro Tacca. Tacca also is responsible for the *fountains* on either side of the piazza, which originally were destined for the port city of Livorno and therefore depict sea monsters.

The most important building on the piazza is the **Spedale degli Innocenti** (17), or foundling hospital. Begun by Brunelleschi and finished by Francesco della Luna in 1445, it is considered one of the first true buildings of the Renaissance in its use of Classical elements and principles. Between the arches of the loggia are Andrea della Robbia's ten ceramic roundels of infants in swaddling clothes. (The ones at the ends are copies.) Inside are two cloisters and the *Galleria dell'Ospedale degli Innocenti,* a museum containing works by Luca della Robbia, Piero di Cosimo, and Ghirlandaio.

On another side of the piazza is the ***church of the Santissima Annunziata** (18), begun in the mid-13th century by members of the Servite order, founded by wealthy Florentines. The church was rebuilt by Michelozzo and other architects in 1444–1481. There are a number of important Mannerist frescoes inside. Another outstanding work of art is the *tempietto* to the left of the nave entrance, which houses a much-revered image of the Virgin. Works by Andrea del Castagno are found in the first and second chapels to the left. In a chapel off the sanctuary is a *Resurrection* by Bronzino. The *Chiostro dei Morti* contains Andrea del Sarto's *Madonna del Sacco.*

Via della Colonna leads off the piazza to the ***Museo Archeologico** (19). Among the many artifacts it houses are the sixth-century B.C. Greek *François Vase,* the fifth-century B.C. Etruscan *Mother* figure and *Chimera,* and the second-century B.C. Etruscan *Orator.* The museum's Egyptian collection is Italy's most important outside of Turin.

WALK 3: ***Duomo–**San Lorenzo–*Palazzo Strozzi– Ognissanti–**Ponte Vecchio–**Palazzo Pitti–*Santa Maria del Carmine

See map on pages 62–63.

Splendid Florentine churches, chapels and palaces from the Gothic, Renaissance and Baroque periods are featured in Walk 3. In the Capella Medicee you'll be able to see Michelangelo's famous sculptures of Dawn, Dusk, Day and Night, and, a few steps away, his architectural work in the Biblioteca Laurenziana. Borgo San Lorenzo and Via de' Tornabuoni are major shopping streets, where you can find all manner of Florentine specialties. Frescoes by Ghirlandaio, Botticelli and Masaccio grace the churches of the Ognissanti and Santa Maria del Carmine. The famous Ponte Vecchio is included in this itinerary, as is the Pitti Palace with its superb art collection, located across the Arno River. A stroll in the beautiful Boboli Gardens is a memorable highlight of any trip to Florence— from here you'll have a view of the city and its remarkable cathedral.

From Piazza San Giovanni in front of the Duomo, follow *Via de' Martelli* to the Palazzo Medici-Riccardi and turn left on Via de' Gori to the ****church of San Lorenzo** (20), a Renaissance church rebuilt by Brunelleschi and filled with paintings by Rosso Fiorentino, Filippo Lippi and Bronzino, a marble tabernacle by Desiderio da Settignano, and two bronze pulpits that are the last works by Donatello (1460). Brunelleschi's so-called *Old Sacristy* contains four medallions by Donatello, depicting scenes from the life of Saint John and the Evangelists, bronze doors by Donatello, and a porphyry tomb by Verrocchio.

Around San Lorenzo, on the *Piazza di Madonna degli Aldobrandini,* is the entrance to the *Capelle Medicee.* The **Cappella dei Principi,* a mausoleum for the Medici grand-dukes, is decorated

with hard, brightly colored types of stone called *pietre dure.* A passage to the left leads to the ****Sagrestia Nuova,** begun by Michelangelo and never completed. On the left is the *tomb of Lorenzo,* Duke of Urbino, which supports Michelangelo's allegorical figures of *Dawn* and *Dusk;* to

San Lorenzo

the right is the *tomb of Giuliano,* Duke of Nemours, with the figures of *Day* and *Night.* Another work by Michelangelo (constructed in collaboration with Vasari) may been seen by going through the cloister of the church: The *Biblioteca Laurenziana,* noted for its staircase, is considered one of the first examples of Mannerist architecture.

From the front of San Lorenzo, follow the shopping street *Borgo San Lorenzo* south to Via de' Cerretani, where you turn right and walk through the *Piazza Santa Maria Maggiore* (its church dates from the 13th century) and angle left on Via Rondinelli to the *Piazza Antinori. Palazzo Antinori,* on the right of the piazza, is a small, 15th-century palace with a beautiful garden, and the *church of San Gaetano,* on the left, is a rare example of Baroque architecture in Florence. Continuing, the street becomes Via de' Tornabuoni, Florence's most elegant shopping street, lined with fabric, leather, and jewelry shops. Among the grand palaces lining the street is the 15th-century ***Palazzo Strozzi** (21), one of the most stately Renaissance buildings of the city. Via della Vigna Nuova angles off from the corner of the palace past the early Renaissance *Palazzo Rucellai* (22), designed by Alberti, to *Piazza Goldoni,* where the Arno River is bridged by the *Ponte alle Carraia* (23). This span, like all the bridges in Florence except the Ponte Vecchio, was reconstructed after

being destroyed during the German retreat from the city in 1944. From the Piazza Goldoni it is a short walk along *Borgo Ognissanti* to the **church of Ognissanti** (24), a 13th-century church rebuilt during the Baroque period. In the church proper are frescoes by Ghirlandaio and Taddeo Gaddi, as well as a crucifix by a follower of Giotto. In the refectory are more frescoes by Domenico Ghirlandaio and Botticelli. From *Piazza d'Ognissanti,* head upriver along the Arno past Piazza Goldoni to **Palazzo Corsini** (25), a Baroque palace enlivened by the terraces, statues, and busts on its façade. The next bridge across the Arno is the *Ponte a Santa Trinita* (26), built by Ammannati with assistance from Michelangelo, and reassembled after World War II using as much of the original material as could be dredged from the river, including the statues of the *Quattri Stagione* (Four Seasons) at either end. From the bridge you have an excellent view of the Ponte Vecchio. The nearby *Piazza Santa Trinita* is the site of the Renaissance *Palazzo Bartolini-Salimbeni* and the Gothic *church of Santa Trinita,* which contains a lovely triptych of the *Annunciation* by Lorenzo Monaco, frescoes by Ghirlandaio in the *Cappella Sassetti,* and a marble tomb decorated with a ceramic frame by Luca della Robbia.

Continuing along the river, you will come to the ****Ponte Vecchio** (27), which spans the Arno at its narrowest point in Florence. The present structure was built in 1345, and the small goldsmiths' and jewelers' shops that line it were the idea of Ferdinand I de' Medici, who replaced blacksmiths' and butchers' shops with more elegant enterprises. Midway across the bridge there is a small square, which has excellent views of the city downstream.

The Ponte Vecchio leads to the Oltrarno section of Florence (literally, "the other side of the Arno"), a former working-class suburb filled with old palazzi. The most sumptuous of these is the ****Palazzo Pitti** (28), reached from the end of the Ponte Vecchio by Via Guicciardini. Begun in the 1450s for Luca Pitti, the rival of Cosimo de' Medici, it was acquired in 1549 by the Medici, who increased its splendor by adding works of art and expanding the original building. (It reached its present state in the early 19th century, with the addition of the two front wings.) After being home to the grand dukes of Tuscany, it became the royal residence of King Victor Emmanuel II when Florence was the capital of Italy; after World War II it was the original home of the Florence fashion shows, which have since been moved to the Fortezza da Basso.

The most important of the museums housed in the Palazzo Pitti is the ****Galleria Palatina,** which contains masterpieces by Titian, Rubens, Van Dyck, Tintoretto, and Raphael, as well as many Baroque and other paintings. In addition, the *Galleria d'Arte Moderna* houses primarily Italian 18th- to 20th-century paintings; the *Museo degli Argenti* displays the Medici collection of antique stone vases and extravagantly crafted objects; the *Appartamenti Monumentali* once were occupied by the House of Savoy; and, in the *Palazzina della Meridiana,* the *Collezione Contini-Bonacossi* is noted for its costume collection and Italian and Spanish paintings. The extensive ***Boboli Gardens** (29), just behind the palace, are among the most beautifully landscaped gardens in Italy. The layout dates from the mid-16th century, when Eleonora di Toledo and Cosimo I de' Medici moved to the Pitti Palace and commissioned the formal gardens, with their fountains, statues, and cypress allées. The gardens extend up the slope of the hill of San Giorgio, crowned by the *Forte di Belvedere,* which has magnificent views of the city.

After returning to Piazza Pitti, in front of the palazzo take Sdrucciolo dei Pitti across Via Maggio (where many fine antiques shops are located), where it becomes Via dei Michelozzi, to the remarkable **church of Santo Spirito** (30), designed by Brunelleschi in the 15th century. Among the highlights of its interior, surrounded by 38 semicircular chapels, are a *Madonna and Child With Saints* by Filippino Lippi, and the *Cappella Corbinelli,* designed by Andrea Sansovino.

At the other end of Piazza Santo Spirito, turn right on Via Sant'Agostino to Via Santa Monica and the **church of Santa Maria del Carmine** (31). This Romanesque-Gothic church was rebuilt after a fire in 1771, which fortunately did not damage the frescoes in the *Cappella Bran-cacci*. The *Expulsion from Paradise* and *Tribute Money,* painted by Masaccio in the early 15th century, profoundly influenced Renaissance painting; there are other frescoes in the chapel by Masaccio, Masolino and Filippino Lippi.

WALK 4: ***Duomo–**Museo del Bargello–*Piazzale Michelangelo–*San Miniato al Monte

See map on pages 62–63.

Highlights of Walk 4 include the Museo del Bargello, which displays masterpieces of sculpture by the greatest artists of the Renaissance, and the church of San Miniato al Monte, located on a hill overlooking Florence and the surrounding countryside. On your way to this superb example of Tuscan Romanesque architecture, you'll be able to stop at the monumental Piazzale Michelangelo.

From the east side of the Piazza del Duomo, follow Via del Proconsolo south for several blocks to the **Badia Fiorentina** (32), a 10th-century Benedictine church, altered in the 13th-century and rebuilt in the Baroque style in the 17th century. It houses Filippino Lippi's *Madonna Appearing to St. Bernard,* as well as Mino da Fiesole's tombs for Bernardo Giugni and Count Ugo. Across from the church is the ****Palazzo del Podesta** or *del Bargello* (33), built in the 13th–14th centuries as the city hall. It now houses the ***Museo del Bargello,* the most important collection of Renaissance sculpture in Florence. Among its masterpieces are three by Michelangelo: *Drunken Bacchus, Pitti Tondo,* and *Brutus.*

Other superb works include Sansovino's *Bacchus;* a *Narcissus, Ganymede,* and bust of *Cosimo I* by Cellini; Giambologna's *Mercury;* and two versions of *David,* one by Donatello and another by Verocchio. Here, too, are Brunelleschi and Ghiberti's competitive panels of *The Sacrifice of Isaac* for the baptistry doors.

From *Piazza San Firenze* in front of the Bargello, Via dell' Anguillara leads east to *Piazza Santa Croce.* From there it is a short walk toward the Arno along Via de' Benci to No. 6, a small 15th-century palazzo. It is home to the **Museo Horne** (34), a collection of 14th–16th century paintings, as well as furniture, household utensils and decorative arts, assembled in the early 20th century by the English art historian Herbert Percy Horne, who lived in the palazzo.

Beyond the Horne museum is the *Ponte alle Grazie* (35), which crosses the Arno to *Piazza de' Mozzi* and the *Museo Bardini*. The present structure was built in 1883 on the site of the 13th-century church of San Giorgio della Pace from parts of other buildings (the façades' windows are framed with fragments from a Pistoian altar). It houses an art collection, which includes Classical, Renaissance, and Baroque sculpture as well as paintings by such masters as Antonio Pollaiuolo and Francesco Salviati.

From Piazza de' Mozzi, *Lungarno Serristori* leads to *Piazza Giuseppe Poggi*, where a series of terraced steps leads up to ***Piazzale Michelangelo** (36). This vast piazza surrounds a monument to Michelangelo, which consists of bronze copies of his marble statues of David and the allegorical figures from the Medici tombs in San Lorenzo. The place is celebrated for its magnificent view of Florence and the surrounding hills, including Fiesole and Settignano. The stairs at the side of the restaurant in the piazza lead to the simple, 15th-century **church of San Salvatore al Monte** (37), and above it the **church of San Miniato al Monte** (38), one of the best examples of Tuscan Romanesque in existence. Its façade is composed of the same green-and-white marble found on other monuments in

Florence. Inside is the *Cappella del Crocifisso,* designed by Michelozzo, with a vault by Luca della Robbia; a 13th-century marble screen and pulpit; and the 15th-century *Cappella del Cardinale de Portogallo,* which contains the tomb of the Cardinal of Portugal by Antonio Rossellino and a ceiling with fine medallions by Luca della Robbia.

Excursions from Florence

**Fiesole (8 km., 5 miles, from Florence): *By car: Take Viale Allessandro Volta to Via di San Domenico, which climbs the hill to Fiesole. By bus: take the No. 7 bus from the Stazione Centrale, the Duomo, Piazza San Marco, or other points in Florence.*

Founded in the 7th century B.C. by the Etruscans, Fiesole became an important Roman colony in 80 B.C. and vied for predominance with Florence until the latter city captured it in 1125. Its charming views of Florence from *Piazza Mino da Fiesole,* and interesting Roman theater and baths make it a pleasant trip. It also has a Romanesque *Duomo* (which contains columns with Roman capitals and works by Mino da Fiesole and Giovanni della Robbia), the 14th–15th-century *convent of San Francesco* on the site of the ancient acropolis, and the *Museo Bandini,* with Etruscan tombs and Renaissance paintings.

*Settignano (8 km., 5 miles, from Florence): *By car: Follow signs from Via del Campofiore. By*

bus: take the No. 10 from Stazione Centrale, the Duomo, or Piazza San Marco.

Settignano, the home of Desiderio and other 15th-century sculptors, is a small village with many villas nearby, among them *Villa I Tatti,* once the home of art connoisseur Bernard Berenson (occasionally open to specialists by appointment); and the 15th-century *Villa Gamberaia,* which has a noteworthy garden. The cypress-and-olive clad hills between Settignano and Fiesole, in particular the villages of *Monte Ceceri* and *Maiano,* are excellent for hiking.

*Certosa del Galluzzo (8 km., 5 miles, from Florence): *By car: Follow Route S 2 south toward Siena; signs mark the road to the monastery, on the right past the village of Galluzzo. By bus: Take the No. 36 or 37 from Piazza Santa Maria Novella.*

This Carthusian monastery, built in the 14th century, has a *pinacoteca* in its *Palazzo degli Studi,* which contains early-16th-century frescoes by Jacopo Pontormo. The adjacent *church of San Lorenzo* has underground Gothic chapels with a number of tombs, notably those of Niccolò Acciaiuoli, who founded the monastery in 1341, and Cardinal Agnolo II Aciaiuoli.

***Venice

Venezia (Venice) is entirely the work of human hands. For centuries the most important sea power in the world, the city is built on 117 islands separated by canals, and connected by more than 400 bridges. It has manifold individual treasures and attractions, but perhaps the main one is the visual delight it offers no matter which way you look, or at what time of the day, or from land or water. It is undoubtedly this special quality, together with the absence of motor traffic, that continues to draw visitors here from all over the globe. G. K. Chesterton once described Venice as a city "whose very slums are full of palaces, whose every other house has a battered fresco, or a Gothic bas-relief . . . a sky fretted with every kind of pinnacle . . ." Its visual seduction is as complex and interesting as its history.

History

Conflicting dates are given for the founding of Venice. An Illyrian tribe, the *Veneti,* originally occupied the area, forming a defensive alliance with Rome in the third century B.C. In A.D. 452, the invading forces of Attila the Hun drove the inhabitants from the mainland to the islands in the lagoon. The island communities formed a naval confederation under a doge (from Latin *dux,* "leader") in 697, and in 811 *Rivus Altus* (Rialto)—the present-day Venice—became the seat of government. The Evangelist Mark, whose remains were brought to Venice in 829, became the patron saint of the Venetian Republic; his symbol, a lion, became the city's emblem.

By the tenth century, Venetians had created an empire that extended all the way to Asia Minor. The city became so powerful and well-defended that, in 1502, it resisted a combined attempt at invasion by Emperor Maximilian I, Louis XII of France, Ferdinand of Aragon, and Pope Julius II.

The golden age of Venetian art and culture peaked during the 15th and 16th centuries. Its character was most vividly expressed by such masters as Titian, Tintoretto, and Veronese, whose works are very much on display in Venice today. Although aspects of the economic and political decline of the city were apparent as early as the 16th century, its culture continued to flourish, as the works of Tiepolo, Canaletto, Guardi, and Longhi make clear.

In 1797, the once mighty republic yielded to the strength of Napoleon's armies. Later, Venice was ruled by Austria until 1866, when it was incorporated into the United Kingdom of Italy.

Attractions

See map on page 77.

The heart of Venice is *****Piazza San Marco** (St. Mark's Square), one of the largest and most ravishing urban spaces in the world. It is surrounded by the cathedral, which magnificently dominates the square, a picturesque *campanile* (bell tower), and two long colonnaded palaces, each housing a world-famous café—*Florian* and *Quadri*. In season, their tables spill out into the piazza, and their bands sometimes compete to entertain. The space is usually flooded with tourists, pigeons, and—in the winter months—the rising waters of the Grand Canal.

***Basilica San Marco (1), which John Ruskin termed "a treasure heap," is a unique structure, the crowning glory of the Venetian Republic, and an edifice that truly merits the adjectives "exotic" and "fantastic." The effect it has on a visitor entering the piazza for the first time and seeing the basilica from afar cannot be described. It stands on the site where two earlier churches were built to house the remains of Saint Mark. The churches were destroyed, and the present building dates from the 11th century. It is a combination of Venetian and Byzantine styles, with doors in arched portals, the central one the highest. Five domes echo the five pointed arches above the cornice line. Eight centuries of artists have made the basilica—inside and out—one of the world's most colorful assemblages, filled with sculpture, mosaics, frescoes, and ornaments made of precious materials. On a terrace above the doors are replicas of four ****bronze Graeco-Roman horses** that were brought from Constantinople to Venice in 1204. The originals have been removed to the basilica museum (*Museo Marciano*) because pollution had seriously damaged them. The replicas convey the dynamic effect of the originals, however, and now the marvel of the originals' artistry can be examined at close hand.

The basilica's interior is darkly gleaming, and the wealth of decoration can best be appreciated from the galleries around the walls. From there you can see the column capitals and the extraordinary Medieval mosaics on arches and walls, and get an overview of

Basilica di San Marco

the famous **Pala d'Oro* behind the high altar above the tomb of Saint Mark. This altarpiece is a masterwork of Byzantine goldsmiths, richly inlaid with gold and precious stones, and covered with intricate cloisonné enamelwork. The cathedral *Tesoro* (Treasury) is rich with booty taken from Constantinople in 1204, and the museum had, apart from its newly acquired horses, a wealth of Byzantine sculptures, icons, gems, metal objects, and other church treasures. Enter from the museum to the front terrace, where the horses are located, for a superb view of the piazza.

In front of the basilica is the

*Campanile, a faithful restoration of the tenth-century bell tower that suddenly and inexplicably collapsed in 1902. The 16th-century *Loggetta* at its base also was crushed in the collapse and was restored; an elevator takes you to the top of the tower, where you can relish another marvelous view.

On the north side of the piazza is the **Torre dell'Orologio** (3), a 15th-century clock tower. Two bronze figures, known as "I Mori" (the Moors), signal the hour by striking a bell with their hammers. The clock tower stands over the entrance to the *Mercerie,* a busy (and in the summer, very crowded) shopping area of wind-

VENICE (Venezia)

0   Miles   0.25

Kilometers

Train Station
Ponte degli Scalzi
S. Geremia
To Murano, Burano, and Torcello
C.po dei Gesuiti
Giardino Papadopoli
Corte Canal
Ponte degli Scalzi
Canal
Canal Grande
Strada Nuova
Fondamente Nuove
S. Giacomo di Rialto
C.po S. Polo
Riva del Vin
C.po S. Bartolomeo
C.po S. Maria Formosa
C.po S. Rocco
Salizzada S. Pantalon
Calle della Mandola
C.po S. Luca
C.po S. Margherita
C.po S. Manin
Markusplatz
C.po Morsini
Calle Larga 22 Marzo
Ponte dell'Academia
Punta della Dogana
Canale di S. Marco
Canal
Canale della Giudecca
Isola di S.Giorgio Maggiore
To Lido

Palazzo Ducale and
Piazza di San Marco

ing streets that lead toward the Rialto Bridge. In the Mercerie a bewildering number of shops aim to break down your resistance on every possible level.

To the left of the clock tower stretch the early 16th-century *Procuratie Vecchie,* the offices and residences of the administrators of San Marco. The buildings directly opposite are the **Procuratie Nuove** (5), begun toward the end of the same century; during Napoleon's occupation of the city in 1797, they were a royal palace. This building now also houses the ***Museo Correr** (4), with its varied collection of items related to the city—ceramics, ceremonial clothes of the doges, weapons and trophies, as well as important paintings, among them Dirk Bouts' *Madonna and Child,* and Giovanni Bellini's *Transfiguration.*

The extension of Piazza San Marco between the basilica and the waterfront is called the *Piazzetta.* The *Marciana Library*

(designed, like the Loggetta, by Sansovino) occupies the west side; it contains frescoes by Titian, Tintoretto, and other masters. Directly opposite is the **Palazzo Ducale,** the seat of the doges' government and their courthouse from the ninth century to the fall of the republic of Napoleon.

The subtly dazzling exterior, with its pink-and-white geometrically patterned walls, pointed arches, and pierced rosettes, dates from the 14th–15th centuries. In the magnificent Renaissance courtyard is the *Scala dei Giganti* (Giants' Staircase), where Sansovino's colossal statues of Mars and Neptune lead to the loggia. From here the *Scala d'Oro* (Golden Staircase) leads to the second floor (or *piano nobile*). The sumptuous rooms on this floor were once the doges' private apartments and are decorated with paintings by the great Italian masters. The *chiesetta* (chapel) contains a marble group by Sansovino. Apartments throughout the palace, including state chambers, cabinet rooms, and council halls, contain some of the city's finest works, in almost overwhelming abundance. On the far side of the palace, in front of the entrance to the *Old Prison,* a staircase leads to the legendary **Ponte dei Sospiri* (Bridge of Sighs), which spans a narrow canal, and gives access to the New Prison.

Leaving the Palazzo Ducale, it is a short walk, if a confusing one (with only an occasional signpost), through a maze of alleys to the second most important square in Venice, the ****Campo Santi Giovanni e Paolo** and the *church* (7) of that name (also rather confusingly called *San Zanipolo* in the Venetian dialect). The church is the principal one in the eastern part of Venice. In the interior, built between 1246 and 1430, are the monumental tombs of many doges and other famous Venetians. Its important art works include a monument of Doge Pietro Mocenigo by Pietro Lombardo and, in the San Domenico chapel, a famous 18th-century ceiling painting by Piazzetta. The Gothic window at the end of the right transept is decorated with stained glass from drawings by Vivarini and Mocetto, the only 15th-century stained glass remaining in Venice.

Just south of the church, in the piazza, is the monument that Ruskin deemed "glorious," the equestrian statue of Bartolommeo Colleoni (general of the condottieri, or mercenaries) by the Florentine sculptor Verrocchio (Leonardo da Vinci's teacher). The statue captures Colleoni's power and air of fierce pride. Adjacent to the church is the Renaissance **Scuola di San Marco,** originally the seat of a philanthropic society, now a hospital. It is notable for the very persuasive trompe-l'oeil panels on the lower façade.

From the southwest corner of the piazza, the *Ponte Rosso* leads to the Calle delle Erbe. Continue on this street, cross the Ponte delle Erbe, and follow the Calle Castelli to the small but exquisite ***church of Santa Maria dei Miracoli** (8). This many-colored 15th-century marble building by the Lombardo brothers, is one of the gems of Renaissance architecture. The coffered barrel vault of the single-nave interior is embellished by heads of saints and prophets, its choir stalls by charming figures.

One of the most wondrous ways to view Venice is from a boat on the *****Canal Grande;** its curving route is flanked by more than 200 entrancing palaces. You may hire a gondola (romantic but expensive), take a motor launch (the Venetian version of a taxi), or simply ride on one of the *vaporetti* (water buses) that are the city's public transportation system. The *vaporetti* ply up and down the waterway at frequent intervals, with many stops, giving access to different parts of the city. Sights to look for, beginning at the Piazza San Marco and moving toward the railway station include: ***Santa Maria della Salute** (9). This Baroque church, crowned by an impressive dome, stands on the point of land opposite the piazza. It was built by Longhena as an offering of thanks for Venice's deliverance from the plague of 1630. The sacristy contains remarkable paintings by Titian and Tintoretto, and there is an altarpiece by Giordano.

**Accademia di Belle Arti (10) houses in its *Galleria* the largest collection of paintings in Venice; it constitutes a complete survey of

Venetian painting from the 14th to the 18th centuries, as well as offering works of other artists.

**Palazzo Franchetti (11), also called *Palazzo Cavalli,* was built in the 15th-century lancet style, and is one of the city's most beautiful palaces.

*Palazzo Rezzonico (12), perhaps the most opulent palazzo on the Grand Canal, dates from the 17th century, although it received its top story a hundred years later. It contains the *Museo del Settecento Veneziano,* which authentically recreates the ambience of an 18th-century palace, with its pictures, furnishings, and objets d'art. Next door is the *Palazzo Foscari* (13), now part of the university; in the 16th century, King Henry III of France stayed here as a guest.

**Santa Maria Gloriosa dei Frari (14). Usually referred to as "I Frari," and one of the city's most beautiful churches, it was constructed between 1330 and 1443 in the Gothic style, with a Venetian-Byzantine bell tower. The interior contains tombs of such important personages as Titian and the sculptor Canova. The carved choir stalls and the high altar date from the 15th century. The chief masterpieces in the church are Titian's *Assumption* (on the high altar), and his *Madonna di Ca'Pescaro,* the triptych of a *Madonna and Child between Saints* by Giovanni Bellini on the sacristy altar, and Sansovino's baptismal font.

Just west of I Frari is the *church of San Rocco* (15th century, renovated in the 18th century), with eight works by Tintoretto. Across the little *campo* is the ****Scuola Grande di San Rocco** (1515–1560), one of the six great Venetian charitable confraternities that flourished during the Renaissance. Dedicated to Saint Roch, patron of plague victims, the school was built with donations from Venetians seeking protection from the plague. The white marble façade, with its colored discs, is in Renaissance style. Inside is a series of 56 canvases by Tintoretto on the ground floor and upper floors, as well as paintings by other Venetian masters.

**Ponte di Rialto (15), the most elaborate bridge in the city, was built in the last years of the 16th century on the site of an old wooden bridge. It crosses the Grand Canal with a single arch. Now, as for centuries past, the Rialto area is the business center of Venice. Where once silks and spices were traded, souvenirs, vegetables, fish, and clothing are now sold. The Rialto provides an extremely animated and colorful scene and perhaps an occasional bargain.

**Ca' d'Oro (16) is a richly decorated and romantically fanciful Gothic palace built between 1425–1440 by Bartolomeo Bon and several others, and seems to embody the essence of Venetian style. It derives its name from the gilding that once adorned its

Venice: Ca' d'Oro

façade. The palace houses the *Galleria Franchetti,* beautifully disposed in the handsome chambers. Among its treasures are masterworks by Mantegna, Titian, Carpaccio, Lippi, Ghirlandaio, Signorelli, Tintoretto (of course), and others, along with sculpture and other works of art.

*Palazzo Pesaro (17), a sumptuous Baroque palace adorned with masks, is home to the *Museo Orientale* and a large collection of contemporary art in the *Galleria d'Arte Moderna.*

The 13th-century Venetian-Byzantine-style palace **Fondaco dei Turchi** (19) was the residence of Emperor Frederick III when he lived in Venice from 1452 to 1469. It served as an embassy in the early 17th century; then, for two centuries, was a warehouse for Turkish merchants. Now it is the *Museo di Storia Naturale* (Museum of Natural History). There is an exhibition of Venetian fountains on the ground floor.

Chiesa degli Scalzi (20) or Gli Scalzi, was built by Longhena in the 17th century in Baroque style for the barefoot (scalzi) order of Carmelites. It contains paintings by Tiepolo and the tomb of the last doge. The church is close to the *main train station,* Santa Lucia, (21) and the *Piazzale Roma* (22), the terminus for buses connecting Venice with the mainland, where huge parking garages store the cars of many visitors to Venice. The piazza is also the point of departure for the airport.

Near the mouth of the Grand and the Guidecca canals, and standing on an island of its own, is the majestic white **church of San Giorgio Maggiore,* one of the most splendid sights of Venice. It was begun by the architect Palladio in 1566, and completed in 1610 by Scamozzi. Its campanile affords an unsurpassed view even in a city so rich in vistas.

Excursions from Venice

*Lido (1.4 km.; 1 mile from Venice): *By vaporetto: numbers 6 or 11 from Riva degli Schiavoni; Number 2 from Piazzale Roma or Rialto.*

The Lido is known throughout the world for its sandy beaches and cosmopolitan atmosphere. The once highly fashionable resort is still a pleasant retreat from the city, with its casino (open only in summer) a main attraction. Some visitors come for a dip in the sea or an uninhibited sunbath, and some take the boat just for the very pleasant ride and the unforgettably romantic views of the city.

*Burano: *By vaporetto: numbers 5 or 12 from Fondamenta Nuova.*

This lagoon island is the center of the Venetian glass industry, which began in the 13th century. Remnants of its former splendor still are visible. There is the Gothic *church of San Pietro Martire;* the Gothic *Palazzo da Mula;* the *Museo Vetrario* (Glasswork Museum) in the *Palazzo Giustiniani;* and the Venetian-Byzantine-style *basilica of Santi Maria e Donato,* with its strikingly beautiful apse facing the canal. There are, of course, numerous shops selling glass objects.

*Burano: *By vaporetto: Number 12 from Fondamenta Nuova.*

Burano, with its small, neat, brightly painted houses, is a picturesque fishing island, whose lace-making schools have been known since the 16th century. Islanders still make and sell lace, and visitors may tour the *Scuola dei Merletti* (Lace School) on the main square, *Piazza Baldassare Galuppi.* The *church of San Martino* houses a Tiepolo *Crucifixion* and several Mansueti paintings. Restaurants serve delicious fish dishes; *da Romano* is the best known.

**Torcello: *By vaporetto: Number 12 from Fondamenta Nuova.*

Torcello, perhaps the most romantic of the lagoon islands, was the main town of the lagoon from the seventh to the ninth centuries. This once prosperous and well-populated wool center is now almost deserted, yet still a place of pilgrimage for its church and cathedral. **Santa Fosca,* dating from the 11th century, has an interesting apse and columns with Byzantine capitals. ***Santa Maria Assunta,* the seventh-century Byzantine cathedral (rebuilt in 1008), contains magnificent Greek columns, remarkable Byzantine mosaics, a seventh-century bishop's throne, and other friezes and mosaics. A pair of 14th-century palaces, *Palazzo del Consiglio* and *Palazzo dell'-Archivi,* now serve as museums, with collections of Roman vases, inscriptions, small bronzes, and other excavated artifacts, as well as religious objects from the cathedral and from demolished churches on the island.

Ernest Hemingway used to fish on Torcello. Another note of sophistication is its famous and expensive restaurant, *Locanda Cipriani,* which looks simple and homely enough from outside. There are two other more modest restaurants on the island.

*Chioggia (25 km.; 6 miles from Venice): *By vaporetto: Number 11 from the Lido (makes bus connections). By bus: from Piazzale Roma. By car: causeway to Mestre, Route S 309 along the lagoon to Chioggia.*

A picturesque and pleasant fishing port, Chioggia is like Venice, built on islands, and connected with the mainland by a long bridge. The 11th-century *Duomo* (rebuilt by Longhena in the 17th century) was erected next to a 14th-century Romanesque bell tower and the small 14th-century *church of San Martino*. A more secular attraction is the fish market held daily behind the early 14th-century *Granaio*. As might be expected, the restaurants on the Corso always serve fresh fish. *Sottomarina Lido*, connected to Chioggia by a bridge, has a long, sandy beach, a church with an altar by Sansovino, and a 14th-century *castello*.

***Naples

Naples, or *Bella Napoli* to its admirers, is situated on the Bay of Naples and still is lovely despite massive traffic and industrial pollution. The curve of the *bay,* with Mount Vesuvius in the distance, is one of the most beautiful sweeps of land in Italy. Naples is the third largest city in Italy, after Rome and Milan, and it is the major city of the south.

Napoli is known for its survivalist population who specialize in *l' arte d' arrangiarsi:* (the art of making do—of inventing and improvising and getting by with a little help from their friends).

History

Greek settlers from Cumae, just north on the coast, came down and built the city of Partenope about the 8th century B.C. Then Greeks from Sicily moved in and built the new city, or Neapolis, a name which has become Napoli.

Under Norman rule during the 12th century, Naples became part of the Kingdom of Sicily, where Roger II ruled. In 1266 the city belonged to the Angevins and in 1458 to the Spanish. Later, Naples was ruled by the Spanish House of Bourbon until 1860, when Garibaldi began the unification of Italy. The city was badly bombed during World War II.

Attractions

The five sightseeing routes described here depart from the Piazza del Municipio, which commands a wonderful view of the bay.

WALK 1: Piazza del Municipio–**Castel Nuovo– *Palazzo Reale–**Castel Dell'Ovo–**Santa Lucia

See map on page 86.

This walk, encompassing an area adjacent to the Bay of Naples, includes two royal palaces, the famous Neapolitan opera house, a 12th-century fortress, and ends in the picturesque quarter of Santa Lucia. Along the way there are splendid views.

At the enormous *Piazza del Municipio* (1) there is a bit of everything—city park, equestrian statue of Victor Emmanuel II, bus and trolley outdoor terminal, the Classical *Palazzo Giacomo* (1819), and the **church of*

San Giacomo degli Spagnoli, founded by Don Pedro de Toledo in 1514. Don Pedro's impressive tomb lies within, the work of Giovanni da Nola.

At the side of the piazza, turn up the hill into the **Castel

Nuovo (2), the former residence of Neapolitan kings and viceroys. It was built for Charles of Anjou during the 13th century and much rearranged under Alfonso of Aragon. The gem of the castle is the newly restored *Triumphal Arch,* an early Renaissance masterpiece built to welcome Alfonso to Naples. Inside, the *Cappella di Santa Barbara* (or Palatina) has a lovely portal with a *Madonna* by Laurana atop it. Laurana was a superb interpreter of the Madonna, and his statues of her with the Child grace many churches in the south of Italy. A stairway leads to the *Sala dei Baroni,* now the seat of the city council. On the waterfront below the castle is the **Stazione Marittima** (3), where large ocean liners and cruise ships dock. (Also the overnight boat to Palermo, in case you decide to take it.) The ferries for Ischia and Capri leave nearby, while the hydrofoil harbor is north along the bay.

Next to the Castel Nuovo is the ***Palazzo Reale** (4), the royal palace whose 168-meter- (550-foot-) façade is decorated with statues of eight of the major rulers of Naples: Roger the Norman, Frederick II Hohenstaufen (Stupor Mundi); Charles I of Anjou; Alfonso I of Aragon; Emperor Charles V; Charles III of Bourbon; Joachim Murat; and Victor Emmanuel II.

Within the palace, which was constructed during the 17th and 18th centuries, are the *royal apartments,* an art gallery, and the *Teatro di Corte,* the royal theater.

The *Biblioteca Nazionale,* with more than a million and a half books, also is housed here.

Alongside is the ***Teatro San Carlo** (5), the opera house, whose acoustics are among the best in the world. It was built in 1737 in a classical style and rebuilt after the fire of 1816. After La Scala in Milan, San Carlo is Italy's most famous opera house. Go inside to see the golden royal box and the scarlet velvet seats. Even if a bit worn, the royal atmosphere still recalls the genius and artistry of Puccini and Verdi. Facing the Palazzo Reale across the car-infested *Piazza del Plebiscito,* a semicircular monument with equestrian statues of the Bourbon King Charles and Ferdinand of Aragon flanks the **church of San Francesco di Paola** (6), which is beautiful on Sunday or in the early morning before the piazza becomes a garage. It was modeled after the Pantheon in Rome, and its 53-meter- (174-foot-) coffered dome is supported by 34 marble columns.

From the Piazza del Plebiscito, Via Cesario Console passes the public gardens, with sweeping views of the busy harbor and Mount Vesuvius, and curves into the port and district of ****Santa Lucia,** which forms a small peninsula in the bay. This quarter is filled with hotels that command fine harbor and Vesuvius views, and alleyways of typical Neapolitan trattorias, where moderately priced food and wine can be enjoyed while watching the gusto of Neapolitan life. Via Nazario

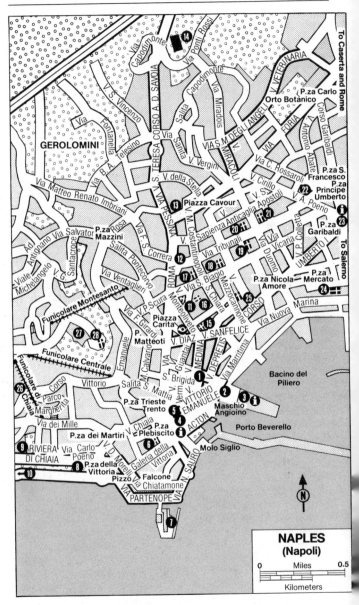

To Caserta and Rome

Via Ponti Rossi

Capodimonte

14

Via Capodimonte

V. S. Vincenzo

Salita Capodimonte

Via Miradois

V. VETERINARIA

P.za Carlo

Orto Botanico

Corso Garibaldi

Via Fontanella

Via

Via B. A. Telesino

GEROLOMINI

Via Matteo Renato Imbriani

S. TERESA CORSO A. D. SAVOIA

Santa v. Vergini

V. della Stella

VIA S. M. DEGLI ANGELI

VIA S. MIRACOLI

FORIA

Antonio Abate

Via C. Rossaroli

P.za S. Francesco

P.za Principe Umberto

V. A. Poerio

22

Ad Antignano Via Salvator Rosa

P.za Mazzini

Via F. S. Correra

Salita Pontecorvo

V. Cirillo

V. SS. Apostoli

V. S. Costantinopoli

Sapienza Anticaglia

20

21

13 **Piazza Cavour**

V. M.

Via Tribunali

Via Duomo

V. P. Colletta

P.za Garibaldi

23

Viale Michelangelo

V. G.

Santacroce

Via Ventaglieri

ROMA

12

17

18 19

V. S. Biagio

V. San Mezzocannone

V. Vicaria

UMBERTO

P.za Garibaldi

To Salerno

Funicolare Montesanto

Via P. Scura

Via F. Girardi

V. S. Chiara

V. S. Anna

25

P.za Nicola Amore

CORSO

Via Nuova

Marina

24

27 28

Funicolare Centrale

Emanuele

PIAZZA Carita

P.za Matteoti

V. DIAZ

V. SANFELICE

15

16

11

V. Medina

V. DEPRETIS

Via Marittima

Vittorio

Salita S. Mattia

S. Brigida

V. Guanta

V. VITTORIO EMANUELE

1

Bacino del Piliero

Funicolare di Chiaia

26

Corso Parco Margherita

Via dei Mille

P.za Trieste Trento

5

S. Chiara

P.za Plebiscito

4

ACTON

Maschio Angioino

2

3

Porto Beverello

9 **RIVIERA DI CHIAIA**

Via Carlo Poerio

P.za dei Martiri

6

Molo Siglio

8 **P.za della Vittoria**

V. D. Morelli

Galeria della Vittoria

Pizzo

Falcone

Chiatamone

10

Via PARTENOPE

N. SAURO

7

N

NAPLES (Napoli)

0   Miles   0.5

Kilometers

The 18th-century Spanish Steps, one of the most popular areas in Rome, lead up to the church of Trinità dei Monti.

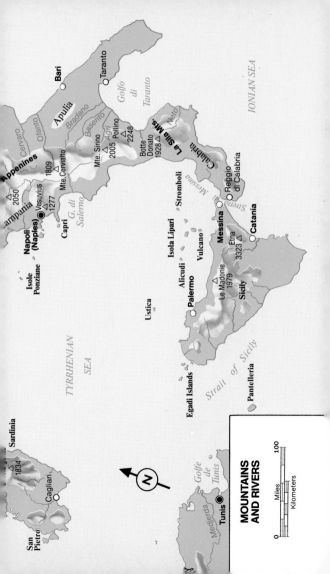

MOUNTAINS AND RIVERS

Colonnades, statues, and fountains such as this one grace the spa of Montecatini Terme.

The Renaissance city of Florence, dominated by Brunelleschi's famous dome, remains an important cultural center in contemporary Italy.

Bizarre rock formations, created by centuries of erosion, are a distinctive feature of the South Tyrolean landscape.

The Faraglioni rocks rise in majestic beauty off the island of Capri.

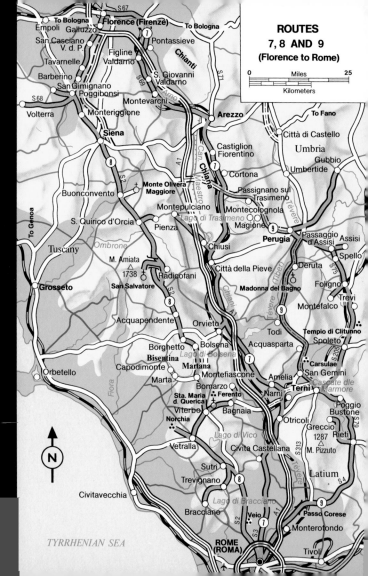

Sauro is a **seafront promenade* with particularly fine views. From Via Partenope a jetty leads to the **Castel dell'Ovo** (7), on a little island shared with harbor-view trattorias. It's called the "Castle of the Egg" because of an ancient legend in which Virgil placed an egg under the castle's foundation and linked it through the structure in such a way that if the egg moved, the castle would fall, and with it, Naples. Come back at night for a folk-dancing program arranged by the Tourist Office.

Just beyond the castle at the bend in the street, the *Fontana della Immacolatella* is a Baroque monument that celebrates the bay and its grandeur, past and present.

Heading away from the center of Naples will take you to the glorious windswept promenade, Via Francesco Carracciolo, which follows the semicircle of the bay.

WALK 2: Piazza della Vittoria–Villa Comunale–Mergellina–Santa Maria di Piedigrotta

See map on page 86.

Walk 2, a continuation of Walk 1, takes you through the lovely bayside gardens of the Villa Comunale, where there is an aquarium, to the harbor area known as Mergellina. The walk leads on to the Neoclassical Villa Pignatelli, which houses a major porcelain collection and has several 19th- and 20th-century carriages, the church of Santa Maria di Piedigrotta, and ends at the slope of Monte Posillipo.

Just beyond the Castel dell'Ovo, back on the mainland, the *Piazza della Vittoria* marks the beginning of this walk. The park that borders the bay is the **Villa Comunale** (8). It was designed in 1696 as a royal garden and was not opened to the public until the late 18th century. Now, besides attractive walks and statues, it includes the *Aquarium,* wonderfully constructed and filled with more than 200 different types of sea creatures, but often poorly maintained. On the landward side of the park is the lovely **Villa Pignatelli** (9), a patrician Neapolitan villa from the 19th century in a splendid garden that houses a collection of 19th-century furniture, china, and paintings, and an interesting carriage collection.

The Riviera di Chiaia, which follows the park on this side, leads to Via Piedigrotta and, at its end, the **church of Santa Maria di Piedigrotta** (10), known especially for the ancient and popular festival that takes place here each year (for three days at the beginning of September) to celebrate the Madonna of Piedigrotta. During the festival, with its music, floats with allegorical representations, food, and fireworks, all of Naples takes to the street to enjoy the merriment. Near the church, tunnels lead beneath Monte Posillipo to the far side of Naples. The slope of this mountain shelters the *Tomb of Virgil* and the *Tomb of Giacomo Leopardi* (1798–1837), the poet-lyricist.

Monte Posillipo slopes down to the harbor of **Mergellina** at this point, and farther along it reaches out to the beautiful *Cape Posillipo*, where the views of the **Bay of Naples* and the seafood at waterfront restaurants are superb.

To return to Piazza del Municipio, you may take one of several buses—numbers 15, 106, 150, and 152.

WALK 3: Piazza Municipio–*Piazza Dante–***Museo Archeologico Nazionale–*Palazzo Reale di Capodimonte

See map on page 86.

This route leads to some of the most beautiful churches in Naples, through the old quarter of Spacca-Napoli, and to two outstanding museums. The antiquities in the Museo Archeologico Nazionale are among the world's finest and include finds from Pompeii and Herculaneum; the painting collection in the Palazzo Reale di Capodimonte is varied and excellent.

Just west of the *Piazza del Municipio* (1) runs **Via Roma,** also called Via Toledo because the Spanish viceroy Pedro de Toledo laid out this section in 1540. It's Naples main traffic artery, which means bumper-to-bumper for most of the day and night.

Shortly after the Piazza Carità, the narrow Via Morgantini bears right to the ****church of Sant'Anna dei Lombardi** (11), also called Monteoliveto. Built in the early Renaissance style in 1441 and renovated two centuries later, the church contains some of Naples' most interesting Renaissance sculptures. The *San Sepolcro chapel* contains a dramatic ***Pietà* group, consisting of eight life-size terra-cotta figures, sculpted in 1510 by Guido Mazzoni. The elegant, 16th-century ***Palazzo Gravina** is just a few steps away, on the Piazza Monteoliveto.

Return to Via Roma, turn right and walk to the ***Piazza Dante** (12), where a semicircle of 18th-century buildings is decorated with 26 marble statues representing the virtues. Dante himself presides above it all from his pedestal at the center. From the north end of the piazza a Baroque gate, the *Port'Alba,* leads into Via Port'Alba and the heart of Spacca-Napoli, Naples' old quarter of Gothic and Baroque churches, apartments, university buildings, and wonderful pizzerias with brick ovens that are often wood-fired. Stop for a "Margherita," Naples' favorite pizza, made with only tomato sauce, fresh mozzarella and fresh basil to complement the delicious crust. *A word of warning:* it is best to dress simply and unobtrusively here, and to explore the quarter during the day. Keep purses and cameras close to you—a shoulder strap around your neck is recommended—and carry your money in a belt, if you can. Follow Via Port'Alba until it becomes Via San Pietro a Maiella; to the right, on Piazza Luigi Miraglia, is the *church of San Pietro a Maiella* (1300). Next to it is the *Old Conservatory* (1537), now a museum. It has recently been closed, but you may be in luck. In any case, it's rare not to hear some violin notes wafting through the air. From here, retrace your steps a short distance and turn right on ***Via Santa Maria di Constantinopoli,** which is lined with churches, palaces, and antiques shops. You will come to the **Accademia di Belle Arti* where 19th-century Neapolitan paintings are displayed.

The street then continues north for some distance to the *****Museo Archeologico Nazionale** (13), which houses one of the world's finest collections of antiquities, thanks in part to the nearby excavations of Pompeii and Herculaneum. The building was constructed in 1586 as a barracks, served from 1612 to 1777 as a university building, then as the Academy of Fine Arts. Finally it was remodeled into this great museum (1790). Among the greatest treasures are the marble sculptures of the ***Farnese

Bull—the largest extant marble group of antiquity, dating from the third century B.C.; the ****Farnese Hercules,* a colossal statue attributed to Glycon of Athens, found in the Baths of Caracalla in Rome; a ****Torso of Aphrodite* (fourth century B.C.); and the ****Mosaic of Alexander at the Battle of Issus,* from Pompeii. The remainder of this huge collection is made up of bronze statues, antique glass, the most valuable collection of ****antique vases* in Italy; *wall paintings*—some of the best of Pompeii; silver and gold jewelry; and an outstanding ***Egyptian collection.* The Museo Nazionale Archeologico is 2 km. (about 1 mile) from the Capodimonte palace at the top of the hill, reached by following the Corso Amedeo di Savoia. You may take bus number 110 or 127 to the ***Palazzo Reale di Capodimonte** (14), the royal palace, built between 1738 and 1839 in a wonderful ***park.* The 100-room palace now houses the ***Museo e Gallerie Nazionali di Capodimonte,* with an excellent painting collection, fine **porcelains,* and valuable *tapestries.* The ***painting collection* (Pinacoteca) exhibits major works by Masaccio, Botticelli, Correggio, Giovanni Bellini, Perugino, Titian, Lucas Cranach, Velázquez, El Greco, and Goya. In the royal apartments, ask to see the *Salottino di Porcellana,* a delightful room exquisitely decorated entirely in porcelain tile.

Just outside the main gates of Capodimonte and down the hill are several interesting sights.

After leaving the park you will come first to the modern pilgrimage *church of the Madre del Buon Consiglio* (1920–1960); near the traffic circle known as the Tondo di Capodimonte there is a restored fifth-century church, *San Gennaro extra Moenia;* and just beyond are the second-century *Catacombe di San Gennaro,* enormous chambers on two levels in which the saint is buried along with countless other Christians. Mosaics and frescoes are well preserved. Stop at the office on the left to buy a ticket.

Bus number 110 or 127 will take you back to Piazza del Municipio.

WALK 4: Piazza del Municipio–**Santa Chiara–**San Domenico Maggiore–**San Gennaro Cathedral (Duomo)–**Porta Capuana

See map on page 86.

This tour leads through another part of *Spacca-Napoli,* the old city, and visits some of the most beautiful Gothic and Baroque churches. One of the most fascinating sights of Naples, however, is the Neapolitans themselves—their melodious voices, gestures and attitude of being able to cope with anything that comes their way. You can see street life especially at dusk, when residents put chairs outside in the small piazzas to create a living room *al fresco,* especially necessary during the hot summer. Clotheslines with laundry drape once-elegant palaces, and the street *ragazzi* play and scheme where lords and ladies strolled a century ago. (This is not the place to wear jewelry or to leave your camera dangling by a strap. Moneybelts are definitely called for. If your wallet is showing, a local resident is likely to tug your sleeve, point to it, and say, "Attenzione." They have the same problems every day, after all.)

From *Piazza del Municipio* (1) follow the wide Via Medina to the *church of Santa Maria Incoronata* (14th century), with interesting old frescoes. A few blocks farther, turn right on Via Santa Maria la Nova to the **church of Santa Maria la Nova** (15), built in 1268 and given a Renaissance façade in 1599. The interior contains interesting ceiling paintings and sculptures, and there are two lovely cloisters. In this section you also will notice two of Naples' new structures: the 32-story *Grattacielo* (skyscraper) *della Cattolica,* near the end of Via Medina, and just to the left, on the Piazza Matteotti, the *Postal and Telegraph Building.* Via Medina changes its name and continues north as Via Monteoliveto. Follow this avenue past the *Palazzo Gravina*, turn right on *Calata Trinità Maggiore*, and you will soon come to the *Piazza del Gesù Nuovo*. Just off the south side of the piazza is the **church of Santa Chiara** (16), whose plain exterior conceals the beautiful **tomb of Robert of Anjou*. The stunning Gothic lines of the church are even more impressive since its renovation. Santa Chiara is called the Pantheon of Naples because of the exquisite tombs of famous people that it contains. It was built between 1310–1340 in a Provençal-Gothic style, remodeled, and then—after the bombs of World War II—restored to its original appearance. The wife of Robert of Anjou had this church built for the order of the Poor Clares. Look for the splendid ***fresco cycle* (14th century) in the nuns' choir. The ****cloister* is one of Naples' most beautiful places, a perfect blend of an outdoor garden and brilliant *faience* tiles that cover benches, colonnades and walls of the quiet retreat with scenes of rural life and of mythology.

Across the Piazza del Gesù Nuovo, the *guglia*—that curious steeplelike monument style found throughout southern Italy—is very well carved and topped with a statue of the Madonna (1721).

At the ***church of Gesù Nuovo** (17), also called Trinità Maggiore, the plain front with diamond rustication yields a surprise when you enter. After the somber exterior, the interior bursts into color, almost like a Baroque carol. The frescoes are excellent, especially the one over the main door, *Heliodorus Driven from the Temple,* by Solimena.

From the Piazza del Gesù Nuovo follow Via Benedetto Croce past the historian-philosopher's house at number 12, where he lived and created a school. (Croce lived from 1866 to 1952.) When you see another guglia, a simpler version—erected by Naples' citizens as a thanksgiving for being spared by the plague— you will also see the ***church of San Domenico Maggiore** (18). (Before entering, have a *sfogliatelle* (zfo-lya-tellay) at the bakery directly across. It's a Neapolitan specialty that is especially good here.) The church was built in 1283 on the remains of an eighth-century church, and it's been remodeled several times. Among the church's many works of art are the 14th-century *caryatids* by Tino da Camaino, which represent the virtues and support a huge candelabrum in the chancel near the entrance. Set into the walls of the sacristy are *tombs* of the dynasty and court of the Aragons—45 in all—and a brilliant *fresco* by Solimena on the ceiling. Saint Thomas Aquinas (1225–1274), the Neapolitan philosopher-saint, lived and taught in the adjacent monastery, which was destroyed and rebuilt. The small painting of the "Cross that talked to Saint Thomas" is in the chapel near the main altar, easily recognized by the numbers of candles lit and usually by people praying in the little chapel.

In back of San Domenico on the side street is the bizarre *Sansevero Chapel,* in which the prince of that family created a funeral chapel, known especially for the *Veiled Christ,* an amazing work in marble, and the mummies in the cellar, which are supposedly preserved—by the prince's witchcraft or genius. The Piazza San Domenico in front of the church is surrounded by beautiful Renaissance and Baroque palaces. To the east, adjoining, is the *Piazzetta Nilo,* named for its reclining figure of the River Nile. Continue on Via San Biagio ai Librai to *Via San Gregorio Armeno,* turn up Via San Gregorio to the left and you will see ***San Lorenzo Maggiore** (19), erected on the remains of a sixth-century church of the same name, which was, in turn, built on the ruins of a Roman basilica. Of particular interest are the *Gothic portal* (1325), the *Tomb of Charles of Anjou,* and the soaring Gothic polygonal *apse,* a French design created by Thibaud de Saumur. Boccaccio first saw his great love, whom he wrote of as Fiammetta, in this church; and Petrarch stayed in the adjoining monastery.

Next to San Lorenzo is the church's *Museum* of relics accumulated throughout its distinguished history. Across the street is the ***church of San Paolo Maggiore** (20), rebuilt in 1603 over the remains of a Roman temple, from which two Corinthian columns are incorporated in the façade.

From here, turn right on Via dei Tribunali, then left on Via del Duomo, and you will soon come to the ****Duomo di San Gennaro** (21), built by the Angevins in the 13th–14th centuries. In the triple-naved interior, many original decorations remain intact, including the floor (1423) and the wall frescoes by Luca Giordano. But the main attraction is the splendidly and richly decorated ****Cappella di San Gennaro,** built in 1608 to contain the skull of the saint and vials of his congealed blood, which liquifies, according to tradition, twice here every year—on December 16th and September 19th—before an awestruck congregation. (On the first Saturday in May, the "miracle of the blood" takes place in Santa Chiara.)

Façade of the Duomo

The *Cappella Carafa,* a masterwork of the Renaissance, is located beneath the high altar. A door at the center of the left aisle of the nave leads to the **basilica of Santa Restituta,** built in the year 510 on the site of Naples' first known church, which was in turn—in good Italian tradition— built atop a temple to Apollo. Recent excavations have yielded some interesting objects of Naples' Greek past, now on view. As the oldest church in Naples, Santa Restituta served as the city's cathedral until 1299. Although it was rebuilt in 1690, it still has ancient columns with Corinthian capitals (from the earlier structure) and fifth-century mosaics.

Two interesting churches are only a few steps to the north of the Duomo: the 13th-century *Santa Maria di Donnaregina,* in the Largo Donna Regina (to the right of the Duomo in the first block past it). Inside are notable frescoes by Pietro Cavallini. The 15th-century *San Giovanni a Carbonara,* with a Renaissance tomb of King Lancelot of Anjou, is located on Via San Giovanni a Carbonara (turn right on Via Pisanetti from Largo Donna Regina, then left on Strada San Giovanni a Carbonara to the church). If, instead, you turn right on Strada San Giovanni a Carbonara, you will soon reach the *Piazza Capuana* (from the Duomo, walk south to Via dei Tribunali and turn left to the Piazza). At the end of the Piazza is the **Porta Capuana** (22), considered the most beautiful Renaissance gate in Italy. Built in 1484 according to plans by Giuliano da Maiano, this main entrance to the city during the reign of the House of Aragon is flanked by two powerful round towers. The marble reliefs are the magnificent contribution of Sangallo.

Adjacent to the Porta Capuana is the Renaissance *church of Santa Caterina a Formiello* (1523), and across from it is the imposing *Castel Capuano* (12th century), residence of past rulers of the Kingdom of Naples—the Normans and the Hohenstaufens— and later the Court of Justice.

From the Porta Capuana, it is a short walk to the right, down the Via Poerio, to *Piazza Garibaldi,* where the *central train station* (23) (built 1960–1964) is located. From the station you may return to the Piazza del Municipio by way of the picturesque *Piazza del Mercato.*

Follow Corso Garibaldi almost to the waterfront; turn right at the Piazza Guglielmo Pepe onto Via del Carmine, and you will come to the market square. It is dominated by the large Baroque *church of Santa Maria del Carmine* (24), with a soaring bell tower, and the *university* (25), founded by Emperor Frederick II and now occupying a huge new building constructed in 1908.

To return to the Piazza del Municipio, follow any of the streets at the west end of the Piazza del Mercato to the nearby Corso Umberto I; turn left and walk to the *Piazza Bovio,* where the *Borsa*

(Stock Exchange) and the *Neptune fountain* are located. From there, Via Depretis leads to the Piazza del Municipio.

WALK 5: *Villa Floridiana–*Castel Sant'Elmo– **Certosa di San Martino

See map on page 86.

The sights described on this route—a 19th-century villa and 14th-century castle and monastery, with its collection of traditional Neapolitan art—are located on the *Vomero,* a hill reached either by bus (numbers 182, 185, or 186 from Piazza del Municipio) or by cable car (Funicolare di Chiaia, Funicolare Centrale, or Funicolare di Montesanto). The terminus of the Funicolare Centrale is closest to the Piazza del Municipio, near the intersection of Via Roma and Via Santa Brigida.

Much of the Vomero is a large **park** commanding a spectacular view of Naples. Near the southern end stands the ***Villa Floridiana** (26), erected between 1817–1819. The villa now houses a major ceramics collection of the Duke of Martina, the *Museo Duca di Martina,* with Chinese vases and porcelains from Sèvres, Meissen and Capodimonte, as well as objects in silver and ivory, and other works of art. On the eastern edge of the Vomero is the ***Castel Sant'Elmo** (27), constructed in 1329 by King Robert of Anjou, one of Naples' most beloved rulers, on the highest point of the hill (224 meters; 735 feet), enlarged many times over the next 300 years, and surrounded by massive walls.

The ****Certosa di San Martino,** or Carthusian Monastery of St. Martin (28), is located below the castle on the Vomero slope (the view is marvelous). It was constructed during the 14th century but was given a Baroque transformation during the 17th–18th centuries and is a fine example of this style in Naples. Since 1876 the monastery has housed the ****Museo Nazionale di San Martino,** a treasure trove of Neapolitan paintings, tapestries, traditional costumes, gala carriages, majolica, and a magical collection of **crêche (presepio) figures.* The *presepio,* a strong tradition in Naples, is an entire Christmas village, usually arranged a bit eclectically, with Classical columns and Neapolitan kitchens in the same setting as the Nativity at Bethlehem. At San Martino, entire rooms are devoted to the more elaborate *presepi.* The ****Belvedere** commands a spectacular view of the bay and

Crèche, Museo Nazionale
di San Martino

beyond. The large *chiostro* (cloister) (1623) is lent grandeur by the addition of 63 columns. The **Monks' Chancel** can be reached through the chapter room; it's an example of Neapolitan Baroque in all its glory, a sumptuous world of marble and stucco and a wealth of statues and paintings. The *choir stalls* in the chancel are exquisitely carved.

Excursions from Naples

See map on page 96.

***Capri

The island of Capri, in the Tyrrhenian Sea, is 35 km. (22 miles) from Naples. Ferries (*traghetti*) leave regularly from the pier in front of the Castel Nuovo (see page 85), or you can make the trip faster in the *aliscafo* (hydrofoil), which leaves from Mergellina. You also can take one of the guided tours organized by major tour operators in Naples. But the island, famed since antiquity for its ethereal beauty, is so exquisite that you will probably want to wander about on your own with enough time to enjoy this precious part of the world. Boats anchor in the small harbor of *Marina Grande,* from which visitors can transfer to a smaller boat to enter the ***Grotta Azzurra* (Blue Grotto), a large watery cave that you tour by a third, smaller boat. If possible, plan a visit early in the morning, when the slanted rays of sunlight create glorious effects of a blue light known only to Capri.

From the port of Marina Grande, a funicular, a highway, and a staircase lead to the town of ***Capri,** 138 meters (450 feet) above sea level. At the center of town is the *Piazza Umberto I,* which could be the stage set for an operetta, surrounded as it is with white houses bedecked with flowering balconies, café terraces, the town hall and clock tower, and the *church of Santo Stefano* (17th century), with a freestanding staircase that serves as a resting place for an ever-more-international set of tourists. From the piazza it is only a short walk along Via Vittorio Emanuele, past busy tiny shops of souvenirs and luxury items, to Viale Matteotti, where you turn left for the **Giardini di Augusto* (Gardens of Augustus), with its narrow pathways and unworldly panorama of beauty. You'll also see the remains of the *Certosa di San Giacomo* (14th century), a Carthusian monastery. In front of the gardens, the narrow Via Krupp winds its way down to Marina Piccola (a half-hour walk), where there is a beach, spectacular rock formations, and restaurants with fine views.

Another favorite choice for excursions is the **Punta Tragara,* the southeastern promontory of the island. It offers an impressive view of the *Faraglioni,* three statuelike rocks that rise from the sea, just offshore. From here a road leads to the *Grotta Matromania,* transformed in Roman times into a luxurious bathing facility. A staircase ascends to the *Arco Naturale,* a

natural stone arch that affords one of Capri's frequent superlative views.

The most important archaeological treasure on the island is the ***Villa Iovis* (Jupiter's Villa), where the Emperor Tiberius spent the last years of his life. It's reached from the town of Capri by following a footpath, Via Tiberio, for about 45 minutes. Whether Tiberius really had his enemies hurled from the cliffs here is uncertain, but several ancient writers claimed that he did. A small chapel, *Santa Maria del Soccorso,* crowns Monte Tiberio and offers yet another splendid view. The site of greatest antiquity on the island is the **Palazzo a Mare,* which probably belonged to the Emperor Augustus. The section lying on the sea is called *Bagni di Tiberio* (Baths of Tiberius).

From Capri, a corniche road with dizzying panoramas leads

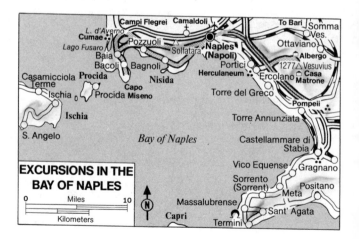

to **Anacapri,** a lovely, less crowded village at 310 meters (1,017 feet) above sea level, with narrow streets and white houses reminiscent of Moorish architecture. From the village, Via San Michele leads to *Villa San Michele,* built some 100 years ago by the Swedish writer and physician Axel Munthe, on the site of another villa of Tiberius. (He wrote of his life there in *The Story of San Michele,* which usually is for sale on the premises.) Now a museum, the villa is filled with antique furniture and Roman sculpture (some pieces were retrieved from the sea near the villa). His beautiful garden is still well tended, and the villa is the site of concerts during the summer. Above the villa, the *Castello di Barbarossa,* impressive ruins of a

Capri: Sant'Antonio

fortress built about 1100 to protect the island from pirates, makes an attractive destination for a walk. A chairlift from Anacapri slowly ascends to **Monte Solaro** (589 meters, 1,932 feet), the highest point on the island, where there is a superlative panoramic view.

From the *St. Anthony chapel* in Anacapri, the **Scala Fenicea** (Phoenician stairs) descends to Marina Grande. In earlier times, this was the only way to get from the Roman city on the sea to the Greek city (Anacapri) on higher ground.

**Ischia

The sister island of Capri in the Bay of Naples, Ischia is 20 km. (12 miles) from Naples. Ferries (*traghetti*) leave from the pier in front of the Castel Nuovo (see page 85); hydrofoils (*aliscafi*) leave from Mergellina. From Capri, boats from Marina Grande go to Ischia. Tours of the island can be arranged in Naples; once there, local buses will take you almost anywhere.

Ischia, volcanic in origin, is a quiet island that maintains ancient appearances and ancient ways. Lush semitropical vegetation— palms and fig trees, orange and lemon groves, and pines everywhere—make this very green island a favorite retreat, especially for families. Beautiful swimming beaches, a rarity on this coast, appeal to everyone.

The boat arrives, after passing a dramatic castle, at **Ischia Porto,** situated in the crater of an extinct volcano that was linked to the sea by a canal in 1854. The town's Greek, Roman, and Medieval past is portrayed in the *Museo* (the town museum). Nearby is the castle you saw when coming into port, the **Castello d'Ischia*, built in 1441 on a 91-meter- (300-foot-) cliff where the House of Aragon once enjoyed the sea air and minded the port.

From Ischia Porto, a circumferential road leads around the island (the 33-km.-, 20-mile-, drive takes about one hour); it passes through pine groves and whitewashed villages where many of the houses have domed roofs and outdoor staircases, and it's almost always in view of the sea. The road leads first to *Casamicciola Terme,* where 17 therapeutic hot springs cater to international aches and pains; then on to another hot spring at **Lacco Ameno*, which is the most fashionable part of the island, thanks to the luxury hotels on the harbor and the fine swimming facilities. (Your mud bath may be a celebrity event.) Offshore is *Il Fungo,* a mushroom-shaped rock.

The road continues around to the **Bay of San Montano*, encircled by cliffs, and comes to another popular resort, **Forio**, with beautiful beaches and gardens. There is an interesting *Maltese Museum.*

From here the road winds up the foothills of **Monte Epomeo* (400 meters; 1,300 feet) to the **Rotonda Belvedere*, with magnificent views. The interior routes passing ancient cliffside villages, are among the most fascinating. From the town of *Panza* you may follow a narrow road to **Sant'Angelo*, a picturesque fishing/tourist village on the southernmost edge of the island. From Panza you can also follow a path (15 minutes walk each way) to *La Guardiola,* a promontory overlooking the sea. The radioactive **Lido del Maronti* (Maronti Beach), with fumaroles hissing gas and steam, can be visited by boat from Sant'Angelo. The *Valley of Cavascura,* where a hot spring emerges from the cliff to feed a thermal bath below, is not far off.

From *Serrara Fontana* the road winds through *Fontana* (where you can begin to climb *Monte Epomeo,* Ischia's beloved and quiet volcano (788 meters; 2,585 feet) to *Barano,* nestled in the midst of green hills and vineyards, where some of Ischia's wonderful wines begin as grapes. Try Ischia DOC wines—white and red—while you're there. The DOC added to the name means that the wine production has been regulated by law.

***Vesuvius

A round trip to the volcano, with ascent of the west face, is about 46 km. (29 miles) from Naples; shorter ascent on the south face; the choice depends on weather conditions. The trip can be arranged through tour operators in

Naples, or you can take the bus from *Herculaneum* (see below). Driving around Naples is usually more pain than pleasure, but if you do drive, take A 3 to *Ercolano* for the ascent of the west face, or to *Torre Annunziata* for an ascent of the south face. The easiest ascent follows the west face, where a road leads to a chairlift, which takes you to the crater. A guide is obligatory.

Mt. Vesuvius (Il Vesuvio) is surely Europe's most famous volcano, and it vies with Mt. Fuji for world renown. It is admired for its lovely profile, which adds a melodious curve to the romantic Bay of Naples. Its fame is also the result of the eruption of A.D. 79, which buried the coastal city of Pompeii with hot lava and Herculaneum with mud. The lower slopes of Vesuvius are covered with orchards and vineyards which produce a variety of good wines, including the well-known Lacrima Cristi (Christ's Tears).

***Herculaneum and ***Pompeii

The two ancient cities are 11 km. (7 miles); and 24 km. (15 miles) from Naples, respectively. *By car: Autostrada A 3 or Route S 18. By train: the Circumvesuviana from Naples' Central Railroad station—a clean, pleasant train, to both. By trolley: from Piazza del Municipio in Naples to Herculaneum (very slow) (see page 84.)*

***Herculaneum (Ercolano):

Herculaneum's plight was different from Pompeii's. It was covered with mud churned up by the eruption of Vesuvius in A.D. 79. Because the covering was mud and not burning ash, Herculaneum was well preserved, down to the familiar details of daily life, including furnishings, murals, and other combustibles that were destroyed down the coast in Pompeii. The town began as a Greek settlement named Heraklion and dedicated to the god Hercules. At the time of its destruction the town was a Roman fishing port and resort of some 10,000 people. Its daily life has been preserved almost too well. Casts can be seen of the last agonies of the inhabitants, struggling to get away.

But on the whole, Herculaneum is a delightful experience, on a smaller scale than Pompeii. Typical of the well-preserved buildings is the beautiful *Casa dei Cervi* (House of the Stags), a patrician villa richly decorated with frescoes and works of art. The atrium leads to the dining room—a typical pattern of houses here—where there is the fine sculpture of a *Deer Pursued by Dogs* that gave the house its name. A wonderful statue of a *satyr* can be seen in another room, and the surprising *Drunken Hercules,* looking all too human.

Among other buildings in the excavated area (digging continues, and a new museum is being prepared on the site) are the

Casa dell'Albergo—a huge villa divided into apartments; *Casa a Graticcio* (built with simple wooden trellises, *graticcio,* as walls, containing apartments and a shop); *Casa dell'Atrio a Mosaico* (with intact mosaic-paved atrium); *Casa Sannitica,* a simple Samnite-style dwelling with a lovely atrium; *Casa del Mosaico di Nettuno e Anfitrite* (with mosaics in the nymphea and a well-preserved shop); and the *Baths* (where the skeletons of attendants huddle in a corner).

Continuing through the cities of *Torre del Greco* (where coral and mother-of-pearl cameos are a leading industry) and *Torre Annunziata,* you'll reach *****Pompeii,** where excavation has revealed a large city, allowing us to see the details of ancient Roman life as never before. Pompeii probably was founded by the Oscans, an early group that predated the Greeks in southern Italy, and it became a thriving Roman community of 25,000 inhabitants. Excavations have been extensive, and many of the objects found here are in the Museo Archeologico Nazionale in Naples (see page 89). Plan to spend much of the day at Pompeii, for the site is very large and includes an entire city of buildings.

The best way to enter Pompeii is through the *Porta Marina,* which opens on one side to the sea and on the other onto the *Via dell'Abbondanza,* one of the streets (all streets in Pompeii intersect at right angles). To your left is the *Forum,* with several important public buildings, including *temples to Apollo and Jupiter* and the *Macellum,* the covered market where food once was sold. Just beyond the Forum you will come to the *Terme Stabiane,* with a swimming pool, dressing rooms and such intricate detail work as a stucco-decorated ceiling. Just across from the baths, on the Via Stabiana, is a large complex that includes the *Foro Triangolare* (Triangular Forum), with a stunning propylaeum (vestibule) and small temple; the *Teatro Grande,* built in the fifth century B.C. and seating 5,000 spectators (today, open-air performances are given here in the summer); the *Odeon,* a covered theater accommodating a crowd of 800; and the *Caserma dei Gladiatori* (gladiators' barracks). Just to the east is the *Casa di Menandro,* a large villa that has its own baths and is decorated with mosaics and frescoes. From here, the Via dell' Abbondanza continues past several other private dwellings.

To the north of the Forum stands the *Casa dei Vetti,* once the home of wealthy merchants and perhaps the finest house in Pompeii, with impressive frescoes, some of them pornographic (shown only to adults). *Via dei Sepolcri,* lined with tombs, leads to the *Villa dei Misteri,* so called because frescoes in one of its rooms depict scenes from the Dionysian mysteries).

Other Excursions in the Bay of Naples

***Phlegraean Fields Campi Flegrei; 75 km. (46 miles) from Naples. *By car: take Route S 7 Quater, which cuts through the region. By subway: to Pozzuoli (last stop), then continue by bus to Cuma.*

The *Campi Flegrei* is a volcanic area whose name derives from the Greek word meaning "to blaze." Known for volcanic activity since ancient times, this became a popular area for thermal baths when the Romans settled here. Leaving Naples from the west, continue along the coast road S 7 Quater around Capo Posillipo and you will come to ***Pozzuoli,** a famous port under the Romans and the first commercial city of the Empire. Remains from this period include the **Macellum* (large market hall), also called the *"Temple of Serapis"* because previously it was thought to be a temple to the Egyptian god Serapis; and, in the upper city, the ruins of an **amphitheater.* Seismic activity has thrust Pozzuoli upward in areas and sunk the city in other places. Follow the coast to *Lago Lucrino,* known for oyster cultivation in ancient times. From here you can ascend the *Epitaffio Hill,* site of the so-called *Oven of Nero,* a natural thermal bath that is part of the Roman bathing complex. The coast road continues to ****Baia,** named for Baios, a companion of Ulysses, who was buried here. The *Termae Baiene* (Roman Baths) are

reminders of the luxurious days when this was an elegant spa. Next to the *Springs of Venus* there is a 16th-century fortress built on the ruins of a Roman imperial villa to offer protection against pirates. Another 2 km. (1 mile) farther is the town of *Bacoli,* location of the ***Piscina Mirabile,* covered by a heavy, vaulted roof supported by 48 pillars; this reservoir once supplied the Roman fleet anchored in the nearby Bay of Miseno.

As the road continues around the foot of Monte Miseno, which dominates the Phlegraean landscape at this point, you will come upon **Mare Morto* (the Dead Sea), considered in antiquity to be the River Styx, over which Charon ferried the souls of the dead. From *Capo Miseno* there are beautiful views of the sea and of the nearby island of *Procida.* The road now turns north and after some 9 km. (6 miles) reaches **Lago Fusaro,* from which an ancient canal runs to the sea. Just beyond are the ruins of the town of ****Cuma (Cumae),** the oldest Greek settlement in Italy (eighth century B.C.). From the ***Antro della Sibilla* (Hallway of the Sibyl), in the acropolis of the upper town, the famous oracle made her predictions. Accordingly, Cumae was a place of great sanctity for the ancients. The Greeks ingeniously cut a gallery through calcareous rock to the Oracle Room, which was a small cave. Above this complex is a lava hill covered with the ruins of Cumae, the temples of Apollo and Jupiter—both of which were transformed into Christian basilicas.

Soon after leaving Cuma you will pass the *Arco Felice,* a triumphal arch dating from the time of the Emperor Domitian (A.D. 81–96), now on the road that links the town to Route S 7 Quater. Heading inland on that road, you will pass *Lago d'Averno,* Virgil's entrance to the underworld. The Roman general Agrippa, a more practical sort, transformed the lake into a military port and connected it to the sea by a canal. Ruins of a bathing complex are left.

Before returning to the outskirts of Naples the road passes ***La Solfatara,* a volcanic crater from which steam and vapors escape through cracks and crevasses in the ground, giving the whole area an otherworldly look. The temperature of the fumes arising from the main fumarole is 162° C.(324° F.).

**Camaldoli is located 18 km. (11 miles) from Naples. This mountain can also be reached by bus from the Vomero hill in Naples. The best views are within the mountainous grounds of a monastery, prohibited to women (and to men in the summer). The same view can be seen by everyone from the *Belvedere della Pagliarella,* reached by a footpath.

**Milan

While many Italian cities wear their past like a comfortable old robe, Milan (Milano) drapes itself in the new. Soaring, modern towers and reserved people poised for business define this city, which to first-time visitors seems disconcertingly "un-Italian." As Italy's chief center of industry and finance, Milan has a commercial motor that never stops running. But the patient and curious soon uncover Milan's hidden charms: stately residences embracing grand courtyards, so beloved by the writer Stendhal, quaint antique neighborhoods, such as the Brera, and more eccentric ones, like the Navigli—which still has a few of the many canals that laced the entire city in the 16th century—and where antiques scouters and jazz enthusiasts can readily indulge their desires. From the renowned La Scala opera house to the rich museums and churches brimming with treasures, Milan is a city of world-class cultural stimulation. As for shopping, Milan—as the center of Italy's fashion industry—is a veritable wellspring of variety and design. Strategically placed at the foot of the Alps, Milan has been attracting foreigners for ages, making it one of the most appealing continental cities of Europe.

History

A Gallic settlement in the fifth century B.C., Milan later became the capital of the Celts, who shaped it into a powerful city that was all too attractive to the Romans, who seized control in 222 B.C. Mediolanum, as it was called, prospered greatly under Augustus' rule (27 B.C.–A.D. 14), and in the fourth century A.D., when the Emperor Diocletian split the Empire, he made Milan the capital of the western half. Christianity received its legitimate status here in A.D. 313, when Constantine the Great issued his famous Edict of Milan, declaring tolerance for Christians, and no one did more to empower the new religion than Saint Ambrose, spiritual father and bishop of Milan (A.D. 374–379).

As the Empire declined, Milan was hit with waves of barbarian attacks, starting with the Huns and Goths, who all but destroyed the city. Then the Lombards seized it and resurrected it from its ruinous condition. When Charlemagne incorporated the Lombard region into his dominions, Milan grew more prestigious, reaching great independence under its ruling archbishops in the 10th and 11th centuries. A prosperous city-state, Milan struggled with its neighbors and caught the rapacious eye of Frederick I Barbarossa, who tried to bring Milan under the control of his Holy Roman Empire, which now was governed from German soil.

His aggression catalyzed the formation of the Lombard League—made up of Milan and its neighbors—which eventually lead to Barbarossa's defeat in 1176. The city's independence was recognized in the Peace of Constance (1183). A mere hundred years of peace and prosperity followed, until the city's new power brokers arrived. From 1260 onward, powerful families ruled Milan with a combination of treachery and art. The Torriani family ruled until the Visconti family took control in 1277. Under Gian Galeazzo Visconti, Milan enjoyed splendorous wealth, but the city's artistic and cultural acclaim was achieved by the Sforza family, particularly Lodovico il Moro, who brought Leonardo da Vinci and Donato Bramante to this court, and actively patronized the arts while escalating the level of intrigue in his palaces. But after Milan fell in 1499 to Louis XII of France, it became a political volleyball and bounced between the hands of the French and the Spanish Hapsburgs, who assumed power under Charles V. Under Spanish rule, which lasted until 1713, Milan sank economically and politically until the Austrians took control, ceding power briefly to Napoleon (1796–1814) who made Milan the capital of his Cisalpine Republic in 1797. The Austrians reestablished their claim and ruled until 1859, when Milan welcomed Victor Emanuel II. Two years later it joined the newly unified Italy. World War II heavily damaged the city, though miraculously some of its art treasures were spared.

Attractions

See map on page 105.

Banks and office buildings may be the lifeblood of the city, but its heart is still the *****Duomo** (1), which stands almost in the center of the city and directs the flow of activity. Beyond its reputation as the third largest Gothic cathedral in the world and the largest one in Italy, the Duomo is a monumental masterpiece of Italian eccentricity. A blaze of white marble with a filigreed forest of spires, it stretches heavenward some 108 meters (354 feet). Constructed over a period of several centuries, it was begun in 1386 under orders of Gian Galeazzo Visconti, who dedicated the cathedral to the Virgin, to whom he prayed for assistance in fathering a son and heir.

Italian, French, German, and Flemish craftsmen and masters lent their services, and Leonardo da Vinci was a collaborating architect. Its statistics are dazzling: 135 spires, 150 gargoyles and over 3,000 statues, some of which can be closely admired at the top of the roof, from which you can see the sprawling city, the plains, and the snow-capped Alps, all under the eye of the small gilded statue of the Madonna that crowns the topmost spire. Napoleon ordered the completion of the façade in 1805–1809, and the last of five bronze doors was added as recently as 1965. The enormous ******pointed windows*** in the apse (14th century) are beautifully intricate, the work of Nicolas de Bonaventure in 1389. Said to be the largest church windows in the world, they admit a kind of half light that gives the interior a mysterious and hushed atmosphere. The 52 soaring columns divide the massive interior space. Among the several altars, the sixth one on the north aisle has the famous *Crucifix* carried by Saint Charles Borromeo during the plague of 1576, and on the *high altar* is the large bronze *ciborium* by Tibaldi. Of particular interest in the north transept is the majestic seven-

armed *bronze candelabrum,* almost 5 meters (16 feet) high, of French or German origin. Just south of the cathedral, on the grand *Piazza del Duomo* is the **Palazzo Reale** (2), a former 14th-century ducal palace, redesigned by Piermarini in the 18th century, that houses the *Museo del Duomo* on the ground floor. The museum displays an exceptional collection of Italian, French, and Flemish sculpture

from the 14th–15th centuries and a sterling array of religious vestments, tapestries, paintings, and fascinating drawings of the 600-year construction of the cathedral. The second floor of the palace is the home of the **Civico Museo d'Arte Contemporanea*, dedicated to modern Italian art since World War II.

On the north side of the Piazza del Duomo you enter the famous **Galleria Vittorio Emanuele** (3), an enormous cross-shaped, glass-domed arcade that serves as the city's public salon: Here people debate the latest political follies, tryst at the numerous cafés, and shop at the elegant stores. Designed in 1865 by Giuseppe Mengoni, who unfortunately fell from the top and died just a few days before the inauguration ceremony in 1878, it is the artery connecting the Piazza del Duomo with the *Piazza della Scala,* where a monumental statue of Milan's favorite adopted son, Leonardo da Vinci (who lived and worked here on and off for 30 years) rises from a cluster of his adoring pupils. On the northwest side of the square is the world-famous **Teatro alla Scala** (4), a honey-colored, Neoclassical building, begun in 1776 by Piermarini. Some of the greatest operas premiered here: Puccini's *Madama Butterfly* and *Turandot;* Verdi's *Otello* and Bellini's *Norma,* to name a few. Blessed with perfect acoustics, La Scala was home to Toscanini, who conducted some of his best performances here. Today, the Milanese

continue to enjoy the *stagione lirica*—the season's opera schedule, which runs from December to May, and the many concerts of the *stagione sinfonica,* which covers spring through fall. (For both, reserve tickets well in advance.) The adjacent *Museo Teatrale* has some wonderful memorabilia, including busts and portraits of some of the greats: Rossini, Verdi, Bellini.

Opposite La Scala is the *Palazzo Marino,* dating from 1558, today the city hall. The beautiful *Cortile d'onore* (court of honor), whose rear façade faces *Piazza San Fedele,* was designed by Alessi, and preserves the palace's original Mannerist style. Just beyond is the lovely *church of San Fedele,* begun by Tibaldi in 1569. From the end of the piazza, walk past La Scala on Via Verdi, which becomes Via Brera. You will come to the 17th-century *Palazzo di Brera,* where in the courtyard Canova's powerful statue of Napoleon, depicted as Caesar, beckons you into the **Pinacoteca di Brera** (5), one of the finest galleries for northern Italian painting. Inside is a trove of Lombard and Venetian works from the 14th–20th centuries: Mantegna's *Dead Christ,* a miracle of perspective; Veronese's compelling *Last Supper;* the quiet *Madonna of the Rose Tree* by Bernardino Luini; and Raphael's inimitable *Marriage of the Virgin;* plus works of Tintoretto, Correggio, El Greco, Rubens, and Rembrandt. From the palazzo, continue on Via Brera until you come to Via Fatebene-fratelli, where you turn right. This street leads to the *Piazza Cavour,* which opens onto Via Palestro, leading to the **Villa Reale** (6). Built in 1790 and one of the finest examples of Neoclassical design, it houses several museums and sits in a pretty garden. Within are the *Galleria d'Arte Moderna* and the impressive *Grassi Collection,* with French and Italian works by artists such as Gauguin, Manet, Van Gogh, Cézanne, Renoir, Modigliani; and the *Marino Marini Museum,* with over 200 mixed-media works of the famous contemporary Italian sculptor, whose unmistakable horse themes grace many public and private spaces around the world. The villa looks out on the *Giardini Pubblici,* a serene park with trees, monuments, lakes, and a small zoo. On the *Corso Venezia* side, you'll find Italy's first natural-history museum, the *Museo Civico di Storia Naturale,* where the largest sulfur crystal in the world and a 40-kilogram (88-pound) topaz attract the curious and disbelieving.

From the Piazza Cavour, Via Manzoni leads southwest; on the left, at No. 10 Via Morone, you will come to the ****Museo Poldi-Pezzoli** (7), the generous gift of the nobleman of the same name (1879). The museum is full of eye-catchers, such as the luminescent *Portrait of a Lady* by Pollaiuolo; Botticelli's *Madonna and Child,* Bellini's *Pietà,* plus works of the Flemish, German, and Dutch

masters, including Cranach. For antiques lovers there's a host of tapestries, china, bronzes, and furnishings.

For a walk through the gilded past, begin at Piazza del Duomo and walk west on Via Mercanti to *Piazza Mercanti,* where some of the most sumptuous palaces stand waiting to transport you back to the riches of yesteryear. *Palazzo della Ragione* (13th century), with a stunning equestrian relief on its rear wall and the *Palazzo dei Giureconsulti* (16th century, with a tower from the 13th) are both on Via Mercanti. The Baroque *Palazzo delle Scuole Palatine* (17th century), and the black-and-white marble *Loggia degli Osii* (1316) are in the piazza. From here, walk across the adjacent *Piazza Cordusio* to Via Dante, which leads to the ***Castello Sforzesco** (8). This massive square fortress, built in 1451–1466 by Francesco Sforza on the site of the old Visconti castle, was designed to intimidate (his name itself means "the strong") and later was enriched by Bramante and Leonardo da Vinci. Used as barracks during the 18th and 19th centuries, it was restored and remodeled several times over the years, especially after the World War II bombings that destroyed almost two-thirds of the archives and many other treasures. In the main courtyard is the *Piazza d'Armi,* which hosts summer concerts and art shows. A collection of buildings make up the various museums here. From the court-

Castello Sforzesco

yard of the Corte Ducale, you enter the *Museo d'Arte Antica*, which contains Byzantine and Romanesque remains and the noble marble head of the Empress Theodora, plus many sarcophagi and tabernacles. For a look at the Sforza family, ask an attendant to unlock the two small rooms over the moat, which contain the Luini portraits of the rulers. One must-see, in the *Sala degli Scarlioni*, is Michelangelo's ****Rondanini Pietà**, an unfinished sculpture of deep emotional intensity that occupied the artist periodically for over nine years, up until a few days before his death. As part of the *Museo d'Arte Applicata* there is also a room of tapestries and furniture and good period pieces of Lombard style. A *museum of musical instruments* has quite a good collection of lutes, wind instruments and clavichords and even a spinet used by the 14-year-old Mozart. Don't miss the *Egyp-*

tian Museum and a fine *pinacoteca* (picture gallery) with works of Bellini, Filippo Lippi's *Madonna dell'Umiltà*, Lotto's *Portrait of a Boy Holding a Book;* and Titians and Correggios, among others. Beyond the castle is the sprawling *Parco Sempione,* dotted with modern sculptures, a sports arena, exhibition hall and antique building fragments.

The Piazza Castello adjoins the *Piazza Cadorna.* Turn south into Via Carducci and continue to the Corso Magenta, where you turn right to reach the ****church of Santa Maria delle Grazie** (9). This recently restored brick and terra-cotta church is crowned by the striking dome of Bramante. Executed between 1466–1490, it contains the lovely *Chiostrino* (cloister) by Bramante, along with the beautiful frescoes of Ferrari. The real attraction, however, is in the adjacent Dominican refectory, where Leonardo da Vinci's incomparable ***Cenacolo or *Last Supper* (painted from 1495–1497) covers the far wall. Nothing can prepare you—not the posters, postcards or art-book reproductions—for its impact. Commissioned by Lodovico il Moro (Sforza), it was painted during one of the most stimulating periods for Leonardo, a time when he experimented with mechanics, optics, and a host of scientific theories that he applied to painting. Its powerful force derives from its genius perspective, and the placement of the apostles is said to correspond to the various ways light is reflected. The painting has undergone several good and bad restorations, for ironically it was the artist's life-long experimentation that proved the near-undoing of this painting. Unlike a true fresco, which is painted on wet plaster, this one Leonardo executed in tempera, on a dry wall, which resulted in much fading and crumbling over the years. On the wall opposite this painting is Donato da Montorfano's fresco of the *Crucifixion*.

By returning to Via Carducci and following it south until it ends at Via San Vittore, you will see on your left the ****church of Sant'Ambrogio** (10), founded in the fourth century by Saint Ambrose, Bishop of Milan. A Roman lawyer who embraced Christianity late in life (he wasn't even Christian when the crowd elected him bishop), Ambrose lived at the height of the Arian and Orthodox controversy and was a friend to many an emperor, including Gratian, Valentinian I, II, and Theodosius the Great, whom he humbled into severe penance for an unjust massacre at Salonica. The church, expanded in the ninth century and again in the 11th, is a prototypical Lombard basilica with a vibrant historical past. Holy Roman Emperor Henry VI married Constance of Sicily here in 1186, and it is believed that Saint Ambrose baptized Saint Augustine within. In front of the church is an 11th century atrium that conceals the rather austere façade marked with

intricate bas-reliefs on the doorway. The beautiful interior, where Lombard kings were crowned, has the typical women's galleries over the side aisles and an elevated apse above the crypt, which holds the remains of Saint Ambrose and those of two martyrs, Saint Gervase and Saint Protasius, who flank him. Particularly interesting are the pulpit, reconstituted from fragments from the 11th and 12th centuries; the magnificent ciborium in the sanctuary above the golden altar, a masterpiece of ninth-century Carolingian goldsmiths, glimmering with gems, enamels, and gold and silver reliefs depicting scenes from the lives of Christ and St. Ambrose. Don't miss the mosaics and marble throne of Saint Ambrose in the apse. Off the right aisle you'll find the *Sacello di San Vittore in Ciel d'Oro* (fourth century) whose dome contains "crudely solemn mosaics," according to Henry James. From the left aisle you can enter the *Portico della Canonica* (which Bramante left unfinished in 1499 and which was completed in 1955 according to his plan.) The *Museo di Sant'Ambrogio,* in the upper part, has a fine collection of Early Christian mosaic fragments, lovely frescoes by Bergognone and Luini, and the illuminated missal used by Gian Galeazzo Visconti (1395).

Just up Via San Vittore is the 16th-century *basilica of San Vittore al Corpo,* built on the site of an Early Christian church. Among the many fine works it contains is a fabulous collection of Luini frescoes. Attached to the church is the 16th-century Olivetan convent whose rooms now house part of the *Museo Nazionale della Scienza e della Tecnica Leonardo da Vinci,* which extends to two other buildings. Here you can pore over Leonardo's prophetic designs and models in optics, horology, astronomy, navigation. The *Galleria Leonardesca* is devoted solely to the models of machines and contraptions invented by Leonardo.

Heading back toward the Duomo from Basilica di Sant'Ambrogio, go north on Via Carducci to Corso Magenta, turn right and continue straight (the street becomes Via Meravigli) to *Piazza Cordusio* (the financial center), from which Via Mercanti leads directly to the Duomo. Just south of the Piazza Cordusio is the *Borsa* (Stock Exchange) and south of here, at *Piazza Pio XI,* you'll find the *Biblioteca Ambrosiana* (11), the library founded in the 17th century by Cardinal Federico Borromeo, and housed in his palazzo. The first-floor ****Pinacoteca Ambrosiana** has some fine works: Botticelli's serene *Madonna and Child with Angels;* still lifes by Brueghel; Luini's charming *Holy Family with Saint Anne and Young Saint John;* Raphael's cartoon for his painting of the *School of Athens* (in the Vatican), plus some fine Titians and Caravaggios. A large room in the famous library is devoted to Leonardo's scientific and nature drawings, the *Codex Atlanticus,*

and a handsome assortment of manuscripts, such as the Virgil illustrated by Simone Martini that Petrarch owned.

The southern part of the city is alive with interesting sights and historic churches and can be reached easily from the Duomo by taking Via Torino southwest to *Piazza Carrobbio* and then turning south on Corso di Porta Ticinese, which leads to the **basilica of San Lorenzo Maggiore** (12), perhaps the most important relic of Roman and Early Christian Milan. This fourth-century church, which was rebuilt in the 12th century after its vault collapsed and again in the 16th century by Martino Bassi, faces a cemetary and is made up of a series of buildings that date from various periods. The most impressive is the late Romanesque *Cappella di Sant'Aquilino* on the right, which contains lovely fourth-century mosaics and a third-century sarcophagus; it covers part of a Roman bath-house. The apse of San Lorenzo faces the *Parco delle Basilica,* a long and narrow stretch of grass that parallels the Corso di Porta Ticinese and curves around to the right to the ***church of Sant'Eustorgio** (13). A Medieval gem, it contains but a few stones of the original ninth-century basilica. All of its earlier remains were integrated into the new church in the 11th century, and since that time it has undergone many restorations, the most ambitious one being in 1958–1959. The façade (rebuilt in 1862–1865) is one of the finest examples of the Lombard style, with a tall *campanile* (1297–1309) beside the apse. Milanese nobles, such as the Visconti, lie at rest in the many chapels within; the most appealing is the *Cappella Portinari,* designed by Michelozzi and decorated with flamboyantly colored stucco angels on the drum of the dome and superior frescoes by Vincenzo Foppa. Outside the church, a few steps farther south bring you to the **Porta Ticinese.** The 16 Corinthian columns that stand like historical exiles beside tram tracks were taken from a fourth-century temple and are the most palpable memory of imperial Rome.

Excursions from Milan

The Italian Lakes

See map on page 112.

From early imperial days to the present, the glorious lakes that form a kind of azure crescent across the top of Lombardy have been oases of silence and beauty. Definitely nature's best poetry, the area has retreats to satisfy a number of tastes—from the lovely and serene Lago Maggiore to the more rugged and mountainous Lago d'Iseo. The three widely known lakes of the area are: Lago Maggiore, Lago di Como and Lago di Lugano. The smaller ones of Orta, Varese, Iseo—and the largest one of the area, Garda—have their own special appeal.

The lake district, which runs from the Veneto and the northern reaches of Lombardy through to the Piedmont (Piemonte) and up to Switzerland, is surrounded by sylvan mountains overlooking crystalline blue waters. Flowers of all varieties provide color and fragrance, and everything is heightened by a brilliant sun and nurtured by the mildest climate. Spring is the best time to come, from April to June, when the air is heavily perfumed. Resorts abound and range from the simple to the sumptuous. The legendary beauty of these glacial lakes has attracted everyone from Virgil and the Plinys to Bryon and Mark Twain.

**Lago Maggiore, surrounded by fragrant subtropical vegetation, is roughly 67 km. (40 miles) long and 5 km. (3 miles) across at its widest part, and its northern end is claimed by Switzerland. Fed primarily by the Ticino River, the lake acts as a boundary between the Piedmont and Lombardy. The more gentle face of the lake is seen from the lovely resort town of *Stresa,* which sits on the western side. For those inclined to the Swiss temperament, there are the resorts of *Locarno* and *Ascona;* Italy's resorts are *Intra Verbania, Pallanza, Baveno, Stresa, Arona, Laveno, and Luino.* There are any number of ways to get around. *By car: Autostrada A 8 to Route S 33, which follows the western shore of the lake, becoming Route S 34. By train: frequent service from Milan to Stresa and other major lakeside resorts. By boat: frequent steamer*

Lago Maggiore

service in the summer along the route of Arona-Stresa-Baveno-Intra-Luino-Cannobio-Ascona-Locarno.

LAKES OF NORTH ITALY

Lago Maggiore's four lovely *Borromean Islands* can be reached by boat from Stresa, Bavena or Pallanza. The largest, *Isola Madre,* the first to be built on and landscaped with plants, has a simple Renaissance-style villa overlooking stately cypress, pine, and laurel trees. Plant-lovers find the extensive botanical garden appealing for its rich abundance of exotic plants. *Isola dei Pescatori* (Fishermen's Island) is aptly named and well preserves the old fishing village image, with narrow, cobbled streets and good, unpretentious seafood restaurants, along with, unfortunately, the usual souvenir stands. For a dreamy retreat, stay at the small Hotel Verbano, perched on the shore. *Isola Bella* is true to its name and is the inspiration of Count Carlo III Borromeo, who in 1630 decided to transform this rocky island into a paradise, with an impressive degree of success. A garden of ten rising terraces frame his beautiful baroque *castle* (1650–1671), which houses a valuable art collection. During the days of the 18th-century Grand Tour, many an Englishman made his way here, filling his diary with accounts of the incomparable gardens filled with camellias, acacias, agaves, rhododendrons, jasmine, lemon and orange trees, and probably becoming heady from the bounty of botanical delights. There is no admission to the small island of *San Giovanni.*

*Lago di Como (the town of Como is 48 km.; 30 miles from

Milan), is the deepest lake in Europe. *By car: take Route S 35 north to Como and then lakeside Route S 340 for the western shore or Route S 36 northeast to Lecco and the eastern shore. By train: frequent service to Como and Lecco. By boat: steamer service between Como-Argegno-Bellagio-Menaggio-Colico and hydrofoil service between Como-Tremezzo-Bellagio-Menaggio-Dongo-Gravedona-Domaso-Colico-Lecco.*

Como is ringed by soaring mountains that rise over 2,600 meters (8,500 feet) high on the north side. It is graced by an astonishing variety of greenery—olives, mulberries, figs, and oleanders—and splashed with flowers from an Impressionist's palette. The writer Alessandro Manzoni splendidly describes the lake in his famous novel, *I Promessi Sposi* (*The Betrothed*). The lake is in the form of an upside-down Y; you can take the eastern arm, *Lago di Lecco,* or the western arm, which leads to the modern resort town of *Cernobbio,* site of the grand 16th-century Villa d'Este hotel. At the point where the arms of the Y join is *Bellagio,* a charming, serene town with spectacular views, surrounded by flowering parks that weave among the town's best hotels and sumptuous patrician villas, several of which should not be missed: *Villa Melzi-d'Eryl,* which has wonderful archaeological finds on its grounds, a fine art collection, and the lingering spirit of Franz Liszt

and his mistress, Countess Marie d'Agoult, who enjoyed some ravishing times here; and the *Villa Serbelloni* (not open to the public), whose lush gardens sprawl across the top of the promontory.

*Como, which sits at the southern tip of the western arm, is a prosperous resort. The city and surroundings have a rich artistic vein, having produced the *maestri comacini,* master craftsmen, architects, and sculptors of the Middle Ages and the Renaissance, who beautified the area and spread the Lombard style throughout Italy and abroad. Silk manufacturing has been an important part of Como's economy since the 16th century. Between shopping, sightseeing and luxuriating, there's enough to occupy you for a few days, if not longer. The **Duomo,* Santa Maria Maggiore, encircled by the picturesque old town, was built between the 14th–17th centuries in the Lombard-Gothic style and is lavishly decorated with statues, including the incongruous ones of Pliny the Elder and Younger, who were native sons. It also contains some beautiful 17th-century tapestries depicting biblical scenes. The old town hall, the *Broletto,* next to the cathedral, dates from the 13th century and has the soaring *Torre del Comune* rising above it. The town walls, which Barbarossa built, include the 40-meter (130-foot) tower of *Porta Torre,* an example of Romanesque military architecture. Several churches in and around the city are worth visiting, among them: the *basilica of San Car-poforo* (11th–12th centuries), *Sant'Abbondio* (1093), with two bell towers; *San Giacomo* (1144, restored in the 16th century); and the Romanesque *San Fedele* (12th century), Como's first cathedral, which fronts on a lovely square of the same name.

To get a truly spectacular view of the area, take the funicular from Viale Geno to the tiny village of *Brunate* (a mere seven-minute ride) which sits 716 meters (2,350 feet) above the lake. *San Maurizio,* at an elevation of 906 meters (3,000 feet), is just 25 minutes beyond Brunate.

Lecco, an industrial town, is saved by its picturesque siting on a little sliver of land between the eastern arm of Lake Como (known as *Lago di Lecco*) and *Lago di Garlate.* It was the home of the novelist Alessandro Manzoni (1785–1873), whose villa contains a small museum. There's also the 17th-century *Palazzo Belgioioso,* Lecco's natural-history and archaeological museum. Lecco draws mountaineers and hikers for the untamed beauty of the mountainous Grigna region.

*Lago di Lugano is shared by the Swiss and Italians, and both have contributed their character to the area—which sometimes makes it confusing for the visitor. Actually, only the northeastern and western parts of this lake belong to Italy (known to the Italians as *Lago Ceresio*).

Campione d'Italia is 72 km. (48 miles) from Milan. *By car:* *take Autostrada A 9 to the exit for Campione d'Italia and then lakeside Route S 340. By train: There is service from Milan to Lugano and other lakeside resorts. By boat: steamer service between Lugano-Porlezza-Gandria-Campione-Capolago-Morcote-Ponte Tresa.*

Campione d'Italia, the Italian enclave in Switzerland and the principal Italian resort on the lake, has a bustling, well-known casino and uses Swiss money and postal services. Lovely villas dot the shore, and excursion boats travel to Lugano, the city on the other side of the lake.

Two smaller lakes in the region, *Lago di Varese,* located between Lago di Lugano and Lago Maggiore and *Lago d'Orta,* just west of Maggiore, offer pleasant alternatives to the more crowded, popular resorts. Orta is particularly favored for its densely wooded hills and its delightful country resort, *Orta San Giulio,* located at the tip of a peninsula and lined with gracious old houses at the base of the Sacro Monte, a hill dedicated to Saint Francis. At the summit there are 20 chapels that span the 16th to the 20th centuries. From the town one sees the *Isola San Giulio,* reached from Orta by motorboat. It is a tiny garden of delights and contains the fourth-century Romanesque basilica of *San Giulio,* built in memory of the saint, who is reputed to have rid the island of a dragon and many snakes.

24 Routes Through Italy

Modern autostrade (highways) today cover all of Italy, making it possible to reach any major point in the north or along the peninsula without leaving a highway. Although we have mentioned the shortest and fastest autostrade routes between locations in the following 24 Travel Routes through Italy, we have placed greater emphasis on Italy's scenic routes— those smaller highways and roads that reveal far more intimately the country's 3,000-year-old cultural heritage. By following these suggested routes, you can experience the incomparable beauty of the Italian landscape, and become better acquainted with Italy's artistic and historic treasures. Whether you take a main highway or a road less travelled, the most important and remarkable sights are described along with information that allows you to stop off at noteworthy cities and places of scenic, cultural, or historic interest along the way.

Northern and central Italy, including itineraries to Venice, Florence and Rome, are covered in the first 11 travel routes. The following seven routes traverse both coasts of southern Italy from Rome in the west and Pescara in the east down to the toe of the Italian boot. Travel Routes 19 to 24 are devoted to the islands are Sicily and Sardinia. Before choosing and travelling on any one of our self-guided travel routes, you may wish to read the chapter called *Getting Your Bearings,* which briefly describes the characteristic landscapes and cities in each region of Italy.

TRAVEL ROUTE 1: Brenner–*Bolzano–*Trento– *Riva–**Bergamo–**Milan (350 km.; 217 miles)

See maps on pages 117 and 121.

Travel Route 1 begins in the Alpine region of the Alto Adige (or South Tyrol), where the cultures, customs and languages of Italy and Germany overlap. The first section of the route, from Brenner to Bolzano, passes through cool alpine spa towns and allows you to make a side trip to the international resort of Merano. Traveling through well-preserved Medieval cities such as Bolzano and Trento—with towers, churches, castles and fortresses—you may well wonder what century you're in. The shores of beautiful Lago di Garda—lined with lakeside towns and bursting with colorful subtropical vegetation—form the next leg of this itinerary. Brescia and Bergamo are ancient cities with a lively contemporary pace, and both are full-scale introductions to some of the variety and beauty of Italy's priceless historical and architectural heritage.

Note: Both Italian and German names are given for locations in the Alto Adige (South Tyrol) region.

Travel Route 1 begins on the Italian side of the Brenner Pass, which at 1,375 meters (4,511 feet) is the lowest pass over the Alps. Follow either Autostrada A 22 (autostradas are toll roads) or Route S 12, which runs parallel to it. Both roads follow the Isarco River through the small resorts of *Terme del Brennero* (*Brennerbad*) and *Colle Isarco* (*Gossensass*) to *Vipiteno* (*Sterzing*), a scenic town known to the Romans as Vipitenum. Here you can admire the Medieval *Torre di Città* (City Tower) and the pointed arches, rib vaulting, and flying buttresses that characterize the Gothic *Palazzo Comunale* (1473) and the nearby *church of Spirito Santo,* which has 15th-century frescoes inside.

From Vipiteno you can take a side trip to **Merano* by following routes A 22 to Bolzano (Bozen), or take the more scenic Route S 44 over the *Passo di Monte Giovo* (*Jaufenpass*) (2,094 meters; 6,870 feet). ***Merano** (Meran), the regional capital of the Tyrol from 1317 to 1420 and now an international resort and spa, is known for its excellent tourist facilities and luxurious villas, brought to life by colorful, lush gardens. Most hotels are open from April through October.

Merano's numerous historic sites and wide selection of shops, cafés, and restaurants make it an appealing day or overnight stopover point. You might spend the morning browsing in the many fashionable shops that line the main street, then—after a leisurely coffee break or sumptuous lunch of regional specialties and local wine—spend the afternoon exploring some of the castles and fortresses that surround the town. These include the **Castel Tirolo* (12th century); the *Brunnenburg* (1244); the 12th-century *Castel San Zeno* (*Zenoburg*); and *Scena* (*Scenna*) *Castle* (1350, renovated around 1700). If you prefer to stay within the town, take a walking tour that includes the 14th–15th century Gothic *Duomo,* the *Kursaal,* the town's meeting place, the Gothic *church of Santo Spirito,* the *church of St. Leonhard,* and the *Porta Bolzano* (Bolzano Gate). Before leaving Merano, you may also wish to view the interesting reliefs, frescoes, and paintings inside the *Castello Principesco* or stroll along the *Via dei Portici* (*Laubengasse*), one of Merano's oldest streets, to see the town's most splendid villas.

From Merano, follow Route S 38 along the Adige through *Terlano* (*Terlan*), a wine-growing town surrounded by Medieval fortresses, to **Bolzano* (see below).

The alternate route from Vipiteno to Bolzano (Bozen) follows the valley of the Isarco (Eisacktal), past the 13th-century **Castel Pietra* (Sprechenstein fortress) on the left and the *Castel Tasso* (Reifenstein fortress, dating from around 1100) on the right, to *Fortezza* (*Franzensfeste*), where in

1833 Emperor Francis I built a massive wall to protect the Brenner Road. You will soon come to the town of ***Bressanone** (*Brixen*) (45 km.; 28 miles from Brenner), a popular resort that is currently the economic center of the Isarco valley. The town's *Duomo* (12th century, rebuilt in the 15th and 18th centuries) wears a Baroque façade dating from 1790. The Baroque interior with its finely wrought marble altars and tombs is highlighted by ceiling frescoes painted by Paul Troger in 1750. The lovely Romanesque cloister also is decorated with frescoes. Nearby, the **Palazzo dei Principi Vescovi*, a late Renaissance building with a large, square arcade, houses a small museum displaying *Presepi* (nativity scenes) carved by local craftsmen.

Continue south to **Chiusa** (*Klausen*), a small town that, given its Medieval castles and 13th-century tower, seems an ideal setting for a fairy tale. A 17th-century convent overlooks the town. South of the town follow Route S 242 into the Grödner valley, following signposts for such resorts as *Selva* (*Wolkenstein*) and *Ortisei* (*Sankt Ulrich*), where you will find a museum displaying local woodcarving and other crafts. From the valley, chair and ski lifts, aerial cableways and cable railways ascend the surrounding peaks. Another small valley road leads south through *Castelrotto* (*Kastelruth*) to *Siusi* (*Seis*), a summer and winter resort highlighted by several interesting

churches and a ruined Medieval castle, the *Castelvecchio* (Hauenstein Castle).

From *Castelrotto*, follow the signposts to ***Bolzano** (Bozen) (86 km.; 53 miles from Brenner), an attractive resort city that is strikingly German in character and appearance. (Bolzano also can be reached directly from Chiusa on route A 22 or S 12.) Located in the Dolomites at the juncture of the Talvera and Isarco rivers,

ROUTE 1
(Brenner to Trento)

Bolzano has served as a meeting point for German and Latin cultures since Roman times. At present it is the capital of the mainly German-speaking South Tyrol and the seat of the autonomous local government.

You won't regret including an afternoon or overnight in Bolzano in your itinerary. Among Bolzano's outstanding architectural attractions are the Gothic *Duomo* (14th century), with a Lombard portal and multicolored roof; the Gothic *Chiesa dei Francescani*, with a late Romanesque cloister (14th century); the Gothic *Convento dei Domenicani*, with a beautiful frescoed cloister and a chapel containing frescoes by Friedrich Pacher (14th century); and the *Museo Civico*, a regional museum displaying local antiquities and folk art. You may wish to conclude your tour of Bolzano with a walk along the most charming street in the old quarter, the arcaded *Via dei Portici (Laubengasse)*, which begins at the lively fruit market *(Piazza delle Erbe)*. On this street you'll find the 18th-century *Palazzo Mercantile*, a remarkable building with a fine Baroque façade.

From Bolzano, continue south through the fertile green country along the Adige River to **Salorno** *(Salurn)*, a small town on the border between German- and Italian-speaking areas. The ruins of a 13th-century castle rise dramatically from a rock in the town. Philip Melanchthon and his supporters started spreading Luther's doctrine from this site in 1551. From here, follow the Adige on Autostrada A 22 or Route S 12 to ***Trento** (Trient) (145 km., 90 miles from Brenner).

The center of this bustling city is the spacious *Piazza del Duomo*, the site of the Baroque *Fontana di Nettuno* (1769) that faces the **Duomo of San Vigilio* (13th–16th centuries), a massive Lombard-Romanesque structure worth an unhurried visit, as it contains numerous important frescoes and tombs. Also worthy of note is the *Palazzo Pretorio*, which faces the piazza and houses a collection of paintings, tapestries, and other objects in the *Museo Diocesano;* the *Torre Civica*, a tower on the site of a Roman tower; and the Renaissance *church of Santa Maria Maggiore*, where in 1545–1563 the Pope convened the famous Council of Trent to study ways to combat Protestantism.

While in Trento you might also enjoying seeing the former residence of the prince-bishops, **Castello del Buonconsiglio*, consisting of several buildings dating from the 13th to the 16th centuries. Together, the courtyards, loggias, halls, and gardens create an attractive blend of Medieval and Renaissance elements. Inside the castle is the *Museo Provinciale d'Arte*, where archaeological, ethnological, and painting collections are on permanent display. A circular colonnade commemorating Cesare Battisti, an Italian freedom fighter and native of Trento who was executed by the Austrians in 1916, rises majestically from the top of one of the steep hills to the west of the town.

From Trento, you may continue south to Lake Garda by one of two routes:

1. Route A 22 (or S 12) will take you to *Rovereto,* a hauntingly quiet town that stands guard over Italy's ancient and modern history. In the town center you will find a 14th-century castle containing the most important Italian museum of World War I, the 15th-century *church of San Marco,* and the 15th–16th-century *Palazzo Municipio.* Above the town rises the *Ossario del Castel Dante,* a castle containing the bones of more than 18,000 victims of World War I. From the castle tower the *Campana dei Caduti* (Bell of the Fallen), the largest bell in Italy, tolls every evening in honor of the war dead of all nations. From Rovereto, Route S 240 will bring you back to the lake at *Torbole,* a vacation resort in an idyllic setting, visited by Goethe in 1786 (the house where he stayed bears a plaque). In Goethe's account of his visit, he describes a breathtaking view of Lake Garda from his window at dawn, when "both shores, hemmed in by mountains, glimmered with innumerable small villages."

2. Going west from Trento on Route S 45 bis will bring you to the lake at ***Riva del Garda** (186 km.; 115 miles from Brenner). This highly popular, picturesque resort on the northernmost point of the lake retains its charming old

quarter, where you will find, still protected by Medieval city walls, the *Palazzo Pretorio* (1383); the 15th-century *Palazzo Comunale;* the 13th-century *Torre Apponale;* the castle, or *Rocca* (12th century); and the Baroque *church of the Inviolata* (1611). The forested heights of *Monte Rocchetta* rise above the town.

****Lago di Garda

This lake, called Lacus Benacus by the Romans, is the largest in Italy: 52 km. (32 miles) long, 18 km. (11 miles) wide, and 346 meters (1,135 feet) deep. The beauty of the surrounding landscape, the mild climate and the rich Mediterranean flora (olive, lemon and orange trees, cypresses, cedars, laurel, oleander) attract visitors from around the world to the resorts that line its shores, which are connected by regular ferry service. Those who prefer roughing it rather than staying in hotels may choose from a variety of lakeside camping sites where a relatively modest fee will rent a bungalow, caravan, or tent for the night. (Some sites also provide electricity and telephone; a limited number are open year-round.)

Roads offering magnificent views follow both the eastern and western shores of Lake Garda. The towns that border the water combine quintessential Italian charm and elegance: Their flowered terraces and lakeside cafés, restaurants, shops and bars provide a worldly equivalent to the lake's own natural beauty.

From *Riva del Garda* (the town perched at the northwest corner of the lake), the *Gardesana Occidentale* follows the western shore for 44 km. (27 miles) across 56 bridges and through 70 tunnels to *Salò*. The route first comes to the picturesque fishing port of *Limone sul Garda,* hemmed in by rocks and terraced olive and lemon groves, then to *Tremosine,* where a 6-km. (4-mile) side road leads to *Pieve di Tremosine* (Plateau of Tremosine), which offers spectacular views of the lake. At *Tignale,* you can again leave the corniche and walk up to the *church of Madonna di Monte Castello* at 600 meters (1,970 feet) above the lake, where there is a vast and stunning panorama. In *Bogliaco,* you may wish to view the impressive collection of 17th- and 18th-century art inside the beautiful 18th-century *Villa Bettoni.*

Continuing south, you will reach the twin towns of *Toscalano-Maderno,* nestled on a bay surrounded by rocky hills. In Toscalano, it is well worth an hour or two visiting the Romanesque *church of Santi Pietro e Paolo,* with its 14th-century frescoes and an impressive *Gonzaga portrait* that dates from 1600. In Maderno, note the blend of Roman and Byzantine remains incorporated into the 12th-century *church of Sant'Andrea.*

A short distance south of *Toscalano-Maderno* you will arrive at ***Gardone Riviera,** a popular resort famous for the **Vittoriale,* the magnificent villa of the Italian poet Gabriele d'Annunzio (1863–1938), decorated in an elaborate *fin-de-siècle* style and surrounded by beautifully landscaped gardens. The corniche finally ends at *Salò,* one of the largest towns along the lake and the only one that welcomes visitors through a Renaissance portal. The birthplace of the inventor of the violin, Gaspare Bertolotti (1540–1609), Salò faces the *Isola Garda,* where the powerful Borghese family built an extraordinary villa. If you decide to stop in Salò, don't miss seeing the museum and painting collection inside the *Palazzo del Capitano,* or walking through the centrally located Gothic *cathedral.*

From Salò, Route S 45 bis continues to **Brescia* (260 km.; 161 miles from Brenner; see below).

The **Gardesana Orientale,* beginning north of Riva di Garda in *Arco,* follows the eastern shore of the lake. (From *Riva di Garda,* you also can drive to Brescia by way of Lago d'Idro. Follow Route S 240, a high, winding road, past *Lago di Ledro*—a small lake where you can stop for a refreshing swim—then turn south on Route S 237 past *Lago d'Idro,* a larger lake with peaceful villages, and from there pass through *Vestone* and *Nave* to Brescia.)

*Brescia, probably founded by the Ligurians, became a Roman outpost in 225 B.C.; the existing ruins from that time, well worth seeing, include the *Tempio Capitolino* (A.D. 73) and a *theater.* This rather majestic city, which by the 16th century was known as the City of Beautiful Fountains, was one of the most important cities in Medieval Europe because it specialized in the manufacture of arms and armor. The city is still an iron, steel and arms center. Gaetano Donizetti (1797–1848), the composer of such opera classics as *Lucia di Lammermoor* and *Don Pasquale,* was born here.

Brescia's central *Piazza del Duomo* is graced by two cathedrals. The **Duomo Vecchio* (Old Cathedral) is a circular Romanesque building (11th and 12th centuries) known as the Rotonda: its art treasures include remarkable sarcophagi. Next to it stands the *Duomo Nuovo* (New Cathedral), a white marble structure (begun 1604) with paintings by Romanino. The 12th-century Romanesque *Palazzo Comunale* (better known as the *Broletto*) next to the New Cathedral was the city hall of Medieval Brescia. From it rises the massive 11th-century *Torre del Popolo.*

The new city hall of Brescia is the **Loggia* (in the *Piazza della Loggia*), a graceful Renaissance building from the 15th–16th centuries, designed in part by Palladio. Opposite it, the *Torre dell'Orologio,* a 16th-century clock tower, rises into the sky. Brescia's other sights include the 18th-century *church of San Nazaro e San Celso,* which houses masterpieces by the painters Moretto and Titian, and the Via dei Musei, where the Roman ruins, the *Museo Romano,* containing Roman antiquities, and the *Museo dell' Età Christiana* (Museum of Christian Antiquities) are located. The *Pinacoteca Tosio Martinengo,* housed in the 16th-century Palazzo Martinengo da Barco, has a highly recommended collection of paintings by the Brescian school of the Renaissance. The *Castello*—an old stronghold of the Visconti family—stands in a park above Via dei Musei. Before leaving the city, you may wish to take a memorable drive along the *Via Panoramica,* a well-maintained road that heads east and ascends *Monte Mad-*

To Switzerland · To Splugen Pass · Sarche · To Bolzano
Lecco · Arco · Trento (Trient)
Como · Storo · Riva · Rovereto
Bergamo · Lake Iseo · Torbole
Vestone · Malcesine
Milan (Milano) · Nave · Salò · Gargnano · Toscolano-Maderno
Chiari · Gardone
Treviglio · Brescia · Lake Garda · Bardolino
Desenzano · Sirmione
ROUTE 1 (Trento to Milan)
Lombardia · Peschiera · Verona · A4
0 Miles 50
Kilometers
Adda · To Cremona · To Mantua · To Venice

dalena, 875 meters (2,870 feet) high. From the mountain you can enjoy a wonderful view that extends over Lake Garda, the Po valley, and the Alpine foothills.

From Brescia, Autostrada A 4 leads to ****Bergamo** (312 km.; 193 miles from Brenner). You may also make the trip on the much slower Route S 510, which will take you along the eastern shore of *Lago d'Iseo,* a beautiful lake surrounded by mountains and wild scenery. The island that rises dramatically from its center, *Monte Isola,* is covered by a forest of chestnut trees and crowned by the *church of Madonna della Seriola,* an important pilgrimage site. The shore is dotted with popular resorts connected by steamer service and a lakeside road. At the north end of the lake, pick up Highway S 42 west to Bergamo.

**Bergamo is an ancient city that was an important commercial center during Roman times. Italy's own theatrical form, the *Commedia dell'Arte,* originated here in the 16th century. The city is divided into a modern lower section and an old upper quarter surrounded by walls and reached by car or by a funicular with a terminus at the lovely *Piazza del Mercato delle Scarpe.*

From the piazza, Via Gombito climbs past the *Torre di Gombito* (12th century) to the *Piazza Vecchia,* where you will find another tower, the *Torre del Comune,* and two palaces: the old city hall, *Pa-*

lazzo della Ragione (12th century), which bears on its façade the lion of Saint Mark, and the *Palazzo Nuovo* (1611). The *Piazza Vecchia* adjoins the *Piazza del Duomo,* which includes the Renaissance ****Cappella Colleoni,** a stunning building in multicolored marble, constructed from 1470–1476 as a mausoleum for the condottiere Bartolomeo Colleoni and is one of the most important Renaissance works in Lombardy. Tiepolo painted the frescoes in the cupola. Next to the chapel stands the Romanesque *church of Santa Maria Maggiore* (12th century), with a Baroque, tapestry-hung interior entered through splendid portals designed in 1360 by Giovanni da Campione. On the left side of the square rises the 15th-century *Duomo,* with a baptistry (1340) by Campione and a painting on the high altar by Bellini (*Madonna with Turtle Doves*).

Follow the walkway Via della Noca from *Porta Sant'Agostino* to the lower town to reach the *Galleria dell'Accademia Carrara* (18th century), where you will want to spend an hour or more viewing one of the most important provincial painting collections in Italy. The collection includes works by Lotto, Carpaccio, Bellini, Mantegna, Fra Angelico, Tintoretto, Brueghel the Elder, Dürer, and Tiepolo. From here, take Via San Tommaso to Via Pignola, where you will enter a world of 16th-century churches and palaces. These magnificent structures line both sides of the most picturesque street in Bergamo.

From Bergamo it is 38 km. (24 miles) on the Autostrada to **Milan** (350 km.; 217 miles from Brenner; see page 103).

TRAVEL ROUTE 2: **Milan (–**Turin)–**Genoa– *Alassio–*San Remo–Ventimiglia (312 km.; 193 miles)

See maps on pages 130 and 138-139.

The Italian Riviera is one of the most glamorous places in Europe. This Travel Route hugs the Riviera coastline and takes you to some of its best-known resorts as well as to smaller towns. On the way you can pay a visit to one of the strongholds of the powerful Visconti family and explore Genoa, birthplace of Christopher Columbus and the great musician Nicoló Paganini.

From Milan you may wish to make an optional side trip to **Turin* (approximately 140 km.; 84 miles). The fastest and most direct route is the A 4 west from Milan.

**Turin

See map on page 124.

Turin (Torino), traversed by the Po River and surrounded by a wonderful hilly landscape with a view of the Alps to the west, is an important industrial city with an elegant French air.

The best place to begin a tour is at the *Stazione Porta Nuova* (main train station), (1) on the **Piazza Carlo Felice** (2). The square is surrounded by beautiful palaces and graced by a spring-fed fountain. *Via Roma*, the most elegant and lively street in the city, lined with arcades and luxurious shops, leads from the north end of the piazza. Follow it several blocks to the tree-lined ***Piazza San Carlo** (3), one of the most beautiful 17th–18th century arcaded squares in Italy. The equestrian statue is of Emanuele Filiberto, Duke of Savoy, depicted after the Battle of St. Quentin (1557). (The House of Savoy, Italy's royal family from 1861–1945, resided in Turin for much of the 17th–18th centuries.) Via Roma continues to the **Palazzo dell'Accademia delle Scienze** (4), also built by Guarini in 1679. It houses the **Egyptian Museum* (the second most important in the world after the Egyptian Museum in Cairo), with rare items from 3,350–450 B.C.); the *Galleria Sabauda*, with paintings by Rembrandt,

Van Dyck, Memling, Holbein the Younger, Velásquez, and masters of Piedmontese, Florentine, and Venetian schools, including Fra Angelico, Bronzino, Mantegna, Filippino Lippi, and Tiepolo; and the *Museum of Antiquities*, with prehistoric, Roman and Greek artifacts, among others, excavated mostly in Piedmont and Liguria. To the right is the Baroque *Piazza Carignano* and the **Palazzo Carignano** (5), a typical example of Piedmontese Baroque, built in 1679 from a design by Guarino Guarini. The palace was the birthplace of King Victor Emmanuel II in 1820 and the seat of the first Italian Parliament which chose Rome as capital of Italy in 1861; it now houses the *Museo del Risorgimento* (Museum of the Italian Independence Movement).

Via Roma ends at the huge *Piazza Castello*, in the center of which stands a 15th-century castle, the ****Palazzo Madama** (6), so called because Marie-Christine

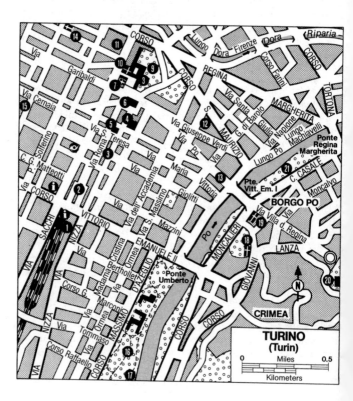

TURINO
(Turin)

0   Miles   0.5

Kilometers

of France, the mother of Charles Emmanuel II, and Giovanna Battista, his widow (both entitled Madama Reale), lived here. In 1718, Filippo Juvarra added the magnificent western wing and façade to the building, which incorporates Roman ramparts. The Palazzo Madama shelters the *Museo d'Arte Antica*, with interesting art collections from the Middle Ages, the Renaissance and Baroque era. The remarkable Baroque *church of San Lorenzo* (7), with an interior by Guarini (1667), is also on the Piazza Castello, and just beyond it is another square, the *Piazzetta Reale*, with the 17th-century ***Palazzo Reale** (8) by Amedeo di Castellamonte. The sober façade of the palace belies its sumptuous interior. You may tour the throne room, the room of the Swiss guards, the ballroom, the apartments of the Kings of Sardinia, and the so-called *scissor staircase*, designed by Filippo Juvarra and leading from the second floor to the third floor. The ground floor houses the *Royal Library*, where drawings by Leonardo da Vinci, Giovanni Bellini, Raphael, Tiepolo, Rembrandt, and Van Dyck are displayed, as well as the *Armeria Reale*, considered to be the richest armory in the world. It contains a remarkable array of European and Oriental weaponry and, in the Galleria Beaumont, 30 suits of armor. The *Palazzo Chiablese*, where there is an impressive *Film Museum*, adjoins the Palazzo Reale.

The *Giardino Reale*, behind the palazzo (9), was designed in 1697 by the famous French landscape architect Le Nôtre, who also designed the gardens at Versailles and the Tuileries gardens in Paris. Part of the park borders the ancient city walls.

The palazzo partly surrounds the ***Duomo San Giovanni Battista** (10), erected between 1492–1498, and Turin's only Renaissance building. In 1668–1694, Guarini added the Baroque *Cappella della Santa Sindone* (Chapel of the Italy Shroud) to house the famous relic in which Christ's body was reputedly wrapped after he was taken down from the Cross. The shroud bears an image of the outline of a crucified body. The campanile of the Duomo adjoins the ruins of the ancient *Teatro Romano*. Just a few steps in front of the Duomo, in Via Porta Palatina, is the ***Porta Palatina** (11), a Roman gate in the city wall erected under Augustus.

If you follow the Via Giuseppe

Porta Palatina

Verdi east from the Piazza Castello and turn left on Via Montebello, you will come to the unusual ****Mole Antonelliana** (12), 167 meters (548 feet) high, with an elevator to the top, where there is a wonderful view. It was designed by the architect Alessandro Antonelli, and was built between 1863–1897. The granite spire broke off in a storm in 1953 and was replaced with an aluminum replica. The building originally served as a synagogue and later became a monument of Italian unity. Southeast of here, opening onto the Po River, is the splendid ***Piazza Vittorio Veneto** (13), built between 1825–1830 and surrounded by arcades.

Near the Porta Palatina, Via Giulio leads northwest to the **Santuario della Consolata* (14), which consists of two Baroque churches, one hexagonal and one oval, constructed from 1679–1703 by Guarini. The church incorporates an 11th–century *bell tower* of the church of Sant'Andrea, the oldest Medieval monument in the city, and a tower of the Roman wall.

From here Via Consolata leads south, across the Piazza Savoia, to the *Mastio* (keep) (15) of the citadel that stood here from 1564–1857. The keep now houses an artillery museum, while just around the corner at Via Guicciardini 7 the *Museo Pietro Micca* has artifacts from the French siege of Turin in 1706, during which the citadel played a crucial role. Micca, a soldier, exploded a mine

and saved the citadel but lost his life.

From the Porta Nuova station (1) you can turn right on the Corso Vittorio Emanuele II and follow it to the banks of the Po River, where you'll find the **Parco del Valentino* (16) with the **Castello del Valentino*, built between 1630–1660, and the **Borgo Medioevale* (17), with replicas of Medieval Piedmontese buildings and a castle. The *Palazzo Esposizioni,* built for the Turin Motor Show of 1948, is at the south end of the park. Here Corso Massimo d'Azeglio becomes Corso Unità d'Italia, and about 2 km. (1 mile) farther is an outstanding car museum, the **Museo dell'Automobile Carlo Biscaretti di Ruffia.* Corso Vittorio Emanuele II ends at the *Ponte Umberto I,* which crosses the Po. Turn left on Corso Moncalieri and right on Via M. Giardino to reach the wooded **Monte dei Cappuccini* (18), 284 meters (932 feet) high, with fine views. Between 1583–1611, a Capuchin church and convent were built on the summit of the hill, where there is now also an interesting museum, *Duca degli Abruzzi,* with relief plans and architectural artifacts.

At the foot of the mountain is the church of the **Gran Madre di Dio* (19), on the piazza of the same name. It was built by Bonsignore in 1818–1831 as a copy of the Pantheon in Rome and has since become a memorial to the victims of World War I. Next to the church, the Via Villa della Regina leads to the **Villa Regina* (20).

The castlelike villa was erected in the 17th century and renovated in 1779 as the residence of the wife of Vittorio Amedeo II of Savoy. Its lovely gardens contain fountains, waterfalls, and terraces adorned with statues.

Upriver from the Piazza Gran Madre di Dio the *Parco Michelotti,* with a zoological garden (21), extends along the banks of the Po.

For travellers with extra time, there are several possible excursions from Turin.

Superga is 10 km. (6 miles) east of Turin. *By car: Take Corso Casale along the Po, then follow the Strada di Superga to the summit. By tram: No. 5 to Stazione Sassi; from there a tram railway makes the ascent.* The summit of *Superga,* 670 meters (2,400 feet) high, is crowned by the basilica of the same name, built between 1717–1831 from designs by Juvarra. The crypts contain the tombs of Sardinian kings from Vittorio Amedeo II to Carlo Alberto, as well as of numerous princes of the House of Savoy. The ascent also affords a grand view of Turin and the Alps.

The *Valle d'Aosta* (or Vald' Aosta) and the city of Aosta offer alpine attractions. *By car:* Autostrada A 5 or Route S 26. *By train: regular service to Aosta and major resorts. By bus: regular service from Turin and Aosta to most spots in the valley.* This lovely valley is ideal for hiking and skiing. Its many resorts are open year round. The valley also has many health spas, the most notable of which are Courmayeur and Borgofranco d'Ivrea.

The largest city in the region is *Aosta,* 120 km. (72 miles) from Turin, attractive mainly because of the mountain peaks that surround it. Known as the "Rome of the Alps," it has a triumphal arch erected by Augustus in 24 B.C. and a gate, *Porta Praetoria,* in the well-preserved Roman city walls. *Courmayeur,* a town stretched out at the foot of the Alps about an hour beyond Aosta on Route 26, is more attractive and glamorous.

Within a 10–30-km.- (6–18-mile-) radius of Turin, there are any number of interesting castles and monasteries, including the Baroque castle of *Stupinigi* (10 km.; 6 miles, southwest), built as a hunting lodge in 1729 by Juvarra; the hunting and pleasure palace in *Venaria* (8 km.; 5 miles, north); the castle of *Agliè* (28 km.; 17 miles, north), which was the summer residence of the dukes of Genoa, with an 18th–century façade; the massive palace of *Rivoli* (12 km.; 7 miles, west), built by Juvarra on the site of a Medieval fortress; the royal palace of *Moncalieri* (10 km.; 6 miles, south), built in the 15th century and restored several times; the abbey of *Sant'Antonio di Ranverso* (18 km.; 11 miles, west), one of the most interesting Medieval buildings in the Piedmont; and the Benedictine monastery of *Vezzolano* (30 km.; 19 miles, east), founded in 773 by Charlemagne and one of the finest groups of Romanesque buildings in Piedmont.

The famous resort of *Sestriere,* which has excellent skiing, is 93 km. (58 miles) west of Turin on Route S 23. *Susa,* 53 km., (33 miles) northwest of Turin on Route S 25, has many noteworthy sights, including an 11th–century cathedral and the so-called Arch of Augustus.

If you leave Turin going south on Route S 20, you'll pass through *Moncalieri,* where the church of Sant'Agostino has an interesting façade, and *Savigliano,* known as the "breadbasket of Piedmont" and the birthplace of the astronomer Giovanni Schiaparelli (1835–1910).

To continue Travel Route 2, return to Milan via Highway A 4, or drive east on A 21 to *Tortona* (see page 131).

Leaving **Milan (see page 103) from the *Corso Porta Ticinese,* enter Route S 35. Shortly after *Binasco,* where there is an interesting *Visconti castle,* a road leaves the highway on the right (follow signposts) for the **Certosa di Pavia** (27 km.; 17 miles from Milan), a Carthusian monastery, built for the most part in the 15th and 16th centuries as a mausoleum for the Viscontis.

The history of Italy, its regions, towns, and cities, is inextricably bound up with the history of the great families that over the centuries acquired, controlled, and then inevitably lost both secular and religious power to yet another clan. In Milan and the region of Lombardy, the Viscontis, followed by the Sforzas, were such a family. In 1277 the Viscontis seized power as the dukes of Milan. As is usual in such power-hungry dynasties, the Viscontis leave behind them a record of ruthless cruelty on the one hand, pious generosity on the other. Gian Galeazzo Visconti (1347–1402) ordered the building of this remarkable Carthusian monastery (*certosa,* in Italian), but he was also a conspirator, assassin, and war leader. The sumptuous decoration of the Certosa, its collection of treasures both inside and out, testifies to the desire of Gian Galeazzo to glorify his family. Six centuries later, you can only marvel at the number of artists who made it what it is, and at the enduring quality of their work.

A visit to the Certosa begins in the great square in front of the building. On the left is the old monastery pharmacy, which now produces a liqueur (there is a tasting room). On the right is the Baroque visitors' lodge. Straight ahead is the extraordinary marble façade of the church, unfinished despite its galleries of superimposed arcades, multicolored marble sculptures, medallions, saints, bas-reliefs, and endless variety of ornamentation. The work of two different sculptors, Amadeo and Lombardo, can be distinguished.

The light and grandiose interior, a unique stylistic product of late Lombard-Gothic melting into Renaissance, creates a profound and luminous impression. At the far end of the nave is a curious *trompe-l' oeil* painting of Carthusian monks viewing their visitors. The fine bronze grilles are late-16th-century work. The church has three naves with side chapels and an impressive transept. In the second chapel is a polyptych with the *Eternal Father* by Perugino and the fragments of a Bergognone altarpiece called *The Four Doctors.* Commanding attention in the center of the nave are marble statues by Cristoforo Solari (1499) for the tombs of Ludovico Sforza, known as il Moro, and his child bride, Beatrice D'Este.

A door with inset medallions of the dukes of Milan leads into the old sacristy, which contains an amazing triptych made from hippopotamus teeth (1409). Some 66 small bas-reliefs and 94 statuettes represent scenes from the life of the Madonna and famous prophets and saints.

On the right of the main chapel and reached through a marble door showing seven duchesses of Milan is the famous *lavabo,* containing a Renaissance fountain and a well. Romano's great monument to Gian Galeazzo Visconti stands outside, in the right transept. Begun in 1497 but not completed until 1562, its bas-reliefs represent the annals of the founder of the Certosa, or at least those deeds he wished posterity to remember. In the apse, Bergognone's frescoes again show Gian Galeazzo, this time accompanied by his children and presenting the model of the Certosa to the Madonna and Child.

The *cloisters,* into which the lavabo and the monks' refectory open, are decorated with charming terra-cottas. Here a Baroque fountain murmurs, and you can get a fine view of the side of the church. From the small cloister you can proceed into the large cloister, surrounded by an arched portico on columns with capitals and rich decoration from the 15th century. Under the portico are the splendid entrance doors of the cells where the Carthusian monks once lived. The monks swore a vow of silence and, when in seclusion, had food delivered through the small swing door at the right of the main doorway.

From the Certosa it is only 7 km. (4 miles) farther on Route S 20 to the city of ***Pavia** (34 km.; 21 miles from Milan), proud and compact, and the location of one of the oldest universities in Italy (established in 1361). Located on the Ticino River near its junction with the Po, Pavia is richly endowed with historic buildings, most of them concentrated along the *Strada Nuova.*

In the Middle Ages, Pavia was known as the city of a 100 towers. Some of these still exist; the three overlooking the Piazza Leonardo da Vinci, behind the university, are the most notable. Some 17,000 students attend classes at this university, whose most electrifying graduate is the man who gave his name to volts, the physicist Alessandro Volta.

In the old center, on Via Diacono, is the magnificent coronation **church of San Michele,* built in 12th-century Lombard-Romanesque style. With its outstanding façade, richly ornamented with a curious assortment of animals, this is the city's most noteworthy structure. Charlemagne, Henri II, and Frederick

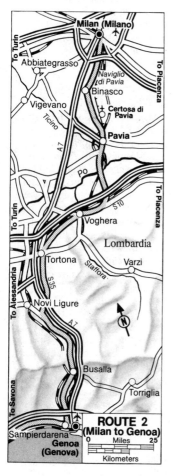

Barbarossa were crowned Kings of the Lombards on this site. In contrast to the exterior, the interior is surprisingly sober, which makes it easier to see and appreciate the superb carvings on capitals, friezes, and the 14th-century high altar.

The vast *Duomo,* or Cathedral, is a strange mixture of architectural styles. Both Bramante and Leonardo contributed to the basic Renaissance building plan in the 15th century, but the huge, dominating dome (the third largest in Italy) was not added until four centuries later. The façade was completed only in 1933. North of the Duomo is *San Pietro in Ciel d'Oro,* where a splendid white marble tomb in the chancel reputedly contains relics of Saint Augustine.

Castello Visconti, the imposing 14th-century fortress at the end of Strada Nuova, is the home of the *Museo Civico.* Designed by Galeazzo II Visconti, father of the Gian who endowed the Certosa di Pavia, the castello passed to the Sforza family. Upon their demise, it was used as a military stronghold by foreign invaders. Now restored, the castle has a collection of civic treasures including Lombard-Romanesque sculptures and intriguing remnants from the city's Roman past. An art gallery exhibits paintings from the 12th to 17th centuries. Other noteworthy reminders of Pavia's great importance are the *Palazzo Mezzabara* (18th century), with its lovely Baroque façade, now serving as the city hall; the *Palazzo Car-minati Bottigella* (15th century); and the *Palazzo Malaspina*, where some 500 paintings are on display, including works by Bellini, Bergognone, Crivelli and Correggio. The *Ponte Coperto* (Covered Bridge), built in 1353 and restored after war damage, spans the Ticino River.

A hearty bowl of the local specialty, *zuppa alla pavese,* is a perfect way to end your visit to this relaxed and charming city. Legend has it that François I of France, before losing the Battle of Pavia (1525) to the Spanish, stopped at a cottage for something to eat. To make her simple minestrone fit for a king, the king's hostess added cheese, eggs, and toasted bread to it.

Some 11 km. (7 miles) from Pavia, Route S 35 crosses the Po River and intersects with Route S 10, which continues through *Voghera* (65 km., 40 miles from Milan), where there is yet another 14th-century Visconti fortress and a cathedral built in 1605, to *Tortona,* with its 16th-century cathedral. *Alessandria,* 21 km. (13 miles) west of Voghera on Route S 10, is worth a side trip because of its pleasant, unspoiled appearance. Most of its buildings date from the 18th and 19th centuries.

At Tortona, get on Autostrada A 7, which provides breathtaking panoramas of the mountains of the Ligurian Apennines on the 150-km.- (93-mile-) stretch to Genoa (231 km., 143 miles from Milan).

**Genoa

See map on page 132.

Genoa, capital of Liguria and the greatest seaport in Italy, has a tumultuous history. Wars and revolutions of one sort or another have been waged by or on Genoa since its first appearance in history, ca. 218 B.C. A rich, independent republic in the tenth century, it fought Pisa for 200 years, then battled with Venice for control of the lucrative Eastern trade. Spanish, French, and Austrian troops have occupied it, and in the 19th century it became part of the Kingdom of Sardinia. During World War II, Genoa suffered severe bomb damage. Like Milan with the Viscontis and Sforzas, Genoa has its own famous family—the Dorias. Christopher Columbus was born and raised in this ancient seaport, as were Italy's great Republican heroes Giuseppe Mazzini and Giuseppe Garibaldi. Genoa has more splendid old palaces of the nobility than any other Italian city, and these help give some impression of what it was like in its heyday, when it was called *"la superba,"* (the proud).

The best place to begin a tour is the **Piazza de Ferrari** (1), hub of the city, with the busiest streets in Genoa radiating from it in every direction. This eternally busy piazza is bordered by the old *Palazzo Ducale* (16th–17th centuries), once the residence of the doges, and monumental buildings from the 19th century, including the remains of the opera house,

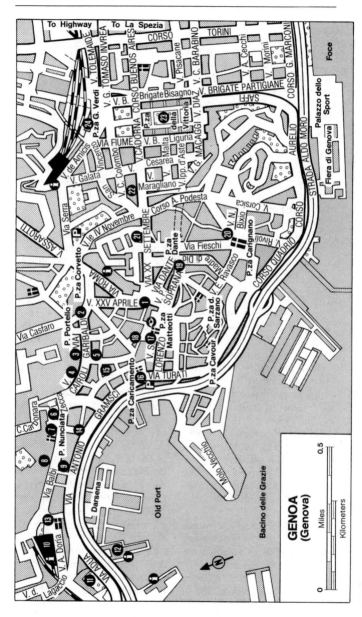

burned down in World War II. To the right of the theater stands the *Accademia Linguistica di Belle Arti,* containing works by Ligurian artists, while the imposing Neo-Baroque *Borsa* (Stock Exchange) stands on the southeast side of the square.

From the north end of the piazza, Via XXV Aprile leads to the ***Piazza Fontane Marose** (2), with three remarkable palaces from the 15th and 16th centuries. Superb views can be had from the terrace of the *Villetta di Negro,* a unique belvedere-labyrinth with cascades and artificial grottoes, situated on higher ground to the northwest. Laid out in the 16th and 17th centuries, the area around the piazza contains a number of churches and the finest palaces in Genoa, approached by magnificent flights of steps, which are one of the characteristic sights of the city. Finest of all is the narrow ****Via Garibaldi,** which is lined with a succession of stunning palaces and is one of the most beautiful streets in Europe.

Built in 1564, the colonnaded ***Palazzo Doria Tursi** (3), now the *Palazzo Municipale* (City Hall), has a splendid interior decorated with Flemish tapestries and displays a violin that belonged to Paganini and a manuscript penned by Christopher Columbus, two of Genoa's most famous sons. Next to it is the ***Palazzo Bianco** (4), so-called because of the once-brilliant whiteness of its stone, with a notable *pinacoteca,* or picture gallery, in an especially luxurious setting. Flemish painting is emphasized, and works by Rubens, Van Dyck, Zurbarán, Murillo, Filippo Lippi and other Dutch and Italian masters are exhibited. Across the street is the splendid ***Palazzo Rosso** (5), which also houses an excellent *pinacoteca,* particularly notable for its fine family portraits and paintings by Veronese, Titian, Caravaggio, Tintoretto and Dürer, as well as ceramics and other works by Genoese artists. Marble sculptures are on display in the beautiful courtyard.

Via Garibaldi becomes Via Cairoli, which you follow to the *Largo della Zecca* (6), from which a funicular ascends to *Monte Righi,* 310 meters (1,000 feet) high. The views of Genoa and the Italian Riviera are breathtaking.

From the Largo della Zecca, *Via Bensa* leads to the *Piazza Annunziata* and the ***church of Santa Annunziata del Vastato** (7), one of the most important and magnificent churches in the city. Constructed in the 13th century, it was transformed in the 16th, given its Neoclassical brick façade in 1848, and severely bombed during World War II. The impressive interior has three naves supported by multi-colored marble columns and filled with 17th-century Genoese paintings.

You are now at the foot of Via Balbi, flanked by handsome palaces that are the finest expression of Genoese Baroque and give the street a regal, monumental character. Immediately on the right is the *Palazzo Durazzo-Pallavicini,* with a Rococo entrance hall, imposing loggia and lovely 18th-century staircase. The *Palazzo dell'Università* (8) at No. 5, with the finest courtyard and gardens in Genoa, was built in the 17th century as a Jesuit college. Statues by Giambologna and a line of imposing lions on the staircase add to the grandeur of the scene. The small *church of San Carlo* (1635) stands next door. The 17th-century *Palazzo Reale* (9), with its brilliant scarlet façade, handsome staircases and richly appointed interior, including a Van Dyck room, was a residence of the royal family until 1817.

Via Balbi ends at the **Piazza Acquaverde** (10), a large square in front of the *Stazione Principe* (main railway station). A *Columbus memorial* by Michele Canzio dominates the center of the square, and the nearby Savoia-Majestic Hotel retains all the grace and elegance of a bygone Vespaless era.

From the piazza, walk west along Via Andrea Doria to the ***Palazzo Doria-Pamphili,** built in 1522–1529 as a country house for Doge Andrea Doria, the much-admired Genoese admiral who ended French and Spanish rule by reinstating the republic in 1528. The fête he arranged for the French king Charles V in 1533 took place on board the Doria flagship, anchored in the middle of the harbor, and lasted for 12 days; when a piece of the silver-gilt tableware was soiled, it was royally tossed into the sea. The com-

poser Guiseppe Verdi (1813–1901) spent the last years of his honor-laden life in this palace.

The *Stazione Marittima dei Mille* (12) (Maritime Station), is only a few steps down the waterfront. Tours of this bustling, noisy harbor, the largest in Italy, begin from the landing stage to the right of the station. Protected by a breakwater, the port has five major basins to handle every kind of vessel from small private yachts to oil tankers. To the west rises the tower of Genoa's oldest lighthouse, the *Lanterna* (1544), with a range of more than 30 miles. The city of Genoa, seen from the perspective of the harbor, rises up in tiers like a honey-colored opera house.

From the Maritime Station, the most direct route back to *Piazza Ferrari* is to follow Via Antonio Gramsci along the harbor. You will pass en route the *church of San Giovanni di Pre* (13), one of the most ancient and impressive of Genoese churches, and the 12th-century *Loggia Commendatori Gerosolimitani.* The Gothic *Porta dei Vacca* (14) leads into the old city. Here you may wish to wander in the ancient streets and twisting alleys called *carrugi,* which are lined with tempting shops. If you're hungry, try a plate of *trenette* with *pesto alla genovese,* a mouth-watering sauce consisting of olive oil, basil, garlic and Parmesan cheese. The Italian ritual of an afternoon stroll, or *passeggiata,* takes place on the elegant Via Luccoli. From the Porta dei Vacca, follow Via San Luca, Genoa's main street in the Middle

Ages, into the heart of the old quarter. On the small *Piazza Pellicceria* a 17th-century palace now houses the *Galleria Spinola* (15), with decorated apartments, fine ceilings, and a collection of paintings from the Italian and Flemish Renaissance. Follow Via San Luca through the old city and you'll be rewarded by the picturesque charm of *Via degli Orefici* (Street of the Goldsmiths).

Here, in *Piazza Caricamento,* near the foot of the street on the waterfront, is the historical ***Palazzo di San Giorgio** (16), consisting of two distinct parts: the Gothic (1260) and the Renaissance (1571). It was first a residence, but was converted in 1408 to the headquarters of the important Banco di San Giorgio, which handled all financial transactions for the rich city-republic of Genoa. A monument to Raffaele Rubattino (1809–1872), the powerful shipping magnate, stands in front of the palace. The square is flanked by lively, half-underground porticoes, called Via di Sottoripa, where you can find specialty restaurants, stores and the famous Genoese fried-fish shops.

Just south of the palazzo, Via San Lorenzo winds away from the harbor to the Romanesque ****cathedral of San Lorenzo** (17), founded, according to legend, in the third century by the Roman Saint Lawrence. The present church has been rebuilt several times since 1100. A relief sculpture of Lawrence being grilled alive can be seen on one of the three French-inspired Gothic por-

San Lorenzo Cathedral

tals. Undaunted by his terrible martyrdom, the saint reputedly put his sense of humor to use by saying, "One side has been roasted, turn me over and eat it!" The bell tower was added in 1522, and two fine 19th-century lions flank the steps. The use of black and white marble in the central nave and galleries gives the interior a look of powerful severity. Rich in works of art and crowned with a Renaissance dome, the cathedral also contains a powerful reminder of the last war: In the south aisle is an unexploded shell that burst through the façade during a naval bombardment in 1941. The **Cathedral Treasury,* housed in the archbishop's palace, contains the famous Sacro Catino, a basin of green Roman glass reputedly given by the Queen of Sheba to Solomon and used by Christ at the Last Supper. According to some, Joseph of Arimathea later collected Christ's blood in it, making this relic the true Holy Grail.

Follow Via San Lorenzo farther to the *Piazza Matteotti,* the location of the *Palazzo Ducale* (Doge's Palace), dating from the end of the 13th century but later rebuilt and restored. It has picturesque pillared courtyards and is now occupied by the law courts. Across the piazza can be seen the solemn façade of *Il Gesù,* a church of very ancient origin, rebuilt from 1589–1606. Its sumptuous interior is covered with marbles and stuccoes and contains major works by Rubens and Guido Reni. *Via T. Reggio* leads off from the west side of the piazza. Passing the 13th-century *Palazzo del Comune* and the early 14th-century *Torre del Popolo,* you come to the narrow Salito allo Arcivescovato, which leads to the **Piazza San Matteo** (18). The houses of the noble Doria family, some of them faced with black and yellow marble and forming one of the most impressive corners of the old city, are found here, as is their small manorial church, *San Matteo,* with its remarkable Romanesque-Ligurian striped façade. The tomb of Andrea Doria, called "Father of his Country" and presented with a house on the square (No. 17) in 1528 by the Genoese republic, is located in the church. Adjacent is the beautiful early Gothic cloister, *Chiostro di San Matteo.*

Piazza Ferrari, where the tour began, is at the end of the Salita del Fondaco. Once back to the piazza, you may wish to make a short additional tour by walking through Via Porta Soprana (reached from the piazza by Via Petrarca) to see the tall Medieval tower, the ***Porta Soprana** (19), erected by the citizens of Genoa in 1155 to protect themselves from yet another invader, this one Frederick Barbarossa. Next to it is the graceful, double-columned 12th-century cloister of a former monastery, and the ivy-covered *House of Columbus,* where the explorer supposedly was born in 1451 and spent his youth.

Other noteworthy sights in this fascinating port city include the 16th-century *basilica of Santa Maria di Carignano* (20), with its large dome and four small ones, located south of the city center in the *Piazza Carignano;* the ancient parish church used by Columbus, *Santo Stefano* (21), first built in the tenth century and almost destroyed by aerial bombardments a thousand years later, and the *church of Santissima Annunziata di Portoria* (22), both in the lively shopping street *Via XX Settembre;* the richly decorated *Triumphal Arch* (23), a monument to the victims of World War I, built over the Tomb of the Unknown Soldier, on the *Piazza della Vittoria* at the end of Via XX Settembre. Models of Columbus's three ships can also be seen in the piazza. A railway station, *Stazione Brignole* (24), is across the square in *Piazza Verdi.*

Autostrada A 10 is the fastest route from Genoa to the French border, but far more appealing is the spectacular coastal route S 1, also known as Via Aurelia, after the old Roman road that covered this same stretch of coastline. With its scenic cliffs, luxuriant vegetation and little Old World port towns beside a brilliant blue sea, this section of the Italian Riviera is worth a visit. An admission fee is charged at many of the beaches.

Pegli, a popular weekend retreat for the Genoese, is a place of beautiful parks and villas. *Villa Durazzo Pallavicini,* with an archaeological museum and splendid grounds, extends up a lushly planted hillside with fountains, grottoes, an underground lake and a Medieval-style castle. *Villa Doria* houses an extensive collection of maritime artifacts, including mementos of Columbus. *Arenzano* is a charmingly situated resort with a good beach, an old castle, and a beautiful park.

Varazze (183 km., 113 miles from Milan), situated among orange groves and with a wide, sandy beach and excellent resort facilities, is much frequented in summer and winter. The old town contains extensive remains of a Roman wall and the *church of Sant'Ambrogio,* with a 10th-century façade. Beautiful walks inland can be made to the *Invrea plateau,* planted with fragrant spruce trees, to the pilgrimage church of *Madonna della Guardia* and to the *Convento del Deserto,* a convent on *Monte Beigua.* Nearby **Celle Ligure,** birthplace of the

Franciscan Pope Sixtus IV (1414–1484), is an attractive resort above which is a fine old pinewood with a landscaped promenade; it also boasts a beautiful, sandy beach for swimming. There are plentiful hikes into the surrounding hills, vineyards and olive groves. In the old town visit the *church of San Michele,* with its Medieval bell tower, and the *Torri Sandra,* from the 14th and 15th centuries.

Albisola Marina has been known since antiquity for its ceramics, and the interior of its 16th-century *parish church* is decorated with multicolored majolica. The luxurious *Villa Gavotti* at *Albisola Superiore,* 1 km. (half a mile) north of the little town and surrounded by magnificent grounds, belonged to the della Roveres, the family of popes Sixtus IV (1414–1484) and Julius II (1443–1513).

Savona (206 km.; 128 miles from Milan), fifth largest seaport in Italy, is a provincial capital that includes a modern quarter and a historic old city with Renaissance palaces. The most interesting streets are Via Paleocapa, lined with shopping arcades, and the narrow, crowded Via Pia. Here may be found most of the town's 15th- and 16th-century towers and churches, including *Santa Maria di Castello,* with its winged altar, *Cristo Risorto,* containing worthwhile ceiling frescoes and choir stalls, and *Sant'Andrea.* The 16th-century Duomo, with its 19th-century façade and inlaid stalls, stands next to the *Papal loggia* and the *Sistine Chapel,* built by Pope Sixtus IV in the 15th century to commemorate his parents. Julius II had the famous Florentine architect Sangallo design the nearby and unfinished *Palazzo delle Rovere.* The 16th-century *Priamar fortress* stands on the ruins of an older castle.

Just up the coast, *Spotorno,* surrounded by wooded hills and olive groves, has an interesting church and the ruins of a castle. The island of *Bereggi* lies offshore. Beyond the town there is a splendid view of *Capo Noli* (Cape Noli).

*Noli, famous for its apricots, is a fishing village and seaside resort of great charm and character. A major naval power in the Middle Ages, the town eventually joined forces with Genoa to form an independent republic. Worth seeing are the late Romanesque *church of San Paragorio,* three

13th-century towers, the ancient houses *Casa Pagliano* and *Casa Repetto,* the *Porta di San Giovanni,* the cathedral, and the imposing *Castello di Monte Ursino.* The town walls are well preserved. There is a pleasant walk (about one hour) to *Capo Noli,* where there is a signal station and church.

From Noli the Via Aurelia runs through a tunnel under Capo Noli and continues along high, overhanging cliffs to ***Finale Ligure** (221 km.; 137 miles from Milan), an internationally known resort formed by four villages, three of them linked by a magnificent corniche road. A wide sandy beach and lush surrounding hills add to the romance. The town is overlooked by a ruined castle and can boast of its fine Baroque church, *San Giovanni Battista,* by the renowned Bernini. Artifacts

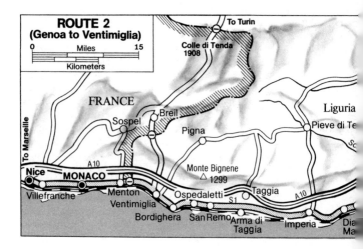

ROUTE 2
(Genoa to Ventimiglia)

0   Miles   15

Kilometers

To Turin

Colle di Tenda
1908

FRANCE

Liguria

Sospel   Breil

Pigna

Pieve di Te

To Marseille

A10

Monte Bignene
△ 1299

Nice   MONACO

Villefranche   Menton   Ospedaletti   Taggia   A10

Ventimiglia   S1

Bordighera   San Remo   Arma di   Imperia   Dia
Taggia   Ma

found in some 50 prehistoric caves nearby (closed to the public) can be viewed in a museum in the Cloister of Santa Caterina. Inland 2 km. (1.2 miles) is the village of *Finalborgo,* former capital of a marquisate, with the beautiful Gothic *collegiate church of San Biago,* built on a tower in the town wall and flanked by a graceful campanile. The elegant 13th-century abbey *church of Finalpia* is used for pilgrimages, and the *basilica of Finale Marina* is fancifully graced with a Baroque façade.

An excursion can be made on a Roman road into the *Valle di Ponci,* where there are several Roman bridges. Stalactite caverns are also to be found in the vicinity.

Plentiful offshore reefs and caverns make **Pietra Ligure,** at the foot of *Monte Trabocchetto,* popular with underwater-sports enthu-siasts. A coastal promenade past palm trees and gardens, and the many Medieval buildings in the town, including the *Chiesa dell'Annunziata* and *Oratorio dei Bianchi,* add to the delights of the place.

Loano, a popular beach resort, is situated on a spacious plain protected by mountains. The *Palazzo Andrea Doria,* now the town hall, dates from 1578 and contains third-century mosaics. The *castle* and a superb loggia are Medieval, while the *Porta dell'Orologio* (clock-tower gate) dates from 1774, and the parish *church of San Giovanni* from 1633–1638.

For a pleasant walk, head toward the hillside just north of town to find the early-17th-century *Convento di Monte Carmelo* and the nearby pilgrimage *church of Santi Cosma e Damiano.*

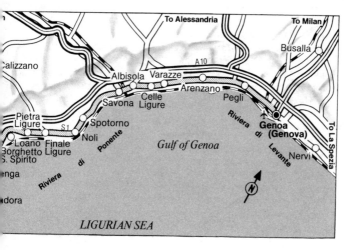

Beyond Loano there is a fine view of *Monte Carmo* in the Ligurian Alps. About 5 km. (3 miles) west, the *Toirano Grotto,* with bizarre stalactite and stalagmite formations and traces of a Paleolithic hunter culture, is a reminder of how long this area has been inhabited.

Route S 1 continues through the beach resorts of *Borghetto Santo Spirito,* with Medieval streets and city walls, and *Ceriale,* with a 16th-century fort, and comes to ***Albenga** (241 km.; 149 miles from Milan), a distinctive city with tall, reddish brick towers and city walls, situated in a fertile plain with plentiful market gardens. Though it is now a short distance from the sea, it was a thriving port in the Roman period. Albenga became independent during the Middle Ages but fell to the greater might of Genoa in the 12th century. The town's Medieval character can be savored in the streets and piazzas of the *Quartiere della Cattedrale* around the 13th-century **Cathedral,* dominated by a late-14th-century campanile and with a Baroque façade. Just opposite stands the tower of the *Municipio* (city hall) and at the end of the square the *Palazzo Peloso-Cepolla,* now the *Roman Naval Museum,* with a collection of amphorae recovered from a first-century ship that sank just off the coast. The 13th-century *Palazzo Vecchio del Comune* beside the Cathedral marks the important architectural transition from Romanesque to Gothic and

provides a splendid panorama from the top of its tower. The archaeological collection of the *Museo Civico* is housed in the palace itself, which is crowned with merlons and contains a Gothic communal loggia. A fifth-century *baptistry* is built on an octagonal plan and contains an Early Christian mosaic and baptismal font. Other houses of Medieval nobility, several of them with attached towers, line the adjacent streets, and near the Via Aurelia a Medieval bridge, the *Ponte Lungo,* spans the former course of the River Centa.

The rocky island of *Gallimara,* with ruins of a 13th-century Benedictine abbey, can be seen just off the coast of Albenga. Saint Martin of Tours fled to a cave on the island in 370. ***Alassio** (248 km.; 154 miles from Milan), with its long sandy beach and bay sheltered from cold winds by a surrounding amphitheater of mountains, is one of the Riviera's most elegant resorts. Edward Elgar was inspired to compose "In the South" here in 1904. The town is famous for its mild climate, which makes possible the beautiful gardens. On and around the Medieval main street are the parish *church of Sant'Ambrogio,* the *Oratorio of Santa Caterina,* and interesting old houses. An old watchtower stands on the seafront promenade. The surrounding hills, dotted with villas, are ideal for walking.

Laigueglia is a closely built little town with a fine beach and a popular mineral spring, the *Fonte* *del Faro*. There is a lovely 18th-century parish church, *San Matteo*. A ruined castle and beautiful 13th-century Romanesque church can be found along the Roman road that climbs through the hills beyond the town.

Beyond the town of *Diano Marino*, Route S 1 winds gently uphill to *Capo Berto*, which provides a magnificent view back as far as *Capo Mele*. The road continues on to the provincial capital of *Imperia*, created in 1923 by merging two adjoining towns and now an important port and center for Ligurian oil production. Just inland there are abundant olive groves.

Taggia, a picturesque and partly fortified little town commanding a view of the *Valle d'Argentina*, was an art center in the 15th and 16th centuries and now hosts an antiques and crafts fair on the last weekend of each month. The *church of San Domenico*, on the upper slopes a little outside the town and containing a noteworthy collection of paintings by Louis Brea, adjoins tranquil cloisters and 15th-century monastic buildings. The town also contains old patrician houses and the 11th-century Romanesque church of *Madonna del Canneto*.

At the end of the valley, a 15th-century bridge with a pre-Romanesque arch spans the River Argentina. The road climbs through lovely countryside (to 1,000 meters; 3,300 feet) to the pilgrimage *church of Santa Maria di Lampedusa*.

The seaside resort of *Arma di Taggia*, with its beautiful beach, lies another 3 km. (2 miles) to the southwest.

*San Remo (293 km.; 182 miles from Milan), with its deliciously warm temperatures and the highest average sunshine in Liguria, is Italy's largest, oldest (since 1861) and most luxurious health resort. Capital of the "Riviera of Flowers," San Remo is the main Italian flower market. In midwinter, from Ventimiglia to Alassio some 9,000 acres are planted with an intoxicating array of carnations, roses, jasmine, hyacinths, narcissi, violets, tulips and mimosa. San Remo's racecourse, casino, lively festivals and excellent tourist facilities have given it a worldwide reputation.

The *old town* is an intriguing warren of winding alleys, staircases and tall houses linked by arches as a protection against earthquakes. The long and elegant main street, Via Matteotti, is in the *new town*, along with the *Casino Municipale*, with gaming rooms and a theater, and continues westward by the famous Corso dell'Imperatrice, a promenade shaded by Canary palms. The *Cathedral*, founded in the 12th century, is located a short distance northeast. One of the longest cable car routes in the world climbs, in 45 minutes, to the top of *Monte Bignone*, 1,300 meters (4,265 feet) above sea level, where there is a spectacular view of the Riviera and the Maritime Alps, and south to Corsica.

Route S 1 continues, through

Ospedaletti, a pretty resort and horticultural center, to **Bordighera.** With its mild climate and villas and hotels scattered among bright flower gardens, the town has long been a popular winter retreat for the British. A horticultural center, Bordighera is especially famed for its date palms, exporting the branches to the Vatican for Palm Sunday and to Jewish communities for the Feast of Tabernacles. The *Sant'Ampelio* reef provides excellent skin diving. There are superb views of the coast from the Via dei Colli, and the old town still has fortified gateways. The former *Villa of Queen Margaret of Savoy,* who died here in 1926, is now a pensione.

Ventimiglia (312 km.; 193 miles from Milan), the frontier town, is situated at the mouth of the river *Roia,* which divides it in two. The old town, on the left bank, is cut by steps, covered ways and alleys known as *scuri,* lined with one old house after another. The Romanesque *church of San Michele,* the *cathedral* and the *baptistry* all date from the 11th century. Breathtaking views as far west as Cap Ferrat can be had from the *Piazzale del Capo,* a little way south. A flower market is held in the *Via Roma* of the new town, on the right bank, where there is also an interesting *Archaeological Museum* in the *Municipio.* Impressive ruins, including an *amphitheater,* are found in nearby *Albium Intemelium,* where the famous Roman soldier Agricola (A.D. 40–93) was raised.

The French border is just 5 km. (3 miles) ahead. Route S 1 continues through Menton, Monaco, and Villefranche to Nice.

TRAVEL ROUTE 3: *Genoa–La Spezia–Viareggio–**Pisa–Piombino–*Elba–*Grosseto–Civitavecchia–***Rome (545 km.; 338 miles)

See maps on pages 145 and 153.

The Romans built this ancient route, which they called the Via Aurelia (now Route S 1) and which follows the coastline. There are beautiful seaside resorts all along this route, and you can easily sneak in a day or two on the beach as you travel south.

If you leave **Genoa (p. 131) going east on Via XX Settembre, which connects with Route S 1, you come first to **Nervi** (11 km.; 7 miles from Genoa), the oldest spa on the *Riviere di Levante* (Eastern Riviera) and now a suburb of Genoa. A promenade along the coast, *Passeggiata Anita Garibaldi,* winds through the rocky cliffs. Among Nervi's lovely gardens are the *Parco Municipale,* the *Villa Gropallo,* and the *Villa Serra,* in which the *Galleria d'Arte*

Moderna is located and in which ballet performances are given during the summer.

After Nervi, the road passes through the coastal towns of *Bogliasco, Pieve Ligure, Sori* and *Recco,* all pleasant, small resorts. The main road turns inland after Recco, but a coast road descends to **Camogli,** a picturesque Medieval town, built steeply along the coast. Camogli was famous for its fleets, and the town's most interesting attractions are the *Museo Marinaro,* with exhibits relating to sailing, and the *Dragonara castle,* which has a large aquarium. From Camogli, you can either walk along the path or take a boat (25 minutes) to *San Fruttuoso,* a pretty village with a Benedictine abbey and cloisters from the 13th century.

Santa Margherita Ligure and *Rapallo* are well-known resorts, both located on the *Golfo Tigullio* (or Bay of Rapallo). The beaches are rocky but scenic, and the settings are lush. There is little of art or architecture to see in these towns, but the blue Mediterranean and verdant green hills should satisfy any visitor's longing for beauty. And should these towns not provide enough seaside charm, then by all means explore ****Portofino,** located just beyond Santa Margherita on a headland. Portofino is an old fishing port that has become very popular with yachtsmen. Atop the promontory is the *church of San Giorgio,* where the relics of Saint George the Dragon Slayer are said to rest.

Back on Route S 1, the road out of Rapallo passes through *Zoagli* and reaches **Chiavari,** a shipbuilding center and a beautiful resort. The main street is arcaded, with many interesting old buildings. The beach is sandy, and there is a port for small boats. A necropolis from the eighth–seventh centuries B.C. has been excavated here, and later remains from the Roman era can be seen in the *Civico Museo Archeologico.* The road continues through the resorts of *Lavagna, Cavi* and *Sestri Levante,* all of which have long, sandy beaches. The beaches become rocky, however, as you enter the ***Cinque Terre (Five Lands), as the area of *Monterosso, Vernazza, Corniglia, Manarola,* and *Riomaggiore* is known. Until recently, these old fishing villages could be reached only by sea or by a footpath that wound around the rocky cliffs. Now a coast road has made these as well as numerous other seaside villages easily accessible, and there are many in Italy who argue that the construction that inevitably follows such accessibility will ruin the landscape and the towns and make it impossible for the inhabitants to continue living as they have for centuries. So far at least, building hasn't occurred in the Cinque Terre, where the villagers still fish and produce the excellent local wines. Should you stop in the Cinque Terre, be sure to visit the small pilgrimage churches around which these towns grew up.

The faster, alternative Route S 1

curves inland at *Sestri Levante* (see above) and crosses the *Passo del Bracco* (615 meters; 2,000 feet) before descending to the coast at **La Spezia** (113 km.; 70 miles from Genoa), Italy's major military port, which lies at the head of the *Golfo della Spezia.* The *Duomo* on *Corso Cavour,* the city's main street, contains a fine polychrome terra-cotta by Andrea della Robbia (*Coronation of the Virgin*). Also on Corso Cavour are the *Musei Civici* (the Municipal Museums), one of which is the *Museo Archeologico Lunense,* which contains Ligurian statues of the Lunigiana cult and remains from the nearby Roman town of *Luni.* The *Museo Navale* contains relics and models that illustrate the naval history of Italy. By far the most beautiful sight, however, is the bay itself, whose crescent shape led the Romans to call it the *portus lunae* (port of the moon). The beauty of the ***Golfo della Spezia* has been extolled by Dante and Petrarch, Shelley and George Sand, D'Annunzio, Ceccardi, and D. H. Lawrence, among others. The bay is best seen by boat, and if you take the boat that leaves from the public gardens, you also can travel to ***Portovenere,** the ancient *Portus Veneris,* a lovely fortified town on the southern tip of the peninsula. The town has maintained its fortified houses, 12th-century fortress, city gate and tower, and the *church of San Lorenzo.* On the promontory at the southern end of the village is the *church of San Pietro,* which has

been closed because of structural failures. But do walk around it—the views of the cliffs of the Cinque Terre are magnificent. Below the church is the *Grotta Arpaia*—or Byron's Cave—from which Lord Byron set out to swim the Gulf and visit Shelley at Lerici in 1822. It was, by the way, from Lerici that Shelley himself set out on the fateful voyage to Livorno that led to his death when his boat capsized. **Lerici** itself, on the eastern shore of the bay, is both a summer and winter resort. The *church of San Rocco* has a 14th-century clock tower and there is also a Medieval castle in the town. Off the coast lies the island of *Palmaria,* with its *Grotta dei Colombi* (Grotto of the Doves), one of the earliest known human habitations in the Mediterranean basin. Palmaria is flanked by the small islands of *Tino* and *Tinetto.* On Tino are the remains of the *abbey of San Venerio,* from the 11th cen-

Riomaggiore

tury, and the ruins of an Early Christian settlement.

From La Spezia, Route S 1 continues to **Sarzana,** the old southeastern outpost of the Genoese republic. The town has several Medieval churches as well as the *Duomo of Santa Maria Assunta,* built from the 13th–15th centuries. The *Medicea citadel* from the 13th–14th century and the *Castruccio fortress,* built in 1322, are evidence of the town's military past.

The road now runs along the edge of the *Apuan Alps,* site of some 300 marble quarries. To the right, access roads lead to the wide, sandy beaches of resorts on the *Riviera della Versilia: Marina di Carrara, Marina di Massa, Forte dei Marmi, Marina di Pietrasanta* and *Camaiore Lido.* To the left, the road branches off to *Carrara,* famous for its marble, which has been used for centuries by sculptors, among them Michelangelo. At Carrara is a beautiful Romanesque palazzo to which a fine Gothic upper story was added in the 13th century. From Carrara it is possible to visit any of the many nearby quarries and then to visit the marble-cutting mills in town. Farther along on the road is *Massa,* with its 15th-century *Duomo* and the *Castello della Rocca,* from the 14th–16th centuries, once the residence of the dukes of Malaspina.

Viareggio (170 km.; 105 miles from Genoa), the most popular beach resort in Tuscany, is the scene of frightful traffic jams in

ROUTE 3
(Genoa to Pisa)

0   Miles   20

Kilometers

To Milan
**Genoa
(Genova)**   M. Antola
                △
                1597
Nervi
Bogliasco   Uscio
Pieve Ligure
        Sori
Camogli   Recco
S. Fruttuoso Rapallo
Portofino   Santa Margherita
        Gulf of   Zoagli Ligure
        Tigullio Chiavari
                    Lavagna
            Cavi
Sestri Levante   **Liguria**

                  Pso. d. Bracco
                  613

        Levanto
Monterosso
al Mare   Vernazza
                  Corniglia
        Manarola
Riomaggiore   **La Spezia**

Portovenere
Palmaria
        Tino Lerici   Sarzana
                  Tinetto
                  ☩ Luni
Marina di Carrara   Carrara
Marina di Massa   Massa
                          Seravezza
        Forte dei Marmi
Marina di Pietrasanta   1858
        Viareggio   Pietra- △
Torre del Lago   santa M. Pania
                          d. Croce
                          Camaiore
                    Villa Puccini
Marina   *Lago di*
di Pisa   *Massaciuccoli*
Tirrenia   **Lucca**

                Pisa
Livorno
        Tuscany
To Rome   To Florence

To Ventimiglia
Riviera   di   Levante

To Parma

To Modena

the summer as visitors, especially from Florence, crowd its long, sandy beaches—or try to! It is a lovely spot for swimming, with a backdrop of dense pine forests and a distant view of the Apuan Alps. Each February a carnival is held here on four successive Sundays; it is one of Italy's most popular events. The road continues through **Torre del Lago Puccini,** a small town near *Lago Massaciùccoli;* it is named after Giacomo Puccini, who composed most of his operas here. Puccini's tomb is near his *villa* on the shore of the lake.

Nearby, Highway A 11 heads inland toward *Lucca* (see page 202) and *Florence* (see page 60). Route S 1 continues south to ***Pisa* (193 km.; 120 miles from Genoa), a city that achieved great power during the Middle Ages and bequeathed Romanesque architectural splendors unequaled anywhere else in Italy.

***Pisa

See map on page 149.

Most tours of Pisa begin in the ***Piazza del Duomo,* which is also known as the *Campo dei Miracoli.* Unlike those in most Italian towns, this cathedral does not provide the focus of civic life. Instead, the square lies well northwest of the city center, and its wide green lawn sets off beautifully the gleaming marble buildings that surround it—the Duomo itself, the leaning tower, the baptistry and the Camposanto. The cren-

ellated city walls that enclose the square on the north side give it an even greater sense of being separate from the city, which certainly seems far away once you're inside the precincts of the Piazza itself. If you have only limited time to spend in Pisa, spend it here on the Piazza del Duomo and in the splendid buildings that had so great an impact on architecture throughout northern Italy.

The ***Duomo** (1) was started in 1063 but was completed only in the 13th century. It is a wonderful example of Pisan-Romanesque architecture and one of the most important Romanesque buildings in Italy. The Duomo stands on a pavement of white marble, and its façade is alternating bands of white and black marble, a decorative device that is continued in the interior as well. The façade itself has four tiers of columns with open galleries, below which are seven tall arches. The interior is especially dramatic and especially beautiful, with many 18th-century paintings and some earlier masterpieces, by Andrea del Sarto, Vanni and Il Sodoma, for example. But by far the most striking and most important work in the Duomo is the **pulpit* by Giovanni Pisano, on which he worked from 1302 to 1311. Its beautifully carved columns and capitals and its intricately sculpted reliefs make it the most important Gothic sculpture in Italy.

At the east end of the Duomo is the ***campanile** (2), the famous Leaning Tower of Pisa,

Leaning Tower of Pisa

built from 1174 to 1350. It was only about 10 meters (33 feet) high when it first began to sink into the subsoil and lean; its drift has been slowed significantly, and the lean now increases by only about 2 mm. (about $1/16$ inch) a year. The tower is made up of six splendidly designed superimposed arcades. Inside, a spiral staircase leads up to the belfry, from which there is a marvelous view of Pisa and the surrounding countryside.

The *****baptistry** (3) is west of the Duomo. It was started in 1152 and finished, in the Gothic style, in 1284. The dome was added in the 14th century. The exterior has four portals; the one facing the Duomo was designed by Giovanni Pisano. Inside is the octagonal font of white marble made by Guido da Como in 1246. The **pulpit was made by Nicola Pisano in 1260; its slender pillars with figures of the

Virtues and panels with bold reliefs of the Nativity, Adoration, Presentation, Crucifixion, and Last Judgment are especially beautiful.

At the north end of the piazza is the *Camposanto (4), a cemetery laid out in 1278. This burial ground is in the form of a rectangular cloister lit by traceried windows. The interior frescoes and sculpture suffered greatly during an Allied bombardment in 1944, but painstaking restoration has made it possible to view once again this magnificent series of paintings by, among others, Benozzo Gozzoli, Taddeo Gaddi, Antonio Veneziano, and the unknown painter who is called the Master of the Triumph of Death, after the series on that theme.

On the south side of the square is the *Museo delle Sinopie del Camposanto Monumentale* (5) housed in the former *Ospedale Nuovo della Misericordia*. This remarkable museum was opened in 1979 to display the sinopias taken from beneath the frescoes in the Camposanto when they were being restored. Sinopias are the underdrawings of frescoes—so called after the red pigment with which they were executed (this pigment came originally from the red earth near Sinope on the Black Sea)—that later were covered with a layer of wet plaster as work on the fresco proceeded. The beautifully designed museum allows visitors to examine closely the fine drawings upon which the frescoes across the square in the

Camposanto were based. It is rare indeed to be able to view such drawings, and they are lovely to look at.

From the eastern end of the Piazza del Duomo Miracoli, *Via Cardinale Maffi* leads to the **Bagni di Nerone** (6), the remains of Roman baths that were uncovered in 1942. From here, turn right into Via Carducci, then left on Via Santa Caterina to reach the *Piazza Martiri della Libertà* and the **church of Santa Caterina** (7), built for the Dominicans in the 13th century; it has a Pisan-Gothic façade completed in 1330. Inside, be sure to note the impressive *tomb* of Archbishop Simone Saltarelli by Nino Pisano, who also made the Annunciation figures that flank the altar.

A short walk west from here leads to the ****Piazza dei Cavalieri**, named for the Knights of Saint Stephen, an order begun by Cosimo I de'Medici. Their church, *Santo Stefano dei Cavalieri* (9), built in 1569 according to

Santa Caterina

a design by Vasari, contains banners won from the infidels, whom the knights battled. To the left of the church is the *Palazzo dei Cavalieri* (8), with marvelous graffiti decorations. The north end of the piazza is occupied by the *Palazzo dell'Orologia* (10), on the site of the old *Torre dei Gualandi*. It was in this tower in 1288 that Count Ugolino della Gherardesca, accused of treason, was condemned to starve to death with his sons and grandsons; Dante tells the story in the *Inferno*.

Leave the piazza on Via V. Dini and follow it to Via San Francesco, past the small Lombard-Romanesque *church of Santa Cecilia* (11), with a façade and campanile covered with majolica, to the ***church of San Francesco** (12) built in the 13th–14th centuries in the Gothic style. The high altar has a reredos by Tommaso Pisano, and the vault was painted by Taddeo Gaddi. The chapels have frescoes by Taddeo Gaddi as well, and recently a sinopia by Gaddi has been discovered and is displayed in the sacristy.

There are several noteworthy churches south of here, including the *church of San Paolo d'Orto* (13), built in the Pisan style of the 12th century; *San Michele* (14); *San Pierino* (15) and *Sant'Andrea* (16). Along the bank of the river, on the Lungarno Mediceo, is the 16th-century *Palazzo Toscanelli* (17), where Lord Byron lived in 1821–1822 and where he wrote *Don Juan*. Nearby is the *Palazzo Medici* (18), for a long time the residence of Lorenzo il Magnifico. It is now the seat of the prefecture. A few steps beyond is the *church of San Matteo* (19), built in the 13th century and changed greatly in 1610. The convent, built in the 13th–15th centuries, was later converted to a prison and now houses the **Museo Nazionale di San Matteo** (20), which, in galleries opening onto the former cloisters, exhibits paintings and sculptures by the Tuscan masters—especially Nino, Giovanni, and Andrea Pisano.

In front of the museum the Ponte alla Fortezza crosses the Arno to the *Giardino Scotto* (21), a lovely park surrounded by the walls of the old fortress. Shelley

once lived in the now ruined *Palazzo Scotto*. The park also contains another fortress, the *Bastione di Sangallo* (22).

Viale *Benedetto Croce* leads west to *Piazza Vittorio Emanuele II,* the business center of modern Pisa, with the *main post office* (23), *government offices* (24), the *church of San Antonio* (25) and the *Palazzo della Borsa* (26).

Corso Italia, which begins here, is the main traffic artery of the new city. Just where the Corso begins, on the right, is the small *church of San Domenico* (27), which has been deconsecrated; it was built in the 14th century. Halfway up the Corso, going north, is the *Piazza del Carmine* (28) and the *church of*

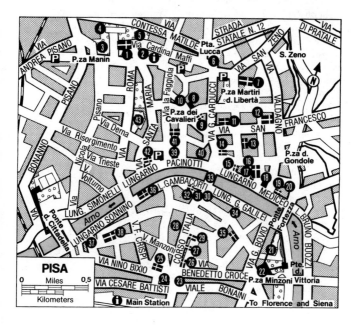

Santa Maria del Carmine (29), built in the 14th century and renovated in 1618. Near the end of the Corso by the river is the *Palazzo Gambacorti* (31), also from the 14th century; it is now the *Municipio*, or city hall.

Opposite the Palazzo Gambacorti is the open portico called the *Logge di Banchi* (30) and nearby is the *church of Santa Cristina* (32), built in the 12th century and renovated many times since then. According to legend, St. Catherine of Siena received the stigmata on this site. The nearby *Ponte di Mezzo* (33) provides a beautiful view over the Lungarni, the promenades along the banks of the Arno. Rather than crossing to the other side of the river, turn right on the Lungarno Galilei and right again after four blocks, to reach the unusual octagonal *church of San Sepolcro* (34) built in 1150. Go south from San Sepolcro and turn left onto Via San Martino to reach the *church of San Martino* (35), with a black-and-white striped marble façade. Most of the church was built in 1610, incorporating portions of a 14th-century structure.

Following the river in the opposite direction, you will come along the Lungarno Gambacorti to the *Ponte Solferino,* where you will find one of the loveliest pieces of Pisan-Gothic architecture, the **church of Santa Maria della Spina* (36). It was built in 1323 to house a thorn from Christ's crown.

Still farther down the river is the **church of San Paolo a Ripa*

d'Arno (37), built in the 11th–12th centuries and a beautiful example of the Romanesque-Pisan style. The façade of this church is remarkably similar to the façade of the cathedral. The small, 12th-century *Oratorio di Sant'Agata* (38) is behind the church. Like San Sepolcro, Sant'Agata is octagonal.

Other important sights in Pisa include the 16th-century *Palazzo Upezzinghi* (39), the 15th-century *Palazzo Agostini* (40), the 12th-century *church of San Frediano* (41), the 13th-century *church of San Nicola* (42), with a leaning bell tower, and the *botanical garden* (43).

A tree-lined road connects Pisa with *Marina di Pisa,* on the Mediterranean. Follow signposts from the road to the mouth of the Arno, where the **basilica of San Piero a Grada* was built in the 11th century on the site where the Apostle

San Paolo a Ripa d'Arno

Peter landed in Italy from Antioch. You may follow the sandy beaches of Marina di Pisa south to *Tirrenia,* another resort with excellent sports and recreational facilities.

The shore road continues to **Livorno** (Leghorn) (213 km.; 132 miles from Genoa), a major port founded in the 11th century by the Pisans. Its present layout is derived from a later design by the Florentine architect Bernardo Buontalenti for a *città ideale* (ideal city) of the Renaissance. Other than the fortifications, little remains of the old city, especially after the terrible destruction during the Second World War. The *Fortezza Vecchia* (Old Fortress) (1534); the *Mastio,* a round tower dating from the 11th century; the *Fortezza Nuova* (New Fortress) (built only a few years after the Old Fortress), the *Torre Marzocco* (Marzocco Tower) from 1423, and the 13th-century *Torre Meloria* (Meloria Tower) are reminders of Livorno's long-standing naval importance. Today, it is one of the largest ports on the Mediterranean.

Leaving Livorno to the south on Route S 1, at *Ardenza* you will come to a turnoff for the 17th-century pilgrimage *church of Montenero,* perched high on a hill and providing spectacular views of the sea and the coastline.

Route S 1 continues through the beach resorts of *Castiglioncello, Rosignano, Marina di Cecina,* and *San Vincenzo,* then turns inland. At *Venturina,* Route S 398 leads back to the coast and **Piombino** (294 km.; 182 miles from Genoa), an industrial town and the main point of departure for Elba and the other major islands of the Tuscan archipelago. There is an interesting 14th-century rectory in the old part of the city.

The Island of *Elba

See map on page 152.

Elba, only 10 km. (6 miles) offshore, is the largest and prettiest of the islands of the Tuscan archipelago. The island is rugged and mountainous (its highest peak, *Monte Capanne,* reaches 1,019 meters or 3,343 feet), but it has sandy and relatively uncrowded beaches. The Etruscans discovered and exploited Elba's rich mineral deposits (especially iron), and the island became famous around the world when Napoleon was exiled here in May, 1814.

The capital of Elba is the small town of *Portoferraio,* where boats from the mainland dock. The *Villa dei Mulini,* the modest residence of Napoleon, is in the upper part of the town. A road going west from town leads to the *Villa San Martino,* the emperor's summer residence and now a museum; it is about 6 km. (4 miles) from Portoferraio. In front of the house is a Neoclassical building erected as a monument to Napoleon by Prince Demidoff. It is now the *Pinacoteca Foresiana,* containing a collection of Tuscan works of the 16th through the 19th centuries.

In the eastern part of the island is *Porto Azzurro,* a fashionable resort on a splendid bay. West of Portoferraio is *Procchio,* which has probably the most beautiful beach on the island. *Marciana Marina* is famous for its sardine and anchovy fishery, but it is also a swimming resort.

From Piombino (see p. 151) follow Route S 398 for 14 km. (9 miles) back to Route S 1 and continue south.

Near *Follonica* you can either follow the coastal Route S 322, which passes through *Castiglione della Pescaia*—a Roman port with a massive fortress—and *Marina di Grosseto*—a popular resort—to *Grosseto* (see below) or Route S 1 through the Tuscan hills. If you take Route S 1, you will pass near the village of *Vetulonia,* located on the site of an Etruscan acropolis of the same name. There you'll find fascinating remains of old walls and the *Tumulo della Pietrera* burial grounds.

*Grosseto (347 km.; 215 miles from Genoa), the center of the *Maremma,* now a prosperous and fertile valley irrigated by the River Ombrone, was the scene of much misery in the Middle Ages, when the low-lying region was ravaged by malaria. In the **old city,* surrounded by walls, there is a fine Romanesque *Duomo* from the 13th century. Its façade and campanile were renovated in the 19th century, and as with so many 19th-century renovations, this one is neither faithful nor particularly attractive. The *Museo Archeologico e d'Arte della Maremma* contains Etruscan and Roman pieces from sites throughout the Maremma. The museum also displays Sienese paintings from the 13th through the 17th centuries, including works by such masters as Guido da Siena, Segna di Bonaventura, and Sassetta.

After leaving Grosseto going south on Route S 1, you cross the Ombrone and return to the coast near *Fonte Blanda.* The nearby resort of *Talamone* was founded by the Etruscans as early as 1300 B.C.

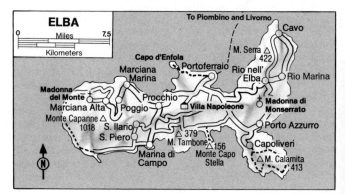

Near *Albinia,* Route 74 branches
off to the left and leads to *Man-
ciano,* near where Route 322
branches off to the towns of *Mon-
temerano* and *Saturnia;* looping
back around through San Martino,
Sorana, and *Pittigliano.* The
Etruscan excavations in the area
are fascinating if you have time for
the short detour. To the right, an
access road leaves Route S 1 for
Monte Argentario (635 meters;
2,083 feet), which rises on land
that was once an island. A lagoon
separates the mountain from
Orbetello, a fashionable summer
resort with a long history: First
settled by the Etruscans, it was
occupied and fortified by the
Spanish in 1557. The *Duomo*
dates from the 14th century,
though it was largely rebuilt in the
16th. The museum at Orbetello
(*Museo Civico*) displays sculpture
of the Etruscans and the restored
pediments of an Etruscan temple.
The view from the town across
the lagoon to Monte Argentario
is beautiful. On the southeastern side of the mountain is
Port'Ercole, and on the northern
side is *Porto Santo Stefano,* both
exclusive resorts. From Santo
Stefano the ferries, hydrofoils and
small boats travel frequently to
Isola del Giglio, with a granite
fortress-village, vineyards and
sandy beaches. It is popular—
and crowded!—in summer.

Back on Route S 1 there is a
short branch off to the right to
Cosa, which was settled by the
Romans in 273 B.C. Ruins of a

Roman temple and forum can be seen, and a small museum displays the findings from the continuing excavations here.

Route S 1 crosses several small coastal rivers and comes to ****Tarquinia,** with some of the most important Etruscan remains yet discovered. *La Cività* hill has yielded the great **necropolis;* other partially excavated necropolises, are located north and east of La Cività.

The ***Museo Nazionale Tarquiniese* is housed in the *Palazzo Vitelleschi,* a Gothic-Renaissance structure from the 15th century. It contains one of the most important collections of Etruscan artifacts and some important items from ancient Greece and Egypt as well. But by far the most interesting view of Etruscan civilization is to be found in the great necropolis itself, which can be reached by following Via Porta Tarquinia, or you can take one of the tours that start at the museum. The paintings and the tombs represent all phases of Etruscan art. Far later in time, but no less splendid, is the *church of Santa Maria in Castello,* which was built from 1121 to 1208; it is a fine example of Romanesque architecture.

Before continuing south, you can make a short side trip, by following the signposts to **Tuscania,* 24 km. (15 miles) northeast of Tarquinia. The town is surrounded by

Tuscany: San Pietro

Medieval walls, and within them are an early Romanesque church from the eighth century, several 15th-century churches, and the ruins of Etruscan necropolises and Roman viaducts and baths.

From Tarquinia, Route S 1 follows the coast south to **Civitavecchia** (472 km.; 293 miles from Genoa) which has been the port of Rome since the second century A.D. Its harbor is guarded by a 16th-century *fortress* that was begun by Bramante and completed by Michelangelo. The *Museo Nazionale* displays local archaeological finds. Today, the city is visited because of its wonderful seafood restaurants and because it is the major embarkation point for Sardinia (see p. 312).

TRAVEL ROUTE 4: ***Venice–*Padua–**Vicenza–**Verona–*Brescia–**Milan (289 km.; 180 miles)

See map on page 157.

From Venice, Travel Route 4 leads west to Milan, Italy's most cosmopolitan city. Stops along the way include some of the country's most charming and fascinating smaller cities. Giotto's luminous and moving frescoes fill the Scrovegni Chapel in Padua, an old university town filled with noteworthy Medieval and Renaissance buildings. Vicenza is a city of architectural wonders—many of them designed by Andrea Palladio, a pre-eminent Italian architect of the 16th century. Shakespeare's star-crossed lovers Romeo and Juliet haunt Verona, a beautiful city second only to Rome in its number of ancient monuments; its spectacular amphitheater, nearly 2,000 years old, is still used every summer for opera performances. From Verona you can make a side trip to Lago di Garda, largest of the Italian lakes. The majestic city of Brescia, with its two cathedrals, and Bergamo, where a funicular connects the upper city with the lower, are both described in Travel Route 1.

Driving from Venice to Milan, you can take either Autostrada A 4 or the slower but more picturesque Route S 11, which passes through Padua, Verona and the many other historic cities on this route. (You also can exit to these places from the Autostrada.) After crossing the causeway from Venice to Mestre, Route S 11 follows the bank of the Brenta toward Padua. In the 16th–18th centuries, Venetian patricians built magnificent villas, many of them designed by the master architect Andrea Palladio (1508–1580), on the banks of this canal and spent their summers here.

The most impressive villa on the canal is the 18th-century *Villa Nazionale (Villa Pisani)* in the town of ***Stra.** Tiepolo painted the frescoes on the ceiling of the ballroom, where Napoleon once entertained royal guests. The French emperor purchased the villa in 1807 and presented it to Eugène Beauharnais, his stepson from Josephine's first marriage. Mussolini and Hitler met here in 1934.

Padua *(Padova)* (44 km.; 27 miles from Venice) is the city of Saint Anthony, a Portuguese Franciscan who preached in and around the city and died here in 1231. He is buried in the Romanesque-Byzantine ****Basilica di Sant'Antonio (also called simply Il Santo), built from 1232–1307, and his tomb is a place of pilgrimage. The high altar in the chancel is decorated with bronzes by Donatello, and the chancel walls have bronzes by Bellano. Four lovely cloisters (13th–16th centuries) adjoin the church.

Next to the basilica is the 14th-century *Oratorio di San Giorgio,* built as a funeral chapel for the Marquess of Soragna and containing frescoes by Altichiero and Avanzo. The adjoining *Scuola del Santo* is decorated with 16th-century frescoes of the life of the saint, including three by Titian, while the nearby *Monastery of Saint Anthony* has been temporarily housing the *Museo Civico,* with important works by Giotto, Tintoretto, and other Italian masters. The museum will eventually move to a new site near the Scrovegni Chapel. The square in front of these buildings, *Piazza del Santo,* is graced by Donatello's 15th-century *equestrian statue of the Venetian commander Erasmoda Narni, known as Gattamelata. It was the first bronze work of its size to be cast in Italy since antiquity.

From the piazza, Via Belludi leads to the *Prato della Valle,* a 17th-century oval garden planted with plane trees and surrounded by obelisks and statues of famous men. The site was once part of the Roman city. Just southeast of the park is the enormous 16th-century *church of Santa Giustina, crowned with eight domes, which has an altarpiece by Veronese. North of the church is the *Orto Botanico,* Europe's oldest botanical garden, planted in 1545. Via Umberto I, the street that begins at the north end of the Prato della Valle, leads to the center of the city and the main squares, which are surrounded by magnificent buildings. The **Palazzo della Ra-

gione, the old law courts of Padua, is between the *Piazza delle Frutta* and the *Piazza delle Erbe,* and dates from the 12th–13th centuries. The loggias and sloping roof (1306) are noteworthy. The large *salone* (hall) inside the building is covered with 15th-century frescoes and contains a lively market and a large wooden horse, copied from one Donatello made for a 15th-century tournament. The building is linked by arcades to the 16th-century *Palazzo Municipio.* West of these two piazzas lies a third, *Piazza dei Signori,* with the 15th–16th-century *Loggia della Gran Guardia* in its southwest corner. Just beyond it is the *Palazzo del Capitanio,* a 14th-century building remodeled between 1599–1605, with Italy's oldest astronomical clock in its tower. From here, an arch leads to the Corte Capitaniato and the *Sala dei Giganti,* part of the palace and gardens (now housing the arts faculty) that once belonged to the Carraras, a ruling family of the 14th century, and with a *Museo di Scienze Archeologiche e d'Arte* on the top floor.

Another arcade leads from the Piazza dei Signori to the Renaissance *Duomo* with its unfinished façade, built in the 16th century to a design, much altered, by Michelangelo. The Romanesque *baptistry* dates from the 13th century and contains 14th-century frescoes and a polyptych.

The *university,* whose main building is in a palazzo just east of the Piazza delle Erbe, was founded in 1222 and was for centuries the most famous university in Europe. Galileo was a professor here in 1592–1610; Copernicus and Tasso were students. Its 16th-century court, reached through a modern courtyard in Via San Francesco, is adorned with the busts and heraldic emblems of past students and professors. A perfectly preserved anatomy theater, the first in Europe, dates from 1594.

Foremost among the sights in Padua is the *Cappella degli Scrovegni,* north of the university on Corso Garibaldi, whose interior is filled with a magnificent series of frescoes, painted by Giotto in 1303–1305, illustrating stories from the lives of Christ and the Virgin Mary. These dramatic and moving works reveal the full genius of a painter who helped to bring drama, life, and perspective to Italian painting. A 14th-century *Madonna* by Giovanni Pisano stands on the altar.

The beautiful *Colli Euganei* (Euganean hills), southwest of Padua, are volcanic in origin and were inhabited as early as the Paleolithic era. For centuries they have been known for their thermal spas, the most famous being *Abano Terme,* with its mud baths used in the treatment of arthritis and rheumatism (12 km.; 7 miles from Padua; leave Padua by Via Euganea and follow signposts; also accessible by bus). The town has an interesting church, *San Lorenzo,* dating from the 12th–14th centuries. Other spas in the region include *Montegrotto Terme,* with the remains of a Roman theater and an ancient bath complex, and *Arquà Petrarca,* where the great humanist poet Petrarch (Francesco Petrarca) died in 1374 and is buried.

Leaving Padua on Autostrada A 4 or Route S 11, you soon come to *Vicenza* (77 km.; 48 miles from Venice).

**Vicenza

See map on page 159.

Vicenza is often called the Venice of the Mainland because of the nearly 100 palaces built here during the 16th century. Many of them were designed by Andrea Palladio (1508–1580), the last

ROUTE 4
(Venice to Milan)

great architect of the Renaissance, who lived and worked here during the last years of his life. Palladio's studies of ancient buildings resulted in a clear, classically noble style that exerted an enormous influence in Italy and abroad.

Route S 11 enters the city on Corso Porta Padova, and passes, on the right, two of Vicenza's finest 15th-century palaces, the *Palazzo Regau* (1) and the *Palazzo Angaran* (2). After crossing the Bacchiglione River, the street comes to the *Piazza Matteotti* (with a large parking area), where two of Palladio's masterpieces are located.

The ****Palazzo Chiericati** (3), one of Palladio's most original designs, houses the *Museo Civico,* with its splendid collection of 14th–18th-century Venetian paintings, sculpture, and works by Hans Memling and Van Dyck. At the far end of the piazza is the ****Teatro Olimpico** (4), Palladio's last work, which was completed by Scamozzi, his pupil and successor, in 1584. Modeled on the theaters of antiquity and constructed of wood and stucco, it has a marvelous stage with a piazza and three streets in forced perspective.

Corso Andrea Palladio, the main street of Vicenza, starts at the piazza and leads first to the graceful *Casa del Palladio* (5), where the architect briefly lived; behind it is the Dominican **church of the Santa Corona* (6), built in 1261, with works by Gio-

vanni Bellini and Veronese. At Corso Palladio No. 147 is the 15th-century Venetian-Gothic *Palazzo da Schio* (7), also called Ca' d'Oro because it once was covered with frescoes on a gold background. From here, a street called Contrà Zanella, lined with a number of fine buildings, leads north to the 18th-century Baroque *church of Santo Stefano* (8), where a painting by Palma Vecchio hangs in the transept.

Farther down Corso Palladio, turn left onto the narrow Contrà Porti and you will come to the *Piazza dei Signori,* the heart of Vicenza, dominated by two Venetian columns and the magnificent ****Basilica** (9), Palladio's masterpiece, begun in 1549. The building was not a religious structure but rather a gathering place for the city's notables. To create it, Palladio reworked the 15th-century Gothic Palazzo della Ragione, adding porticos and loggias to its sides and achieving a perfect pro-

Piazza dei Signori
and Loggia del Capitano

portion. The building now contains the *Museo Palladiano*. A 19th-century statue of Palladio stands in front of the west end of the building. The adjacent *Loggia del Capitaniato* (10), begun to plans of Palladio in 1571 but left unfinished, was the residence of the Venetian governor. The long *Monte di Pietà* (11), in two parts, frames the Baroque façade of *San Vincenzo*.

Just behind the basilica, a lively market is held in the *Piazza delle Erbe*. The narrow surrounding streets are lined with fine old houses, including the 15th-century *Casa Pigafetta* (12) in the Contrà dei Proti, where Magellan's navigator was born. A hump-backed bridge, *Ponte San Michele* (13), leads across the Re-

trone River to the *Oratorio di San Nicolò* (14) (16th–18th centuries), where the interior paintings are surrounded by 17th-century stucco work.

From the Piazza dei Signori, continue down Corso Palladio and turn right on Corso Fogazzaro. Palladio designed *Palazzo Valmarana* at No. 16. Farther down the street is the 13th-century brick **church of San Lorenzo,** (15) with a beautiful Gothic façade and graceful campanile. Return on Corso Fogazzaro to the *Duomo* (16), with its unusual 15th-century red-and-white marble façade. The cupola was designed by Palladio, and the remarkable Romanesque bell tower dates from the 11th century. The foundations of two earlier churches have been

found under the Duomo. A splendid Renaissance loggia adorns the courtyard of the *Palazzo Vescovile* (17) on the piazza, and there is a Roman crypt beneath *Palazzo Proti.*

Corso Palladio ends at the *Porta Castello* (18), with a massive 11th-century tower that was part of the fortress of Vicenza's 14th-century ruling family, the Scaligers. Beyond the gate lies the *Giardino Salvi,* a large park overlooked by Palladio's *Loggia Valmarana* (19). Follow Corso Santi Felice e Fortunato to the *basilica of Santi Felice e Fortunato* (20), which incorporates the remains of a fourth-century building and fragmentary mosaic pavement from the same era.

About 3 km. (2 miles) south of Vicenza is the *Basilica di Monte Berico,* a 17th-century pilgrimage church. In the refectory is Veronese's *Feast of Saint Gregory,* badly damaged by Austrian troops in 1848 and later restored; to the right of the church's high altar is Montagna's masterful *Pietà.* There is a splendid view of the city and the Alps from the square in front of the church. The basilica is easily reached on foot, by bus from the Piazza Duomo, or by car on Viale 10 Giugno.

Nearby, at the foot of Monte Berico, is the 17th-century *Villa Valmarana,* with its renowned cycle of frescoes on mythological subjects, painted by Giambattista Tiepolo and his son Gian Domenico in 1757. A short distance away is the superb **Villa Rotonda,*

begun by Palladio in about 1550 and completed by Scamozzi in 1606.

Leaving Vicenza by Route S 11, you will pass *Montebello Vicentino,* with its castle ruins, and then *San Bonifacio,* with its Romanesque 12th-century abbey and church of San Pietro Apostolo. *Soave,* which produces the well-known white wine, is surrounded by 14th-century walls (with 24 towers) that climb the hill to a castle of the same date. The road continues through the wine region of the Monti Lessini to *Verona* (133 km.; 82 miles from Venice).

****Verona**

See map on page 162.

Verona is a beautiful and prosperous city made almost entirely of the rosy-hued local marble. Located on the banks of the Adige River, Verona is surpassed only by Rome in its number of ancient monuments and has preserved to a remarkable degree its past architectural and artistic grandeur. The city has always been strategically important. It was ruled by the Scaligers from 1260 to 1387 and then by the Milanese Viscontis until 1405, when it submitted to Venetian rule for four centuries; from 1796 until the Risorgimento unified Italy, Verona was ruled mainly by the Austrians. It is perhaps best known as the city of Romeo and Juliet, those star-crossed lovers who lived and died here around 1302 and whose tragic story was immortalized by Shakespeare.

The life of the city centers around *Piazza Bra,* lined with fashionable shops and cafés, and the location of a remarkable ****Arena** (1), one of the largest amphitheaters in the Roman world, probably built at the end of the 1st century A.D. and accommodating 22,000 spectators. It still is used every summer for Verona's internationally famous opera festival. Beside the amphitheater is the 19th-century Neoclassical *Palazzo Municipale* (2), and opposite it, the Baroque *Palazzo delle Gran Guardia,* dating from 1610. An old gateway and tower, the *Portoni della Bra,* links the Gran Guardia to the *Museo Lapidario Maffeiano* (3), housing a collection of Greek, Etruscan, and Roman inscriptions established here in the 18th century.

The elegant *Via Mazzini,* now for pedestrians only, leads from the Piazza Bra to the old center of Verona. Turn right on Via Cappello to reach the so-called *Casa di Giulietta* (4), a 13th-century Gothic house built around a lovely courtyard. It was from a balcony here that Giulietta Capuleti, whose family supported the Emperor Frederick I, was supposedly wooed by Romeo, of the papist Montecchi family. Via Cappello leads north to the ***Piazza delle Erbe** (5), the colorful fruit, flower and vegetable market, filled with sun umbrellas and surrounded by wonderful old houses and towers. This has been a place of bustling activity for some 2,000

Juliet's Balcony

years—it was once the site of the Roman forum, and chariot races were run around its perimeter. There are four monuments of interest here: the 16th-century *Colonna di San Marco,* with its winged lion (symbol of Venice); the 14th-century fountain bearing a Roman statue called the *Madonna Verona;* the *Colonna Antica,* erected in 1401; and the 16th-century *Capitello,* a rostrum from which decrees and sentences were proclaimed.

The piazza is dominated by the 83-meter (272-foot) *Torre del Gardello,* built in the 14th century; beside it is the Baroque *Palazzo Maffei,* and on the corner of Via Pellicciai, the Medieval guild house, *Casa dei Mercanti.* An arcade leads from Piazza delle Erbe to the ***Piazza dei Signori** (6), far more formal in its elegance, with a 19th-century statue of Dante brooding in the center. In the courtyard of the massive *Palazzo della Ragione,* Verona's

Medieval municipal building, there is a Gothic stairway. Opposite stands the *Loggia del Consiglio* (7), built in 1493 and considered to be the finest Renaissance building in the city. A narrow passage at the far side of the piazza leads between two Scaliger palaces to a small Medieval square where the Gothic *Arche Scaligere* (Tombs of the Scaligers) (8) were erected. There are six tombs of this ruling family here, enclosed by fine 14th-century wrought-iron grilles and surmounted by several statues. The *church of Santa Maria Antica*, with its prominent bell tower, was built in the seventh century and renovated in the 12th century.

Return to the Piazza dei Signori, go through the arch next to the Loggia del Consiglio, and turn right on Corso Santa Anastasia to reach the 13th–15th-century *church of Santa Anastasia* (9), Verona's most important Gothic structure. The three-aisled interior contains many works of art, including Altichiero's 14th-century fresco, and the sumptuously decorated *Pellegrini chapel*, decorated with 17 terra-cottas by Michele da Verona depicting the life of Christ.

North of the church, the *Ponte Pietra*, a Roman bridge rebuilt in the Middle Ages, blown up in 1945, and reconstructed using the original materials, crosses the

Adige and leads to the hill of St. Peter. The *Castel San Pietro* (10) was built in the 19th century on the remains of the palace of King Theodoric, which later became a royal castle of the Lombards. At the foot of the hill is a Roman *theater* (11), built during the reign of Augustus (27 B.C.–A.D. 14) and enlarged later. Above the theater is the 12th-century *church of Santi Siro e Libera* and the *Museo Archeologico,* located in the former monastery of San Girolamo, with a collection of Etruscan, Greek, and Roman bronzes, as well as mosaics, glass, and vases. There is a fine view from the terrace.

The Renaissance *church of San Giorgio in Braida* (12), enriched by masterworks of Tintoretto and Veronese, stands on the bank of the river north of the theater. From here, follow the river and cross the *Ponte Garibaldi,* turning left into the Piazza del Duomo, with its 12th-century Romanesque–Gothic *Duomo* (13). The remarkable main doorway, done in the Lombard-Romanesque style, is decorated with figures of the prophets and bas-reliefs. Inside there are red marble columns and, in the first altar to the left, an *Assumption* by Titian.

From the back of the Duomo, follow Via Duomo to the *Palazzo Forti* (14), where Napoleon lived in 1796-1797; today it houses the *Museo del Risorgimento* and the *Galleria d'Arte Moderna.*

From the Piazza delle Erbe, Corso Porta Borsari leads to several other historic sights, including the *Porta dei Borsari* (15), one of Verona's gates during Roman times, which takes its name from *bursarii,* or tax collectors. Farther down the street, which becomes Corso Cavour, is the 12th-century *church of the Santi Apostoli* (16), with its beautiful Romanesque campanile. Just beyond the church are the noble 16th-century *Palazzo Bevilacqua* (17), a masterpiece by the Veronese architect Sammicheli, and, opposite it, the 12th-century *church of San Lorenzo* (18). Corso Cavour continues past the Roman *Arco dei Gavi* (19), dismantled in 1805 and rebuilt with the original material in 1932, to the most important Medieval building in Verona, the 14th-century *Castelvecchio* (20). It now contains the *Civico Museo d'Arte,* with an important collection of Venetian paintings from the 14th–18th centuries, including Tiepolo, Tintoretto, and Crivelli, as well as works from the school of Verona. The battlemented *Ponte Scaligero* spans the Adige behind the Castelvecchio.

Beyond the Castelvecchio, and best reached by following the river northwest to Via Barbarani, which leads into the Piazza San Zeno, is the magnificent **church of San Zeno Maggiore** (21), a masterpiece of Italian Romanesque architecture. Built largely in the 12th century, and with a freestanding *campanile* of the same period, the sober, ivory-colored church is entered through a portal that protects splendid 11th–12th-century *bronze doors* depicting scenes from the Old and New Testaments. On either side are masterful bas-reliefs. On the high altar is an important 15th-century *triptych* of *The Madonna and Saints* by Andrea Mantegna. Relics of Saint Zeno are in the crypt, and a Romanesque cloister with 12th–14th-century paired columns is north of the church.

To make a pleasant side trip to ****Lago di Garda** take Route S 11 from Verona to *Peschiera del Garda* (20 km.; 13 miles from Verona) on the southern tip of Garda, the largest of the Italian lakes. A trip along the western shore of the lake is described in Travel Route 1. The town was founded by the Romans and later became a Venetian border fortress. Route S 249 follows the eastern shore of the lake, coming first to the resort of *Lazise,* where there is an almost complete ring of Medieval walls and a Scaliger castle, and then to *Bardolino* which is renowned for its wine and has two remarkable churches: the small 9th-century Carolingian *church of San Zeno* and the 12th-century Romanesque *San Severo.* From here it is only 3 km. (2 miles) to **Garda,** which sits at the base of the foothills of Monte Baldo. Situated among olive groves and cypress trees, the Roman town here gave its name to the lake. There is an old quarter and an 18th-century parish church with a 15th-century campanile. The monastery of San Giorgio sits on a hill overlooking the town (45 minutes by foot) and provides a splendid view of the lake.

After another 8 km. (5 miles), the road passes through *Torri del Benaco,* with a battlemented 14th-century Scaliger castle. The little 15th-century *church of Santa Trinità* is decorated with frescoes. The popular resort of *Malcesine,* built on a promontory at the foot of Monte Baldo, is one of the loveliest places on the lake; the old center of the town is dominated by the impressive Scaliger *castle* (13th–14th centuries), where Goethe, seen sketching in a lane and arrested as a German spy, was briefly detained in 1786. The Renaissance *Captains' Palace,* now the town hall, stands on the edge of the lake. There is a cable car to the top of Monte Baldo. From Malcesine, Route S 249 continues north to the health resort of *Torbole* and to *Riva* (see Travel Route 1).

Alternatively, instead of following the eastern shoreline of the lake, you can continue past Peschiera on Route S 11. After 8 km. (5 miles) a road branches off to the right and follows a peninsula for 3 km. (2 miles) to ***Sirmione,** an old town with houses clustered around the massive **Rocca Scaligera* (1259), whose keep offers a good view. Hot sulfur springs located just outside the town have made Sirmione famous as a health resort since Roman times. At the tip of the peninsula, reached by a road that runs through olive groves, are the so-called *Grottoes of Catullus,* with the remains of a Roman villa and thermal baths, and a beautiful view of the lake. Route S 11 continues to the southwestern end of Lake Garda and the town of **Desenzano del Garda** (171 km.; 106 miles from Verona), where the road leading north along the lake's western shore begins. Roman ruins in Via Scavi Romani include the *Villa Romana*, a beach villa with beautiful mosaics. There is a *Last Supper* by Tiepolo in the parish church. Beautiful views of the southern portion of the lake are to be had from the Scaliger castle and the shoreline promenade.

From Verona, you can continue the rest of the trip as described in Travel Route 1, either on Route S 11, or take Autostrada A 4 to *Brescia (199 km.; 123 miles from Venice; see page 120) and continue through **Bergamo (251 km.; 156 miles from Venice; see page 122) to **Milan (289 km.; 179 miles from Venice; see page 103).

TRAVEL ROUTE 5: **Milan–**Parma–**Modena–*Bologna–*Rimini (333 km.; 206 miles)

See maps on pages 167 and 176.

The towns and cities covered in Travel Route 5 offer brilliant examples of Italian art and urbanity, and you should give yourself ample time to savor the contrasting charms of each one. Castles and palaces along this route attest to the great wealth and power of Medieval and Renaissance families such as the Farneses, the Viscontis and the Estes, but this itinerary also takes in the humble birthplace of Mother Cabrini, America's first saint. On the way to Parma, a city noted for its opera house, music-lovers can visit the birthplace of the great composer Giuseppe Verdi, in Roncole, and his famous villa at Sant'Agata, as well as the town of Cremona, known for its Stradivarius violins. Modena, home of the Ferrari and Maserati automobiles, boasts a Romanesque cathedral and an excellent art gallery. The arcaded streets of Bologna, a sophisticated university city renowned for its Medieval towers and superb cuisine, offer up one pleasure after another. These are places where you won't encounter crowds of tourists, and will be in the midst of—some say—the best cooking in all of Italy.

If you have time, take the more interesting Route S 9; if not, take the Autostrada.

Leaving **Milan* (see page 103) on *Corso Lodi* to the southeast, take Route S 9, which follows the route of the Roman *Via Emilia,* for 32 km. (20 miles) to **Lodi** the center of a rich agricultural area and a dairy center. Frederick Barbarossa founded Lodi in 1158, and it was later the site of a battle during which Napoleon forced an Austrian retreat, in 1796.

The 12th-century *Duomo* has frescoes dating from the 14th–15th centuries, but the star of the city is the *church of the Incoronata* (15th century), which is considered to be a Renaissance masterpiece because of its finely carved and well-preserved octagonal interior.

If you take Route S 235 west for 13 km. (8 miles), you'll reach **Sant'Angelo Lodigiano,** where the restored *castle* of the Visconti can be visited; its armor collection is especially interesting. The first American saint, Mother Frances Cabrini, was born here in 1850. After years of working with the poor in Italy, she was sent by Pope Leo XIII to America, where she established many hospitals and schools. In 1917 she died and was buried in New York City. Her Italian birthplace became a museum after she was canonized in 1946.

If you take Route S 235 east about 16 km. (10 miles) from Lodi, you will come to *Crema,* where there is a fine Romanesque-Gothic church of the 13th century.

Another side road from Lodi leads west 6 km. (4 miles) to **Lodi Vecchio** (follow signposts). There the eighth-century *church of San Bassiano* (renovated in the 12th and 14th centuries) and the *church of San Pietro* stand with the remains of a Medieval abbey.

Lodi Vecchio (Laus Pompeia), founded by the Romans, was a formidable rival of Milan until the more powerful Milanese completely destroyed it in 1158.

From Lodi, Route S 9 continues through *Casalpusterlengo* to *Piacenza* (68 km.; 42 miles from Milan).

Strongly industrial, with a solid agricultural base, ***Piacenza** has old sections that still bear the familiar Roman imprint of streets running in a grid pattern. At the architectural center of the city is the **Piazza Cavalli,* surrounded by historic buildings. The *Palazzo Gotico* (also called *Palazzo del Comune*) dates from the 13th century. In front of it stand two *equestrian statues* of the Farnese, brilliant 17th-century works of Francesco Mochi that gave the Piazza of the Horses its name. In 1545 Pope Paul III had made Piacenza part of the duchy of Parma, which he gave to his son, Pier Luigi Farnese, and so the Farnese could well adorn the town center. They ruled their duchy from 1545 to 1731. Pier Luigi was finally the victim of a mob murder, apparently because he attacked fiscal and judicial abuses, thus incurring the enmity of the nobility.

The bustling Via XX Settembre leads from the piazza past the *church of San Francesco,* which dates from the 13th century and has a fine Gothic interior. At the end of the street is the **Duomo,* begun in 1122 in Lombard-Romanesque style and completed during the next century, when the Gothic movement began in Italy. On its imposing campanile there is a *gabbia,* an iron cage in which naked miscreants were exposed for the town's edification or amusement. In the cupola are frescoes that show prophets, sibyls, and events from the life of Christ, mainly by Guercino. In the nearby *basilica of Sant'Antonino,* a splendid Gothic porch called the *Paradiso* contains a tablet that records the meeting between Barbarossa and messengers of the Lombard League, establishing the basis for the Treaty of Constance. The church also boasts an octagonal lantern, said to be the first in Italy (11th century).

From the Piazza Cavalli, *Via Cavour* leads to the *Palazzo Farnese* (16th century), which houses the *Museo Civico* and its collection of archaeological artifacts (among them the *Fegato di Piacenza,* an Etruscan bronze depicting a sheep's liver—probably because the Etruscans examined livers and other entrails to divine the future), paintings by such masters as Botticelli, and some fine state coaches. From here it is only a few steps to the *church of San Sisto,* constructed in 1499–1511 in early Renaissance style. Raphael painted his *Sistine Madonna* for the high altar. The original, now in Dresden, was replaced with a copy.

From Piacenza you can make a side trip to *Cremona* (32 km.; 20 miles) by taking either Autostrada A 21 or Route S 10.

*Cremona, has been known since the 16th century for its stringed instruments. Stradivari, Guarneri, and the Amatis built violins, violas, and cellos here of the highest quality. Another musical celebrity of the town is Claudio Monteverdi (1567–1643), the most important Italian composer of the 17th century.

At the center of the old quarter, the *Duomo* stands on the *Piazza*

del Comune. The façade of this 12th–13th-century cathedral is unusual in its Renaissance double loggia, which connects with the 13th-century *Torrazzo,* the highest Medieval bell tower in Italy. If you climb the 487 steps, you'll be charmed with the view of Cremona from the top. There are fine frescoes and tapestries to be seen within the Duomo.

The adjacent *baptistry,* octagonal in shape, was built in the 12th century. Across from it stands the *Loggia dei Militi* (1292), a beautiful example of the Lombard-Gothic style, built as a meeting place for the town's military leaders. Also on the piazza is the *Palazzo del Comune* (rebuilt 1206–1245), the ancient seat of government for Cremona. The 16th-century *Palazzo Affaitati* houses a *Museo Civico* that specializes in works by Cremona artists and the cathedral treasury of missals, beautifully illuminated. The *Stradivarius Museum* at No. 17 Via Palestro contains memorabilia of the great violin makers.

Leave Piacenza on Route S 9 going southeast. You will come to *Fiorenzuola d'Arda,* where you can turn south on the side road along the Arda valley for 11 km. (7 miles) to the walled hill town of *Castell'Arquato.* The Romanesque *Collegiata,* 12th century in origin, has a loggia of pointed arches and a picturesque 14th-century cloister. The road continues south through *Lugagnano* to the picturesque artificial lake of *Mignano* and to *Velleia Romana,* where there are Roman excavations.

Shortly after Fiorenzuola on Route S 9, a side road turns left to *Chiaravalle della Colomba* (4 km.; 2.5 miles), worth a visit for its 13th-century Cistercian abbey and lovely Gothic cloister.

Route S 9 continues to ***Fidenza** (105 km.; 65 miles from Milan) where the Emperor Maximian had Saint Domninus decapitated in 291. The *Duomo,* begun in the 12th century in Romanesque style and completed in the Gothic style in the following century, is dedicated to the saint and is notable for its sculptures by the workshop of the great Antelami, including *David* and *Ezekiel,* which may be by Antelami himself. Opposite the Duomo are remnants of a Roman bridge from the time when S 9 was the more romantically named Via Emilia.

Now you're reaching Verdi land. The maestro might be alive today, so vital is his presence in the towns he made famous. In *Busseto,* 15 km. (9 miles) north of Fidenza, a theater and a museum in his *Villa Pallavicino* celebrate the immortal composer of *Aida* and *La Traviata,* who lived from 1813 to 1901. His simple birthplace in nearby *Roncole* and the church in which he learned to play the organ are also on the pilgrimage route, as is the charming *Villa Verdi* at *Sant'Agata,* 4 km. (2 miles) north of *Busseto,* where he lived and created some of his most celebrated work.

Just south of Fidenza on Route

S 9, a road turns left (signposts) for 7 km. (4 miles) to *Fontanellato,* with its *Rocca,* one of the most beautiful moated castles in Italy, built during the 13th century and expanded during the 16th. In its elegant rooms a fresco painted by Parmigianino when he was 30 is one of the highlights.

Farther on Route S 9, you can turn right on Route S 357 to *Noceto* (6 km.; 4 miles), where another lovely castle of the Po valley is located. The Travel Route then continues on S 9 to *Parma* (128 km.; 80 miles from Milan).

**Parma

See map on page 170.

Parma comes as an elegant surprise to the traveller. It's urbane and sophisticated, yet friendly and charming. Music always seems to be in the air in this city of Verdi, Pizzetti, and the conductor Arturo Toscanini, all of whom were born in the area. Not surprisingly, the *Teatro Regio* is one of the best opera stages in Italy. In the city's art galleries hang masterpieces by Correggio and Parmigianino, also native sons of the region. Parma takes culinary honors as well: It is the home of Parmesan cheese and the best *prosciutto* in Italy. The essence extracted from Parma violets has been famous for centuries.

Founded by the Romans as an outpost along the Via Emilia, and for centuries the site of invasions, Parma began to flower during the Middle Ages, when the great Duomo was built. Pope Paul III made his son Pier Luigi Farnese

duke of Parma and Piacenza in 1545. Even after Pier Luigi was assassinated, the city stayed under Farnese rule for two centuries. After the death of the last Farnese, the duchy was ruled by the Bourbons of Spain, who made Parma a fashionable European capital. At the Vienna Congress in 1815, the city was handed over to France in the person of the former empress Marie Louise, whose reign seems to live on in today's city, where she still is spoken of with affection. Her great love of music helped to shape the cultural life of the city. In 1859 Parma became part of the kingdom of Italy; during the Second World War it was heavily bombed.

The *Piazza del Duomo* is the stage for Parma's beautiful **Duomo** (1), one of Italy's finest Romanesque churches. Entered from a porch beneath a loggia and three tiers of galleries, the interior is crowned with a dome painted by Correggio between 1520–1530. In the right transept is the great *Descent from the Cross* (1178) by Antelami, a native of Parma and one of Italy's finest sculptors. The Gothic *bell tower,* 208 feet high, was built between 1284–1294. Next to the cathedral is the octagonal **baptistry** (2), designed and with elegant sculptural details by Antelami. These buildings, plus the church of San Giovanni Evangelista (see below), form an exceptionally lovely piazza, one best seen in early-morning light and afternoon sun. Even on rainy days this complex exudes a rare charm.

Just behind the cathedral is the

church of San Giovanni Evangelista (3), rebuilt from 1498–1510, with a façade of a century later. Frescoes in the dome and the left transept lunette were painted by Correggio, while those under the entrance arches of several chapels on the left aisle are the work of Parmigianino. The adjacent Benedictine monastery has three beautiful Renaissance *cloisters.* Parmigianino also painted some of the frescoes of the *church of the Madonna della Steccata* (4), but it took him so long that he was imprisoned as punishment. In its crypt are tombs of the Farnese family. North of the Duomo, off the Strada Garibaldi, is the former refectory of the abbess of the *Convent of San Paolo* (5), with a *trompe-l'oeil* pergola complete with *putti* (cherubs), painted by Caravaggio.

Near San Paolo is the **Palazzo della Pilotta** (6) (1583), the former Farnese residence that now houses the ***Museo Nazionale d'Antichità* and the *Biblioteca Palatina,* which contains precious old manuscripts and incunabula, including works by the printer Bodoni, who designed many typefaces still widely in use; his workshops were here in the palace from 1763 to 1813. Also in the palace is the *Galleria Nazionale,* where not only works by Correggio are found, but also works by the Carracci and the *Head of a Young Girl* (sketch) by Leonardo da Vinci. The *Teatro Farnese,* adjacent to the gallery, was faithfully reconstructed after the Pilotta was bombed during the war. It was modeled after Palladio's Teatro Olimpico in Vicenza.

Another famous Parma collection is in the *Pinacoteca Stuard* (7) near the *Piazza le Boito,* where Tuscan and Emilian paintings from the 14th through 19th centuries are on view. The *Museo Bottego* (8), with zoological and mineralogical collections, is nearby. To the south of the city, at Via San Martino 8, is the **Museo d'Arte Cinese* (9), with bronzes and ceramics from the third century B.C. to the present.

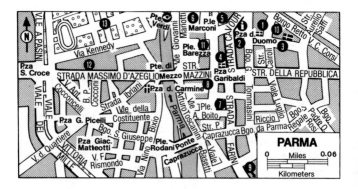

Among the many other sights of Parma are: the *Storica Farmacia di San Giovanni* (10), which functioned as a pharmacy from 1298 until 1881 (restored in 1951); the *Teatro Regio* (11), the famous opera house on Strada Garibaldi, built in 1829 at Marie Louise's behest; and the *Archivio di Stato* (12), across the river from the center of town on Strada Massimo d'Azeglio, with documents from the Farnese and Bourbon eras; and the nearby *Parco Ducale* (13). On this side of the river, along the bank, you'll find some wonderful markets for buying leather goods or tasting Parma ham.

From Parma, Route S 9 continues to **Reggio nell'Emilia,** famous for the Parmesan cheese it produces. In the old quarter are beautiful Renaissance palaces; the Romanesque *Duomo* (13th century), with a later Renaissance façade; the *Palazzo Comunale,* where, in 1797, the red, white, and green tricolor was declared the flag of the Cisalpine Republic (and later adopted as the Italian flag)—the palazzo's tower dates from the 15th century; and the Baroque pilgrimage *church of the Madonna della Ghiara,* of the early 17th century.

Continue on Route S 9 to *Modena* (180 km.; 112 miles from Milan).

**Modena

See map on page 172.

This ancient Etruscan and Roman city became an independent city state in 1135, when the city walls were built. About 50 years later, Modena established one of Italy's earliest universities. Today, Modena proudly counts the singer Luciano Pavarotti among its native sons. From 1452 to 1860 Modena—dominated by the Este family—was a duchy. After the Napoleonic wars, however, Austrians installed a Hapsburg, Francesco IV, as ruler. Modena joined the kingdom of Italy in 1860. The city today is known for its high-class products in the automotive line—Ferrari and Maserati—and for a vinegar so fine it should have another name, but is called simply balsamic vinegar; it is always aged ten years or more in cellars throughout Modena. To see it made, ask the tourist office which cellars are open for visitors when you are there.

All those years of ducal pleasures and warfare naturally endowed the city with some noteworthy treasures. Soaring above the city is a clock tower, 87 meters (285 feet) high, built in 1319 and known as the *Torre Ghirlandina* (1) because of a bronze garland on its crowning weathervane. The tower stands next to the ***Duomo** (2), a beautiful example of Romanesque architecture, built from the 11th–13th centuries. In the nearby ***Palazzo Comunale** (3), the *Sala del Fuoco* is decorated with notable frescoes. The 17th-century *church of San Giovanni Battista* (4), a short distance from the cathedral on the busy Via

Emilia, possesses an impressive *Pietà* (1476) by Guido Mazzoni. From the Palazzo Comunale, Via Farini leads straight to the *Palazzo Ducale* (5), the former palace of the Este family, now a military academy. Beyond it is a lovely public garden, from which the Corso Canal Grande leads back to the center. The **Galleria Estense in the ****Palazzo dei Musei** (6) closes at 2 P.M. on weekdays, so be sure to get to the *Piazza Sant'Agostino* in time to see some of the collections, which include paintings by Veronese, Tintoretto, Correggio, El Greco, and Velasquez. The palazzo also houses the 600,000 books of the *Biblioteca Estense,* and such gems as the richly illuminated Bible of Borso d'Este. Another of Modena's beautiful buildings is the Baroque *church of Sant'Agostino* (7), adjacent to the palazzo.

To the south of the city center, near the broad, tree-lined Viale delle Rimembranze, is the *church of San Pietro* (8), once part of a monastery, with a Renaissance façade ornamented in terra-cotta, a fine bell tower, and a *Pietà* of note. The *church of San Biagio del Carmine* (9) near the university, is decorated with frescoes by Mattia Preti, a great student of Caravaggio.

East of Modena Route S 255 leads to ***Nonantola,** a town graced by the Romanesque abbey ***church of San Silvestro** (12th century), with a sculptured façade and a crypt supported by 82 columns with Romanesque capitals.

Leaving Modena, continue on Route S 9 to *Bologna* (219 km.; 136 miles from Milan).

****Bologna**

See map on page 174.

Bologna of the tall, crooked towers, the intellectual ferment of

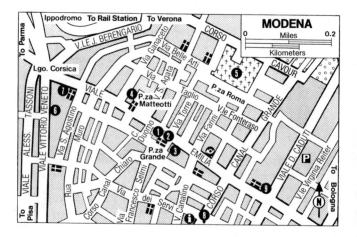

university life, and the pleasure of fine food is also the regional capital of Emilia-Romagna and an important center of cultural life in Italy. Trade fairs often are held here, and so it is important to book ahead no matter what time of year you plan to visit.

During the Middle Ages, the University of Bologna (founded in 1088) was already world-famous, especially in the field of law, and the city was called "Bologna the Learned"; another title, "Bologna the Fat," made reference to the rich yet delicate cooking that has made the city a gastronomic capital.

The city's Renaissance palaces, art treasures, and beautiful arcaded streets give evidence of a past that was colorful and grand. At the heart of the city is the **Piazza Maggiore*, dominated by the ***Basilica of San Petronio** (1), begun in 1390 in the Gothic style of northern Italy, with brickwork that has been admired through the centuries; the nave vault and interior were completed in the 17th century, but the façade has been left incomplete. At the 15th-century portal, sculptures by Jacopo della Quercia illustrate the story of Genesis. The interior, where sessions of the Council of Trent were held, contains remarkable works of fresco, sculpture, stained glass and marble. The crenellated *Palazzo dei Notai* (2), the old College of Notaries, stands next to the basilica, and to the east is the *Museo Civico Archeologico*, with important Etruscan and Greek antiquities. Adjoining the

Palazzo Maggiore is the ****Piazza del Nettuno*, where the ***Palazzo Comunale** (3) is located, a vast Gothic complex enhanced by a terra-cotta Madonna by Nicolò dell'Arca (1478). Over the main gateway is a statue of Pope Gregory XIII, the Bologna-born pontiff who introduced the Gregorian calendar in 1582. Inside the palazzo, the *Collezione Comunale d'Arte,* which specializes in Bolognese art, is at the top of a magnificent staircase ascribed to Bramante.

Across the piazza is the **Palazzo del Podestà* (Governor's Palace) (4), beneath the *Torre dell'Arengo,* a crenellated tower built in 1212. Through an arcade you'll reach the *Palazzo di Re Enzo* (5) built in 1246, and named for Frederick II Hohenstaufen's son, who was imprisoned here from 1249 to 1272. Outside in the piazza the rather bemused figure of Neptune, called *Il Gigante* by his fellow Bolognese, rises high above his *fountain.*

Just to the north of the two squares, Via Rizzoli leads east through the beautiful *Piazza di Porta Ravegnana* to the **Due Torri* (6), two leaning towers remaining from Medieval Bologna. The city once had 180 towers, each important family trying to best the others by going higher. You can climb up for a superb view. These towers are delightful from every angle and change with the sun and shadows, making them sculpture in the round. The nearby *Loggia del Carrobbio* (7), more commonly known as the *Palazzo della*

Mercanzia, is a Gothic merchants' hall dating from the 14th century.

Walking around Bologna, you are bound to notice the prosperity and cleanliness of the streets and the general good humor of its residents. The shopping streets sport top designer boutiques, and the excellent restaurants are always crowded. It comes as a surprise to many travellers that the city has long supported the Communist party, which is still the party in power. But obviously it's communism Italian style, something that would give Marx nightmares.

Via Zamboni, lined with beautiful mansions, leads northeast from *Porta Ravegnana* to the Gothic *church of San Giacomo Maggiore* (8), in which the *Bentivoglio Chapel* and the *tomb* of the jurist Antonio Bentivoglio, by Della Quercia, along with the frescoed *Oratory of Santa Cecilia,* have great charm. Just beyond the church is the *Teatro Comunale* (9), built on the ruins of the Bentivoglio palace, where this important family of Bologna lived and warred. Giovanni II Bentivoglio is credited with bringing the Tuscan Renaissance to Bologna, though the city returned to the control of the papal states in 1506.

Now the sight of bicycles and book bags lets you know the *university* (10) is near. On the alumni

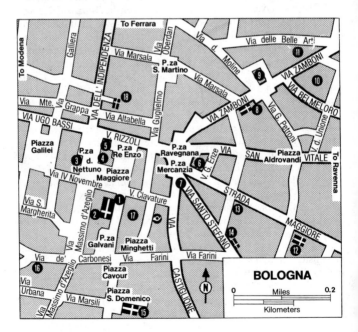

roster are Copernicus and Petrarch. Turn left into Via delle Belle Arti, lined with Medieval houses, and you'll see the *Pinacoteca Nazionale* (11) in front of you; its well-maintained collection displays works by Raphael, the Carracci, Perugino, Guido Reni, and a wonderful life-size *Pietà* by Nicolò dell'Arca.

Walk back to Piazza Verdi at the Teatro Comunale and take Via Petroni to Strada Maggiore and the 14th-century Gothic *church of Santa Maria dei Servi* (12), with a Cimabue *Madonna Enthroned.* Heading back toward the center on Strada Maggiore you'll pass some fine palaces, among them the *Casa Isolani* (13) on the left, fronted with wooden beams.

On the *Piazza Santo Stefano,* reached from the *Piazza Mercanzia* on Via Santo Stefano, is the ***basilica of Santo Stefano** (14). Actually three sanctuaries, which date back as far as the fifth century, Santo Stefano has a pretty courtyard and a little museum.

To the south of the city center is the ****church of San Domenico** (15), on the piazza of the same name. The church is dedicated to Saint Dominic, founder of the Dominican order, who died here in 1221. In the sixth chapel on the right, his tomb, the **Arca di San Domenico,* is notable not only for the angel by a young Michelangelo but also for the angel facing it by Nicolò dell'Arca. In the apse of the chapel is a fine painting by Guido Reni, and there are several other notable chapels, such as the

Madonna del Rosario, adorned by an altarpiece with 15 paintings by Lodovico Carracci, Reni, and others. On the north side of the church are the interesting elevated tombs of the notaries and lawyers in the cemetery.

Via Marsili leads out of the piazza toward the 15th-century **Palazzo Bevilacqua* (16), built in Tuscan style with a splendid colonnade. Members of the Council of Trent, fleeing Trento for fear of the plague, held sessions here as well as at San Petronio in 1547. The *Palazzo dell'Archiginnasio* (17), once seat of the university, is along the *Portico del Pavaglione,* just south of the Piazza Maggiore. As early as the 13th century, Bologna's prestigious university had an enrollment of about 10,000 students. Ask the portiere to show you the *Biblioteca Comunale* and the *Teatro Anatomico (Anatomy Theater)* inside. North of the Piazza del Nettuno, off the busy Via dell'Indipendenza, is the *Duomo* (18), dedicated to Saint Peter. Its bell tower dates from the 12th century, and its Baroque façade from the 18th. In the western part of the city on *Piazza Malpighi* stands the *church of San Francesco,* in which a magnificent altarpiece and many Renaissance tombs can be found, including that of Pope Alexander V.

For wonderful views of Bologna, or for a jogging path if you've enjoyed too many pastas *alla Bolognese,* go to the *Porta Saragozza* and continue out on *Via Saragozza* for about two miles up the hill to the sanctuary of the *Madonna di San Luca,* along an arcaded walkway with 666 arches. Not only is the view lovely, but there is the Madonna, painted, according to tradition, by Saint Luke.

Autostrada A 14 speeds you from Bologna to Rimini on the Adriatic, but Route S 9 provides a more scenic ride. Leaving Bologna by the *Porta Maggiore* on Route S 9, you soon will reach *Castel San Pietro* a popular spa and summer resort, and then ***Imola** founded in 82 B.C. by the Romans, although it probably has an earlier Etruscan ancestry. The town's layout still follows the lines of the Roman urban plan. The 14th-century *castle* displays a collection of arms dating from the time of the battle between troops of Caterina Sforza and Cesare Borgia (1500). On the Via Emilia a former convent houses an interesting painting collection, and some of the palaces are open to the public.

Route S 9 continues to ***Faenza** (268 km.; 166 miles from Milan), a pretty town long

noted for its glazed and colored ceramics, called *faïence* or *majolica.* It was about the year 1200 that Faenza's population began making pottery in a colorful style that swept the Mediterranean. The **Museo Internazionale delle Ceramiche* contains a superb collection that would be relegated to a decorative arts section in a larger museum. The town is filled with craft shops of all qualities and tastes, some quite good.

Forlì, 15 km. (9 miles) farther on S 9, is a thriving agricultural center and has two infamous residents of days gone by: Benito Mussolini, born in the nearby countryside, and Caterina Sforza, whose troops here, as in Imola, battled with those of Cesare Borgia. When Borgia threatened to kill her children, she replied, "I am young enough to have more."

On the *Piazza Saffi* is the Gothic *Palazzo del Podestà* (15th century) and the Romanesque *basilica of San Mercuriale* (12–13th centuries), with a handsome cloister. Its 15th-century Renaissance campanile was once the watchtower of the adjoining pal-

Forli: Piazza Saffi

ace, belonging to the Orgogliosi family, whose name translates as "The Proud Ones." In the Neoclassical *Duomo* is an *Assumption* by Cignani. In *Corso della Repubblica* the *Archaeological Museum* and *Pinacoteca Saffi* has a *Nativity* and *Agony in the Garden* by Fra Angelico. It also has contemporary art and antiquities.

Route S 9 now continues through *Forlimpopoli,* whose castle of the Ordelaffi now contains a museum and theater.

Cesena, surrounded by Medieval walls, lies at the foot of a hill, guarded by the *Rocca Malatestiana,* the 15th-century fortress of the Malatesta family, high above it. Inside the remarkable Gothic *Duomo* are Renaissance altars. Go to see the *Biblioteca Malatestiana* one morning—40 meters (130 feet) long, on a basilica three-aisle plan adorned with white marble columns; precious manuscripts and incunabula are displayed.

Route S 9 crosses the Marecchia River by the *Ponte di Tiberio,* completed under the Emperor Tiberius in A.D. 21, and enters ***Rimini** (333 km.; 206 miles from Milan), which is one of the largest and most popular beach resorts in Europe, complete with a 15-km. (9-mile) sandy beach on the Adriatic and excellent tourist facilities. Unfortunately, pollution has taken its toll on water and marine life here and there are days when it is not safe to swim.

Located at the crossroads of three major Roman trade routes, Via Emilia, Via Flaminia, and Via Popilia, Rimini served as an important colonial center for the Empire. Monuments from imperial Rome include the **Arch of Augustus,* erected in 27 B.C. to mark the junction of Via Emilia with Via Flaminia, and the remains of an *amphitheater.* The ***Tempio Malatestiana,* since 1809 the cathedral of Rimini, was built during the 13th century and then transformed by Sigismondo Malatesta in the 15th century to glorify himself. Scion of the family that ruled Rimini during the Middle Ages, the cultured and utterly ruthless Sigismondo murdered two of his four wives, and took Rimini to the height of its power. The Tempio is considered to be one of the major works of Renaissance architecture; its unfinished façade by Leon Battista Alberti was inspired by the form of the Roman triumphal arch. A crucifix inside is attributed to Giotto. Sigismondo, damned as a heretic in Rome, is gloriously depicted before his patron saint in frescoes by Piero della Francesca.

At the heart of the old quarter on *Piazza Cavour* is the *Palazzo dell'Arengo* (1204) and the Gothic *Palazzo del Podestà*, home of part of the *Museo delle Arti Primi-*tive (Primitive Arts Museum). Between the two is a replica of Brussels' beloved *le pisseur*. Railroad tracks separate old Rimini (birthplace of Federico Fellini, who recalled his boyhood here in the movie *Amarcord*) from the active resort by the sea.

TRAVEL ROUTE 6: (Brenner)–**Verona–**Mantua–*Bologna–***Florence (256 km.; 159 miles)

See map on page 180.

Travel Route 6 heads south from Brenner through Verona to Mantua, a city filled with imposing reminders of the Gonzaga family, which once ruled there. The route continues through Modena and Bologna, described in detail in Travel Route 5, before ending in Florence.

The fastest way to get from the Brenner Pass to Florence (and from there to Rome) is to take Autostrada A 22 to **Modena* (see page 171) and, from there, Autostrada A 1 to Florence and Rome. By combining several other Travel Routes in this book, you can also make the trip on the excellent, and often more interesting, national routes. The first part of the trip, from the Brenner to Trento, is described in Travel Route 1. From Trento, continue south through Rovereto (see page 119) on Route S 12, which runs along the Adige to **Verona* (see page 160). From there Route S 12 continues south to **Modena*, but taking Route S 62 from Verona to **Mantua (Mantova) (39 km.; 24 miles) is a far more fascinating trip, if somewhat longer.

The historic city of **Mantua,** a peninsula washed by the Mincio River, which widens to form large, lakelike basins, was founded by the Etruscans. It was also an important Roman town and was the birthplace of the poet Virgil. During the Middle Ages it was ruled by the Gonzagas, who during a 400-year reign created a city of palaces, castles, and churches. Some of the greatest architects and artists of the Renaissance—Alberti and Mantegna among them—came to Mantua to create this urban splendor.

Virgil is honored in the *Piazza Virgiliana*, a large park adorned with a statue of the poet, but of the Gonzaga clan we have more substantial memories: **Palazzo Ducale,* or *Reggia dei Gonzaga*, the largest palace in Italy after the

Vatican, was started in 1290 and completed—all 15 courtyards and more than 450 rooms—about 300 years later. The sumptuous palace apartments now house important collections of sculpture, with statues from the Hellenic and Roman eras, and a painting gallery with works by El Greco, Rubens, Van Dyck, and other notables. The summer rooms look out on a hanging garden, and the *Hall of Mirrors* has allegorical paintings with bizarre optical effects. The imposing *Scala del Paradiso* leads from the Paradise Apartment (so named because of the view) to the *Appartamento dei Nani,* named for the dwarfs who were the favorite amusements of the Middle Ages; they were here given tiny quarters and a tiny chapel, though apparently as much to amuse the castle guests as to house the little people.

The imposing *Castello di San Giorgio,* a formidable fortress built alongside the palace, dates from the 14th century. In the **Camera degli Sposi** Mantegna painted frescoes that are among the first to create illusions of three-dimensional space. On the second floor are the considerably less comfortable jails for enemies. Isabella d'Este's rooms, created for the brilliant wife of Francesco II Gonzaga, can still be visited, although many of the great works of art she commissioned for them have been removed.

Passing through the arcades of the *Piazza Sordello* in front of the ducal palace you'll see several palaces and the *Duomo,* whose interior is covered with splendid stucco decoration by Giulio Romano (1545).

The *Piazza delle Erbe* still shelters a market under umbrellas and enjoys a view of the *Palazzo della Ragione* (Law Courts) and the Romanesque *Rotonda di San Lorenzo* (built about 1082)—the oldest building in Mantua, whose interior is formed by massive columns supporting the dome. The *clock tower* houses a remarkable astronomical clock installed in 1473.

Nearby is the early Renaissance *basilica of Sant'Andrea* (1472–1494), designed by Alberti with a Neoclassical façade inspired by Rome's triumphal arches. Inside is the tomb of Andrea Mantegna, who came to Mantua in 1459 at Ludovico Gonzaga's request. Mantegna's house, which the artist designed and had built between 1466–1473, stands in the southern part of the city, kitty-corner from the *church of San Sebastiano.* Not to be missed is the **Palazzo del Te,** farther to the south on the Viale Te, a castlelike Renaissance villa, which was the Gonzaga's summer palace. Decorating the walls of the *Sala dei Giganti* are *frescoes* by Giulio Romano and his pupils, dramatically depicting the world of mythology: The titans, attempting to reach Olympus, are crushed by rocks and buildings hurled by the gods.

Leave Mantua going south on

ROUTE 6
(Verona to Florence)
0 Miles 15
Kilometers

Route S 62; after 4.5 km. (3 miles) turn left, towards *San Benedetto Po*, and then south on Route 413 to the town of *Carpi*. (Autostrada A 22 also leads to Carpi from Mantua.)

*Carpi is dominated by the gigantic Medieval *Castello dei Pio* in the *Piazza dei Martiri*. Passing under the 17th-century *Torre dell'Orologio* (clock tower), you'll reach a Renaissance courtyard designed by Bramante. A fine staircase leads up to the *Museo Civico*, with frescoes, a painting gallery, and, in one room, a museum of woodblock printing. The 16th-century *Portico Lungo*, comprised of 52 arches, borders one side of the piazza. There are also several interesting 15th-century houses and the *Duomo Nuovo* (new cathedral), dating from the 16th and 17th centuries. The old *cathedral of Santa Maria* (or *della Sagra*), built in 750 and later given a Renaissance façade by Perruzzi, has an attractive interior with Romanesque elements.

Route S 413 continues south to ****Modena** (111 km.; 69 miles from Milan; see page 171). Route S 9 (or Autostrada A 1) leads from there, as described in Travel Route 9, to ****Bologna** (150 km.; 93 miles from Milan; see page 173).

From Bologna there are three routes over the Apennines to Florence: Autostrada A 1; Route S 64, which leads to Route S 325 through the summer resort of *Castiglione dei Pepoli*; or Route S 65, which is the most scenic. The latter crosses two Apennine passes, *Raticosa* and *Futa* then goes through several popular resorts. Route S 65 becomes *Via Cavour* after it enters ***Florence** (256 km.; 159 miles from Milan; see page 60).

TRAVEL ROUTE 7: ***Florence–*Arezzo–*Cortona–**Orvieto–***Rome (359 km.; 222 miles)

See color map.

The fastest route from Florence to Rome is by way of the Autostrada; however, this Travel Route follows the Arno through the small, pleasant towns of rural Tuscany. Although the landscape is not spectacular, its rolling green hills will remind you of scenes painted by the great Tuscan masters.

Leave ***Florence** (see page 60) from the east on Route S 67. You will soon come to *Pontassieve,* known for its good Chianti. A 16th-century bridge, by Ammanati, spans the River Sieve, which flows into the Arno here.

From Pontassieve, turn south on Route S 69, which follows the course of the Arno past vineyards and olive groves. Just south of Pontassieve, a rural road branches off to the left to *Vallombrosa* (follow the signposts), a resort beautifully situated in a pine forest, with a monastery from the 11th century. The poet Milton stayed here in 1638.

Back on Route S 69, *Figline Valdarno* has two well-preserved churches from the 13th and 14th centuries, as well as the Palazzo Pretorio, with a Medieval tower.

*Arezzo

See map on page 182.

This lovely and prosperous city, the birthplace of the poet Petrarch, flourished under the Etruscans and the Romans. In its *Museo Archeologico,* next to the ruins of a Roman *amphitheater* from the first century B.C., are remnants of its ancient past. Today, old Arezzo, which is on the slopes of a hill surrounded by the rather bland modern city, is still Medieval in character. This is best seen in the busy, sloping *Piazza Grande,* surrounded by Medieval houses and Arezzo's oldest church, **Santa Maria della Pieve** (1). Built in the 12th–13th centuries in a Romanesque style, the interior shows elements of the transition to the Gothic, especially in the arches. The *campanile,* from 1330, is known locally as the "tower of the 100 holes," because of its scores of arched Romanesque windows. Adjacent to the church is the *Palazzo della Fraternità dei Laici* (2). The palazzo is a mixture of Gothic and Renaissance styles.

The sculpted lunette on the façade is by Bernardo Rossellino, and the *loggias* (3) were built by Vasari in 1573. Across from the loggias are the *Palazzo Lappoli* (4) and the *Palazzo Cofani* (5). Near the square on Via dei Pileati are many other historic buildings, including the *Palazzo del Capitano del Popolo* (6), the *Palazzo Camaiani* (7) and the *Palazzo Pretorio* (8), now the public library. As the road curves up the hill, you will come to the *Casa Petrarca* (9) at Via dell'Orto 28, the house where the poet was born and now an institute devoted to the study of his works.

The ***Duomo** (10) was started in 1278 in the Romanesque style and was completed in the 15th century in the Gothic style. The **Arca di San Donato* at the high altar was worked on by several 14th-century artists, including Giovanni di Francesco and Betto di Giovanni; it contains the remains of Saint Donatus, martyred in 361. A *Lady Chapel* off

the north aisle contains five terra-cottas by Andrea and Giovanni della Robbia, and farther down the aisle and to the right is the beautiful *Saint Mary Magdalene* by Piero della Francesca.

From the Duomo, you can walk across the lovely park of *Passaggio del Prato* (11), which overlooks the surrounding countryside and in which is the *Fortezza Medicea* (12), a Medici fortress built in the 16th century by Sangallo. The Via Cesalpino at the back of the Duomo goes past the *Palazzo Comunale* (13) and the Gothic **church of San Francesco** (14), built in the 13th–14th centuries and decorated with Piero della Francesca's fresco cycle, *The Legend of the True Cross*, considered to be his finest work and, indeed, one of the finest fresco cycles of the Italian Renaissance. These frescoes were painted between 1452 and 1466. The stained-glass windows in the façade are by Guillaume de Marcillat.

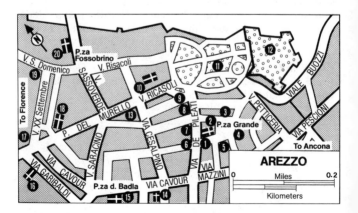

Via Cavour leads from the church of San Francesco to the *Badia,* (15), an abbey designed by Vasari, and slightly farther along, to the *church of the Santissima Annunziata* (16), also built during the Renaissance, and farther still, to the 15th-century *Palazzo Bruni* (17), which houses the *Galleria e Museo Medioevale e Moderno.* The museum has a fine collection of paintings of the Medieval and Renaissance periods and an outstanding collection of majolica.

The nearby *church of Santa Maria in Gradi* (18), just to the east off the *Piaggia di Murello,* has a pre-Romanesque crypt and an altarpiece by Andrea della Robbia.

Via XX Settembre leads north from here to the *Casa di Vasari* (19), which Vasari himself decorated with frescoes. Via San Domenico leads, to the right, from the end of the street to the *church of San Domenico* (20), built in 1275 and decorated with splendid frescoes by local artists of the 13th–14th centuries. On the high altar is a crucifix by Cimabue.

From Arezzo, you can take a wonderful excursion across the mountain pass of *Foce di Scopetone* (526 meters; 1,725 feet high) on Route S 73. Along the way there are marvelous views of the Tiber valley. Go as far as *Sansepolcro* (38 km.; 24 miles from Arezzo), where Piero della Francesca was born. Several of his paintings are in the Pinacoteca there, and en route to Sansepolcro the road passes near *Monterchi,* where Piero's famous *Madonna*

del Porto can be found in the cemetery chapel.

Going south from Arezzo on Route S 71, you will pass *Castiglione Fiorentino,* with two interesting churches and, in the Palazzo Comunale, a picture gallery with works of Tuscan artists. The road soon comes to ***Cortona** (115 km.; 71 miles from Florence). This ancient city, founded by the Etruscans and one of the 12 cities of the Etruscan Federation, is built on terraces that climb a steep hillside. It is surrounded by Medieval walls, and its streets and squares are lined with Renaissance houses.

The *Palazzo Pretoria,* begun in the 13th century, houses the **Museo dell'Accademia Etrusca,* with an outstanding collection of Etruscan artifacts as well as Egyptian art and Tuscan painting. The Gothic *church of San Domenico,* from the 15th century, has works by Lorenzo di Niccolò, Signorelli and a sadly deteriorated fresco by Fra Angelico. In the *Museo Diocesano,* which occupies the former *church of Il Gesù,* is Fra Angelico's splendid *Annunciation,* alongside many other masterpieces.

Next to the Museo dell' Accademia Etrusca is the Romanesque *Duomo,* built in the 10th century and remodeled in the 15th century by Sangallo.

From many places in Cortona splendid views are to be had across the surrounding valley all the way to *Lago Trasimeno* (see below). For a particularly wonderful view you should go up the steep, cypress-lined path to the *church of Santa Margherita.* The tomb of Saint Margaret of Laviano is in the church. Behind the church is the *Fortezza Medicea* from the 16th century. From the fortress you'll get probably the best view in Cortona.

Route S 71 now descends to the shores of **Lago Trasimeno,** which is famous as the site of the battle in 217 B.C. in which Hannibal defeated the Romans. From the shore you can see the three islands of the rather shallow lake, *Isola Polvese, Isola Minore,* and *Isola Maggiore.*

Route S 71 continues along the western shore of the lake through *Castiglione* to *Città della Pieve* (see below).

If you have extra time you may want to take a side trip to **Chiusi* (4 km.; 2.5 miles) and **Montepulciano* (26 km.; 16 miles). Shortly before Route S 71 reaches *Città della Pieve,* you can turn right onto Route S 146 for ***Chiusi,** an ancient town that, known as Chamars, was the most important of the 12 cities of the Etruscan Federation. It enjoyed its finest moments some 25 centuries ago and is now rather drab. The **Museo Nazionale Etrusco* displays numerous artifacts from the Etruscan era, and its sarcophagi are especially important. On the outskirts of the town are excavated Etruscan tombs, which you can visit. Among the most interesting are *Tomba della Pellegrina, Tomba del Colle* and the famous **Tomba*

della Scimmia (Tomb of the Ape) from the fifth century B.C., with important wall paintings.

Chiusi is surrounded by well-preserved Medieval **walls.* Its 13th-century **Duomo* is built with Roman and Etruscan fragments. From Chiusi, Route S 146 continues for another 12 km. (7.5 miles) to the famous spa of *Chianciano Terme,* known since Roman times for its healing waters.

*Montepulciano, picturesquely perched atop a slope 600 meters (2,000 feet) high, is known as the "pearl of the Renaissance" because of the churches and palaces built here in the 16th century by Vignola and Sangallo the Elder. The loveliest palace is the 16th-century *Palazzo Nobili-Tarugi.* On the *Piazza Grande* is the *Duomo,* built between 1593 and 1630, in which you'll find works by Taddeo di Bartolo, Michelozzo, Benedetto da Maiano, Giovanni di Agostino, and Sano di Pietro. The town is known throughout the world for its wines, which you should sample while you're here. And in August the Cantiere d'Arte (art workshop) has become quite popular.

Città della Pieve (160 km.; 99 miles from Florence), surrounded by Medieval walls and built atop a hill, is the birthplace of Il Perugino, and many of the painter's works may be seen here. Particularly lovely is his fresco *The Adoration of the Magi* in the *church of Santa Maria dei Bianchi.* Perugino's paintings in the *Duomo* are also quite fine and recently have been restored.

Route S 71 meanders through a beautiful, hilly landscape, typical of this part of Umbria, past *Ficulle,* with ruins of 13th-century city walls and towers, to ****Orvieto** (208 km.; 129 miles from Florence). This beautiful city, built on a rocky summit, was inhabited by the ancient Etruscans and, much later, provided a refuge for the popes of the Middle Ages who fled revolts in Rome. The ***Etruscan necropolis* at the foot of the hill has tombs from the fifth and fourth centuries B.C. and is very well preserved.

The **Duomo is one of the most impressive Romanesque-Gothic buildings in Italy. It was begun in 1290, but work continued through the 17th century. Lorenzo Maitani, who became the cathedral's master builder in 1310, is responsible for altering the original Romanesque plan and initiat-

Orvieto Cathedral

ing the Gothic style in which the Duomo is predominantly designed. He was followed by some of the most illustrious builders of the late Middle Ages: his son, Vitale; Andrea and Nino Pisano; Andrea di Cecco da Siena; and Andrea Orcagna. The façade is largely Maitani's work and that of Andrea Pisano, though the great rose window is by Orcagna. The design of the Duomo, however, is best seen in the interior. Especially beautiful is the **Cappella della Madonna di San Brizio* at the end of the south transept; it contains frescoes by Fra Angelico and Signorelli, perhaps the greatest treasures of the city and, indeed, of the Italian Renaissance. Opposite, at the end of the north transept is the *Cappella del Corporale,* where, over the altar, is the Reliquary of the Corporal, a silver-gilt tabernacle by Ugolino di Vieri, which contains the chalice cloth (the "corporal") of the miracle of Bolsena—a Host, which, wrapped in this cloth, began to bleed in 1263.

Just south of the Duomo is the *Palazzo Soliano* (or *dei Papi*) where the *Museo dell'Opera* of the cathedral is housed, containing works of art from the cathedral. In the *Palazzo Faina,* also near the cathedral, is the *Museo Civico Archeologico,* with a collection of Etruscan finds excavated in the area.

From the cathedral you can follow Via del Duomo to the *Piazza del Popolo,* dominated by a palace of the same name, built of volcanic rock in 1157. Corso Cavour, which runs through the town, ends in the *Piazza della Repubblica,* the center of city life. Built on the site of the Roman forum, the square now houses the city hall, built in 1581, and the *church of Sant'Andrea,* from the 13th century. Here in 1217 Pierre d'Artois was crowned king of Jerusalem, and in 1281 Martin IV was crowned pope.

The 13th-century **church of San Domenico,* on the northern side of Orvieto on *Piazza 29 Marzo,* shelters the crucifix from which the figure of Christ supposedly said to St. Thomas Aquinas, who taught here, "Bene scriptisti de me, Thomas" ("You wrote well about me, Thomas"), as well as other mementos of the saint. The church is also the resting place of Beata Vanna, the patron saint of seamstresses.

From Orvieto three roads lead to Rome: The quickest is Autostrada A 1. Route S 71 and then S 2 leads to Rome through *Viterbo* (see Travel Route 8). You also can leave Orvieto on Route S 205, which leads through the charming, mountainous countryside of Umbria to **Amelia.** This ancient and beautifully situated resort is surrounded by a massive *wall* from the fifth century B.C. The *Duomo* was built in 1050. The *church of San Francesco* (13th century) and the *Palazzo Comunale* are also interesting.

Narni is a Medieval hill town surrounded by sloping vineyards and cypress groves, with a long history beginning in the third century B.C. The *Duomo,* built in the

12th century, is entered through a Renaissance portal from the 15th century. Narni's other historic buildings include the *Palazzo del Podestà* (13th century), the *Loggia dei Priori* (14th century) and many Romanesque and Gothic churches. The town squares are adorned with Medieval fountains. In the former *church of San Domenico* there is a fine collection of art, including the *Annunciation* by Gozzoli.

Otricoli, on the left bank of the Tiber, harbors ruins of Roman walls. This is where the colossal head of the Zeus of Otricoli, now in the Vatican Museum, was discovered.

*Civita Castellana, slightly to the right of Route S 3, boasts a ceramics industry that goes back to Etruscan times. The *Borgia castle* (15th century) and the *cathedral* (built in 1210) are especially interesting.

West of Civita Castellana you'll find the excavations of **Faleri Novi.** Here Etruscan necropolises and cremation sites from the eighth century B.C. have been uncovered. Later remains—temples dating from the sixth through the fourth centuries B.C.—also have been discovered. Vases from this period are among the most beautiful antiquities in Italy.

Continue on Route S 3 to *Castelnuovo di Porto,* a popular day trip from Rome, with its beautiful view of the Tiber valley, and onward to *****Rome** (359 km.; 223 miles from Florence; see page 35).

TRAVEL ROUTE 8: ***Florence–**Siena–Bolsena–*Viterbo–***Rome (306 km.; 190 miles)

See color map.

There are few areas in Italy more visually (and historically) intoxicating than the one covered here, which begins in the Renaissance city of Florence and ends in the Eternal City of Rome. Heading south through the vineyards and olive groves of Tuscany, you will encounter a splendid variety of places, periods and sights, including San Gimignano, with its Medieval towers (and excellent dry white wine); Volterra, with Etruscan walls; and Siena, one of the most beautiful smaller cities in Italy. Close to the large lake of Bolsena, the route enters the province of Latium, where there are former cities of the mysterious Etruscans, Roman remains, Renaissance churches, and the Medieval city of Viterbo, once a residence of the popes.

From ***Florence (see page 60) travel south on Route S 2 (via Cassia) through *Galluzzo,* where the famous abbey *Certosa del Galluzzo* (14th–18th centuries) stands; then *San Casciano Val di Pesa,* whose Gothic church Misericordia dates from the 14th century; continuing through *Tavarnelle Val di Pesa;* and *Barberino Val d'Elsa,* surrounded by ancient walls, to **Poggibonsi,** a small wine-trading center at the foot of the Chianti hills. Sights here include the *Rocca di Poggio Imperiale* fortress from the 15th century, which was designed by Sangallo, and the *church of San Lucchese,* from the 14th century.

There is a recommended side trip to **San Gimignano and **Volterra (34 km.; 21 miles) from Poggibonsi. Only 11 km. (7 miles) west of Poggibonsi is ****San Gimignano,** where the famous 13 Medieval towers of the nobility encircle the town. These are a small remnant of the original 72 towers, which must have been an impressive sight indeed. The *Piazza della Cisterna,* named for its 13th-century cistern, and the adjacent *Piazza del Duomo* form the center of the old town. Other

Piazza della Cisterna

interesting sights in San Gimignano include the *Palazzo del Podestà*, whose *Torre della Rognosa* set the height limit for all the towers in the town. This was aimed at halting the mad competition among the nobility to build the tallest tower—which, of course, resulted in the 72 original towers of San Gimignano. The *Palazzo del Popolo* was built in the 13th century; it suffered extensive damage in the Second World War and has since been restored. It houses the *Museo Civico* and contains, among other important works, a large fresco by Lippo Memmi, the *Maestà*. The *Collegiata* is a Romanesque structure enlarged in the 15th century by Giuliano da Maiano, with fine frescoes and sculpture by Tuscan masters of the late 14th and 15th centuries. San Gimignano, like other towns in the region, is famous for its local wine, in this case the white Vernaccia. Sampling the wines of this lovely region is at least as much of a treat as exploring the churches and examining the artworks.

Head south from San Gimignano to S 68, which brings you after 16 km. (10 miles) to **Volterra,** portions of whose **Etruscan walls** can still be seen. The city gate *Porta all'Arco* also dates from Etruscan times. Volterra's **Duomo** dates from the 12th–13th centuries. The octagonal *baptistry* faces the cathedral; its font was sculpted by Andrea Sansovino in 1502. You should also see the massive 14th-century

fortress; the *Piazza Maggiore,* on which stand the tall *Palazzo Pretorio* and the *Palazzo dei Priori,* whose 13th-century tower and façade are decorated with coats of arms; and the *Museo Etrusco Guarnacci,* which displays a large collection of Etruscan urns.

From Poggibonsi continue south along Route S 2 through *Monteriggioni,* whose 13th-century walls hold 14 towers, to *Siena* (70 km.; 43 miles from Florence).

**Siena

See map on page 189.

Siena has scrupulously maintained its Medieval appearance, from its towers to its pewter-topped walls. The best place to begin a tour is on the scallop-shaped ***Piazza del Campo,*** where every year on July 2 and August 16 the town holds its famous horse race, the Palio delle Contrade, in which town neighborhoods (*contrade*) compete against one another. The square is dominated by the **Palazzo Pubblico** (1), built from 1268 to 1342, the most elegant palace in Tuscany. Its 102-meter- (335-foot-) high *Torre del Mangia,* built in 1348, commands breathtaking views of the surrounding country. Whether or not you choose to climb the tower, you must enter the palace itself to see Simone Martini's great *Maestà* in the *Sala del Mappamondo,* which he painted in 1315; despite its poor condition, it shows the Gothic spirit at its most ethereal and most elegant. Across the room is Martini's fresco *Guido Riccio da Fogliano*, recently cleaned, with bright colors and masterful lines. In the adjoining *Sala della Pace o dei Nove* (where The Nine, who ruled Siena after 1270, met) is the fresco cycle some consider to be the most important secular paintings extant from the Middle Ages, *The Effects of Good and Bad Government* by Ambrogio Lorenzetti. In its allegorical depiction of the effects of good government, you can see clearly what both town and country life must have been like at the end of the Medieval period.

On the other side of the Campo is the *Palazzo della Mercanzia* (2), built between 1417 and 1428 when architecture was in a transitional phase between Gothic and Renaissance. The *Palazzo Sansedoni* (3) has beautiful triple-arched windows. *Palazzo Piccolomini* (4) houses the state archives; behind this palace stands the church of *San Martino* (5), built in the 16th century. Other interesting buildings around the campo are the *university* (6), which competed with the university in Bologna in the 14th century; the *Loggia del Papa* (7), erected by Pope Pius II in 1462; and numerous Medieval houses and Renaissance palaces.

A short walk from Piazza del Campo leads to the ****Duomo** (8), started in 12th century Romanesque style and finished in 14th century Gothic. Its marble **façade* is one of the most beautiful architectural creations of its time. The left nave of the interior, richly decorated with paintings and sculpture, leads to the **Libreria Piccolomini*, the cathedral library, founded in 1495 and one of the major creations of the Renaissance. Cardinal Francesco Piccolomini, who would later become Pope Pius III, established the library to house the books of his uncle Aeneas Silvius Piccolomini, Pius II. Delightful frescoes of the life of Pius II by Pinturicchio and his students decorate the interior.

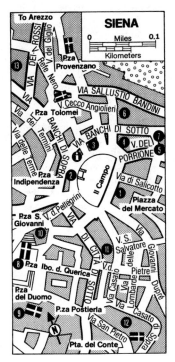

The south aisle of the incomplete *Duomo Nuovo*—which was to replace the existing cathedral—has been converted into the *Museo dell'Opera del Duomo,* which houses some of the art treasures of the cathedral. Among them are statues and sculptural fragments from the façade of the cathedral, probably the most important and impressive groups of Italian Gothic sculpture. On the first floor is the *Sala di Duccio,* which displays the glorious *Maestà* by Duccio di Buoninsegna. It was commissioned for the high altar of the cathedral in 1308, and when it was completed three years later, it was borne in solemn procession around the town by the laity and clergy of Siena, in honor of the Virgin and of the masterpiece Duccio had created. It is a remarkable, indeed, awesome work, and one of the seminal works of the Sienese school.

A Gothic portal leads underneath the choir to the *baptistry,* which contains an uncompleted Gothic façade (1382), a baptismal font by Jacopo della Quercia (15th century), bas-reliefs by Ghiberti, and statues by Donatello and Giovanni di Torino.

Next to the cathedral stands the *Palazzo Arcivescovile* from the 18th century; across from it is the *Ospedale di Santa Maria* (9), built in the 12th–13th centuries. The adjacent *church of Santa Maria* contains a large organ.

There are many other palaces in the city; among the most beautiful are the *Palazzo del Magnifico* (10),

from the 16th century, with bronze reliefs on its façade; the *Palazzo Chigi-Saracini* (11), from the 14th century, which now houses the music academy and a concert hall; and the *Palazzo Buonsignori* (12), built in the 15th century and restored in 1848. The Buonsignori houses the *pinacoteca,* the most important collection of the masters of Sienese painting in the country—from its beginnings in the work of Guido da Siena to its apogee in Duccio di Buoninsegna and the great painters for whom Duccio provided the inspiration: Simone Martini, Pietro and Ambrogio Lorenzetti, Taddeo di Bartolo, Sano di Pietro, Matteo di Giovanni, Sassetta and Giovanni di Paolo. Their generally small, jewellike works are among the finest achievements of Gothic and Renaissance Italy.

If you have the time, try to see some of the other sights in Siena: the *Piazza Salimbeni* (13), where the palaces date from the 12th to the 14th centuries; the *Medici fortress* (16th century), now the site of the city park; the *house of Saint Catherine* (14th century), the patron saint of Italy; the Gothic *church of San Domenico,* with frescoes by Sodoma—the High Renaissance Sienese master—and sculpture by Benedetto da Maiano.

Although Siena is a small city, it is built on a series of ridges and valleys, and the streets are often quite steep. This fact, and the profusion of artworks and architecture to be seen make it necessary to spend several days here to appreciate fully this jewel of a city.

Leaving Siena, follow Route S 2 south through the scenic Arbia valley to *Buonconvento* (97 km.; 60 miles from Florence), whose city walls date from the 14th century.

From Buonconvento, try to make the side trip (10 km.; 6 miles) northeast to the *Convent of Monte Oliveto Maggiore* (14th century), in whose large cloister you will see magnificent frescoes by Luca Signorelli and Sodoma.

Follow Route S 2 to *San Quirico d'Orcia,* where there is an important Romanesque *Collegiata;* inside there is a triptych by Sano di Pietro.

*Pienza, 10 km. (6 miles) east on Route S 146 is often referred to as the "ideal Renaissance city," and indeed its *Duomo* is one of the first Renaissance churches in Italy. Pienza was the birthplace of Aeneas Silvius Piccolomini, who became Pope Pius II. He commissioned Bernardo Rossellino to make Pienza a center of art—and he pretty well succeeded. The Duomo has works by Giovanni di Paolo, Vecchietta and Sano di Pietro. The *Palazzo Piccolomini* is probably Rossellino's masterpiece. The *Piazza Pio II* is the quintessential 14th-century Florentine square.

Return to Route S 2, which winds its way through the Amiata Mountains. Slightly to the left, in *Radicofani* there are ruins of a 15th-century fortress and the church of San Pietro, which contains three altar sculptures by Andrea and Giovanni della Robbia. To the right of the S 2 a small road leads 6 km. (4 miles) to the Benedictine **abbey of San Salvatore* (8th century), with its noble basilica.

The towns in this area are fine summer resorts. Walking paths traverse chestnut and beech forests. In winter, the slopes here provide good skiing.

Continuing for 27 km. (16 miles) on Route S 2 to *Acquapendente,* where there is a cathedral with a 10th-century crypt, and the bare range of the Volsini mountains, you arrive at **Lago di Bolsena,** the largest (115 square km.; 44 square miles) volcanically formed lake in Italy. There are two islands, *Bisentina* and *Martana.* A tour around the lake on the *Giro del Lago* road (62 km.; 38 miles) is highly recommended. Points of interest on the south shore are *Capodimonte,* a castle by Sangallo; and *Marta,* known for its eels. On the lake's north shore, on Route S 2 is **Bolsena** where there are a 12th-century castle and ruins of a 13th-century *fortress.* The *church of Santa Cristina* (11th century) has a Renaissance façade and contains the famous Altar of Miracles—in 1263 in this church the miracle of the bleeding Host occurred, which inaugurated the observance of Corpus Christi Day.

Continue south on Route S 2 along the eastern shore of the lake for 15 km. (9 miles) to **Montefiascone,** surrounded by sloping vineyards and dominated by the octagonal cupola of the *Duomo*, built in 1519 by Sanmicheli. Montefiascone is also the site of the *church of San Flaviano* from the 12th century and the remains of a Medieval fortress, once used as a papal summer residence, and from which there is a beautiful view.

From Montefiascone continue on Route S 2, which now follows the ancient Roman road Via Cassia, which merges with Via Flaminia on the outskirts of Rome, to *Viterbo* (224 km.; 139 miles from Florence).

**Viterbo

See map below.

During the Middle Ages Viterbo vied with Rome as the residence of

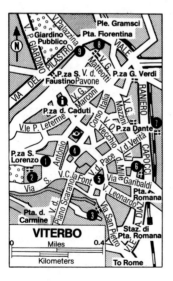

the popes and was often the seat of the papal court. The 13th-century ***Palazzo dei Papi** (1) on *Piazza San Lorenzo* was the site of the longest conclave in Church history; it lasted 33 months and resulted, finally, in the election of Gregory X as pope. After this debacle, Gregory fixed the rules for the conclave that still are observed today.

The Romanesque **cathedral* (2) has a splendid marble façade and a Renaissance-style apse from the 15th century.

The principal sight in Viterbo, however, is the ***Contrada San Pellegrino** (3), a district that has remained unchanged since the 13th century.

In the center of the city, on *Piazza del Plebiscito* (4), visit the *Palazzo Comunale* (16th century), the *clock tower* (1487) and the *church of Sant'Angelo*. The *Fontana Grande* (5) (13th century), the city's largest and prettiest fountain, stands on nearby *Piazza Fontana*. From here, Via Garibaldi leads to the Romanesque *church of San Sisto* (6) from the 11th–12th centuries).

The convent of the **church of Santa Maria della Verità* (7), built in the 12th century, now houses the *Museo Civico*. The museum principally displays Etruscan relics. The Gothic *church of San Francesco* (8), built in 1236, contains the tombs of popes Clement IV and Hadrian V. Nearby, on *Piazza della Rocca* (9) are ruins of a Medieval fortress. Other sights include numerous Gothic and

Renaissance palaces dating from the 13th through the 16th centuries.

Three kilometers (2 miles) east of Viterbo on Route S 204 stands the Renaissance pilgrimage *church of Santa Maria della Quercia,* dating from the 15th–16th centuries. Its portals are decorated with terra-cotta sculptures by Andrea della Robbia, and its interior is rich in art.

In *Bagnaia,* 5 km. (3 miles) east of Viterbo, is the summer residence of the dukes of Lante, with its fountains and superbly landscaped gardens. From Bagnaia, continue for another 15 km. (9 miles) to *Bomarzo,* where the Renaissance Prince Orsini decorated his castle's park with gigantic stone figures of mythological monsters.

North of Viterbo (8 km.; 5 miles) you can visit the remains of the Etruscan and Roman city of *Ferentum.*

Continue south on Route S 2 to *Vetralla* where a side trip leads 9 km. (5.5 miles) west to the Etruscan necropolis at *Norchia,* containing large stone tombs.

From *Quercie d'Orlando,* 9 km. (5 miles) farther, a side road leads 3 km. (2 miles) east to the volcanic *Lago di Vico,* the Lacus Ciminus of antiquity, with its picturesque wooded shores. There is a scenic road, Via Cimina, around the lake. Continue on Route S 2 to *Sutri* which boasts a first-

century Roman *amphitheater* cut out of tufa, and the remains of Etruscan *cut-stone walls* from the fourth century B.C. Two gates, *Porta Furia* (in the north) and *Porta Vecchia* (in the south), date from the same period. One of the many rock tombs from the Etruscan necropolis was used by the Romans for the Mithraic cult and now shelters the small *church of Santa Maria del Porto.*

Just 2 km. (about 1 mile) south of Sutri a side road leads south off Route S 2 for 12 km. (7 miles) to *Trevignano,* a spa set on the northern shore of *Lago di Bracciano.* The spa offers beaches and facilities for all types of water sports. A road runs about 35 km. (22 miles) around the lake. In the town of *Bracciano* stands an Orsini castle, Odescalchi, from the 15th century.

Continue on S 2 to the exit for the ruins of ***Veio** (286 km.; 177 miles from Florence), an Etruscan city that flourished between the eighth and sixth centuries B.C. Sacrificial sites and foundations of the so-called *Apollo Temple* remain. The acropolis contains remains of religious buildings and a cistern. *Isola Farnese,* a nearby Roman city, offers ruins of buildings with mosaic floors, remains of fountains, paved streets and more.

Finally, Route S 2 leads through the *Porta del Popolo* to *****Rome** (306 km.; 190 miles from Florence; see page 35)

TRAVEL ROUTE 9: ***Rome–Terni–**Assisi– **Perugia–***Florence (365 km.; 226 miles)

See color map.

This Travel Route heads north into Umbria, whose hilltowns and some-what dreamy landscapes—often covered in morning or evening mist—have inspired generations of painters and more than one saint. Nearly every small Umbrian town has an artistic, architectural or archaeological treasure worth seeing. Assisi, home of Saint Francis, has been a major pilgrimage site since the 13th century and contains a great basilica filled with superb frescoes by Cimabue, Giotto and others. Perugia, the other major stop on this tour, is an ancient city founded by the Etruscans; built atop a high ridge, it is filled with marvelously preserved Medieval and Renaissance buildings, and an intriguing maze of ancient streets. Side trips will take you to Spoleto, another lovely Umbrian hilltown, or into the Monti Reati range.

From ***Rome** (see page 35) travel north on the Via Salaria, which becomes Route S 4, past the *Villa Savoia* park on the right.

It is possible to drive directly to Terni by picking up Route S 3, but in order to visit Rieti, follow S 4 for 81 km. (50 miles) through a beautifully hilly landscape.

*Rieti, once a major city of the Sabines and a Roman munici-pality, has many beautiful Medi-eval buildings. On the ****Piazza Battisti** is the 12th-century Ro-manesque *Duomo,* which later underwent a Baroque renovation. The campanile was added in 1252, and a 15th-century portal was completed in the Renaissance style. The *Palazzo Vescovile* (Epis-copal Palace), with its Roman-esque **Loggia Papale* (1288), stands next to the cathedral. The 13th-century Gothic hall, *Volte del Vescovado* (Episcopal Ar-cades), is also nearby.

Via Roma leads to the Renais-sance *Palazzo Vecchiarelli* and the *church of San Pietro Apostolo,* with its Romanesque portal dating from the 13th century.

Near the Roman bridge span-ning the Velino River turn left from Via Roma onto Via San Fran-cesco to reach the *church of San Francesco* (1285); it has a Gothic altar and some remarkable fres-coes.

The Baroque *Palazzo Comu-nale* on the *Piazza Vittorio Eman-uele* houses the *Museo Civico,* which displays Roman artifacts, Medieval sculptures, and paint-ings. Colle dei Cappuccini offers a beautiful panoramic view.

Several excursions can be made through the Monti Reatini range and the beautiful Santa Reatina valley. West of Rieti is *Fonte Col-ombo* (6 km.; 4 miles), called the "Franciscan Sinai" because Saint Francis drew up the rules of his order on this 650-meter- (2,130-foot-) hill. In *Greccio* (6 km.; 4 miles northwest of Fonte Colombo), is the "Franciscan Bethlehem," where on Christmas Day 1223 Saint Francis introduced the manger for the first time. In *Poggio Bustone* (29 km.; 18 miles north of Rieti), Saint Francis had his first vision in 1208.

From Rieti drive north on Route S 79 past *Lago Piediluco* and some smaller lakes and the magnificent *Cascata delle Marmore* (the Marble Waterfall) to **Terni** (119 km.; 74 miles from Rome), an important industrial center with interesting Renaissance palaces dating from the 16th through the 18th centuries; several Romanesque and Gothic palaces; and the remains of a Roman *amphitheater.* The *Duomo,* renovated in the 17th century, has a splendid façade (1653) attributed to Giovanni Bernini, a Romanesque portal, and a tenth-century crypt. While here you may wish to sample a local specialty, *pan peppato,* a pepper-flavored chocolate cake.

From Terni there are two driving routes to **Perugia.** The more direct way, north along Route S 3 bis, travels by way of Medieval *San Gemini;* the ruins of the Roman city *Carsulae;* and the much-frequented spa, *Acquasparta,* with its palace from the 16th century. *Todi,* slightly west of Route S 3 bis, was founded by the Etruscans and has Medieval walls and towers as well as numerous Romanesque and

Gothic churches and palaces. From here Route S 3 bis passes *Deruta,* a town known for its ceramics production; just before Deruta you can make a side trip to the pilgrimage *church of Madonna del Bagno* and on to **Perugia** (see page 198).

The second way is to travel north on Route S 3. The first stop should be ***Spoleto** (147 km.; 91 miles from Rome), a picturesque old city at the foot of Monte Luco (830 meters; 2,720 feet) where every June the renowned Festival of Two Worlds offers theater, film, concert performances, and art exhibits. In Spoleto be sure to walk along the *walls;* they date from the sixth to the fourth centuries B.C. and even withstood Hannibal. The **Teatro Romano* (the amphitheater), the *Ponte Sanguinario,* and the *Arco di Druso* (Arch of Drusus) remain from the Roman period.

Spoleto also has many remarkable Romanesque and Gothic churches and a *Duomo* (1198) with a mosaic façade, a Renaissance portal (1491) and a bell tower (12th century). The cathedral's interior displays frescoes by Pinturicchio and Filippo Lippi, who is buried here.

Other sights in Spoleto include a *fortress* built in the 14th century by Gattapone; the *Ponte delle Torri* (13th century), which spans a gorge; and the *Palazzo Comunale,* with its *Pinacoteca Comunale,* or picture gallery.

Continue north for 14 km. (8 miles) along Route S 3 to the

*Tempio del Clitunno (Temple of Clitumnus), a fourth-century Early Christian church erected on top of a Roman sanctuary. A 25-minute walk leads from here to the *Fonti del Clitunno* (Springs of Clitumnus), the source of the Clitunno River, nestled in the midst of a romantic ash and poplar grove.

In **Trevi,** 4 km. (2 miles) farther, the *Duomo* (12th century) and the churches of *San Francesco* (13th century), *San Martino* (14th century), and *Madonna delle Lacrime* (1487) are worth visiting. There is a marvelous view over the valley from *Piazza Garibaldi.*

Continue north on Route S 3 to **Foligno,** a modern industrial city in which there are, nevertheless, many old buildings. Visit the *Duomo* (1122); the *Palazzo Trinci* (1389), with its archaeological museum and picture gallery; the Romanesque *basilica of Santa Maria Infraportas* (12th century), with its remarkable Byzantine and later frescoes; the *Palazzo Comunale* (13th century), with its 15th-century façade and tower; and the *Palazzo Orfini,* where Dante's *Divine Comedy* was first printed.

A side road leads 12 km. (7 miles) southwest to **Montefalco,** a town in the mountains that is surrounded by walls. In its old churches are frescoes produced by three generations of Umbrian painters.

Another side road from Foligno leads 6 km. (4 miles) east to the **Abbey of Sassovivo,** an 11th-century Benedictine monastery with a Romanesque cloister from 1339.

From Foligno take Route S 75 north to **Spello,** where there are numerous Roman remains, as well as Medieval and Renaissance buildings. The **Belvedere* offers a panoramic view of the Umbrian region all the way to Assisi and Perugia. The ascent to the Belvedere starts behind the town hall. From here you also can see the ruins of an old fortress.

Continue northwest along Route S 75 for 5 km. (3 miles) to *Passaggio d'Assisi* and turn north to ****Assisi** (191 km.; 118 miles from Rome), the birthplace of Saint Francis, who founded the Franciscan order here. Saint Clare (Santa Chiara in Italian), was also born in Assisi, and founded a Franciscan order for women, the Poor Clares. The city is a major pilgrimage site. The **basilica of San Francesco* (1226) consists of a lower church, from which steps lead to the crypt that houses the saint's tomb, and an upper church

Basilica di San Francesco

(1253), the earliest Gothic church in Italy. In the 13th century the building was decorated with a majestic ****fresco cycle** that includes some of Giotto's first known works. Cimabue, Pietro Lorenzetti, Simone Martini and scores of unknown pupils of these masters also worked on the frescoes. The chapel of Saint Catherine in the lower church leads to a fine *cloister* (which once served as a cemetery) and the *monastery*, with a 13th-century chapter house and a second cloister dating from 1476.

Via San Francesco leads uphill from the basilica to the city center, which is overlooked by a Medieval fortress (*Rocca Maggiore*), where Frederick II spent time as a child. The old Roman Forum was located on the site of the *Piazza del Comune*. Here, the most noticeable building is the Roman **Tempio di Minerva* (first century B.C.), with fluted columns, Corinthian capitals and a pediment; the temple was later converted into a church. Follow Via San Gabriele delle Addolarato to the Romanesque **Duomo San Rufino* (12th century, rebuilt 1571), in which Saint Francis, Saint Clare and the Holy Roman Emperor, Frederick II, were baptized. The fine, square-sided *campanile* also dates from the 12th century. Nearby is the *church of Santa Chiara*, with a pink and white façade. Built between 1257–1265, this is where Saint Clare is buried. An enormous 14th-century painted crucifix dominates the otherwise austere interior; from the terrace outside there is a good view out over the Umbrian countryside.

Santa Maria Maggiore, to the west of Santa Chiara, was once Assisi's cathedral. From here, follow Via Sant'Apollinare and then Via Borgo San Pietro to the 13th century Romanesque-Gothic *church of San Pietro*, with its lovely rose windows. If you have the time, explore the maze of picturesque old streets that make up Assisi. You can climb to the Rocca Maggiore above the city by going back to the Duomo. Follow the charming Via Maria delle Rose, and then continue along a lane and up the slope. The present structure dates from the 14th century, and there is a good view from the keep.

Highly revered Franciscan sanctuaries are found all around Assisi, among them the convent of **San Damiano* from the 13th century, where Saint Francis first heard the order that decided his vocation and where Saint Clare lived with her nuns; the **L'Eremo della Carceri*, a cave hermitage where Francis often went for retreat and devotions; and the 16th-century *basilica church of Santa Maria degli Angeli*, where the saint died.

From Assisi you can follow Highway 47 to Perugia, or pick up Highway 75 south of town. If you choose 75, go north to Ponte San Giovanni and the nearby **Ipogeo dei Volumni*, a subterranean Etruscan necropolis. Both 147 and 75 lead to *Perugia* (212 km.; 127 miles from Rome).

**Perugia

See map below.

This beautiful and somewhat mysterious Umbrian city, lying on a hill above the Tiber Valley, possesses a rich treasury of art from all epochs. Massive Etruscan walls testify to the city's great age, but on Perugia's ancient, winding streets you'll also find Medieval and Baroque buildings. Perugia has a lively, elegant, international atmosphere, thanks in part to its well-known *University for Foreigners.* Late every afternoon the

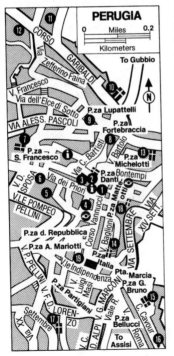

Corso Vannucci is thronged with residents making their *passeggiate.*

The artistic heart of the city is the great *Piazza IV Novembre* with the **Fontana Maggiore* (1) (1275), one of the most beautiful Medieval fountains in Italy. Here stands the **Duomo* (2), dating from the 14th and 15th centuries, with a carved and inlaid wooden choir, and noteworthy cloister, which leads to the *Museo Capitolare.* The stately 13th-century **Palazzo dei Priori* (3) houses the **Galleria Nazionale dell' Umbria,* with its rich collection of painting and sculpture dating from the Middle Ages and Renaissance. In the main hall of the 15th century *Collegio del Cambio* (4), the former money exchange, you'll find magnificent frescoes painted by Perugino (and possibly Raphael) between 1496–1500.

Return to Piazza IV Novembre, where there is an arch leading to Via dei Priori and the Medieval quarter of the city. The Gothic *church of Sant'Agata,* with 14th-century frescoes inside, is on your left. Further on, to your right, is the *church of San Filippo Neri,* with a Baroque façade. Continue on this street to the *Torre degli Sciri* (5), a tower that dates from the 12th century, and on to the ancient Etruscan gate, the *Porta Trasimena.* Beyond, in a charming piazzetta, is the 16th-century Renaissance *church of the Madonna della Luce.* Just northwest of here is the ***Oratorio dí San Bernardino** (7), whose façade, decorated with terra-cotta in 1461 by Agostino di Duccio, is one of the principal achievements of Early-Renaissance art, and, adjoining it to the north, the Gothic *church of San Francesco* (1230).

Another route through the city leads from the **Palazzo dei Priori* (3) along the old Via della Gabbia, one of the most impressive Medieval streets in Italy, to the **Maestà delle Volte*, an oratory with a 14th-century red-and-white arch. Farther along lies the *Piazza Morlachi*, from where Via C. Battisti leads to the *Arco Etrusco* (8), a third or second century B.C. Etruscan gate. The Baroque *Palazzo Gallenga* (9) stands nearby; it is the seat of the world famous Italian University for Foreigners, founded in 1925. Perugia's State University is located farther west. Follow Corso Garibaldi north from here to the 13th century *Church of Sant'Agostino* (10), with its remarkable carved choir from 1502, and the round Early-Christian **church of Sant'Angelo* (11), (dating to the fifth or sixth century) with its 16 antique columns. The old city gate, *Porta Sant'Angelo*, is adjacent to the church.

Other interesting churches in Perugia are *San Severo* (13), where there is a fresco by Raphael; *Sant'Ercolano* (14); *San Domenico* (15) and its adjacent monastery (now the *Museo Archeologico Nazionale*, with prehistoric and Etruscan-Roman sections); *San Pietro* (16) (10th century), which

has a 17th-century arcaded courtyard, a wooden ceiling in the nave, and which displays paintings by Guercino and Perugino; and *Santa Giuliana* (17) with its convent and Gothic cloister (14th century).

The *Palazzo dell'Università Vecchia* (Old University Building) (18) and the elegant *Palazzo del Capitano del Popolo* (both from the 15th century) are located on *Piazza Matteotti*.

Rocca Paolina (19), incorporating the Etruscan *Porta Marzia*, offers a beautiful, panoramic view and leads to *Via Bagliona*, a curious underground street lined with Medieval houses.

From Perugia you can make many excursions into the mountains of the Umbrian Apennines, whose valleys shelter towns with considerable art treasures. For one such trip, drive northeast on S 298 for 39 km. (24 miles) to ***Gubbio,** an important city in Etruscan and Roman times whose Medieval appearance has been magnificently preserved. It has numerous *Romanesque* and *Gothic churches, palaces* dating from the 13th and 14th centuries, remains from a *Roman theater,* and—in the surroundings—many remarkable old *fortresses.*

Leaving Perugia, take S 75 bis northwest to *Magione* where a *castle* of the Knights of Malta (1420) can be seen. Drive 1 km. (.6 miles) farther west to the east bank of *Lake Trasimene* and the village of *Montecolognola*, surrounded by Medieval fortified walls, which boasts a notable 14th century church. Route S 75 bis runs from here along Lake Trasimene. *Passignano sul Trasimeno* is a pretty beach resort, its old center situated on a promontory in the lake. From there S 75 bis leads directly past the battle-field where Hannibal slaughtered the Romans in 217 B.C. At the northwest bank of the lake, pick up S 71 north to ***Florence** (365 km., 226 miles from Rome; see page 60).

TRAVEL ROUTE 10: Circular Tour ***Florence–*Montecatini Terme–**Lucca–***Pisa–San Miniato–***Florence (182 km.; 113 miles)

See map below.

This route is designed especially for those who will be spending some time in Florence and want to see the surrounding Tuscan countryside as well as the artistically important cities nearby.

Leaving ***Florence** (see page 60), take Autostrada A 11 for 13 km. (8 miles) or local roads 20 km. (12 miles) to **Prato,** a city whose textile industry has led to affluence, as proved by the modern public sculpture here by such artists as Henry Moore and Gio Pomodoro, interspersed with its more venerable works of art. A walk on the 13th-century *Castello dell' Imperatore,* built for Emperor Frederick II Hohenstaufen, provides a good overview of the city. Across from the castle is the *church of Santa Maria delle Carceri,* which was designed by Giuliano da Sangallo in 1485, based on Renaissance principles of Alberti and Brunelleschi, and contains medallions of the evangelists by Andrea della Robbia.

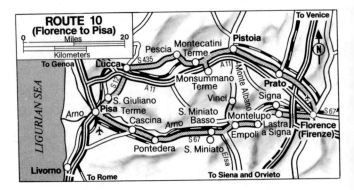

The Romanesque *Duomo* has Donatello and Michelozzo's famous *pulpit* on the right corner of its façade, as well as a lunette of the *Madonna e Santi Stefano e Lorenzo* over the main portal. Inside are a Renaissance pulpit by Mino da Fiesole and Antonio Rossellino; frescoes by Agnolo Gaddi and a *Madonna and Child* by Giovanni Pisano in the *Cappella del Sacro Cingolo;* frescoes of the lives of Saint John the Baptist and Saint Stephen by Filippo Lippi in the apse; frescoes by Uccello; and a 15th-century tabernacle. The *Museo dell'Opera del Duomo* contains a number of masterpieces, including the original reliefs of dancing putti by Donatello from the pulpit in the Duomo and the *Reliquary of the Holy Girdle* by Maso di Bartolomeo. Prato's *Galleria Comunale*—housed in the Medieval *Palazzo Pretorio* with its interesting 14th-century outdoor staircase—has a number of Tuscan paintings, including works by Filippino Lippi.

Continue to **Pistoia,** famous in Dante's and Machiavelli's time for its violent citizenry (pistols were named for the town), but today a quiet agricultural center. At Pistoia's center is the *Piazza del Duomo,* surrounded by a number of notable buildings: The predominantly Romanesque *Duomo* contains a silver altar in the chapel dedicated to Saint James (there are sculptures by Brunelleschi and others) as well as many other works of art; the octagonal Gothic baptistry, designed by Andrea Pisano, is covered with green-and-white marble; and the 13th–14th-century *Palazzo del Comune,* which houses two museums—the *Centro Marino Marini,* dedicated to the sculptor, born in Pistoia in 1901, and the *Museo Civico,* which displays paintings from the 13th century onward. Other sites include the *Ospedale del Ceppo,* which has a frieze by Giovanni della Robbia depicting *The Seven Acts of Mercy;* the 12th-century *church of Sant'Andrea,* with its pulpit by Giovanni Pisano; the 12th-century *church of San Bartolomeo in Pantano,* with its pulpit by Guido da Como; and the *church of San Giovanni Fuoricivitas,* built between the 12th–14th centuries, which has a polyptych by Taddeo Gaddi, a terra-cotta *Visitation* by Luca or Andrea della Robbia, a pulpit by Fra Guglielmo da Pisa, and a holy-water stoup by Giovanni Pisano.

Heading southwest from Pistoia on *Viale Marcallè,* angle south for 1 km. (about half a mile) to the road to ***Montecatini Terme** (50 km.; 31 miles from Florence), a famous spa whose warm springs are frequented for a variety of ailments. There are many hotels and thermal-bath facilities, and most visitors tend to congregate around the café at the *Stabilimento Tettuccio.*

Follow Route S 435 to *Pescia,* known for its *Nuovo Mercato dei Fiori,* or flower market, located just outside of town. In town there is *Piazza Mazzini,* with buildings dating from the 13th century (including the 15th-century *Oratory of the Madonna di Piè di Piazza* and the 13th-century *Palazzo dei Vicari,* a small *Museo Civico* containing 14th–16th-century paintings, a Baroque *Duomo,* and the Gothic *church of San Francesco.*

Continue on Route S 435 to ****Lucca** (78 km.; 48 miles from Florence), originally a Roman colony, which became the capital of Tuscany under the Lombards and Franks during Medieval times and is one of the few towns in Italy to preserve its *ramparts,* in this case dating from the 16th century. A walk on top of the ramparts provides an excellent orientation to the city's many monuments from the Middle Ages. The Roman presence in Lucca may be seen in the regularity of the street plan and in the oval *Piazza del Anfiteatro,* which once was occupied by the Roman amphitheater.

Lucca: San Michele

The city's Romanesque ***Duomo di San Martino* contains the *Volto Santo,* a wooden likeness of Christ, and the 1406 *tomb* of Ilaria del Carretto, a masterpiece of the Sienese sculptor Jacopo della Quercia. Especially noteworthy is the ***basilica of San Frediano,* which contains reliefs by Jacopo della Quercia. A few steps farther west stands **Palazzo Pfanner,* with a Renaissance staircase.

Via Calderia leads to the Medieval quarter of the city near the Romanesque *church of *San Michele in Foro,* which has a painting of *Quattri Santi* (Four Saints) by Filippino Lippi and a *Madonna and Child* attributed to Luca della Robbia. Across the street is *Palazzo Pretorio,* built in 1492 and remodeled in 1590 in Renaissance style. Slightly to the west is the 11th-century *church of *Sant'Alessandro,* a fine example of Romanesque-Luccan design and the oldest preserved church in the city.

Lucca: San Frediano

In the *Palazzo Mansi* the *Museo Nazionale* contains rooms with 17th- and 18th-century furnishings, tapestries and works by Tintoretto and Veronese, while the *Pinacoteca Nazionale* has works dating from the Renaissance onward. There is another fine collection of paintings and sculpture in the *Museo Nazionale Guinigi* in Villa Guinigi.

From Lucca, Route S 12 leads through the ancient spa town of *San Giuliano Terme* and ***Pisa** (see page 146). From Pisa, turn east on Route S 67 to tiny *Cascina* and *Pontadera* and on to *San Miniato Basso* and the Medieval town of **San Miniato** (141 km.; 87 miles from Florence) on a hill. Among its sights are the 13th-century *Duomo* and the *Museo Diocesano*, which contains many regional works of art.

About 9 km. (6 miles) farther on is *Empoli,* a small city famous for its glass industry. Its *Museo della Collegiata* contains paintings by Lorenzo Monaco and Pontormo as well as sculpture by Antonio and Bernardo Rossellino, among other fine works. The 14th-century *church of Santo Stefano* has frescoes by Masolino.

Near Empoli, a country road leads north to **Vinci,** a pretty town near which (on Monte Albano) Leonardo da Vinci was born. Its small *museum* houses models of the Renaissance genius's machines, and the font in which Leonardo was baptized is in the *church of Santa Croce.*

Continue on Route S 67 to **Montelupo** (168 km.; 104 miles from Florence), a town long famous for its ceramics, many of which are on display in a small *museum*. Its *church of San Giovanni* contains a *Madonna Enthroned* by Botticelli and his workshop, and its *Villa Ambrogiana* was designed by Buontalenti.

Return to Florence on Route S 67.

TRAVEL ROUTE 11: ***Venice–***Ravenna–*Rimini–*San Marino–Riccione–**Urbino–*Ancona–Pescara (425/501 km.; 264/311 miles)

See maps on pages 211 and 212.

This itinerary leads through famous beach resorts on the Adriatic favored by Europeans, and takes you to port cities of great historical interest. Ravenna, the last capital of the Roman Empire, has exotic Byzantine churches filled with glittering mosaics from as early as the fifth century A.D. The Roman, Byzantine, Medieval, and Renaissance elements in Rimini make for an equally fascinating trip through the centuries.

Two suggested driving routes from Venice to Ravenna are by Autostrada through Padua and Ferrara or along the coast through Chioggia and Comacchio. The first two cities are rich in Medieval monuments and are vibrant cultural centers today. The last two are for those who want to relax in fishing villages and let the tourist world go by.

To Ravenna through **Padua and **Ferrara

Follow the route marked "A" on the map on page 211.

Leave Venice by the *Ponte della Libertà* and drive southwest on either Autostrada A 4 or Route S 11 to **Padua** (44 km.; 27 miles). This stretch is described in Travel Route 4.

From Padua, travel south on either Autostrada A 13 or Route S 16. Just outside of Padua you can make a worthwhile detour to the *Euganean Hills* and *Abano Terme* (see Travel Route 4). Continuing south on Route S 16 for 36 km. (22 miles), cross the Adige River to **Rovigo.** In Rovigo visit the octagonal *church of Beata Vergine del Soccorso,* built during the 16th century by a student of Palladio; nicknamed the Rotonda, it's a veritable art gallery of paintings and sculpture. Among the attractive sights of the *Piazza Vittorio Emanuele II* are the city hall in the *Loggia dei Notai* and the *Palazzo Roncale,* both built during the Renaissance. In the *Palazzo*

dell'Accademia dei Concordi, the picture collection includes such gems as a *Madonna and Child* by Bellini.

Continue south on Route S 16, across the Po River, to *Ferrara* (119 km.; 74 miles from Venice).

**Ferrara

See map on page 205.

In the 13th century the brilliant Este family came to full power and kept control for almost 400 years. The sight of dazzlingly turreted Ferrara thrills hearts jaded by tourism, for in many ways this is the true city of the romantics. It's also good for walkers and bicyclers, for the city is flat enough to explore comfortably. Enter Ferrara through the *Porta Po* and follow the Corso Porto Po. The *church of San Benedetto* (1) will be on the right.

Ferrara could well inspire poets, and Ludovico Ariosto, author of the famous *Orlando Furioso,* came to live here during the 16th century in the *Casa dell'Ariosto* (2) (turn left on Via Ariosto). The *Palazzo Sacrati-Prosperi* (3) stands at the corner of Corso Ercole I d'Este and has an elaborate Renaissance portal. Across the street is the wonderful **Palazzo dei Diamanti** (4), named for the diamondlike faceting on its elaborately rusticated exterior. A bit of advertising is involved here, for the diamond was the symbol of the Estes. The treasures are inside, however, especially the *pinacoteca,* with fine works by Carpaccio, Dossi, and many other artists of the Ferrara school.

From here cross the parks to the north to reach the *Certosa* (5), a former Carthusian monastery whose church is dedicated to Saint Christopher, the traditional saint of travellers.

Follow Corso Ercole I d'Este south to the ****Castello Estense** (6), a masterwork of Medieval fortification, begun in 1385 and later renovated into the sumptuous palace it is today—moat, drawbridge and all. The frescoes have survived in some rooms, and the *chapel of Princess Renée of France* is

one of the few Calvinist chapels in Italy to survive the Counter-Reformation. In the dungeons Niccolò III's wife, Parisina, and her lover, Ugo (Niccolò's natural son), were imprisoned and killed. Across the street from the castle is the *Tourist Office* (7).

Near the castle stands the Romanesque-Gothic-Lombard ****Cathedral** (8), from the 12th century. The tall, elegant arches and ornaments in the apse were designed by Biagio Rossetti, a town planner *par excellence,* who was largely responsible for Ferrara's human proportions and grandeur at the same time. (He even camouflaged the town walls

with greenery, making them a pleasant jogging track in today's city.) The cattedral, with its bell tower, is a fine sight from the back, too, so have a look. The *Museo della Cattedrale* has some good works by the talented Ferrarese school, including an *Annunciation* and *St. George Slaying the Dragon* by Cosmè Tura. The Sienese Jacopo della Quercia also is represented by the *Madonna with a Pomegranate.*

Across from the cathedral, the *Palazzo Comunale* (9), former residence of the dukes of Este, will command your attention. It's now the city hall.

East of the cathedral, the Medieval *church of San Francesco* (10) soon comes into view as Via Savonarola begins, although the two men are a most unlikely pair. The *university* is next in line, and across from it is the lovely *Casa Romei* (11), with two pretty courtyards and frescoed rooms, a typical noble residence of the 15th century. Nearby is the *church of Corpus Domini* (12), resting place of the Estes and of Lucrezia Borgia, who married Alfonso I d'Este and whose name has been almost cleared of the bad deeds now attributed to her brother, Cesare. Two blocks from the church, on Via Borgo di Sotta, is the *Oratorio dell'Annunziata* (13), whose walls are frescoed with the legend of the Cross. Via Scandiana leads from here to **Palazzo Schifanoia** (14) (1385 and later enlarged), one of the most beautiful Renaissance palaces in Italy. It provided a hand-

some setting for the escapades of the Estes and now elegantly houses the *Museo Civico,* where the Salone dei Mesi is a joyful round of frescoes depicting the months in allegorical form; a painting collection of the Ferrara school adds to the enjoyment.

The *Palazzina di Marfisa d'Este* (15) is a small palace of the 16th century with painted ceilings, a garden, and an outdoor theater with *trompe-l'oeil* trellis and birds. Nearer the town's center on the *Corso della Giovecca* the *Palazzo Roverella* (16) presents a grand façade to the world, and across from it is the *Ospedale di Sant'Anna,* with its beautiful cloister where the poet Ariosto died in 1533. His tomb is in the *Palazzo Paradiso* (17), built in 1391.

One of the most evocative quarters of Ferrara for wandering is the southeast area near the delightful Via delle Volte, where covered alleys and old dwellings add to the city's ever-present enchantment— even on rainy days. In this section, at the city walls, are the *monastery of Sant'Antonio in Polesine* (18), with delightful frescoes of the 13th–15th centuries; and the *Palazzo di Ludovico il Moro* (19), the palace of Beatrice d'Este's husband, still interesting to visit for its arcaded courtyard and the *Museo Archeologico Nazionale di Spina,* where finds from the sixth–third century B.C. Graeco-Etruscan port of Spina are well displayed. The collection is enormous, and mostly of Greek ceramics taken from tombs at the site, for

Spina was an important Adriatic trading station for Greece.

A superstrada connects Ferrara with *Spina* and the nearby Adriatic Sea (59 km.; 37 miles). As the tourist industry has increased along the shore, the coast has been built up. Still, sandy beaches and pine trees are a frequent sight, along with hotels and restaurants.

Leave Ferrara on Route S 16 and drive south to *Argenta,* where you may want to stop to see the interesting Romanesque parish *church of San Giorgio.* Continue on S 16 to Ravenna (194 km.; 120 miles from Venice).

***Ravenna

See map on page 208.

This ancient city was the last capital of the Western Roman Empire, and is still a capital of mosaics. Although the coastline is now farther east, Ravenna once was a busy port and a critical link between the Eastern and Western Empires. The barbarians—who weren't all that barbarous, comparatively speaking—and the Byzantine Greeks created a golden city here, the envy of the world. Now the superbly decorated churches are isolated within a relatively new city.

Ravenna's main traffic artery is *Via di Roma,* running from the northern city gate, *Porta Serrata* (1) to the southern gate, *Porta Cesarea* (2). Coming into the city on Route S 16, turn left onto the

Circonvallazione. Continue past *Porta Serrata* on the *Circonvallazione alla Rotonda,* cross the railroad tracks, and on your left will be the ****Mausoleo di Teodorico** (3), dating from A.D. 526. Situated in a grove of cypresses that forms its backdrop, this is not one of Ravenna's mosaic treasures but conveys instead a poignant mood. Built of massive stone blocks that hold up a dome hollowed out of a single piece of limestone, it represents the highest technology of its time and provides a resting place for the Ostrogoth King Theodoric, who became a Christian. Return to Via di Roma and turn right on Via Paolo Costa to the **Battistero degli Ariani* (baptistry of the Arians) (4), where you'll see some wonderful sixth-century mosaics on the vaulted ceiling.

Ravenna's mosaics, unlike some of the best of Constantinople, were not destroyed by iconoclasts in the 8th and 9th centuries. Their glittering charm is most enjoyable on sunny days when the full golden effect can be attained. The bits of mosaic, called *tesserae,* are laid irregularly to catch the light and create a rippling effect.

Continue along Via di Roma and turn left on Viale Farini to the *basilica of San Giovanni Evangelista* (5), a fifth-century church—well restored after war damage—with fine columns and with 14th-century frescoes. Its marble portal, courtyard, and tenth-century bell tower give it added interest. Close by is the *main railroad station* (6).

Continue along Via di Roma to the **basilica of Sant'Apollinare Nuovo** (7), built by Theodoric in the sixth century. Here are some of the most famous Early Christian mosaics in the world, whole processions of martyrs leaving Ravenna and moving toward Christ enthroned, and virgins and magi going toward the Madonna and Child. See these by all means.

To the right of the church stands the so-called *Palace of Theodoric*

(8), built during the late seventh and early eighth centuries, and with a rich façade; also on Via di Roma is the *basilica of Santa Maria in Porto* (9), with an 18th-century façade and 16th-century interior.

In the public gardens behind the church is the **Loggetta Lombardesca* (10), formerly owned by the convent of St. Mary. The *Accademia di Belle Arti,* which displays copies of Classical sculptures and a variety of paintings, in rooms around a lovely cloister, is adjacent to the church.

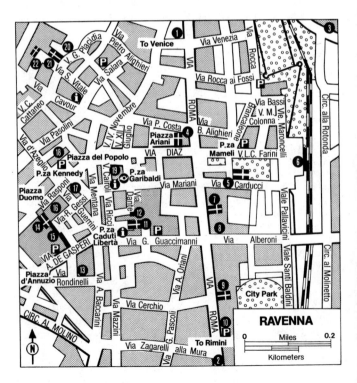

RAVENNA

On *Piazza San Francesco* are the *church of San Francesco* (11) from the fifth century, largely rebuilt in 1793, and the **Sepolcro di Dante* (Dante's Tomb) (12), built in 1780 to house the tomb of the poet, who died here in exile from Florence in 1321. Try as they may, the Florentines have never gotten his illustrious remains transferred to their domain—their just deserts for the exile, say the good folk of Ravenna. The *Biblioteca Classense* (13), in a former convent of the 16th century, has about 200,000 volumes, codices, and incunabula.

Farther west is the Baroque *Duomo* (14), founded in the fifth century and rebuilt in the 18th century, with a bell tower from the tenth. In the adjacent *Museo Arcivescovile* (15), the Throne of Maximian is on display, a superb work of ivory sculpture by sixth-century artists from Alexandria.

The *Battistero degli Ortodossi* (Orthodox baptistry) (16), also called the Battistero Neoniano, stands next to the cathedral. Its fifth-century mosaics have been partly reworked but are still enchanting.

On Piazza Kennedy (many streets and piazzas in Europe are named for the late president), visit the 16th-century *Palazzo Spalletti* (17) and the *Palazzo Rasponi dalle Teste* (18), with its impressive 18th-century façade.

Nearby, on *Piazza del Popolo*, visit the *Palazzo Comunale* (city hall) and the *Palazzetto Veneziano* (19), which are connected by a portico with eight Gothic columns in granite. In front of the latter are two Venetian columns topped with statues of Ravenna's patron saints, Apollinare and Vitale.

Near the western city gate, the *Porta Adriana,* is the domed fifth-century *****Mausoleo di Galla Placidia** (20), tomb of the powerful empress whose father, brother, husband, and son all became emperor. It is in the shape of a Latin cross and on the walls are beautiful mosaics, the oldest in the city.

The *****basilica of San Vitale** (21), next to the mausoleum, is one of the outstanding examples of Early Christian art. The ****mosaics* of *Justinian and His Court* and *Theodora and Her Court* provide enough visual interest for a long visit. There is also a triumphal arch constructed from antique fragments, among which are the lovely *Throne of Neptune* and the columns with lacework capitals.

The nearby monastery of San Vitale (22) houses the **Museo Nazionale,* with valuable collections of ivories, ceramics, Byzantine miniatures, arms, and medallions. The two cloisters contain works in marble from the Roman, Early Christian, and Byzantine eras.

South of the city stands a basilica well worth the 5-km.- (3-mile-) car or bus ride. *****Sant'-Apollinare in Classe,** one of Christianity's earliest architectural gems. Classe was Ravenna's port before silting moved the

Sant'Apollinare in Classe

coastline farther out, and today only this church remains, consecrated in 549 on the spot where the martyred saint, who was also bishop of Ravenna, was buried. Twelve great arches on marble columns line the interior, which contains wonderful sixth- and seventh-century ***mosaics** that show a later development in style, typified by more freedom and relaxed movement. On top of the triumphal arch, Christ is surrounded with the symbols of the Evangelists, and 12 lambs, representing the Apostles. On the apse the Transfiguration is depicted, with a great Latin cross in a sparkling, starry sky. Above the cross is the hand of God the Father, the ultimate director of Creation.

Modern resorts with wide beaches and shady pine forests are spread along the Ravenna seacoast. Camping, vacation villages, and hotels appeal to a wide selection of tastes and pocketbooks.

To Ravenna through *Chioggia and *Comacchio

Follow the route marked "B" on the map on page 211.

From ***Venice* (see page 75), drive on Route S 11 past *Mestre* and turn south on Route S 309, which runs along the lagoon to ***Chioggia** (48 km.; 30 miles from Venice; see page 82).

Continue on Route S 309, crossing the Adige and Po rivers. Stop for a bit in *Mesola* to see the castle Alfonso I d'Este created, and the park where the Estes went to hunt. Then follow S 309 another 12 km. (7 miles) to *Pomposa*, where the pre-Romanesque Benedictine abbey of ****Santa Maria di Pomposa** was founded in 523. A series of 14th-century frescoes and the stunning ****bell tower** (1063) make the trip worthwhile. The 11th-century *Palazzo della Ragione* with its attractive colonnade, stands across from the abbey.

After Pomposa, several roads turn east off Route S 309 to the *Lidi Ferraresi,* the beach resorts of Ferrara, including the *Lido delle Nazioni* and the *Lido di Pomposa.* At the intersection of the turnoff to *Porto Garibaldi,* there is a road that branches west about 5 km. (3 miles) to ***Comacchio,** a fishing village spread over 13 small islands in a lagoon lake well stocked with marine life. During the Middle Ages the city flourished as a trading port. This little Venice of canals is set in a land of rice and eels, which are dried and cured here. While wandering the streets and canals, make sure you see the *Trepponti,* an unusual bridge that enables the town to cross four canals with five converging paths. The handsome *Palazzo Bellini* is another reward for canal walkers, as is a *walkway* of 140 arches leading from Via Mazzini to the *church of Santa Maria in Aula Regia.* All around you is mist and marsh, with the Venetian brand of cattails—the land that Hemingway, who once lived near here, immortalized in *Across the River and into the Trees.*

About 6 km. (4 miles) west of Comacchio lie the large excavations at *Spina,* once a major Graeco-Etruscan port that flourished from the sixth to the fourth centuries B.C.

On the way to Ravenna many roads branch off eastward to resort towns such as *Casal Borsetti* and *Marina Romea.*

Follow S 16, which leads south near the shore of the Adriatic. Should you wish to avoid the main tourist cities (which is often a good idea in summer), take one of the roads that branch off for the resorts of *Milano Marittima, Cervia,* and *Cesenatico.* All have fine sand beaches, small fishing ports, hotels and excellent tourist facilities.

At *Gatteo a Mare* Route S 16 crosses the Rubicon, the famous river that Caesar crossed in defiance of Pompey in 49 B.C., start-

ROUTE 11
(Venice to Rimini)

0   Miles   20

Kilometers

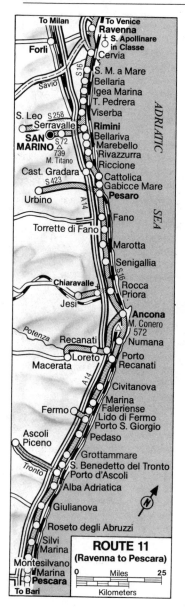

ROUTE 11
(Ravenna to Pescara)

0   Miles   25

Kilometers

ing a civil war in Rome. More side roads lead to the coast, all the way to ***Rimini** (198 km.; 123 miles from Venice; see page 177).

From Rimini, continue down the coast, either on Autostrada A 14 or on Route S 16.

For an intriguing excursion, follow Route S 72 from Rimini southwest for 27 km. (17 miles) to ****San Marino,** the smallest (61 sq. km.; 24 sq. miles) and oldest republic existing in the world. The country, with its capital of the same name, is dominated by Monte Titano, whose three peaks allow you to see where you've been and where you're going. The entrance to the capital city is at the *Porta di San Francesco* (no cars are allowed in the narrow streets of the town). Nearby, the 14th-century church of the same name has a pretty cloister, a museum, and a bell tower for good measure.

Palazzo Valloni contains the *Museo e Pinacoteca dello Stato,* with antiquities, a library and picture gallery.

On **Piazza della Libertà* the *Palazzo Pubblico* (or *Governo*) is an attractive 19th-century Tuscan-Gothic−style structure with a panoramic view. The Neo-classical *Basilica di San Marino* (1836) has some beautiful sculptures of saints, and paintings from Titian's school.

The *three towers* of San Marino, atop the three peaks of Monte Titano, are the thing to see if you want to know how an eagle feels. From these eyries, you can see the Apennines, Rimini, and the sea as far as the Dalmatian coast. One tower, called the *Cesta*, offers not only the dazzling panorama, but also a weapons collection, apparently to keep you from feeling too peaceful. San Marino's souvenir sellers are legendary, and you'll probably develop tunnel vision before you leave this strange republic.

For another panoramic excursion from Rimini, drive 33 km. (20 miles) southwest on Route S 258 to *Villanova,* where you turn off south to the Medieval town of ***San Leo.** The town is situated atop a huge limestone rock, at the edge of a sheer cliff that inspired the Romans to build a temple to Jupiter on it. A 12th-century *Duomo,* whose bell tower offers a splendid view, stands on the site of the ancient temple. Machiavelli praised the *Montefeltro fortress* here as the best example he knew of a military structure and this fortress—on an enormous rock above steep cliffs—kept the town powerful in the Middle Ages. From the fortress there is an immense panorama.

Besides the fortress you'll want to visit the nearby *monastery of Saint' Igne,* founded by Saint Francis of Assisi in 1213.

From Rimini, you can go beach hopping along Route S 16 to **Riccione,** where the coast is inviting and the town sports an aquarium of dolphins, and **Cattolica,** where the Malatestas built a fortress, located on Via Pascoli. You can also watch the fishing boats come home.

From Cattolica, you can take a detour inland to *Gradara* (4 km.; 2.5 miles) to see an almost intact Medieval town with walls and battlements.

Continue southward on Route S 16. There is a splendid corniche road between Gabicce Mare and **Pesaro** (236 km.; 146 miles from Venice), a popular Adriatic resort that sits snugly in a sandy bay at the foot of the eastern range of the Apennines. Its past—when the ruling families were Sforzas, Malatestas, and della Roveres—is visible in the 15th-century *Palazzo Ducale* built by Alessandro Sforza. The grand court and some rooms are open to the public. The birthplace of Gioacchino Rossini (1792–1868) will interest his many fans and is easily found near the *cathedral* at Via Rossini 34. The opera house, *Teatro Rossini,* is a tribute to the composer.

In the *Musei Civici,* the *Museo delle Ceramiche* (ceramics museum) and the *pinacoteca* (picture gallery) are excellent. Bellini's *Pala di Pesaro,* an altarpiece showing the Coronation of the Virgin and scenes from the lives of the saints, is the highlight of the latter. Pesaro has several other interesting 15th-century structures, including the *Rocca Constanza* (fortress) and the *church of Sant'Agostino* with its magnificent Gothic portal. In the vicinity of Pesaro there are several interesting sights, including **Villa Caprile,* 2 km. (1.5 miles) towards Gabicce on S 16, with its beautiful fountains; and the *Castello Imperiale,* about 6 km. (3.5

miles) on the panoramic road to Gabicce, a splendid Sforza palace in the forest, which is, alas, not open to the public. You may want to follow the corniche road to Gabicce Mare, just for the views.

For an especially rewarding excursion from Pesaro, drive southwest for 36 km. (22 miles) on Route S 423 through the scenic Foglia valley to **Urbino,** Italy's "open-air museum," situated on top of two hills. By giving us Raphael and Bramante, the walled city of Urbino did more than its share to foster the Renaissance. It's a city of the Montefeltros, especially the luminary Duke Federico, who sometimes was called the perfect Renaissance prince.

Urbino is nicely contained, you can see everything on foot, from the concentrated center to Raphael's house. The stunning **Palazzo Ducale* by Laurana now houses the *Galleria Nazionale delle Marche,* where a panoply of Renaissance lights appear: Bellini, Raphael, della Francesca, and Botticelli. The museum's best-known work is Berruguete's portrait of Federigo da Montefeltro (with his nose of rare distinction) and his son. The duke's study, one of the splendors of the golden age, is on the tour. In the courtyard the free-floating staircase is airily grand.

Opposite the palazzo, the Romanesque and Gothic *church of San Domenico* has a beautiful Renaissance portal. The *Duomo,* at the end of the piazza, is a Neoclassical work by Valadier. Several other churches are noteworthy, including *San Francesco* and *San Giovanni Battista.* You'll also want to see the stucco *Nativity* at the *Oratorio de San Giuseppe. San Bernardino,* outside of town, is the last resting place of the Montefeltros. Art lovers will want to make a pilgrimage to *Raphael's house* on Via Raffaello, and perhaps leave a flower in memory of the great artist who died so tragically young at the age of 37. At the end of that street, enjoy the panorama from the *Piazzale Roma.*

From Urbino continue south on Route S 423 for about 6 km. (4 miles) to a broad branch in the road, where you bear left on Route S 73 bis toward Fossombrone. This road will merge with Route S 3, the Via Flaminia, to **Fano,** another Malatesta town that, as an Etruscan city, predated its Roman residents. The Emperor Augustus left a *triumphal arch* (when did he not?) on the Via Flaminia, in A.D. 2, and there are some other Roman remains. The *Palazzo Malatesta* houses noteworthy collections of paintings and ceramics. The Malatestas were laid to rest at *San Francesco,* of which only the portico and tombs still exist. At *Santa Maria Nuova* you can see Perugino's *Madonna Enthroned* and an *Annunciation.* If you want a wonderful landscape view, travel a few minutes outside of town to the monastery *Eremo di Monte Giove,* 5.5 km. (3 miles) southwest.

Continue on Route S 16 through the beach resorts of *Torrette di*

Fano and *Marotta* to **Senigallia** a well-known resort by the sea. The *Rocca,* a fortress restored in 1480 for the della Rovere family, dominates the main piazza, which is graced by a lion fountain. Also on the piazza are the *Palazzo del Duca,* a 16th-century ducal residence, and the 15th-century *Palazzo Baviera* (now city offices), with interesting stuccos on the top floor on historical and biblical themes. A few minutes' drive west (3 km.; 2 miles) leads to a museum of rural and agricultural history, the *Centro di Ricerca, Studio i Documentazione,* housed in a former monastery next to the Renaissance *church of Santa Maria delle Grazie,* which is graced by a Perugino *Madonna and Saints.*

Near *Rocca Priora* Route S 76 turns inland for 18 km. (11 miles) by way of *Chiaravalle,* where there is a Cistercian abbey dating from 1172, to **Jesi,** the birthplace of the Emperor Frederick II of Hohenstaufen, whose mother was travelling through the town at the time, and of the 18th-century composer Pergolesi. The city walls, erected on Roman foundations, were built during the fortification-minded 14th century. The *Pinacoteca Comunale,* in the Renaissance *Palazzo della Signoria,* has some important works, including paintings by Lorenzo Lotto. Another noted resident was Maria Montessori, born in 1870 in nearby Chiaravalle, who developed a teaching method widely used in the United States.

Continue on Route S 16 to ***Ancona** (296 km.; 184 miles, from Venice), Italy's principal port on the central Adriatic. Ancona was hard hit in 1972 by an earthquake which made over half of the houses in its historic center uninhabitable and necessitated the closing of several churches and palaces. Some of the sights listed here may still be in the process of restoration. **Trajan's Arch* in the port district was erected in A.D. 115 in honor of the emperor, who built the port. The *Arch of Clement,* seaward of Trajan's Arch, was created by Vanvitelli in 1738 to honor Pope Clement XII.

Climb up Via Giovanni XXIII to the **Duomo di San Ciriaco,* begun in 1140 on the remnants of a temple dedicated to Venus. Its façade and porch were completed about 1270, and its Gothic portal is lovely.

Nearby are the remains of a Roman amphitheater and some

Ancona: San Ciriaco

attractive palaces, as well as the *Museo Nazionale della Marche,* which focuses on the Paleolithic to Roman eras and has some good Greek vases.

Stop at *San Francesco delle Scale* to see not only its lovely Venetian-Gothic portal but also the Lotto altarpiece within.

The charming Romanesque façade of the *church of Santa Maria della Piazza* leads to a lovely interior with mosaics from two earlier churches (fifth–eighth centuries). Nearby is the ever-busy *Loggia dei Mercanti,* whose Venetian-Gothic façade is adorned with statues. On Piazza Roma, the *Fontana del Calamo* boasts 13 water-spouting bronze masks. Titian's *Crucifixion,* painted when he was 70 years old, is one of the treasures of *San Domenico,* not far away.

Air raids destroyed much of Ancona during World War II, but fortunately many historic buildings were spared. Ferries leave the port for Greece and Yugoslavia.

From Ancona a scenic coastal road leads around *Monte Conero,* near the interesting Renaissance *church of Santa Maria di Portonovo* (2 km.; 1.5 miles to the left) and through *Numana,* a town surrounded by gardens and woods; below the surface of the sea here, the remains of an ancient city come mysteriously into view, evoking the Graeco-Roman past.

Just before *Porto Recanati,* Route S 77 branches west from S 16 for 2 km. (1 mile) to ***Loreto,** famous throughout the world for its shrine, the *Santa Casa,* the

house of the Virgin Mary, which was transported, according to legend, by angels from Nazareth. Loreto's name comes from the laurel grove (*lauretum*) where the Santa Casa came to rest. It's set atop a hill that adds to its charm. Some of Italy's finest architects worked on the *Santuario della Santa Casa,* including Giulianoda Sangallo, Da Maiano, Bramante, and Sansovino—as impressive a roster as can be found. Wonderful frescoes surround the Casa, which is beneath the dome. The great architect Bramante also began work on the *Palazzo Apostolico* next to the church, but it never was completed. Inside is a good picture collection. Fountains and a public garden provide calm oases in Loreto.

Shortly after *Porto Recanati,* Route 571 leads west from S 16 for 23 km. (14 miles) through the Potenza valley to the ruins of the

Loreto

Roman city of *Helvia Ricina* and, just south, the vast Roman theater at *Villa Potenza*. Going 6 km. (4 miles) farther south, you will reach *Macerata,* a flowery town of old palaces and churches from the Renaissance.

Continue along Route S 16 through the resorts of *Civitanova Marche, Marina Falariense,* and *Lido di Fermo. Fermo* (8 km.; 5 miles inland) displays the chasuble of Saint Thomas à Becket, a 12th-century gold-and-silk garment, in its *Duomo.* The *Roman cistern* near *San Domenico* consists of 30 underground rooms that were used to hold and to purify water, and in part are still used today.

Fine palaces are not lacking; Sangallo the Younger's *Palazzo Azzolino* is one of them, and there are more to be found around the attractive *Piazza del Popolo.*

Continue south on Route S 16 to *Porto d'Ascoli,* then travel west on S 4 for 28 km. (17 miles) to the provincial capital, **Ascoli Piceno.** If it happens to be the first Sunday in August, lucky you. The Quintana festival turns the town back to the 15th century, and you may think you've entered Brigadoon. Walk about to the *Duomo* and to the nearby *Palazzo Comunale,* which has a picture gallery where Titian and other fine painters are exhibited, and to see many of the old palaces and churches. The Gothic *church of San Francesco* has a rare women's gallery. Stop, too, at *Santi Vincenzo e Anastasio,* a delightful church with mullioned windows.

Follow Via delle Torri, and its continuation, Via di Solestà, to see the Medieval *towers* and houses and the wonderful *Roman bridge.*

Continue along the coast on the faithful Route S 16 through the resorts of *Alba Adriatica* and *Giulianova,* where the octagonal *Duomo* has a Renaissance cupola. Fields of corn provide an unusual view for Italy here. Soon you'll reach *Roseto degli Abruzzi,* where the beaches and mountain views may seduce you. The pines and beaches around *Pineto* are fine, *Silvi Marina* has lovely vegetation, and there is another stretch of white sand at *Montesilvano Marina.* Follow the highway to **Pescara** (452 km.; 280 miles from Venice). Because of its 15-km.- (9-mile-) sandy beach, Pescara is one of the most popular beach resorts in the central Adriatic, filled with hotels, cafés, restaurants, cabanas, and sunning visitors, whose shades range from pale olive to maraschino cherry red. The city was an important crossroads for the Romans (it is at the seaward end of the Via Valeria), and, fortified since the 15th century, it successfully withstood invasions by the Turks in 1566 and the Austrians in 1707. It is also the birthplace of the poet Gabriele d'Annunzio (1863– 1938), who praised the evocative pinewoods that cover the surrounding hills; the house on Corso Mantoné where he was born is now a museum. Severely damaged in World War II, the town has been rebuilt on an impressive scale.

TRAVEL ROUTE 12: Pescara–Termoli (–**Gargano Peninsula)–*Foggia–*Bari (–*Taranto)–*Brindisi–**Lecce–Santa Maria di Leuca (566 km.; 351 miles)

See map on page 219 and color map.

This travel route follows the Adriatic coast south from Pescara to the southern tip of Apulia (Puglia) on the Ionian Sea. It is a continuation of Travel Route 11 (see page 203), which runs along the Adriatic from Venice to Pescara. Travellers who are in a hurry can take the Autostrada. On the smaller roads, however, you will discover far more in the way of authentic regional treasures and interesting sites along the way.

Leaving *Pescara* (see page 217), take Route S 16 south, through the beach resorts of *Francavilla al Mare* and *Ortona,* where there is an interesting cathedral, old palaces and a ruined castle with good views. Some 12 km. (7 miles) southwest of *San Vito Chietino,* is the walled city of *Lanciano,* where there are many Medieval buildings, including a 13th-century cathedral. *Fossacesia Marina,* has a Romanesque *basilica of San Giovanni in Venere,* built in the eighth century, rebuilt in the 11th and 12th centuries, and decorated with frescoes.

Vasto has several interesting sights: the *Duomo* (13th century), the *Palazzo D'Avalos* (18th century) on the same square, and Medieval churches. Continue along the coast on Route S 16 to **Termoli** (103 km.; 64 miles from Pescara), a well-known beach resort with a picturesque old quarter, which is situated on a promontory that allows good views in all directions. It is worth a visit for the Pisan-Apulian–Romanesque *Duomo* and the *castle* of Frederick II Hohenstaufen.

From Termoli, you can take a ferry to the *Isole Tremiti,* a beautiful cluster of limestone islands off the Gargano promontory in the Adriatic. The islands have preserved their traditional character, although they are becoming more and more popular with tourists. *San Domino,* the most westerly and scenic of the islands, was a place of exile until 1943; there is a large pine forest, several camping sites and the legendary grottoes, *Grotta del Bue Marino* and *Grotte delle Viole,* both of which enchant with their beautiful play of light. In this area, the waters abound with fish and are perfect for underwater sports. *San Nicola* contains a small walled village of the same name, which is the capital of the archipelago; it has an 11th-century abbey church, *Santa Maria a Mare,* a castle built around the eighth-century Benedictine abbey, and several other interesting Medieval buildings. Other islands, isolated and almost uninhabited, are *Capraia, Cretaccio* and *Pianosa.*

About 25 km. (15 miles) after Termoli, Route S 16 leaves the coast, travels west of the **_Gargano peninsula_ (see below) and past _San Severo_, to ***Foggia** (192 km.; 119 miles from Pescara) a lively, modern-looking city on the high plateau of _Tavoliere di Puglia_, the granary of Italy. Foggia's most interesting sight is the *_Duomo_, first built in 1172 in Apulian-Romanesque style and rebuilt in 1731 after a disastrous earthquake destroyed almost all of the town. The _Museo Civico_, primarily devoted to local archaeology and folk traditions, also has a collection of modern paintings.

North of Foggia about 4 km. (2.5 miles), you can visit the ruins of the ancient town of _Arpi_. Another worthwhile excursion leads 23 km. (14 miles) southwest on Route S 546 to _Troia_, whose 11th–12th–century _cathedral_ has a Romanesque façade that is considered the most beautiful in southern Italy.

Those who have time can make a trip from Foggia northeast on Route S 89 to the ****Promontorio del Gargano** (Gargano Massif), which forms a mountainous peninsula into the Adriatic and belongs geologically to the Dalmatian limestone formations. The Gargano reaches at _Monte Cavo_ a height of about 1,065 meters (3,500 feet) and then slopes gently toward the sea. Cliffs, steep drops, reefs, grottoes, scenic inlets, clear water and white villages characterize the coast here, which offers an ideal environment for local fishermen and amateurs alike. The so-called Riviera Garganico includes

the resorts of *Rodi, San Menaio,* with villas set amidst pinewoods, *Peschici,* dizzyingly situated on a crag rising straight up from the sea, and *Vieste,* with its charming little port and Medieval appearance; there are fine views from its 16th-century fortress. The coastal valleys and slopes of the Gargano are covered with olive groves and pine forests. Inland there are mixed forests of beech, pine, and oak.

The first stop along Route S 89 is a square Apulian-Romanesque church on a hill, *San Leonardo alle Matine,* with a beautifully sculpted 13th-century doorway. About 10 km. (6 miles) farther is ***Manfredonia,** in the southern "corner" of the peninsula, a famous resort with a sandy beach and tourist facilities. It was founded in the 13th century by Manfred, Frederick II's son, several miles from the Roman town of *Sipontum;* destroyed by the Turks in 1620, it was rebuilt on a regular plan, with streets intersecting at right angles. The Hohenstaufen *castle* dates from the 13th century. While there, visit the nearby **cathedral of Santa Maria di Siponto* (1117), which contains an unaltered crypt. The remains of an ancient *temple* remind us of the town's earlier incarnation as Sipontum.

*Monte Sant'Angelo is a town dominated by the handsome ruins of a Norman *castle* and the *Santuario di San Michele,* containing an ancient grotto basilica dedicated to the Archangel Michael (where an estimated million pilgrims come every year). According to legend, the church, which occupies a cave in the center of town, was chosen as a shrine by the Archangel when he appeared to Saint Lawrence in 490. The bronze door was cast in Constantinople in 1076, and there is a fine 11th-century bishop's throne. Nearby is the so-called **Tomba di Rotari* (Lombard tomb), a domed building that dates from about A.D. 1200 and was probably a baptistry. Between here and *Vico del Gargano* to the north along Route S 528 lies the *Foresta Umbra,* a beautiful forest of beech trees, pines, lindens, maples, gigantic yews, ash trees, cedars and chestnuts.

San Giovanni Rotondo, located west of Sant'Angelo, below Monte Calvo, is the home to the monastery where the controversial Padre Pio da Pietralcina (died 1969) lived. Padre Pio, who received the stigmata, is buried in the modern church near the convent of *Santa Maria delle Grazie.* The town is a destination for many pilgrims seeking cures for their ailments.

Now either take Route S 89 back to **Foggia* to connect with the Autostrada A 14 and Route S 16, or drive along the coastal road, Route S 159, through *Margherita di Savoia,* known for its iodine and bromine extraction, large saltworks, and therapeutic baths, directly to **Barletta* (see page 222).

From Foggia, on either Route S 16 and then S 98 (after Cerignola) or the Autostrada, continue to ***Canosa di Puglia** (244 km.; 151 miles from Pescara), built on the site of an important Roman town (Canusium) and containing remains of Roman walls, a town gate, a bridge and an amphitheater. There is an interesting Romanesque *cathedral* (11th century) with five Byzantine domes and 18 ancient columns; the marble bishop's throne in the choir is supported by carved elephants. In a chapel in the courtyard to the south is the **Tomb of Bohemond (12th century), shaped like a cubiform mosque and crowned by a dome; its massive bronze door is by Roger of Melfi. The tomb's Eastern-inspired architecture reminds one that Bohemond, son of the Norman Robert Guiscard, ruled over the kingdoms of Antioch and Syria.

From here to Bari you can either stay inland on Route S 98, travelling past *Andria* and *Bitonto,* or take Route S 93 to the coast and then S 16 along it through *Barletta* and *Trani* (see page 222).

To Bari through *Andria and *Bitonto

Follow the route marked "A" on the map on page 219.

Leaving **Canosa,* drive east on Route S 98 to ***Andria** (271 km.; 168 miles from Pescara), the birthplace of Conrad, a son of Frederick II Hohenstaufen. This lively market town has several interesting sights: the *Ducal palace (16th century); the Gothic

cathedral of San Ricardo, which contains the tombs of Iolande of Jerusalem and Isabella of England, the second and third wives of Frederick II; and the Gothic *cloister of the *church of San Domenico.*

A highly recommended excursion from Andria leads 17 km. (11 miles) south on Route S 170 dir. to ****Castel del Monte,** Frederick II's massive octagonal hunting castle (1240) and the most imposing Hohenstaufen castle in Italy. Probably built to Frederick's own design, this early Gothic structure is surrounded by eight towers and has eight rooms of the same size on each floor. On the top floor of the castle are royal apartments that offer a magnificent view over the Apulian countryside.

From the castle take Route S 170 and then Route S 98 east to ***Bitonto,** where the splendid **cathedral (12th century) is considered to be the finest example of Apulian-Romanesque style. On the cathedral's right side are deep arches and six-arched windows. Other noteworthy buildings include the Renaissance palace of *Sylos Labini and the Benedictine abbey of *San Leo (11th century), with its beautiful cloister and 14th-century frescoes.

If you bypass Castel de Monte and take S 98 directly from Andria to Bitonto, it is worthwhile to stop in *Ruvo di Puglia,* which has a 12th–13th-century Apulian-Romanesque *Duomo with a richly decorated central portal, and an excellent collection of 5th–

3rd-century B.C. vases in the *Palazzo Jatta*. Then go east 6 km. (4 miles) to *Terlizzi*, where the small church and palaces date from the 16th and 17th centuries.

From Bitonto it is only a few minutes drive to ***Bari** (332 km.; 206 miles from Pescara; see page 223).

To Bari through *Barletta and *Trani

Follow the route marked "B" on the map on page 219.

Leaving *Canosa di Puglia*, take Route S 93 northeast toward the coast. After 13 km. (8 miles) turn left to ***Cannae,** where Hannibal defeated the Romans in 216 B.C. The archaeological zone here includes a large area of excavation containing parts of the Apulian, the Roman, and the Medieval city. Continue on Route S 93 to ***Barletta** a busy port rich in historic monuments and also a popular resort with a large sandy beach. In the city center stands the early Gothic **church of San Sepolcro,* with its Baroque façade and canopy portal. Next to the church is the *Colosso,* a 5-meter- (16-foot-) bronze statue probably representing an Eastern Roman emperor, perhaps Valentinian I, and the finest piece of bronze colossal sculpture from ancient times. The **Duomo* was built in Romanesque style and later enlarged in the Gothic style. Situated on the water beyond the cathedral is the massive Norman ***castle,* enlarged

under the Hohenstaufens, the Angevins, Aragonese, and Charles V. Other sights in Barletta include the Baroque *Palazzo della Marra,* the *church of Sant'Andrea* and the *Museum and Picture Gallery* displaying ancient artifacts as well as works by De Nittis (19th century).

*Trani, (30 km.; 19 miles) further on Route S 16, is a typical Apulian port and beach resort, the see of an archbishop, and has many rewarding historical sights. The large Apulian-Romanesque ***cathedral,* with its beautiful bronze doors (1175) and octagonal spire, stands at the edge of the sea; its impressive interior is the only extant example of an Apulian church with double columns. The *church of the Ognissanti,* formerly a Knights Templar hospice, dates from the era of the Crusades. The elegant **Palazzo Caccetta* (1458) is late Gothic. The 13th-century *castello,* now being restored, was built by Frederick II and was greatly altered later when it was used as a prison. In the municipal gardens east of the harbor are three Roman milestones and a lovely view of the harbor and cathedral. Also worth a visit are the two small Romanesque churches *Sant'Andrea* and *San Francesco* (which has three Byzantine domes), as well as the 11th-century *Benedictine abbey of Santa Maria della Colonna* on the peninsula of Capo Colonna, where there is a beautiful beach.

Continue along the coast on Route S 16 past *Bisceglie,* a resort town in which there are the ruins of a Norman castle, to ***Molfetta,** a large fishing port. Molfetta's principal sight is the Romanesque *Duomo Vecchio (San Corrado)* (12th–13th centuries), with its three domes in the nave and two bell towers. The monastery complex of *Madonna dei Martiri* (13th century) and the **Hospital of Crusaders* (1095) stand outside of town.

Only 2 km. (1 mile) southwest of Molfetta is a karst limestone area dotted with grottoes and large caves that were inhabited as long ago as the Stone Age.

Follow Route S 16 down the coast for 7 km. (4 miles) to the small fishing town of **Giovinazzo,** with its well-preserved old quarter. The Romanesque *cathedral* was altered in the 17th and 18th centuries but still retains parts of its original structure in the portal on the right side, the apse and the bell tower.

From Giovinazzo continue down Route S 16 to ***Bari** (350 km.; 217 miles from Pescara).

*Bari

The capital of Apulia, it is known as the Gateway to the East and is a major transit port for the eastern Mediterranean. Every September it hosts the *Fiera del Levante,* the largest trade fair in Italy after Milan's.

Bari is composed of two distinct cities. Old Bari, the *Città Vecchia,* is located on a promontory between the old and new harbors.

It is a twisted and fascinating labyrinth of Medieval alleys (frequently spanned by arches), squares, stairs, blindingly white houses and Romanesque churches. The complicated alleyways are said to protect the inhabitants from the wind and from foreign invaders, who became hopelessly confused when trying to unravel them. In direct contrast is the new Bari, *Città Nuova,* which resembles a chess board with straight avenues that divide the city into squares. The *Corso Vittorio Emanuele II* separates the two parts of the city.

In new Bari on Piazza Umberto near the train station is the **Museo Archeologico,* with its rich collection of prehistoric and Graeco-Roman antiquities. Of particular interest are the ceramics and the bronze and gold objects from the sixth through the second centuries B.C. Note also the Attic black- and red-figure vases.

The showcase of new Bari— the grand *Corso Cavour,* lined with palm trees—is the site for the *Teatro Petruzzelli* (1898–1903), the fourth largest opera house in Italy (only the ones in Milan, Rome, and Naples are larger). A magnificent seafront promenade, *Lungomare Imperatore Augusto* and *Lungomare Nazario Sauro,* leads from the *Porto Vecchio* to the *Pinacoteca Provinciale* (fine-arts museum), which displays paintings dating from the 11th–19th centuries. Bartolommeo Vivarini's *Annunciation* is the museum's high point.

In the center of four piazzas known as *Conti del Catapano* in the old quarter, is the ****Basilica di San Nicola** (1087–1197), one of Italy's most impressive examples of Apulian-Romanesque architecture. The fourth-century Saint Nicholas of Myra, in Asia Minor, was famed for resurrecting three children whom a butcher had chopped up and put in brine. In 1087 sailors from Bari stole the saint's relics, said to exude a miraculous fluid, and brought them home; the present church was founded to house them. The feast of Saint Nicholas is still celebrated at sea in early May, when the faithful come in boats to pray before his statue.

The majestic façade of the basilica, with its elongated windows, contains three portals flanked by two truncated towers. Three great transverse arches added in 1451 are immediately apparent when you enter. The 12th-century **ciborium (canopy) above the main altar, supported by four columns that differ in color and shape and have different capitals, is the oldest in Apulia. Behind it is an Arabic *mosaic floor* with, in its center, the marble *throne* of Abbot Elia (11th-century church founder), decorated with relief figures. The basilica also contains a rich *treasury* and *sacristy*. Two wide marble staircases lead down to the **crypt, interesting for its columns with magnificent capitals. The main altar of the crypt shelters the tomb of Saint Nicholas, who died in 326. The altar and the mosaics behind the tomb are from the 12th century. The best time to visit the basilica is in the late afternoon, when the sun creates striking light effects through the windows of the façade.

Also visit the basilica's *courtyard* and the *Portico of the Pilgrims*. The small *church of San Gregorio* (11th–12th centuries) is located to the right, beyond the 14th-century arch of San Nicola.

A narrow street, *Strada del Carmine,* leads from the basilica to the ***Duomo,** built in the 12th century and renovated in 1292 in Romanesque style. The façade carries an elaborate frieze and a rose window surrounded by sculpted beasts and monsters. On the sides, the *arcades supporting galleries are magnificent, as are the large window and the decorations above the architrave in the apse. The 12th-century pulpit, the ciborium and the old bishop's

Basilica di San Nicola: Crypt

throne in the presbytery are all admirable reconstructions from fragments of the originals. Remains of an Early Christian church with mosaic pavement have been uncovered in recent restoration work.

From the cathedral it is a short distance west to the Hohenstaufen *castello* (1233–1239), built on an earlier Norman fortress. The corner bastions and inner courtyard were added in the 16th century.

From Bari drive to Lecce either through *Taranto* (see page 231) or through *Monopoli* and *Brindisi* (see page 226).

To Lecce through Monopoli and *Brindisi

Follow the route marked "A" on the color maps.

Leaving *Bari,* follow Route S 16 southeast along the coast. You may wish to leave the highway to drive through the small towns of *Mola di Bari,* where there is a mid-16th century cathedral and Angevin castle, and *Polignano a Mare,* with its scenic sea grottoes, to **Monopoli.** In this port city visit the Hohenstaufen *castello* and the Romanesque *chapel of Santa Maria Amalfitana.* The 18th-century *cathedral* contains treasures from a considerably older church.

Worthwhile side trips from Monopoli (or from Polignano) include one to *Conversano* (18 km.; 11 miles west from Monopoli), whose sights include a large

Norman castle, the Romanesque *church of San Benedetto* (with its Baroque bell tower), and a Romanesque-Gothic cathedral, and one to **Castellana Grotte,** (15 km.; 9 miles southwest from Monopoli) which takes its name from the largest and finest **stalagmite and stalactite caves** in Italy, the *Grotte di Castellana.* The artificially lit caves contain fantastic stone formations and continue for over 2 km. (1 mile). Visitors enter the grottoes in a chairlift to a depth of about 60 meters (200 feet). The longer (two-hour) tour includes the *Grotta Bianca,* unsurpassed in Europe for the perfect condition of its formations.

About 23 km. (14 miles) south of Monopoli is **Alberobello,** the "town of the trulli." Trulli are whitewashed, round, unmortared-stone structures, often linked in groups, with conical roofs formed by overlapping stone slabs. Of uncertain origin, they lend a distinctive and pointed charm to the Apulian landscape. In recent years, however, Alberobello has become commercially self-conscious, and its trulli now house endless gift shops. The surrounding countryside, with its rust-red earth, gray-green olive groves, and clusters of pointed white domes, is undeniably picturesque.

From nearby *Locorotondo* (9 km.; 6 miles east of Alberobello), set on a hill and circular in plan, there is a beautiful view of the valley dotted with clusters of trulli.

From here follow Route S 172 dir. north to S 16 near *Fasano,* whose town hall is in the former palace of the Knights of Malta.

From Monopoli there are again two ways to get to Brindisi: Route S 16 travels inland through *Fasano, Ostuni,* whose 15th-century cathedral has an unusual, Spanish-inspired façade, and *San Vito dei Normanni* to Brindisi (435 km.; 270 miles from Pescara). Or you can take the new coastal road, S 379, which leads first to *Egnazia Terme* and the ruins of ***Egnazia.** The Messapian and Greek town of Egnatia was also important to the Romans. Excavations reveal that it flourished in the fourth and third centuries B.C. Archaeologists have uncovered some interesting sections of the *Via Traiana,* with polygon-shaped Roman stones.

Continue along Route S 389 for 10 km. (6 miles) to *Torre Canne Terme,* a spa well-known for its modern hydrothermal facilities and comfortable resorts offering a variety of underwater sports. Route S 379 then continues to **Brindisi* (432 km.; 268 miles from Pescara).

*Brindisi

See map on page 227.

Brindisi's famous *marble column* (19 meters; 62 feet), one of a pair that overlooked the port and marked the end of the Via Appia—the "Queen of Roads," coming from Rome and Taranto—

is a reminder of the town's strategic and commercial importance in the Roman era. The capital of the column is decorated with figures of Roman gods and sea tritons. The second column, which fell in 1528, was taken to Lecce (see page 228). Near the harbor are other Roman ruins, including the house where the Roman poet Virgil is said to have died in 19 B.C., on his return from Greece.

Brindisi has always been an important port. During the Middle Ages the Crusaders left from here for the Holy Land, and several buildings in the old quarter remain from this period. Near the **port buildings** (1) where the large passenger liners dock, the Corso Garibaldi begins. This street leads to *Piazza del Popolo,* where it becomes Corso Roma. Corso Umberto I angles to the right from the piazza and leads to the *main train station* (2). These three streets form the main commercial and shopping district of the city.

Across from the column marking the end of the Via Appia (3), on the northern side of the inner harbor, stands the 53-meter- (174-foot-) *Monument to the Italian Sailor* (4), a naval war memorial built in 1933 in the shape of a massive ship's rudder; take the elevator up to see the beautiful view.

From here follow *Via Colonna* to the old quarter where the Baroque *cathedral* (5) (1749) was built on the remains of a Romanesque church (11th century; parts of the apse and a mosaic pavement remain). Nearby is the Romanesque *Palazzo Balsamo* (6) (13th–14th centuries), with its remarkable loggia. Facing it, the *Museo Archeologico Provinciale* contains material collected in the area, including ceramics, Attic pottery, votive statuettes, and Roman sculpture fragments. To the southwest is the round Romanesque ***church of San Giovanni al Sepolcro** (7) (11th–12th centuries), a former baptistry erected by the Knights Templar. A few blocks farther is the former monastery **church of San Benedetto* (8) (1080), a Romanesque structure with a very beautiful cloister with fine relief carving. While exploring this old quarter it's a good idea to keep an eye on purses, cameras, and wallets.

Via San Benedetto and Via Carmine lead to the city gate, *Porta Mesagne* (9) (13th century), with its large pointed arch and its pewter-capped towers carrying the weapon of Charles V (16th

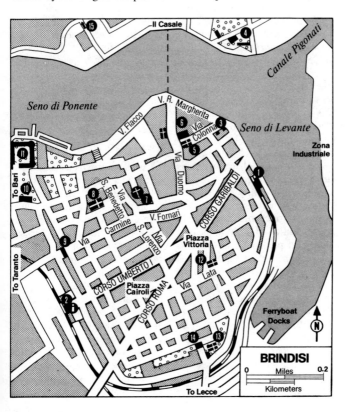

BRINDISI

century). Nearby is another Medieval structure with strong Eastern architectural overtones, the *Fontana Tancredi* (10), built in 1192 by the Norman King Tancred to honor the wedding of his son Roger to Urania of Constantinople. The Crusaders watered their horses here.

The western arm of the harbor is dominated by the ***Castello Svevo** (11), Frederick II Hohenstaufen's castle, erected in 1227 and renovated and expanded in the 15th and 16th centuries (not open to the public).

Other sights here include the *church of Santa Lucia* (12), built in 1225 in Romanesque style and later given a Gothic veneer (note the Byzantine frescoes in the crypt); the Romanesque *Chiesa del Cristo* (13) built in 1230; and *Porta di Carlo Quinto* (14), a city gate built in the 16th century under Charles V. This gate is also called *Porta Lecce* because it leads to the road to Lecce.

Northeast across the western arm of the harbor is the Romanesque ***church of Santa Maria del Casale** (15) (1300), the best Medieval monument in Brindisi. Decorated with pointed arches, its impressive polychrome façade has a unique portal. The single-aisled interior is covered with 14th-century Byzantine frescoes.

Worthwhile excursions from Brindisi lead to: *Mesagne,* (14 km.; 9 miles southwest on Route S 7), which boasts an 11th-century Norman castle (later rebuilt and enlarged) and the *church of Santa Maria del Carmine* (14th century); beyond it, *Francavilla Fontana,* (32 km.; 20 miles from Brindisi) contains some interesting palaces and the *Palazzo Imperiali* (1450; rebuilt 1730); and **Oria* (6 km.; 4 miles south of Francavilla Fontana), whose magnificent **castle of Frederick II* stands on the site of an ancient Greek acropolis. All these towns are on or near the route to Taranto, S 7.

Leave Brindisi through Porta Lecce (see above) and drive southeast along Route S 16 through *Squinzano.* Four km. (2.5 miles) northeast is the Romanesque abbey *church of Santa Maria di Cerrate* decorated with frescoes from the 13th–16th centuries.

****Lecce**

See map on page 230.

Lecce is the provincial capital of a fertile area that produces wheat, tobacco, olive oil, wine, and vegetables and is one of the most interesting towns in southern Italy because of its many Baroque buildings. In addition, *San Cataldo,* with its splendid sandy beach, is only 12 km. (7 miles) from the city center.

Because this southern part of Apulia is surrounded on three sides by water (the Adriatic, the Ionian, and the Gulf of Taranto), many beach resorts are within easy reach.

Baroque reigns supreme in Lecce, thanks to intensive building in the 16th and 18th centuries, which created a unique stylistic uniformity. Architects used a local yellow sandstone, easily carved when first excavated and becoming harder with time, for most of the ornately decorated buildings. The most impressive Baroque structure in Lecce is the sumptuous ****basilica of Santa Croce** (1) (1549–1679), whose exuberant façade is crowded with sculptures strongly reminiscent of the Spanish *Plateresque* style. Next to it, the **Palazzo del Governo* (2), formerly a Celestine convent, also has a richly decorated Baroque façade; a lovely public garden (*Giardino Pubblico*) (3) extends in back of the palace.

Via Templari leads to the ****Piazza Sant'Oronzio** (4), the cobblestoned square in the center of the city. The second *marble column* of the Via Appia (the other one is in Brindisi, see page 226), stands here; a bronze statue of Saint Orontius, patron saint of the city, crowned the top until 1985, when it was removed to protect it from the corrosive effects of smog. The ruins of a Roman **amphitheater* are visible in the southern half of the square. The **Palazzo del Seggio,* or Sedile (1592), the former city hall, with its Gothic arcades and loggia, and the little Renaissance *chapel of San Marco* (1543) stand to the west of the column.

Several blocks south of the square is the **church of San Matteo* (5) (1710), an octagonal build-

ing adorned with a remarkable Baroque façade flanked by two columns. Other nearby churches built in a beautiful Baroque style are the *Gesù* or *Buon Consiglio* (6), *Santa Chiara* (7) and *Sant'Irene* (8). Near Santa Chiara there is a small Roman *theater,* the only one of its kind known in Apulia.

Corso Vittorio Emanuele leads from *Piazza Sant'Oronzio* to ****Piazza del Duomo,** a superbly harmonious square surrounded by still more wonderful Baroque buildings. It is the site of the **Duomo di Sant'Oronzio* (9) (rebuilt 1569–1570), with one lavish façade in Baroque style and another, older and more austere, in Renaissance style, and a 74-meter- (243-foot-) bell tower. Ornately covered with stone fruits, flowers and figures, the altars inside typify the local sculptural style. The *Palazzo Vescovile* (10) rebuilt in 1632, with its loggia and balustrades, fits perfectly between the cathedral and the ***Palazzo del Seminario* (11), a seminary for priests. The seminary, constructed between 1694–1709, has a beautiful façade with a monumental portal. The inner courtyard, with its arcades and Baroque **fountain,* is also worth a look.

The picturesque Via G. Palmieri leads from the Piazza del Duomo to the **Arco di Trionfo* (12), also called Porta Napoli, a triumphal arch erected in 1548 in honor of Emperor Charles V.

The buildings of the *University* (13), in front of the arch, are surrounded by beautifully landscaped gardens. Via San Nicola (also called Via del Cimitero) leads from here to the ***church of Santi Nicola e Cataldo** (14), built by the Norman Count Tancred in 1180, with his richly decorated Romanesque portal at the center of a Baroque façade. Influenced by Byzantine, Arabic, and early Gothic styles, the church is one of the most important Norman monuments in Italy. The interior, with splendid capitals, shows strong French-Gothic influence. The municipal cemetery lies next to the church.

Among the many other churches in Lecce, of particular interest are the large Dominican *del Rosario* (15), *Santa Teresa* (16) and *Santa Maria del Carmine* (17), all built in Baroque style.

The **Museo Provinciale* is located just south of the old city, at the corner of Viale Gallipoli and Viale Francesco lo Re; its extensive archaeological section and picture gallery are built around a modern spiral ramp. *Porta Rusce* (18), a city gate dating from 1703, refers to the ruins of the nearby Roman town of *Rudiae*. Finally, one should also visit the *castello* (19), built in the 16th-century reign of Charles V on the ruins of a Norman castle and renovated several times since then.

Places of interest south of

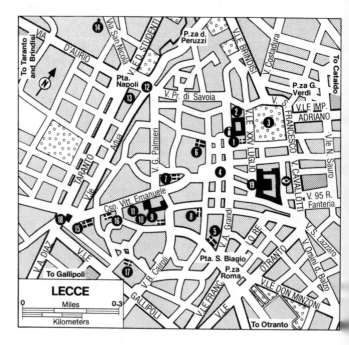

LECCE

Miles 0.3
Kilometers

Lecce, and the route to *Santa Maria di Leuca,* are described on pages 235–236.

To Lecce through *Taranto

Follow route marked "B" on the color maps.

If you opt to drive from Bari to Lecce through Taranto, you can take the Autostrada, a rural road through Mottola, or the route through Altamura (see page 232). The fastest way to get to Taranto is on the Autostrada A 14 or highway S 100, but the trip is much more interesting along the excellent rural road that passes through *Acquaviva delle Fonti,* where there is a large Renaissance cathedral and the 17th-century *Palazzo dei Principi,* to *Gioia del Colle,* just west of S 100, worth a visit for its Norman *castle,* enlarged by Frederick II around 1230. The courtyard is surrounded by Gothic windows with two and three arches. A free-standing outdoor staircase leads to an elegant loggia.

Northeast of the town, on *Monte Sannace,* archaeologists are excavating an ancient Apulian town.

Drive southeast along Route S 100 to *Mottola,* called the "overlook" of Taranto province because of its 390-meter- (1300-foot-) elevation. The area contains numerous *cave churches,* the so-called Basilian *laure,* which are decorated with frescoes; two of them, *San Gregorio* and *San Nicola,* are especially fine. The

13th century *parish church* is also worth a visit.

Massafra, 8 km. (5 miles) farther, is a pretty town with white Eastern-style houses built into the terraced slope of a deep ravine. The many mountain caves here were inhabited during the Middle Ages to escape Saracen massacres, and later some were used as churches (*laure*). Deep, narrow ravines (*gravine*) contain numerous crypts decorated with Byzantine frescoes from the 10th through the 14th centuries. Noteworthy among these fascinating sub-terra sights are the *Chiesa-Crypta di San Marco,* located just below the *Ponte Nuovo* at the bottom of an unmarked staircase (ring for key at house next door), with a good fresco of St. Mark, and the *Gravina della Madonna della Scala* at the edge of town on Via del Santuario. Serious explorers wishing to visit the more extensive series of churches and crypts called *Capella-Cripta della Candelore* must apply in the morning to the Polizia Urbana in the *Piazza Garibaldi* for a guide. Above ground, the Angevin *castle* has a good view, and the old, domed *church of Santa Lucia* may be visited.

Taranto (408 km.; 253 miles from Pescara), one of Italy's two principal naval bases, was founded as Taras in the eighth century B.C. by the Spartans and was the most powerful and wealthy city of Magna Graecia. By the fourth century B.C. it had a population of 300,000 and a city wall

15 km. (9 miles) in circumference. Like other cities of Greek origin on this coast, Taranto became a center of Pythagorean philosophy and was even visited by Plato. It remained a major city under the Romans, and ruins remain from both civilizations. Today Taranto is an important commercial and industrial center (shipyards and iron works), a military port and a tourist city offering many facilities. It is renowned for its honey and fruit, as well as for fishing and oyster and shellfish cultivation. There are beautiful beaches nearby, but they are sometimes marred by pollution.

Of special interest is the *Città Vecchia,* or old quarter, a labyrinth of narrow streets, stairs, alleys, covered passages and small squares located on an island between the *Mare Grande* and the *Mare Piccolo* and reached by a swinging bridge flanked by the *castello* (15th century). Near the beginning of Via del Duomo is the *church of the Trinità,* which contains the remains of a Doric temple.

The *cathedral of San Cataldo* was rebuilt in the 11th century on the site of an earlier building and given a Baroque façade in the 18th century. The cathedral's triple-aisled interior is supported by antique columns with Byzantine and Romanesque capitals.

A few blocks from the cathedral is the *church of San Domenico Maggiore* (built at the end of the 11th century, remodeled in 1302), whose high façade rises above a freestanding Baroque staircase.

The **Museo Nazionale,* in the new part of the city, is rivaled only by Naples' Museo Archeologico for the glories of its collection of antiquities. Splendid examples of Greek and Roman sculpture abound, and there is an outstanding series of ancient mosaics and ceramics; the Corinthian vases are particularly fine. Nearby, a beautiful park—the *Giardini Comunali*—is laid out on a terrace overlooking the *Mare Piccolo* and contains luxuriant exotic plants. The shore road, *Lungomare Vittorio Emanuele III,* with its avenue of stately palms and vibrant oleanders, offers magnificent views of the *Mare Grande,* particularly at sunset; view-lovers will also want to seek out the *overlook La Rotonda* on the Lungomare.

Another possible route from Bari to Taranto is southwest on S 96 past *Bitetto,* with its Romanesque cathedral, and through **Altamura,** partly surrounded by its 5th-century B.C. walls, where the large Romanesque-Gothic *cathedral of Santa Maria Assunta* (13th–16th centuries), has an impressive and richly decorated *portal.* Its 14th-century *columns* carried by lions support a round arch whose rich decorations and bas-reliefs (scenes from the Old and New Testament) are unique in Apulia. Inside are a 16th-century pulpit and bishop's throne and particularly fine carved choir stalls. Altamura also has several palaces dating from the 17th and 18th centuries.

From Altamura, take Route

S 96 west for 12 km. (7 miles) through the Murgia Massif for a side trip to ***Gravina di Puglia,** picturesquely situated above a deep gorge whose walls contain many caves (*laure Basiliane*). In Byzantine times some of these rock-hewn caves were organized into chapels, and the walls were covered with frescoes. The most famous cave church is the **San Michele dei Grotti*, which has five aisles separated by piers and three semicircular apses.

The **Duomo*, of the town, originally built in the 11th century, and rebuilt in 1482, sits on the remains of an older church and contains the 16th-century tomb of a duchess of Gravina. The *church of Santa Maria della Grazie* has an unusual façade shaped like an enormous eagle. The ruins of a Hohenstaufen castle are scattered on a hill north of the town.

For another intriguing side trip from Altamura, take Route S 99 south to ****Matera** (the town can also be reached directly from *Gravina di Puglia* over a country road). This remarkable and very old town sits on the edge of a high cliff whose caves were inhabited from prehistoric times until quite recently; some may still be occupied, although the government is trying to resettle the occupants. The old rock-cut cave houses, called *sassi*, of the lower town were built in the Byzantine era; gradually, as humans and livestock took up residence within their dank confines, the walls were painted with frescoes and the interiors became shrines. Laid out in

Santa Maria della Grazie

the shape of a chaotic amphitheater among the dry, wheat-colored calcareous rocks, they form a unique, ingenious and highly picturesque sight. To visit the *sassi* and the many old **cave churches* decorated with Byzantine frescoes in the now almost-deserted lower town, you may want to hire an official tourist guide; far less expensive, and sometimes just as knowledgeable, are the boys who will crowd around your car to offer their services (arrange a price in advance). The upper part of town is the modern center.

The two most famous frescoes, the *Madonna del Latte* and *San Michele Arcangelo*, both dating from the 13th century, are found in the sassi *church of Santa Lucia* in the main part of the town. The nearby **Duomo*, built in Apulian-Romanesque style on the highest point of the old town, has an interesting exterior with a square campanile, a rose window and a single doorway. Below the cathedral rock, skirting the gorge, lies the panoramic *Strada dei Sassi,* partly hewn out of the rock, like the cave-dwellings along it. The Baroque *church of San Pietro Caveoso* stands at one end of the Strada at the foot of the rock; above it, cut into the rock, is the *church of Santa Maria in Idris,* with Byzantine frescoes. A wonderful view of the old town may be had from the terrace in front of a small Baroque monastery in *Piazza Pascoli* in the upper town. The **church of San Francesco d'Assisi* (1218, rebuilt in Baroque style in the 17th century) houses a remarkable 15th-century polyptych, a *Madonna between Saints,* by the Venetian Bartolommeo Vivarini.

At Via Ridola 24 the **Museo Nazionale Ridola* has a large archaeological collection from the Stone Age, artifacts from Greek tombs from the Bronze Age, and Greek-Italian amphoras from various burial grounds; a picture gallery with an important collection of 17th–18th century paintings is located in the *Palazzo Emanuele Duni* on the same street.

A fortified hill in town is crowned by the unfinished Angevin **castello* with massive walls and round towers.

From Matera, drive east on Route S 7 to **Taranto* (see page 231).

Leaving Taranto, continue east on Route S 7 to *San Giorgio Ionico* and angle right on Route S 7 ter to *Sava* (note its old castle) and continue to ***Manduria,** an ancient

Messapian Walls, Manduria

Messapian city with preserved **megalithic walls* dating from the fifth–third centuries B.C. The gigantic blocks, stacked without mortar, formed a defensive wall around the city. Other interesting sights in the archaeological zone north of the town are the **necropolis* and the **Well of Pliny,* so named because Pliny the Elder referred to it as *Lacus Manduriae* in his *Natural History.* It is located in an artificial cave. The *Duomo,* remodeled in Gothic and Renaissance style and with an interior restored in 1938, houses considerable works of art.

A worthwhile side trip leads north for 11 km. (7 miles) to **Oria,** where Frederick II built a massive **castle* on the site of the ancient Greek acropolis. The complex dominates the entire Salentine peninsula and is one of the best examples of fortifications from the Hohenstaufen era.

Continuing on Route S 7 ter from Manduria through *San Pancrazio Salentino* and *Campi Salentina,* we arrive finally in ****Lecce** (492 km.; 305 miles from Pescara; page 228).

The trip from Lecce to Santa Maria di Leuca at the southern tip of the Salentine peninsula can be made by several routes. One route, along the eastern coast, follows Route S 543 to the beach resort of *San Cataldo* and then scenic Route S 611 along the coast through *San Foca, Torre dell'Orso* with its old watch tower, *Sant'Andrea,* and the Alimini lakes to ***Otranto,** a small, beautifully situated fishing town overlooking a bay. The easternmost point of Italy, it was the Greek and Roman city of *Hydruntum,* often referred to in ancient and Medieval sources as a port of embarkation, and is full of historical monuments. The powerful **castle* built by Alfonso of Aragon

Otranto Cathedral: Rose Window

offers a view across the 60-km.-(37-mile-) Strait of Otranto to the mountains of Albania. Architecturally, the most important building is the **cathedral of Santa Maria Annunziata* (begun 1080), a triple-aisled Romanesque basilica supported by numerous antique columns and adorned with a unique mosaic floor from 1163–1165, showing biblical scenes, heroic subjects, and the months. There is a splendid rose window from the 15th-century and an 18th-century portal. The little ninth-century Byzantine *church of San Pietro* in the upper part of the town, supposedly built on the spot where St. Peter first preached in Italy, is crowned with a Byzantine dome and has frescoes from the tenth to the 13th centuries.

From Otranto, take Route S 173 south to *Santa Cesarea Terme,* a spa famous for its hot springs in large caves in the cliffs. The sulfureous water is used for the treatment of skin conditions and rheumatism; mud baths are also available. You can take a boat trip from here along the rocky coast to several nearby caves, including the **Grotta Zinzulusa,* known for its interesting stalactite and stalagmite formations and unique fauna. This grotto and Grotta Romanelli (see below) were inhabited in the Upper Paleolithic period.

Continue south, and just before arriving at *Castro* there is an access road to Grotta Zinzulusa. The town has Medieval fortifications. In *Castro Marina* you can rent boats to explore the many caves along the coast. One of the most famous is the *Grotta Romanelli,* which contains prehistoric stone engravings and drawings. From Leuca at the tip of the peninsula, it is also possible to visit prehistoric caves by boat, including the *Grotta Treporte* and the *Grotta dei Giganti,* which contains Paleolithic artifacts.

At the southern tip of the Italian "boot heel," where the Adriatic and the Ionian seas meet, is **Capo Santa Maria di Leuca** (566 km.; 351 miles from Pescara), named for its white limestone cliffs (the Greek *leucos* means "white"). The *church of Santa Maria Finibus Terrae* (St. Mary of the Ends of the Earth) stands on the site of a Roman temple dedicated to Minerva and contains a much-revered image of the Virgin. On top of the 102-meter- (335-foot-) *Punto Meliso* rises a 50-meter- (164-foot-) *lighthouse* whose round balcony (260 steps up to it) offers a superb view extending, in clear weather, as far as Albania.

Another possible route from Lecce to Santa Maria di Leuca cuts across the Salentine peninsula and follows its west coast.

From Lecce, drive southwest through *Copertino,* with its powerful 16th-century castle, and turn south to *Nardò,* whose Romanesque-Gothic *cathedral* was given a Baroque appearance in the 18th century; the palacelike Baroque *church of San Domenico*

is also noteworthy. From Nardò, drive to the little beach resort of *Santa Maria al Bagno* on the Gulf of Taranto, where four massive Medieval fortified towers, the *Quattro Colonne,* dominate the scene. A scenic road, partly hewn from the rock, runs along the Riviera Neretina to **Gallipoli,** a port town on an island in the Gulf of Taranto, connected to the mainland by a bridge. Near the bridge is the Baroque 16th-century fountain, *Fontana Antica,* decorated with ancient Greek reliefs. The powerful towers of the 13th–16th-century *castle* stand in the sea. Fine choir stalls may be found in the Baroque *cathedral of Sant' Agata;* the Baroque *church of San Francesco,* dating from the 16th century, is at the western edge of the island and contains outstanding wooden carvings by Vespasiano Genuino.

From here, S 274 leads south to Santa Maria di Leuca.

A third, inland route from Lecce to Leuca follows S 476 south to *Galatina,* whose 14th-century Franciscan church cathedral, *Santa Catarina d'Alessandria,* is rich in treasures. Turn east 5 km. (3 miles) to *Soleto,* where the five-story bell tower, *La Guglia di Raimondello,* is a masterwork of transitional Romanesque-Gothic architecture. From here you may drive west to pick up S 101 or east to pick up S 275; both will take you to Santa Maria de Leuca on the tip of the peninsula.

TRAVEL ROUTE 13: ***Rome–Terracina–*Gaeta– Castel Volturno–***Naples (245 km.; 152 miles)

See map on page 239.

The two tours described in Travel Route 13 go south from Rome to Naples, passing from the province of Latium into Campania. The first route, through Velletri, begins inland, winding through the Castelli Romani, an area south of Rome filled with Medieval fortresses built by Roman popes and patricians, before reaching the sea at Terracina. The second route follows the coastline of the Tyrhennian Sea for the entire tour. From Terracina it is possible for you to make an excursion to the Ponza Islands. Both routes combine memories and ruins of imperial Rome with romantic views of the coastline and sea.

From Rome several good roads lead to Naples. The fastest is the Autostrada A 2. If you do not want to travel on the Autostrada, you can take Route S 6 (described in Travel Route 14) or Route S 7 through Velletri (see below). If you would like to travel along the coast (see page 238), make a detour along the Tyrrhenian Sea.

To Naples through Velletri

Follow the route marked "A" on the map on page 239.

Leave ***Rome (see page 35), follow the Via Appia Nuova (Route S 7) south through the Alban hills, dotted with old fortresses. This is the area of the *Castelli Romani* (see page 57), built in the Middle Ages by the popes and patrician families of Rome.

This route passes through several interesting towns before reaching Velletri: *Castel Gandolfo* (see page 59), the pope's summer residence on Lago Albano; *Albano Laziale* (see page 59); *Ariccia,* where there is a beautiful 17th-century square designed by Bernini that is surrounded by fine buildings; and *Genzano di Roma,* from which you can make an interesting side trip to a volcanic crater lake, **Lago di Nemi* (see page 58).

Velletri (41 km.; 25 miles from Rome) is near Monte Artemisio (842 meters; 2,750 feet) in a scenic vineyard setting. The Emperor Augustus was born here. On *Piazza Cairoli* is the *Palazzo Ginetti,* which contains a beautiful Baroque staircase and loggia, and the Romanesque-Gothic tower, *Torre del Trivio,* from the 14th century.

From Velletri you can make an interesting side trip to **Cori, *Norma* and **Ninfa* by following Route S 7 to *Cisterna di Latina* and then heading northeast for 13 km. (8 miles).

*Cori consists of the lower *Cori a Valle* and the higher *Cori a Monte,* with remains of an ancient **cyclopean wall.* The **Temple of Hercules* (Tempio d'Ercole) in the upper town dates from 90 B.C. and has an atrium surrounded by 9-meter- (30-foot-) high Doric columns. There is a splendid view. The little **church of Sant'Oliva,* with its two-story cloister and ancient columns, is located in the lower town, as is the collegiate church, which is built on the remains of a temple to Fortuna. The Via del Portico is a covered street between Medieval houses.

From Cori, go south towards Norma. In ***Norma** a path leads to the ruins of the old town of *Norba,* destroyed in Sulla's time. Here there is a well-preserved **cyclopean wall* (fourth century B.C.) about 2.5 km. (1.5 miles) long. Inside the wall are the remains of a temple complex and a museum displaying artifacts excavated from the site.

About 5 km. (3 miles) south of Norma stand the ruins of the Medieval city ***Ninfa,** deserted by its inhabitants in the 14th century because of continuing outbreaks of malaria. A fortress from the 13th century and a late Romanesque church and convent from the 12th–13th centuries remain. The surrounding Pontine Marshes were drained about 50 years ago and are now fertile fields.

By way of *Faiti,* Route S 7 reaches the coast at ***Terracina** (104 km.; 64 miles from Rome), a popular beach resort and an attractive fishing port. The **old district* around the *Piazza del Municipio,* where stone paving slabs of the Roman forum can be seen, is especially interesting. The **Duomo,* built on the remains of an ancient temple, contains fine mosaics from the 12th century, a portico, and a campanile in a Romanesque-Gothic transitional style.

Off the coast lie the volcanic **Isole Ponziane** (Ponza Islands), which can be reached by ferry from Anzio, Terracina, Formia or Naples. The main island, *Ponza,* consists of a crater 8 km. (5 miles) in diameter and 283 meters (930 feet) high. The towns of *Ponza* and *Santa Maria* lie at the base of the crater. Ponza is a beautiful, lush island whose inhabitants cultivate grapes and catch fish and lobsters. Pontius Pilate was governor of Ponza before becoming governor of Judea. The three other tiny islands—*Palmarola, Zannone* and *Ventotene*—are generally uninhabited, although there is a simple hotel on Ventotene and a summer restaurant on Palmarola.

To Naples along the Coast

Follow the route marked "B" on the map on page 239.

The trip along the coast from Rome to Naples is 40 km. (25 miles) longer than the drive through Velletri.

Leave ***Rome (see page 35) by *Porta San Paolo* and continue on Route S 8, also called Via del Mare, until you reach the sea at

Lido di Ostia (p. 57). From here, take the coastal road, Route S 601, southeast along the Tyrrhenian Sea through numerous resorts and campgrounds to ***Anzio** (73 km.; 45 miles from Rome), the birthplace of both Nero and Caligula; in the ruins of Nero's villa the *Apollo Belvedere* was discovered. Anzio was the scene of one of the bloodiest and most important battles of World War II. In January 1944 Allied troops landed here and at nearby *Nettuno* to draw German troops from Cassino in order to break through to Rome; after five months of intense fighting, they succeeded.

From Anzio several roads lead east to **Latina,** a city founded in 1939 after the Pontine Marshes were drained. It is the capital of Latina province and the center of a thriving agricultural industry.

Continue along the coastal road through *Sabaudia.* Between *Lago di Sabaudia* and the sea, atop the 541-meter- (1,775-foot-) *Monte Circeo* is **"Cape Circe,"** where Odysseus is supposed to have met the enchantress. The "Cave of Circe" is only a few feet from the road. The entire cape is protected because of its natural beauty. **San Felice Circeo,** the nearby town, is nestled in a scenic setting. Its Medieval fortress (13th century) offers a panoramic view of the area. From here it is a short drive to **Terracina** (144 km.; 89 miles from Rome; see page 238).

On Route S 7 head inland from Terracina, driving on a very beautiful stretch of road between *Lago*

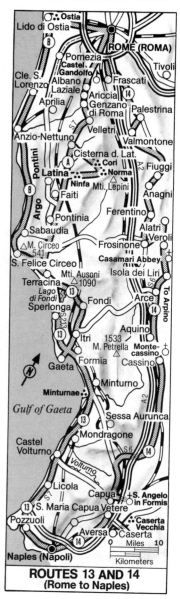

ROUTES 13 AND 14
(Rome to Naples)

di Fondi and the *Monti Ausoni* (up to 1,090 meters, or 3,576 feet high) to *Fondi,* an old city filled with palaces. The *church of San Pietro* contains a Romanesque pulpit and a remarkable Renaissance tomb. Route S 7 then heads southeast to *Itri,* nestled between cliffs and filled with Medieval buildings and a fortress. From Itri, follow Route S 7 through orange and olive groves and vineyards, praised by the Roman poet Horace, to *Formia* (see page 241).

Alternatively, the beautiful new coastal road, Route S 213, leads from *Terracina* to **Sperlonga,** a picturesque town set on a promontory with good swimming beaches. Among the many grottoes along the coast here, the *Grotta di Tiberio* is undoubtedly the most beautiful. Excellent muscatel grapes are grown on the slopes behind the town.

Farther along Route S 213, on a narrow peninsula, is ***Gaeta** (140 km.; 87 miles from Rome), a town that has preserved much of its Medieval heritage. It is dominated by a massive **Lombard castle* from the eighth century, renovated by successive princely houses— Hohenstaufen, Anjou and Aragon. Near the outer port stands the **Duomo* (Sant'Erasmo), dating from the 12th century, but renovated in the 17th century, with its campanile in a Renaissance-Moorish style and its many sculptures from the 12th and 13th centuries. Two ancient columns flank the main portal. Inside, note the **Paschal candelabrum* adorned with 48 reliefs representing scenes from the lives of Christ and Saint Erasmus.

On the summit of *Monte Orlando* stands the *Torre di Orlando,* the mausoleum of Lucius Munatius Plancus (20 B.C.), one of Caesar's generals, where there is a magnificent view.

Also on the Gaeta peninsula is the *Santuario della Montagna Spaccata,* with its pilgrimage church. The three unusually shaped crevasses in the 100-meter- (328-foot-) cliffs near the church were supposedly formed during an earthquake at the time of Christ's death.

Leave Gaeta by *Porto Salvo,* and you will shortly arrive at a Roman tomb on the left, known as **Tomba di Cicerone.* It is believed that Cicero, murdered in 43 B.C., is buried here. Continue on to

Minturnae

Formia, a popular resort with a wide beach. The ruins of ancient villas testify that Formia was a resort even in Roman times.

From Formia, Route S 7 follows the coast past the Aurunci Mountains. Continue on through the beach resort of *Scauri* and then alongside the arcades of an ancient aqueduct to the ruins of an old Roman city, ***Minturnae** (167 km.; 104 miles from Rome), which contains the remains of an ancient port, a forum, an amphitheater and several temples. A Roman aqueduct disappears into the mountain toward Minturno and the old baths of *Suio*.

Minturno lies about 7 km. (4 miles) inland. This Medieval town has a *castle* and the *church of San Pietro* from that period.

The coastal road continues to *Mondragone,* crosses the estuary of the Volturno near *Castel Volturno* and reaches the *Phlegraean Fields* near *Licola.* Passing through **Pozzuoli (see page 101) you will arrive in *****Naples** (245 km.; 152 miles from Rome; see page 84).

TRAVEL ROUTE 14: ***Naples–*Caserta (–*Benvento)–*Capua–**Montecassino–Frosinone–***Rome (240 km.; 149 miles)

See map on page 239.

There's a bit of everything in this route north from Naples to Rome. At Caserta you can explore a Baroque palace that was once the residence of the King of Naples. Extensive Roman ruins are found in Benevento, and there are more Etruscan and Roman remains in Santa Maria Capua Vetere. If you like things Medieval, there's the town of Capua and, closer to Rome, Altari, with its marvelous Medieval quarter. A side trip will take you into the Abruzzi National Park to enjoy the natural beauty of the Abruzzi mountains. Outside of Cassina is the Benedictine Abbey of Montecassino, founded in the sixth century; and the 13th-century Carthusian Trisulti monastery is found in the mountainous area of Collepardo.

This route can be covered on Route S 6 or, if you don't have much time, on the Autostrada A 2. The two roads run parallel and cross several times.

You can easily make this travel route a round trip by returning to Naples inland along Route S 17.

***Naples** (see page 84) to Capua (32 km.; 20 miles) can be reached directly on Route S 6 through *Aversa*. However, you may find it more interesting to make a short detour north along Route S 87 to ****Caserta** (28 km.; 17 miles from Naples), the former residence of the king of Naples. The Baroque ****palace** was commissioned by King Charles III of Naples and Sicily from Luigi Vanvitelli in 1752. A freestanding staircase of 116 marble steps leads to the royal apartments and palace chapel. The rooms are richly appointed and generously decorated with works of art. The palace's 253-meter- (830-foot-) long façade has a colonnade modeled after the one at Versailles. The surrounding ****park** is particularly beautiful, with magnificent fountains, cascades and statues. It was at Caserta that German forces formally surrendered to the Allies on April 29, 1945, a date which is now a national holiday in Italy.

From Caserta drive 8 km. (5 miles) northeast to ***Caserta Vecchia** on *Monte Tifata*, where you can visit the *castle* of the counts of Caserta and a **Duomo* (12th–13th centuries) in the Normano-Sicilian style.

About 42 km. (26 miles) east of Caserta on Route S 7 is **Benevento,** a once powerful city where in 265 B.C. the Romans won a decisive battle against King Pyrrhus of Epirus—the same king who had won his costly "Pyrrhic victory" over the Romans just a few years before. Benevento (then

called Beneventum) stood at the junction of the Via Appia and four other important roads, and thus it became one of the most important cities in the south. From the 6th to the 8th centuries it was the seat of the Lombard dukes. Later it was part of the Papal States.

The Romans built the **Arch of Trajan* (or *Porta Aurea*), considered one of the finest of its kind. Other Roman remains include a **theater* (second century B.C.); the *Leproso bridge,* which marks the Via Appia; and the Egyptian *obelisk* installed here by Domitian in A.D. 88.

The city walls, together with the *Torre della Catena* and the *Porta Arsa* (both built with Roman cut stones), date from the Lombard regime. The *Rocca dei Rettori* on *Piazza V Novembre* is a Lombard fortress rebuilt in the 14th century. On *Piazza Orsini* stands the Romanesque **Duomo* with its gigantic campanile. Another important church is *Santa Sofia,* whose **cloister* (12th century) houses the *Museo del Sannio,* which has collections of Egyptian, Greco-Roman, and Samnite antiquities, a good coin collection, and Medieval and modern paintings.

Leaving Caserta and driving west on Route S 7, you will come after 33 km. (20 miles) to ***Santa Maria Capua Vetere,** the site of ancient Capua, founded by the Etruscans. After the battle of Cannae in 216 B.C., Hannibal and his army occupied Capua, but they were defeated by the Romans under Scipio in 211. In the ninth century Capua was destroyed by the Saracens, and refugees from the city founded present-day Capua.

The *amphitheater (first century A.D., renovated under Hadrian) is certainly the most interesting site in town. Nearby, in an underground passageway, is an ancient *Mithraic temple* containing some splendid frescoes. Also nearby is the gladiatorial school where the slave revolt under Spartacus broke out in 73 B.C. The *cathedral of Santa Maria Maggiore* contains 51 columns from the ancient amphitheater.

A few miles farther is *Capua (40 km.; 25 miles from Naples), founded in the ninth century. The city has retained its Medieval appearance and numerous churches, among them the *Duomo di Santo Stefano* (built around 860), with its marble and granite columns remaining from the time of the Lombards. The campanile, too, dates from this period. You should also try to visit the Gothic *Palazzo Fieramosca* and the *Museo Campano, which, after the Museo Nazionale in Naples, contains the most important archaeological collection in this part of Italy. It displays Etruscan, Samnite, Roman, and Lombard artifacts, Greek vases, mosaics and many other important antiquities.

The *town hall* dates from the 16th century, and the Norman *castle* (11th century) was built with stones from the ancient amphitheater in Santa Maria Capua Vetere.

If you have the time, make the short drive northeast to the *church of Sant'Angelo in Formis,** built in 942 in Campanian-Romanesque style with Byzantine features. It was restored in 1071 and decorated with magnificent Byzantine **frescoes.*

Route S 6 continues parallel to the Autostrada. From Route S 6, pick up Route S 85 north to *Venafro* and then about 44 km. (27 miles) northeast to **Isernia,** set on a hill between the Sordo and Carpino rivers. Walk past the Medieval gateway lined with Roman statues to the *cathedral.* Other sights include the *campanile* and the *Fontana della Fraterna,* a Romanesque fountain with a beautiful loggia. West of the city lie the sparse remains of an ancient acropolis.

Isernia is a good point of departure for excursions into the *Abruzzi National Park.*

Route S 17 runs north from Isernia to *L'Aquila* (see page 246). On the way, numerous roads branch east, leading over the mountains to the Adriatic.

After returning to Route S 6, continue northwest to **Cassino** (101 km.; 63 miles from Naples), a city colonized by the Romans in 321 B.C. The ancient buildings were destroyed during World War II in the battle of Montecassino (1943–1944). After the war the city was rebuilt in a more modern style. Italian, English, Polish, French and German military cemeteries remind visitors of the bitter battle fought here in order to liberate Rome and northern Italy. A winding road leads through the *Zona Archeologica,* the remains of the ancient city, to the ****Abbey of Montecassino,** which was destroyed by bombs but rebuilt after the war according to the original plans. Montecassino is the cradle of the Benedictine order; Saint Benedict founded the abbey in 529. His tomb and that of his twin sister, Saint Scholastica, fortunately survived the war. In the 11th century, the monastery was the richest in the world and was a center of spiritual and artistic activity. The monks had achieved a high degree of skill in book illumination, fresco painting, and mosaic work, and they were imitated all over Europe.

About 12 km. (7 miles) past Cassino a road branches south off Route 6 to *Aquino,* birthplace of the Roman poet Juvenal and the family seat of Saint Thomas Aquinas.

From here to Rome, roads branch north off Route S 6 through the magnificent natural beauty of the Abruzzi. From *San Donato Val di Comino* there is an excellent tour of the Abruzzi National Park; take Route S 509 north from Cassino. From *Arce* drive north for 15 km. (9 miles) to **Arpino,** at an elevation of 500 meters (1,640 feet). This picturesque town is where Cicero, Caius Marius and Marcus Vipsanius Agrippa were born. The old quarter preserves part of a megalithic *city wall,* a pointed-arch *gate* and a Medieval *tower.*

Instead of returning to the main road and from there to Frosinone (see page 245), a short detour of about 25 km. (15 miles) will lead you from Arpino to the industrial town of *Isola del Liri* and the **Liri Falls.* Turn west on Route S 214 and drive 9 km. (6 miles) to ***Casamari Abbey,** founded in 1005 and restored in 1151 in a Gothic-Burgundian style. In subsequent centuries various extensions were added to the Cistercian abbey.

Shortly before the abbey a road branches south to *Monte San Giovanni Campano,* a picturesque town with Medieval walls and towers, where Saint Thomas Aquinas once was held prisoner.

Beyond the abbey a road leads 7 km. (4 miles) north to the old town of **Veroli,* at an elevation of 570 meters (1,870 feet), where an ancient cyclopean wall can be seen. From here the road leads to ****Alatri,** with its splendid Medieval quarter. Here you should see the Romanesque-Gothic **church of Santa Maria Maggiore* (12th–13th centuries) and its fortified campanile; the **church of San Francesco,* whose 14th-century façade is decorated with frescoes; and the remains of a pre-Roman **acropolis,* perhaps built by the Pelagians. From there you have a wonderful view of the surrounding countryside, including the Monti Ernici, ranging in height from 1,700 to 2,000 meters (5,500 to 6,500 feet). An interesting excursion from Alatri leads north about 7 km. (4 miles) through fine mountainscapes to **Collepardo,* where the Carthu-

y was built in
ent III.
Route S 155
e S 6 at **Frosi-**
97 miles from
he above detour).
he Cosa River. It,
point of departure
is to the towns
ove.

*Ferentino has preserved its
Medieval appearance and still
has its fortified *walls from the
Roman era.

From here you can follow S 6,
or pick up Autostrada A 2 a few
miles further on, to *****Rome**
(240 km.; 149 miles from Naples;
see page 35).

ROUTE 15: ***Rome–**Tivoli–Carsoli–
a (251/244 km.; 156/151 miles)

on page 247.

inerary leads east across the Apennine ranges. It is particularly
l for those who arrived in Rome via Tuscany and Latium and want
urn via the Adriatic coast. The route also connects the Tyrrhenian
Adriatic seas. Stops along the way allow you to explore the extensive
remains of the Emperor Hadrian's villa near Tivoli, a favorite excursion
spot of the Romans; Subiaco, famous for the monasteries founded by
Saint Benedict and Saint Scholastica; and the lovely mountainside town
of L'Aquila, with numerous Baroque palaces and a fascinating old quarter. Medieval Sulmona is surrounded by mountains where you can hike,
ski, or relax in an alpine setting; and Chieti, perched on its mountain
ridge, has Roman remains. Throughout this itinerary you'll come across
unfolding panoramic views and cable cars that ascend to wonderfully
scenic points. Soon the final stretches of a new autostrada will be completed; however, the trip along Route S 5 (via Tiburtina) is historically
more interesting.

Leaving ***Rome (see page 35),
travel east on S 5 across the Aniene
River to *Bagni di Tivoli,* a spa
whose thermal springs were used
even in Roman times. Quarries in
the area produce the *lapis Tibur-*
tinus used in the construction of
Saint Peter's and the Roman Colosseum. Cross the Aniene a second time and take the road leading
south to the historically significant **Villa Adriana (Hadrian's

Villa) (see page 57). Return to S 5
and continue to ****Tivoli** (31 km.;
19 miles from Rome; see page 57),
a favorite excursion spot for
Romans.

Continue along S 5 to *Roviano*
where it is possible to make an 18
km. (11 mile) side trip to *Subiaco.*
Just after Roviano turn south onto
S 411 and follow the Aniene River
to ***Subiaco,** located in the upper
Aniene valley at the foot of Monte

Livata (1,429 meters; 4,688 feet). Saint Benedict (San Benedetto) and his twin sister, Saint Scholastica, founded several monasteries here at the end of the fifth century. In Subiaco, the **Monastero di San Benedetto* is impressively set at the foot of a steep cliff. The monastery's entrance is cut into the rock. The present structure dates mostly from the 13th–14th centuries; Saint Benedict lived in the *Sacro Speco* (Holy Grotto). The monastery church and many of its rooms are richly decorated with Medieval frescoes.

In the gorge of the Aniene lies the *Monastero di Santa Scolastica*. The oldest part of the present monastery is the Romanesque *bell tower* (1053). The other buildings were constructed in the 13th century. The *cloisters* are particularly interesting.

In Subiaco itself is the *Rocca*, an 11th-century fortress that Pope Pius VI used as his palace in 1778; now the structure belongs to the Benedictines.

Route S 5 winds its way north to *Carsoli;* at this point you can continue through L'Aquila or Avezzano.

Through *L'Aquila

Follow the route marked "A" on the map.

To avoid the winding, steep mountain road, it is best to follow Autostrada A 24 from Carsoli to *L'Aquila.** The city stands at the foot of Monte Luco, which can be circled on a beautiful panoramic road. L'Aquila was the second city to be founded in the kingdom of Naples; it has preserved its old appearance. Be sure to visit its Baroque palaces.

The best place to start a tour of L'Aquila is at the *Duomo*, with its 18th-century Neoclassical façade. From the *Piazza del Duomo*, which has two fountains and is the scene of a daily market, continue north on Via Cavour to the Romanesque *church of Santa Maria di Paganica* (1308), with numerous palaces from the 15th century nearby. Next, visit the 16th-century *castello,* which houses the *Museo Nazionale d'Abruzzo*, displaying archaeological finds, sculptures, paintings, and other works of art. To the south is the 15th-century *basilica of San Bernardino*, with its beautiful Renaissance sculptures, its carved and gilded Baroque ceiling, and the tomb of Bernardino of Siena, who died in L'Aquila in 1444.

The picturesque *Via Fortebraccio* begins at the foot of a free-standing staircase across from the basilica. West of the city gate, *Porta Bazzano*, and dominated by the Romanesque *church of San Giusta* (13th–14th centuries) is the *old quarter* of the city.

Go through the Porta Bazzano to reach the *church of Santa Maria di Collemaggio* (13th century). In 1294, Pope Celestine V, the founder of the Celestine order, was crowned pope in this church, which he had commissioned. He is buried here in a Renaissance tomb

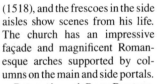

(1518), and the frescoes in the side aisles show scenes from his life. The church has an impressive façade and magnificent Romanesque arches supported by columns on the main and side portals.

Return through Porta Bazzano, turn left down the stairs to Via Celestino V, and follow this to Corso Federico II. Turn right for a block, then left to the *church of San Marco,* with its two portals from the 14th–15th centuries. One block west of the church is the picturesque *Via Arcivescovado,* lined with *palaces.* Around the

Santa Maria di Collemaggio

nearby 14th-century *church of Santa Maria di Roio*, there are more old palaces.

Via Fontesecco leads to the unique **Fontana delle 99 Cannelle*, a 13th-century fountain made from red and white stone. Its 99 water-spouting masks commemorate the 99 castles that, according to legend, originally made up the town.

L'Aquila is a good point of departure for excursions into the Abruzzi mountains, especially to the *Gran Sasso d'Italia* (Great Rock of Italy) area. An excellent new Autostrada, A 24, leads north for 10 km. (6 miles) to **Assergi,** where the *church of Santa Maria Assunta* has a Gothic façade, a rose window and a 12th-century crypt. From Assergi a panoramic road leads to the cable car that ascends the western edge of **Campo Imperatore* (2,130 meters; 7,000 feet) and provides a splendid view of the entire

Abruzzi range. There is a modern chapel and a new observatory near the cable-car station. This area is a popular walking and climbing center and ski resort; experienced climbers who reach the top of the *Corno Grande,* the highest peak, will be rewarded with a magnificent vista that extends over the whole of central Italy to the Adriatic on the east and over the Sabine mountains as far as the Tyrrhenian Sea on the west.

Leaving L'Aquila, travel west on Route S 80 to the ruins of *Amiternum,* where S 80 turns northeast. Continue on this scenic winding road over the *Passo delle Capannelle* (1,299 meters; 4,262 feet), where there is another fine view. On the way down from the pass, detour 4 km. (2.5 miles) north to *Lago di Campotosto,* an artificial lake. To the south towers the mighty *Gran Sasso.* Continue northeast on Route S 80 past *Nerito* and *Montorio al Vomano* with its fine Medieval church to **Teramo** (189 km.; 117 miles from Rome), whose 12th-century *cathedral* in the center of town has a fine Romanesque-Gothic portal dating from 1322, a 15th-century silver altar frontal and a particularly beautiful **polyptych* (15th-century) by Jacopo del Fiore. Southeast of the cathedral are the ruins of a *Roman theater.* The *church of Sant'Agostino,* located in largo Melatini, dates from the 13th–14th centuries; nearby is the Medieval *Casa dei Signori di Melatino.* A small museum is located in the municipal park.

Route S 80 now continues along the Tordino River, reaching the Adriatic coast at *Giulianova*. From here, continue south on Route S 16 through the popular seaside resorts of *Roseto degli Abruzzi, Pineto, Silvi Marina* and *Montesilvano Marina* to **Pescara** (251 km.; 156 miles from Rome; see page 217).

Through Avezzano

Follow the route marked "B" on the map.

From *Carsoli*, go east to Avezzano on Autostrada A 24 and then A 25 or on Route S 5. Route S 5 passes through beautiful landscapes, winding its way up to *Tagliacozzo*, a popular summer resort perched 900 meters (3,000 feet) above sea level in a beautiful pine forest.

Avezzano (116 km.; 72 miles from Rome), in the northwest corner of the Fucino basin—which was Italy's largest lake until it was drained in 1854–1876—is a major commercial and agricultural city. Tragedy struck in 1915 when an earthquake claimed the lives of 30,000 people and almost completely destroyed the town. The surrounding area is particularly suited to growing vegetables and there are vineyards and groves of almond and olive trees. Some 7 km. (4 miles) north are the mysterious and massive remains of an ancient fortified town, *Alba Fucens*, which belonged to the Aequi tribe and became a Roman *municipium*. In the town of *Albe*, an 11th-century Romanesque church has been built into the former temple of Apollo.

From Avezzano, Route S 5 heads northeast, across the Forca Caruso pass (1,107 meters; 3,632 feet), to **Popoli**, a busy town on the bank of the Pescara River and dominated by the ruins of an old fortress. The 15th-century *church of San Francesco* in the *Piazza Grande* has a Romanesque façade surmounted by a Baroque summit. A curious little Gothic structure, the *Taverna Ducale* (14th century), used to be a storehouse for tithes payable to the local duke; on its façade are dynastic coats of arms and lively bas-reliefs of animals, musicians and dancers.

To make a side trip to *Bominaco* (26 km.; 16 miles), drive northwest from Popoli on Route S 17 toward L'Aquila (see page 246). After about 20 km. (12 miles), on the left a mountain road turns south to Caporciano and Bominaco, which boasts two beautiful Romanesque churches, *San Pellegrino* and *Santa Maria*.

Another possible side trip takes you from Popoli to *Sulmona* (18 km.; 11 miles). From Popoli follow Route S 17 south to **Sulmona**, a market town in a fertile basin surrounded by 2,000-meter (6,500-foot) mountains. Sulmona was the birthplace of the Roman poet Ovid (43 B.C. to circa A.D. 17). The ruins of a Roman aqueduct, renovated in the 13th century, remain. The town has preserved its Medieval character, and during its Easter celebration a statue of the Virgin is carried to a meeting with the Risen Christ; her dark clothes of mourning are exchanged for joyous robes of verdant green when she comes within sight of her Son.

The *Palazzo dell'Annunziata*, built in Gothic style in 1415 by a Brotherhood of Penitents, was enlarged in Renaissance style in the 15th–16th centuries and is considered the most beautiful civic building in the Abruzzi region. It houses the *Museo Civico*. Other sights here include the Gothic *Porta Napoli*, built in the 14th century and embellished with historiated capitals and roses; and a Romanesque-Gothic portal, all that remains of the *church of San Francesco della Scarpa*, which was destroyed in several earthquakes. In the *Piazza Garibaldi*, where a large market is held twice a week, a Renaissance fountain, *Fontana del Vecchio*, is fed by the aqueduct that borders the square on two sides; a great Gothic door, once belonging to the church of St. Martin, stands at the end of the piazza.

Around Sulmona there are many winter and summer resorts. Well-preserved Romanesque churches are found in abundance.

From *Popoli*, Route S 5 continues northeast along the Pescara River. ***Torre de' Passeri** is dominated by the monumental **monastery of San Clemente a Casauria*, founded by the Emperor Louis II in 871 and rebuilt by the Cistercians in the 12th century. It is the oldest of many Cistercian monasteries in the Abruzzi.

*Chieti (227 km.; 141 miles from Rome) is an old town on a mountain ridge, and was founded, according to legend, by Achilles. Three small Roman temples of the first century A.D. remain. To the left of *Corso Marrucino*, the town's busiest street, is a first-century Roman cistern dug into the mountain to provide water for the baths. The *cathedral of San Giustino* has a beautiful bell tower (14th–15th centuries) and a Baroque crypt. The pre-Roman, Roman Republic, and Roman Empire collections in the *Museo Nazionale di Antichità* are well worth seeing; in particular, look for the sixth-century B.C. *Warrior of Capestrano*, found in a necropolis and remarkably preserved.

From Chieti you can make pleasant trips into the forests and high plateaus around *La Maielletta* (1,995 meters; 6,545 feet), an hour or so away by car. Route S 5 begins a gentle descent into **Pescara** (244 km.; 151 miles from Rome; see page 217).

Roman Temple, Chieti

TRAVEL ROUTE 16: ***Naples–***Pompeii–***Sorrento–***Positano–**Amalfi–**Salerno–***Paestum–Sapri–Paola–*Cosenza–Catanzaro (539 km.; 334 miles)

See map on page 252.

This Travel Route takes you south from Naples along, perhaps, the most beautiful coastline in the world. En route you'll pass through the eerie excavated sites of Herculaneum and Pompeii, the cliffside resorts of Sorrento and Amalfi, and the old Greek city of Paestum. The route terminates in the region of the majestic Sila Massif. Bear in mind that nothing but a prayer stands between the twisty road with its hairpin curves and the steep cliff precipices along which it travels and that the drive between Sorrento and Amalfi can be extremely dangerous for all but the most expert drivers.

Leave ***Naples (see page 84) by Corso Umberto I and Via Stella Polare to connect with Route S 18. Follow S 18 southeast through Portici to **Herculaneum (Ercolano, see page 99), where part of an ancient city has been excavated from under the mud of Vesuvius' A.D. 79 eruption.

Route S 18 then continues through *Torre del Greco* and *Torre Annunziata* to the excavations of *****Pompeii** (see page 100). Here one should set aside at least half a day for a visit. From Pompeii head south on Route S 145 to **Castellamare di Stabia,** where the Roman springs of Stabiae were destroyed in A.D. 79 by Vesuvius. Now the town is again a favorite resort in the area because of its thermal springs and beach resorts. The name Castellamare (castle on the sea) is derived from Frederick II Hohenstaufen's castle, later occupied by the Angevins. The public park (*Villa Comunale*)

offers a splendid view of the Gulf of Naples, as does the higher part of town, where Robert of Anjou lived in his country estate, *Villa Quisisana.*

A winding private toll road leads to the 1,103-meter- (3,619-foot-) peak of ***Monte Faito,* whose mountain landscape of pine forests, rock walls and steep cliffs is reminiscent of the Alps. The view of the Sorrentine peninsula and the isle of Capri is magnificent.

Continue along the coast on Route S 145 through the vacation resorts of *Vico Equense, Seiano, Meta,* and *Sant'Agnello,* to *****Sorrento** (51 km.; 32 miles from Naples), a populous resort with wonderful panoramic views from its terraces. The steep cliffs permit no beaches, but colorful bathing pavilions have been erected along the shore, beneath cliffs planted with grapevines and orange groves.

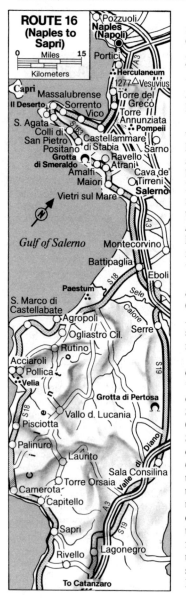

ROUTE 16
(Naples to
Sapri)

Points of interest in Sorrento include the *Piazza Tasso*, with its Carmelite church and statues of Sant'Antonino and Torquato Tasso—the Renaissance poet who was born here and wrote *Jerusalem Delivered*—and the elegant hotel *Excelsior Vittoria;* the *Palazzo Veniero* in *Strada Pietà;* the **Palazzo Correale**, which houses an archaeological museum and an art gallery, and has a fine belvedere; the *Duomo*, with a Romanesque façade and numerous works of art inside, and the *church and monastery of *San Francesco* (14th century), now housing an art school. The nearby municipal park offers stunning views from the belvedere terrace.

From the port of *Marina Piccola* boats leave regularly for Capri and towns south along the Amalfi Drive—another way to see the beautiful coast in the summer months.

A pleasant walk through gardens and olive groves leads to **Punta di Sorrento** and a panoramic view. To get there, leave Sorrento going west on Via del Capo; at the junction, take the Sant'Agata road on the right. You can leave your car in the piazza at *Capo di Sorrento*. Take the road on the right, past the modern church, then follow the valley down through gardens and olives. At the end there is a magnificent view of the Bay of Naples. Sorrento is famous for its intarsia work, a technique utilizing paper-thin sheets of lacquered inlaid wood. Intarsia work can be seen in some of the nearby factories and outlet stores.

Leave Sorrento along the panoramic Route S 145, past *Massalubrense* and through *Sant'Agata* to the monastery of *Il Deserto* (455 meters, 1,460 feet, above sea level), whose terraces look in every direction—back to Naples, out to sea, and along the Sorrentine peninsula.

Now S 145 joins S 163, which follows a ridge along the top of the peninsula's hilly terrain to ***Positano** (80 km.; 50 miles from Naples), one of the most picturesque towns in Europe, a hill of pastel houses brimming with bright flowers and backed by dramatic cliffs. Tiny, pebbly beaches allow some swimming, but hotel swimming pools are needed for the real thing. Painters and poets have celebrated Positano, and tourists crowd the steep, narrow paths all summer, especially in August, when cars and buses fill the coast road and people jam the town's mini-arteries. (Spring and fall are magnificent.)

Route S 163 winds along the coast to Capo di Conca where, far below, the **Grotta di Smeraldo* (Emerald Grotto) rivals Capri's Blue Grotto. The stalactite and stalagmite formations are impressive, and a Nativity scene in ceramics glows from beneath the clear water. Take the trip by boat from Amalfi.

**Amalfi* (93 km.; 58 miles from Naples) is another lovely town, more obviously a real fishing port than postcard-perfect Positano. Lying in a gorge of the mountains, its impressive cliffs, castles and cathedrals create a dramatic sight.

During the Middle Ages Amalfi was an independent and very prosperous maritime republic; navigation in those days was based on the *Tavole Amalfitane,* Amalfi Navigation Tables, the first written naval code known.

At the center of the town is a **piazza* with a charming fountain, and one of the most beautiful cathedrals of southern Italy— the Arab-Norman ***Duomo di Sant'Andrea,* a fantasy of color and design, impressively situated at the top of a long staircase. The tomb of Saint Andrew, patron saint of sailors, is located in the crypt, which is beautifully decorated with statues and columns. The cloister, **Chiostro del Paradiso* (12th century), is a harmonious

Duomo di Sant'Andrea

blend of Arab arches and strong Norman forms, enlivened further by a lovely tiled *campanile and palm trees, all typical of the Moorish style prevalent in Sicily during the 12th century.

Other sights in Amalfi include the *town hall,* where memorabilia from Amalfi's past grandeur are displayed, and the busy seafront promenade, *Corso Flavio Gioia,* named for the Amalfitano inventor of the compass, who also is honored with a statue in the piazza.

Atrani is a delightful old fishing village that is protected from intense tourism by the unfortunate highway that rises over the town, cutting it off from full view. The town's old Moorish quality is enchanting, and although there is little to see in the way of monuments, it is a wonderful place to walk through (up steep streets and steps). To reach Atrani, take the street that leads to the right and down from Amalfi, at the far end of town where the highway turns left up the hill. The Duomo, *San Salvatore,* has 11th-century bronze doors forged in Constantinople.

From here you can make a side trip to Ravello (5 km.; 3 miles) by continuing northeast on Route S 163 just past Amalfi, turning left onto Route S 366, a **panoramic road* and following it to the town. **Ravello,** about 350 meters (1,150 feet) above sea level, is one of the loveliest towns in Italy, and commands unequaled coastal views. The **Duomo di San Pantaleone,* from 1086, has a restored

façade with doors from the earlier façade. The marble *pulpit with mosaics is magnificent, as is the 12th-century lectern, both with intricate carvings. The cathedral museum, entered from the cathedral, also contains some fine works of art. The **Villa Rufolo is one of the most romantic villas ever created, with crumbling vine-covered walls that still reflect the grace of Moorish arches. The view from the gardens is breathtaking. Several popes and emperors have been on the guest list here, and Richard Wagner wrote sections of *Parsifal* after seeing this site. Each summer a Wagner Festival adds music to the beauty of the architecture and natural surroundings. The unusual **Villa Cimbrone has a wonderful cloister, and the *Belvedere boasts exhilarating views of the entire coast; a hidden grotto, gardens, and statuary complete the enchantment.

While in Ravello, be sure to walk along the scenic *Via Annunziata,* which leads under arches and down the mountain, opening onto views of the coast.

Return to the coast road, Route S 163, and continue northeast through *Maiori,* a beach resort surrounded by lemon groves, and through the steep *Capo d'Orso,* with its 16th-century watchtower.

Vietri sul Mare, a town near Salerno, is devoted almost entirely to ceramics. Artisan shops and galleries cluster around the town square and fill the streets beyond, up the hillside. The Tourist Office

in the central piazza has information about watching the potters at
work.

From Route S 163, turn east on
Route S 18 and continue to
*Salerno (117 km.; 73 miles
from Naples), once a Greek settlement, then a Lombard duchy in
the early Middle Ages. Under
Robert Guiscard the Norman,
Salerno became capital of the Norman empire in southeastern Italy.
From this era the ****Duomo**
remains (1076–1085), founded on
the ruins of an ancient church that
contains the tomb of the apostle
Saint Matthew. The cathedral has
a massive tower and a Norman
atrium resting on 28 classical columns. The Romanesque *Lions'
Portal* leads to an attractive courtyard. The triple-aisled interior
contains an impressive ***pulpit*,
richly decorated with mosaics and
resting on 12 columns whose capitals are adorned with figures. The
*Paschal candelabra also is richly
inlaid with mosaic patterns. The
cathedral museum has a fine art
collection; note especially the
ivory manger.

The most picturesque street of
Salerno, which was largely rebuilt
after heavy bombing during World
War II, is the Medieval **Via Mercanti,* just south of the cathedral,
which leads to the western side of
the town at the *Arechi Arch,*
erected during the eighth century
by Lombards and rebuilt later by
Normans. The *Lombard castle*
that dominates parts of Salerno
commands some fine views of the
area and has a picture collection.

The **Museo Provinciale* displays archaeological artifacts,
ceramics, and other works of art,
as well as diplomas of Salerno's old
medical school, founded in the
11th century. The school's Medical Codex was long the standard
text of the field.

Leaving Salerno, follow Route
S 18 east and inland. At *Battipaglia,* pick up Route S 19 east
through *Eboli* to the **Grotta di
Pertosa* (50 km.; 31 miles, from
Salerno), interesting for its stalactite caves, where Neolithic objects
have been found.

From Eboli follow the Autostrada A 3 east for about an hour to
make a side trip to ***Potenza** (96
km.; 60 miles from Eboli; 823
meters, 2,700 feet, above sea
level), in the Basento river valley.
The city's history begins in Roman
times, and the Medieval section is
filled with old alleyways and
nooks that recall this period as
well. Farther down on the slopes is
the colorful modern district. Of
the many churches, *San Francesco* (1274), with its attractive
15th-century portals, is one of the
most interesting to visit. Also
notable are *San Michele* (11th century); *Santissima Trinità,* with its
remarkable apse; *Santa Maria del
Sepolcro* (13th century), for its
interesting façade; and the
Duomo, elaborate in frescoes and
18th-century decorations.

The *Museo Provinciale Lucano*
displays archaeological artifacts
and a rich folklore collection,
which includes the creative work
of shepherds.

From Potenza Route S 96 heads northeast through Altamura (see page 232) to Bari (see page 223), and Route S 407 continues east across the "boot's instep" to Metaponto (see page 264).

The inland route to *Cosenza* leaves Grotta di Pertosa, following Route S 19 southeast, parallel to the Autostrada and along the Tanagro River. The road here is flanked by mountains 1,600 to 1,800 meters (5,250 to 5,900 feet) high. Drive by way of *Sala Consilina, Lagonegro, Morano* (Gothic church of San Bernadino), past Monte Pollino (2,248 meters; 7,375 feet) to arrive in *Castrovillari,* where there is an interesting church, Santa Maria del Castello (built on Roman ruins), and the fortifications from the time of Ferdinand of Aragon. Cross the Coscile River and continue south to Cosenza (see page 258). (This is a good, fast route to Calabria.)

Along the coast from *Battipaglia* (see page 255), take Route S 18 south across the Sele River to *****Paestum** (157 km.; 97 miles from Naples). The overwhelming temples here, built by Doric Greeks from Sybaris around 650 B.C. in the city they called Poseidonia, are among the most impressive Greek temples in Italy. They are exquisitely situated in fields of wildflowers, and the grounds are beautifully tended. In 273 B.C. the city fell to the Romans, who made it a naval base.

The exquisite ****Temple of Neptune,* now known to have been dedicated to Hera (Juno), dates from about 550 B.C. An impressive structure in the honey tones typical of the south (though, in their day, the temples were whitewashed), this is the best-preserved Doric temple anywhere. With 14 columns on each side and six at the ends, it creates a magnificent feeling of Classical strength amid a natural setting of fields and, in the distance, the mountains and the sea.

The **Basilica (circa 640 B.C.) is the oldest building in Paestum and probably was also a temple to Hera. As with most temples in southern Italy, we do not know for sure to which god each was dedicated, and most are misnamed. This temple was called a basilica during the 18th century, when excavations were carried out. It's a large structure, of 18 columns per side, and is imposing rather than poetically beautiful, as is the Temple of Neptune.

The ***Temple of Ceres,* though far less well preserved, is still evocative of its period. The cella apparently was transformed into a church during the Middle Ages, because Christian tombs have been found. Since the area then was largely abandoned, because of malaria and pirate raids, little is known about the site until the 18th century, when excavations were begun.

The **Museum is a delight, especially for the murals from the recently excavated Tomb of the Diver (about 480 B.C.), as it has been called from the graceful form of a man diving as if into a pool, but actually into eternity. Other murals in the tomb have made it one of the most talked-about archaeological finds of the century. The metopes from the Temple of Hera near the mouth of the Sele River, placed as if along a temple top, are wonderfully presented. On the whole this is one of the most attractive small museums in Italy.

The museum is a short walk down the road from the entrance to the archaeological area. For an overview of the city, walk along the town walls, which date from the fifth century B.C. There is a restaurant on the grounds. You can also go toward the sea and the cove of *Palinuro,* where there is a small village, and you can visit nearby *Velia* (see below) as well.

From Paestum you can continue along the coast (Route S 267) or go inland on Route S 18. Both alternatives offer lovely scenery. The slowly rising mountain road, S 18, leads south to the Cilento region on the mountainous peninsula between the gulfs of Salerno and Policastro and then follows the wide valley of the Alento River. Along the way the small, picturesque towns are enjoyable to explore. Stone houses with bright-colored roofs, huddled around a church, are a frequent sight.

If time and weather permit, you might travel by mule from *Novi Velia* (just east of *Vallo della Lucania*) to *Monte Sacro,* or **Gelbison,* where there is a marvelous view. About a three-hour ride will take you up 1,700 meters (5,600 feet).

The coast along Route S 267 is entirely different, a still unspoiled seascape of fishing villages and coves with sandy beaches. At *Agropoli* there are ruins of a Medieval fortress. Offshore, *Punto Licosa,* a lonely rock formation, rises from the sea—a siren turned to stone, who waits and waits for redemption, according to legend.

Shortly after *Acciaroli,* cross the Alento River to the ruins of the city of ****Velia.** In 540 B.C., in the Greek colony then called Elea, Xenophanes, a Greek philosopher and poet, founded the Eleatic school of philosophy, which counted Parmenides and Zeno among its followers. The ruins are not in good condition, but excavation and restoration projects have begun. You can make out the original plan of city walls, streets and squares, baths and temples. A watchtower from a Medieval castle holds its own amid the ancient Greek world.

At nearby *Marina di Ascea* there is a wide sandy beach for a swim. Continue along the coast on Route S 447 (from which roads branch north to Route S 18) to *Palinuro,* whose pretty position amid rocky cliffs, sandy beach and sea brings lots of Italian vacationers throughout the warm weather.

Return to S 18 by Route S 562 along the slopes of *Monte Bulgheria,* 1,225 meters (4,000 feet) high, where the Cilento coast ends, and arrive, in a short time, at **Sapri** (280 km.; 174 miles from Naples on Route S 18; 309 km., 192 miles, from Naples on the coast road). The city is located on the *Gulf of Policastro,* in an area with relatively few tourists. Its blue inlets, mountain ranges dotted with chestnut groves and scrub forests, small towns towering on cliffs above the sea, and ruined watchtowers that once told of approaching pirates, are all distinctive sights in this region. Then Route S 18 continues along the coast. Just past *Porto di Maratea* there is another swimming beach.

*Praia a Mare has a tourist resort at the beach and a church that attracts pilgrims because of the miraculous *statue of the Madonna* that was brought here in 1326 from Sicily.

Scalea, is built in a pyramid shape above the coast and shelters the *church of San Nicola* and a Medieval castle.

Diamante is known for its scenic beach and the sweet-smelling shade of its cedar groves. Stop beyond it at *Belvedere Marittimo* for a splendid view. The next coastal valley (overdeveloped) is *Belvedere,* also with a nice beach.

Continue through several more villages to **Paola,** birthplace of San Francesco da Paola (1416–1506), who founded the Minims, a strict Franciscan order. The monastery he founded, the *Santuario di San Francesco,* lies 1.5 km. (1 mile) north of the town. It is built in Renaissance style and contains lovely Gothic cloisters. In the part of town called *Guadimari* is an eighth-century Byzantine church.

From Paola there are two routes to Catanzaro. The coast road, S 18, goes south by way of *San Lucido, Fiumefreddo* and *Amantea* to *Sant'Eufemia Lamezia,* where Route S 280 branches east toward *Catanzaro* (see page 259). Or you can make a detour through *Cosenza.* If you opt for the latter, take Route S 107 from Paola, which climbs steeply inland over the 900-meter- (2,950-foot-) *Crocetta Pass,* providing views of the sea, to join Route S 19, and continue to ***Cosenza,** which stands at the confluence of the Crati and Busento rivers and still has many buildings from its past glory— Norman, Hohenstaufen, Anjou, and Aragon palaces and churches. Although earthquakes have destroyed much of the city, the picturesque **old town,* built on the slopes of the Colle Pancrazio, retain a note of fascination. The new town extends north from the Busento.

At the confluence of the rivers, the *church of San Domenico* raises its Gothic façade. Cross the *Ponte Alarico* to the *church of San Francesco da Paola,* which has an interesting **triptych* (1522). Climbing higher to the **Duomo,* we find a 12th-century Romanesque building that was later finished in Gothic style, with three portals of pointed arches and beautiful rose windows. Inside, the aisles are made on horseshoe arches, supported by Romanesque pillars. The **tomb of Isabella of Aragon,* wife of King Philip III of France, is a noteworthy example of French Gothic art. She took a fatal fall from her horse near here while returning to France from Sicily. In the *Tesoro dell'Arcivescovado* behind the cathedral is a magnificent Byzantine gold and enamel cross, with enamel panels depicting religious themes. (It can be seen on request.) It was a gift of Frederick II Hohenstaufen to the cathedral upon its consecration.

Routes S 107, S 108 bis, and S 109 are some of the scenic roads that traverse this unusually beautiful region, allowing you to make a noteworthy side trip to the mountainous **Sila Massif,** known as the Italian Switzerland for its dramatic beauty. The northern part is called *Sila Greca,* the central *Sila Grande,* and the southern part *Sila Piccola.* All are rich with vegetation and pine forests, rushing mountain streams, meadows and herds of cattle. The average altitude is 1,200 meters (3,900 feet), but several peaks top 1,600 meters (5,250 feet). The highest is the *Botte Donato*—1,930 meters (6,330 feet). Because the area is off the main roads, the towns have retained some of their Medieval character and present village scenes of Italy long ago. Some of the best hotels can be found at *Lorica* by *Lago Arvo,* where there is also skiing, and *Villaggio Mancuso* (south on Route S 179 dir.), another winter-sports village.

One possibility is to take scenic Route S 107 eastward from Cosenza, around Monte Botte Donato, over passes offering wide-angle views, through rocky landscapes, mountain towns and dark forests, all the way to *Crotone*

(see page 267) where Route S 106 then continues southward to *Catanzaro.* Another possibility—this one not leading so far to the east—follows S 107 eastward from Cosenza to the scenic town of *San Giovanni in Fiore;* backtrack from here to S 108 bis, and take this to Coraci, where you can pick up highway S 109, east to *Catanzaro.*

Several Albanian colonies have created a life apart here in the mountains of the *Sila Greca.* Descendants of Albanians who fled the Turks during the 15th century, they still preserve their own language and culture, though they've clearly been influenced by their Italian neighbors.

We leave Cosenza on our way south on Route S 19, driving parallel to the Autostrada as far as *Rogliano,* a scenic town at 700 meters (2,300 feet). From here S 19 meanders through *Carpanzaro, Coraci, Soveria Mannelli,* and *Tiriolo* to **Catanzaro.** The capital of its province, Catanzaro is the industrial, agricultural, and commercial center of the area and the episcopal seat. *San Domenico,* or *Chiesa del Rosario,* has an 18th-century Neoclassical façade and a late Baroque interior. The statue of the *Redeemer* (15th-century) by the Flemish artist Dirk Hendricksz and a portrait of the *Madonna of the Rosary* are especially noteworthy. The *Museo Provinciale* has a good collection of antiquities, and a *Madonna* by Gagini adorns the *church of the*

Osservanza in the modern section of town. The *basilica of the Immacolata* has some lovely Neapolitan paintings.

The *church of San Giovanni*, built in 1532, stands next to the remains of an old Norman castle, which has been altered several times.

From the *city park* there is a splendid view all the way across to the Ionian Sea.

The beach of *Catanzaro Lido* is 13 km. (8 miles) away on the *Gulf of Squillace* (see page 268);

Other excursions include the ruins of the 11th-century *church of Santa Maria in Rocella*, 3 km. (2 miles) south; *Taverna* (28 km.; 17 miles) to the north, where the *church of San Domenico* contains many paintings by the famous Baroque artist Mattia Preti, who

Santa Maria in Roccella

was born here; and trips in the **Sila Massif (see page 259).

You can continue the trip south from Catanzaro using Travel Route 17.

TRAVEL ROUTE 17: Catanzaro–Pizzo–*Vibo Valentia–*Palmi–*Reggio di Calabria (174 km.; 108 miles)

See map on page 262.

This route is a continuation of Travel Route 16. The fastest connection is the Autostrada, as always, but S 18 is a better route for scenery that includes fishing villages and seaside resorts.

Leave *Catanzaro* (see page 259) going west, and follow Route S 19 dir. for 42 km. (26 miles) along the Amato River to **Sant'Eufemia Lamezia** and the coast of the Tyrrhenian Sea. Near there, at *Gizzeria Lido*, the beach is pleasant, and the vineyard-covered slopes make a nice backdrop. Northeast of Lamezia is the charming mountain-slope town of *Nicastro*, where you might stop before proceeding south on Route S 18, along the coast, to **Pizzo** (67 km.; 42 miles from Catanzaro) a vacation resort on the *Gulf of Sant'Eufemia.* The town has a nice beach and a fortress where Joachim Murat, Napoleon's brother-in-law and King of Naples, was executed in 1815.

Continue on Route S 18 inland to ***Vibo Valentia,** a resort on the high plateau of *Tavolato del Poro,* at an elevation of 556 meters (1,825 feet), near an ancient site that the Greeks called Hipponion. From these lofty heights you can see Sicily, the Aeolian Islands and the snow-capped peak of Mt. Etna. The town was an intellectual center in the 18th century and, under Murat, was the provincial capital. Sights include the partially excavated walls of the Greek *Acropolis, the Doric *Temple of Persephone; the Medieval *Norman castle renovated by Frederick II (who built castles throughout southern Italy); and churches such as the Baroque *Leoluca,* (Santa Maria Maggiore) where Antonello Gagini's marble group of the *Madonna and Saints* is excellent, and the delightful little *San Michele,* in Renaissance style. The *State Archaeological Museum* houses relics of the proud history of this region.

From Vibo Valentia it is possible to make a side trip 41 km., (25 miles) to *Serra San Bruno* (800 meters; 2,600 feet above sea level). This summer resort, located at the foot of *Monte Pecoraro* amid forests of beech

and fir, is known for its mineral water, which has medicinal properties. The nearby Carthusian monastery of *Santo Stefano del Bosco* was built by Bruno of Cologne (founder of the order) in 1090 on a site given to him by Count Roger the Norman.

Backtrack a bit to detour along the *coast road,* Route S 522, to *Gioia Tauro.* The road starts in *Pizzo* (see above) and leads to the beach resorts of *Briatico* and *Parghelia.*

*Tropea, just beyond Parghelia, is a small town, scenically situated, with an interesting *cathedral* whose artworks include a 14th-century wooden crucifix and a fine statue of the Madonna. Down near the beach on a large rock stands *Santa Maria dell'Isola,* a Medieval Benedictine church.

Continue along the coast road, past more beaches at the foot of cliffs stretching all the way to *Capo Vaticano* and *Nicotera,* an ancient Greek city that was laid out later in the Norman plan with a cathedral at its center and streets radiating out like spokes from it. Its Jewish quarter, called the Giudecca, still manufactures cloth. The castle houses an *archaeological museum.* Here you turn inland and rejoin Route S 18; continue to Gioia Tauro.

From Vibo Valentia continue south on Route S 18 in a scenic landscape through *Mileto* and *Rosarno* to **Gioia Tauro,** situated

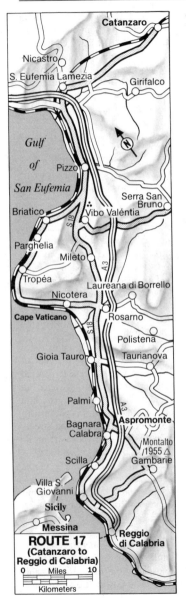

ROUTE 17
(Catanzaro to
Reggio di Calabria)
0   Miles   10
Kilometers

on the coast. It's a resort of sandy beaches at the *Marina di Gioia Tauro,* and the town itself is an important commercial center. The Violet Coast begins here, a stretch of seaside resorts for swimming and catching swordfish.

*Palmi (128 km.; 79 miles from Catanzaro) is located on the north side of *Monte Sant'Elia,* 582 meters (1,909 feet), which offers a rare view of two volcanoes: Etna to the south and Stromboli out at sea to the northwest. The *Museo Calabrese di Etnografia e Folclore "Raffaele Corso"* provides a glimpse of traditional Calabrian daily life. Its three sections are devoted to agriculture and hunting, shepherds' crafts, and religious customs. Look for the *babbaluti,* bottle-shaped figures shaped by the locals to look like detested rulers, a means of showing their feelings. Old customs are deeply rooted in this area, and the traditional style of dress can often be seen—especially as worn by women on Sundays and holidays. Traditional cooking is derived from fresh products of land and sea, as when swordfish is grilled with a sauce of chopped parsley, marjoram, and lemon in olive oil.

Just south of Palmi, Route S 18 ascends to a plateau, *Piani della Corona,* and descends again amidst unforgettable panoramas. ***Bagnara,** a seaside resort at the foot of green hills, has an attractive beach. Here swordfish hunting is the sport (and often livelihood) in spring, while olive-oil production occupies the less nautically-minded. Sandy beaches line the coast, with few interruptions, to the tip of the Calabrese boot. Most of the resorts are popular with Europeans but rarely see Americans. A phrase book and pocket dictionary are particularly useful, although most young Italians study English.

*Scilla is named for Scylla, the rock that Greek legends personified as a marine monster who, together with the whirlpool Charybdis on the Sicilian side, plotted the destruction of ships passing through the Strait of Messina. This channel, which separates Calabria from Sicily, comes into view here. The orange groves and sea cliffs make this area a charming sight. Near the town of **Porticello-Santa Trada** you can see the enormous pylons that carry high-voltage cables across the strait, providing electricity for Sicily from the Scilla mountains.

At **Villa San Giovanni** car ferries provide access to Messina in Sicily.

Route S 18 continues along the coast, offering views of the Sicilian shore, until you reach the capital of the region, ***Reggio di Calabria** (174 km.; 108 miles from Catanzaro), a modern city that has few remnants of its ancient past. It is attractively situated, with a *seaside park* and *promenade* that provide lovely places to stroll and view Sicily and the strait.

Founded in 750 B.C. as one of the principal cities of Magna Graecia, it later was ruled by Romans, Normans, French, and Spanish, like most of southern Italy. Earthquakes have taken their toll of the buildings of antiquity, but the sea recently gave back an ancient treasure: two statues of warriors, known as the *Riace bronzes.* These magnificent forms, with their eerie, otherworldly look, are in the ***Museo Nazionale della Magna Grecia,* along with other fine objects excavated from Greek sites.

In the museum's Medieval to modern collections are paintings by Antonello da Messina, one of the greatest painters of the Renaissance, and the *Return of the Prodigal Son* by another southern Italian, Mattia Preti. At the end of the **Lungomare Marina* promenade are the remains of a Roman bath. Reggio has some excellent restaurants for seafood and other regional specialties. The *Duomo,* rebuilt after the 1908 earthquake, has a beautiful sacramental chapel from the 17th century. Around the block stands the *Chiesa degli Ottimati,* with tenth-century Alexandrian mosaic floors and Arab-Norman columns. Two round towers recall the castle the Aragonese built during the 15th century.

A curiosity of Reggio is the *fata morgana,* a mirage named for Morgan le Fay, that occurs under certain atmospheric conditions. It looks like a fantastic city rising from the sea, then slowly dissolving into thin air. One theory has it that the town of Messina across the strait is being reflected in the water and air.

You may wish to take a side trip to *Gambarie* (42 km.; 26 miles from Reggio). Go north on Route S 18 and at *Gallico* take Route S 184 east to *Gambarie,* a summer and winter resort at 1,370 meters (4,500 feet) in the midst of the *Aspromonte Massif,* the last rise of the Apennines in mainland Italy. The town, surrounded by beech, chestnut, and pine forests, is a point of departure for hiking and mountain walks. A chair lift takes you to the top of *Monte Scirocco,* named for the hot African wind that periodically torments the south during the summer.

Several mineral springs, the largest being *Tre Aie,* cool the region around Gambarie. The town is a popular resort in summer, as a way to escape the heat, and in winter for skiing. In a nearby pine grove Garibaldi was captured during the fight for independence.

TRAVEL ROUTE 18: *Taranto–*Rossano–*Crotone–*Locri–Brancaleone–*Reggio di Calabria (496 km.; 308 miles)

See map on page 265.

This route skirts the coast of the Ionian Sea and turns west to Reggio di Calabria, exploring the far southern reaches of the Italian mainland. En route you'll pass through the "Riviera of the Sun" and a number of resorts and spas.

Leave *Taranto* (see page 231) heading west on Route S 106. Shortly after crossing the Bradano River, 44 km. (27 miles) from Taranto, you will reach **Metaponto,** near the ancient city of Metapontum, whose extensive excavated ruins are nearby. Founded in 743 B.C., this was one of the major Greek settlements in Italy. Temples, houses, and tombs remain to show us elements of the ancient civilization. During the sixth century B.C. the philosopher Pythagoras founded one of the most influential schools of philos-ophy here. Throughout its Greek period Metaponto saw battles among the Greek colonies, and the fighting continued under Roman domination. In later years malaria led to abandonment of the city. Go first to the *Antiquarium,* or museum, where there are models of what the city looked like. In the *Tavole Palatine,* next to the museum, are the remains of a Doric temple. Farther on, turn left on S 175 to see other temples, a theater, and a sanctuary in a fascinating site, set above the sea.

Near the excavations is the *Lido*

di Metaponto, which is a fully developed resort, as is *Marina di Ginosa* to the north.

From Metaponto continue south on Route S 106 to *Policoro,* another excavated city, which was called Heracleia by the Greeks. The famous battle between Pyrrhus and the Romans, in which Pyrrhus won at too great a cost (source of our familiar term, a Pyrrhic victory), took place here in 279 B.C. The *Museo della Siritide* in Policoro exhibits material found at the ancient sites of the area. The hills along this route are dotted with castles and fortresses, which you can explore, along with the pleasant sandy beaches below—which are a rarity in Italy. The area is called the Riviera of the Sun.

At *Rocca Imperiale Marina,* which also has a beautiful beach, a road leads inland for 4 km. (2.5 miles) to *Rocca Imperiale,* where one of Frederick II Hohenstaufen's many castles is located. Another, the Castello di Roseto, is south at *Cape Spulico* (95 km.; 59 miles). South of the resort of *Villapiana Lido,* Route S 106 crosses the *Raganello River,* which irrigates the plain of Sybaris (*Piana di Sibari*).

Sybaris was one of the largest trading centers of early antiquity. It was founded during the eighth century B.C., and its splendor and reputed decadence were so great that the word sybaritic became synonymous with overripe luxury.

After being destroyed by the

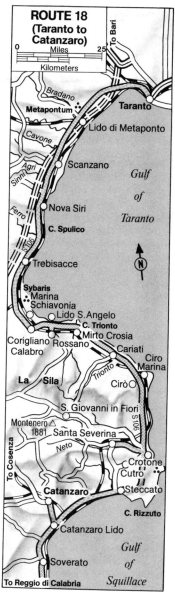

ROUTE 18
(Taranto to Catanzaro)

0   Miles   25

Kilometers

To Bari

Bradano

Metapontum

Taranto

Cavone

Lido di Metaponto

Agri

Scanzano

Gulf

Sinni

Nova Siri

of

C. Spulico

Ferro

Taranto

S 106

Trebisacce

N

Sybaris
Marina
Schiavonia

Lido S. Angelo

C. Trionto

Mirto Crosia

Corigliano
Calabro

Rossano

Cariati

Ciro
Marina

La **Sila**

Trionto

Cirò

S. Giovanni in Fiori

Montenero △
1881   Santa Severina

S 106

To Cosenza

Neto

Crotone

Cutro

Catanzaro

Steccato

C. Rizzuto

Catanzaro Lido

Gulf

Soverato

of

To Reggio di Calabria

Squillace

Crotonians, who flooded the city with the waters of the Crathis (Crati) River in 510 B.C., the town was resurrected by the Romans but never regained its legendary opulence. Its location has been determined only recently, as a result of excavations for a drainage project in the area. The most important traces found are in the *Parco del Cavallo* on the plains. A collection of pottery decorated with cable patterns and the famous silver coins of Sybaris, showing a bull (symbol of fertility) looking backward, are among the discoveries. Today the area is heavily industrialized and gives hint of the *dolce vita* that was its past.

Continue south on Route S 106 for a side trip to **Spezzano Albanese** (16 km.; 10 miles), to Route S 534, which goes west, and then turn south on Route S 19 to *Spezzano Albanese,* one of the best spas of the south. Waters with alkaline, saline, and sulfuric properties ease tired muscles and other ailments, and the facilities here are modern.

ROUTE 18
(Catanzaro to Reggio di Calabria)

A fascinating side trip to ***Corigliano Calabro** and the **"Patirion"** is 12 km. (7 miles) from Marina Schiavonea where a road branches inland from S 106 r. to the fortified town of **Corigliano Calabro;* a second side road off S 106 leads to the "Patirion." The *Convento del Patire* (Santa Maria del Patirion), was founded by Saint Nilus on a rocky peak in a dramatic setting, and it rivaled the greatest of Greek monasteries as a seat of learning during the Middle Ages. You still can see traces of the mosaic pavement but the reason to come here is more the setting than the structure.

From S 106 Route S 177 branches south to ***Rossano**

(155 km.; 96 miles from Taranto), birthplace of Saint Nilus in 910. The town is full of Byzantine relics, so many that it is sometimes called the Ravenna of Calabria. The *cathedral museum* has one of the rarest and most precious of the Greek codices, the **Codex Purpureus,* with miniatures from the sixth century. It is the oldest manuscript in Greek of the Gospels of Matthew and Mark. Note also the *basilica of San Marco* and the *church of Santa Panaglia;* both are from the 11th century, when Normans imported Byzantine craftsmen, and both are gems of this eastern style.

To the south of Rossano the dark-green slopes of the **Sila Massif* (see page 259) begin to appear; on this high, forested plateau originate streams and rivers that course down the mountainous terrain. Small resorts made of mountain granite are beautified by lakes and thick woods (Sila is derived from the Latin *silva,* meaning woods) and meadows. Both winter and summer are well provided for—skiing, hiking and fishing all have their facilities.

Rejoin Route S 106 and continue along the coast to *Ciro Marina.* Beyond its sandy beaches are slopes with vineyards and olive orchards, and the pilgrimage *church of Madonna d'Itri* is nearby. This town has an important fish market and produces excellent wines, so try to plan on a seaside meal here. The remains of the Doric temple of Apollo Aleus

from the fifth century B.C. are found on the cape of *Punta Alice* 5 km. (3 miles) away.

Continue south on Route S 106 to *Torre Melissa,* where there is a Medieval watchtower. Nearby *Strongoli,* the ancient Petelia (9 km.; 6 miles inland), is a high mountain town with a fortress dating from the Hohenstaufens.

At *Fasana* cross the wide estuary of the Neto River and continue to **Crotone** (243 km.; 151 miles from Taranto), located on a promontory at the ancient site of Crotona, the home of Pythagoras and where his school of philosophy attracted the finest minds in literature, science, and the arts. Another famous son was Milo, who consistently won Olympic wrestling matches—perhaps partly because of his commitment to the strict Pythagorean way of life. The city was founded in 710 B.C. by Greeks and grew to dominate the other Greek settlements in southern Italy, except for Sybaris (see page 265), which the Crotonians destroyed in 510 B.C. They met another strong opponent when Agathocles of Syracuse in Sicily was attracted by the mainland's rising powers, and the city fell to him. Crotone again became important during the 13th century A.D., and most of its ancient buildings were incorporated into palaces for the viceroy Don Pedro of Toledo, who was known for such "robberies."

The *Museo Archeologico* contains excavated artifacts of ancient Crotona. Some remnants of a city wall, an ancient Greek port, the castle dating from the 15th century, and the cathedral from that period make an enjoyable visit; but imagining how things looked in antiquity takes some imagination, as the city is now a busy commercial and industrial center.

From Crotone there are good side trips to the ***Temple of Hera Lacinia** (11 km.; 7 miles) and ***Santa Severina** (32 km.; 20 miles). From Crotone go southeast on the small coast road to *Capo Colonna* and the **Temple of Hera Lacinia*, where the remaining column of the Doric temple base is called the "last column" of the ancient city. More recent excavations have turned up interesting relics. In the temple, a yearly celebration honors the Madonna di Capo Colonna, a wooden statue believed to be miraculous. A fine rural road leads to Capo Colonna, the easternmost point of Calabria, where the cape opens to a panoramic view.

*Santa Severina is west of Crotone on Route S 107 (follow signposts). This ancient Greek city was the birthplace in A.D. 741 of Pope Zachary. Its height (326 meters; 1,070 feet) and its 15th-century fortress made it easily defendable, and several Byzantine churches built from the seventh to the 12th centuries have been preserved.

Route S 106 leads inland and across hills to the wide *Gulf of Squillace*, where pebbly beaches and *fiumare* (dry river beds at the foot of steep slopes) and small

towns high above the sea are interspersed with subtropical plants and flowers. Continue on to *Catanzaro Marina*, also called *Catanzaro Lido*, where a long sandy beach lures watersports fans.

From here take Route S 19, which cuts inland for 13 km. (8 miles) to ***Catanzaro** (see page 259)

Continue about a mile along S 106 to *Roccella*. Amid olive groves are the scenic ruins of **Santa Maria della Rocella* (see page 260), one of the largest Norman churches in Calabria, whose Arab arches and lightness relieve the imposing Norman density. Three miles farther is the turnoff to *Squillace*, the Roman Scolacium, with the remains of a Roman theater, amphitheater, and baths. The jasmine shrubs of the area perfume the air with their sweet scent.

Back on Route S 106, drive through *Copanello* to **Soverato**, a small fishing village with an adjacent resort and a wide white beach. Up above in *Soverato Superiore* the *church* has a marble Pietà and a bas-relief, both by the noted 16th-century sculptor Antonello Gagini.

At *Monasterace Marina* are the remains of a Doric temple from the adjacent Greek colony of Caulonia.

From Monasterace Marina you may wish to take a side trip to ***Stilo** and ***Ferdinandea** (34 km.; 21 miles). Follow the winding Route S 110 for 16 km. (10 miles) to **Stilo*. In the upper part of this hill town, spread over stepped terraces, a small tenth-century church of Byzantine design, called *La Cattolica,* has five cupolas and the remains of frescoes in the triple-aisled interior.

Continue on S 110 for about 18 km. (11 miles). A steep road, Route S 110, branches off to the right, and after about 4 km. (2.5 miles) reaches *Ferdinandea,* the former summer residence of Ferdinand II of Bourbon. To the north of the large, recently restored palace you can see the remains of a Bourbon-era foundry and a steel mill.

On Route S 106 continue through *Marina di Caulonia,* followed by *Roccella Ionica,* atop a steep cliff, with the ruins of a castle and a good beach. Continue along the beach-lined road to ***Locri** (397 km.; 246 miles from Taranto), a resort that sprang up alongside ancient Locri, the Greek colony founded about 700 B.C. A Graeco-Roman temple and the remains of a temple to Persephone can still be seen, and the *Antiquarium,* or museum, has collections of votive offerings from the temple site.

For a side trip to ***Gerace** follow Route S 111 inland from Locri for about 8 km. (5 miles). *Gerace,* about 500 meters (1,600 feet) above sea level, is a picturesque memory of the Middle Ages, spread out along three terraces on a hillside. On the first level, ancient shops were dug out of the rock. The *cathedral* is the largest in Calabria; it was conse-

crated in the 11th century and reveals its Arab-Norman stylistic origins. Inside are some Greek temple pillars taken from Locri. Art and tombs of the Pisan school decorate the vastness; Pisa, a formidable sea power, made frequent incursions into southern Italy. The *church of San Francesco d'Assisi* (1252) has some attractive inlaid woodwork, and the castle offers exhilarating views of the countryside.

Route S 106 continues south along the Ionian coast past *Bovalino Marina* to **Brancaleone.** The town boasts a fine beach and sweet air thanks to its jasmine, which is used to make perfumes and essences. Continue along what is now called the Jasmine Coast to *Capo Spartivento.* Beyond the cape, in the midst of olive groves and orange orchards, is **Melito di Porto Salvo.** A lighthouse marks the spot where Garibaldi landed in 1860.

Just west, a small side road leads inland to ***Pentedattilo,** a mountain town situated picturesquely on the slope of a steep, rocky cone. In Greek the name of the town means "five fingers," and refers to the rock formation in the shape of an extended hand. The ruins of a Medieval castle can be explored.

Capo dell'Armi marks the beginning of the *Strait of Messina,* and now the coast of Sicily comes into view. Continue on Route S 106 to ***Reggio di Calabria** (496 km.; 308 miles from Taranto; see page 263).

Sicily

Sicily, the largest island in the Mediterranean, is a popular destination for travellers seeking a bit of exotica without leaving Europe. Its landscape is richly varied, its historical monuments are magnificent, and its towns are often of unparalleled beauty. Sicilian food is a sophisticated blend of sweet and sour flavors that owes much to its Arab past but is nonetheless purely Sicilian.

Sicily's ancient cultures were overrun by Greek colonists, beginning about the eighth century B.C.; the Sicani and Siculi of the early days were perhaps of Spanish origin. The Phoenicians gradually lost their Sicilian outposts to the Greeks and later to the Romans during the Punic wars. Sicily's Greek period was so brilliant that it was considered greater than Greece itself. Greek rulers, called tyrants, exercised absolute power over their cities, but were not always as cruel and despotic as the word implies. After the Romans came—taking more than they contributed—the barbarians came and took more. Byzantines and Arabs came to stay, and the Arabs created a dazzling culture, especially around Palermo—full of mosques and palaces that attracted poets and intellectuals of east and west. The Normans defeated the Arabs but treated them and all resident Sicilians well. Under the Norman Roger II, Sicily knew one of its finest hours domestically, and as a political and artistic center it was respected throughout the world. Frederick II Hohenstaufen grew up in Palermo and always considered himself Sicilian, no matter how far his travels led. After his reign the country saw a decline. The Angevin French were thrown out during the revolt of the Sicilian Vespers (1282) but they were replaced by the Spanish House of Aragon, who ruled by viceroy and relegated the island to a minor role in world events. After Spanish Bourbon and Savoy rulers, Garibaldi landed on the west coast of Sicily in 1860, and the drive for Italian independence began. At present the region enjoys a degree of autonomy from Rome and has its own parliament.

In recent years tourist facilities have improved a great deal, and the road system links the island conveniently in most directions, especially around the coastal routes. The mountainous center has smaller, tortuous roads that lead to fascinating villages of yesteryear, but the major attractions for the first-time visitor lie along the coast for the most part.

The three routes can be combined into one tour if you prefer and have the time.

TRAVEL ROUTE 19: *Messina–**Cefalù–***Palermo–**Segesta–Trapani–*Marsala (399 km.; 247 miles)

See map on pages 272–273.

This route begins at Sicily's gateway city with its remarkable clock in the Duomo and takes you on a side trip to the Aeolian Islands before you arrive at historic Palermo, an ancient Arab stronghold. A modern Autostrada follows most of the north coast, but Route S 113 is generally more scenic.

Cross the Strait of Messina by ferry from Villa San Giovanni or Reggio di Calabria (see page 263) to Messina.

*Messina, the "Gate to Sicily," is situated at the foot of the *Peloritani mountains.* You can travel in several directions from Messina, circling the island, and then return here. (A car ferry from Naples will take you to Palermo, however, if you want to start there.)

Messina's origins are lost in legend. During the eighth century B.C. it became a Greek colony called Zancle, the Greek word for "sickle," because of the shape of its harbor. The city's modern name comes from the Messenians who, defeated by the Spartans in the fifth century B.C., fled here from Greece.

A long line of rulers passed through after the Greeks—from the Romans to the House of Savoy—but one of the city's greatest enemies has been nature. Earthquakes and tidal waves have periodically flattened the town, helped along by bombs in World War II. Today's lively modern city is not beautiful, but it is full of vitality, with a university, a fine museum, delightful piazzas, a windswept waterfront, and delicious food—not bad for a town that has been repeatedly destroyed.

Among the reconstructed buildings is the **Duomo.* Built during the 12th century by the Normans, it was twice destroyed and reconstructed. Subsequent incarnations added Gothic portals

Messina: Cathedral clock

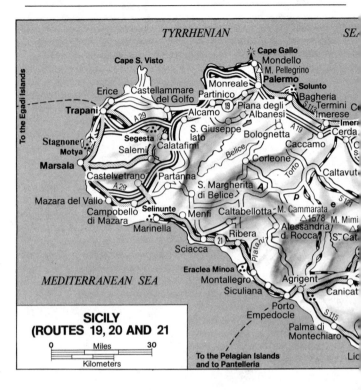

**SICILY
(ROUTES 19, 20 AND 21**

Miles

Kilometers

0 ___ 30

To the Pelagian Islands
and to Pantelleria

and a German astronomical
clock (1933), one of the largest in
the world. Each quarter of an hour,
gilded figures glide from their
niches, and the hours are rung by
two female figures from Sicilian
history. But come to see it at noon
when all the creatures awake: a
lion roars three times, a rooster
crows, a dove flaps its wings, and a
replica of the Montalto church
where the Sicilian Vespers began
appears. At the same time, angels
and magi line up in front of Mary.
One angel hands her a letter,
another retrieves it, and Mary
blesses everyone. Don't be so dis-
tracted by the clock that you forget
to go inside the cathedral, for the
Byzantine mosaics are well worth
a visit.

Just to the southeast of the
Duomo is the smaller but equally
important church of *Santissima
Annunziata dei Catalani,* built in
the 12th century and still showing
its Arab-Norman heritage, with a
touch of later Romanesque.
Santa Maria Alemanna, farther
south, just off of Via Garibaldi, is

a Gothic creation. Once it served as a chapel for German knights who joined the Crusades. Other points of interest in Messina include the *church of Santa Maria della Valle,* called "Badiazza"; and the 16th-century *Fountain of Neptune* on the waterfront, designed by Fra Angelo Montorsoli, who was a student of Michelangelo. The **Museo Regionale* is a well-organized, light and airy museum that houses fine work, such as the *Madonna with Saints*

Gregory and Benedict by Antonello da Messina, the city's most famous son and a leading painter of the Renaissance (this polyptych is badly damaged but still exquisite), and two large works by Caravaggio. Archaeological material and sculpture complete the collection.

The waterfront along the strait has a long *promenade* past ferries, cargo ships, and hydrofoils that leave for Calabria and farther ports, and makes a diverting walk. If you're travelling to the Aeolian Islands (also known as the Lipari Islands), you can take the hydrofoil or ferry from Messina, but on a limited schedule. Milazzo on the northern coast is the more convenient departure point.

For a brief side trip, you can take the coast road north from Messina to the beach at *Mortelle,* on the Tyrrhenian Sea. Nearby is **Capo Peloro,* the easternmost point in Sicily, where the **lighthouse* offers a beautiful view.

To continue Travel Route 19, leave Messina on Via Palermo. Take Route S 113 through the wooded *Monti Peloritani,* with their cedars and pines, and over the *San Rizzo Pass* (410 meters; 1,345 feet) down to the Tyrrhenian coast to *Villafranca Tirrena.* The Autostrada A 20 parallels Route S 113 for part of this Travel Route.

Continue to Olivarella, where you turn north to **Milazzo,** the ancient city of Mylae, which was founded by Greeks in 716 B.C. and

where excavations have revealed tombs dating back to the 14th century B.C.

Outside the industrial zone a vacation resort extends along the coast, dominated by a large castle dating from the 13th century. Other sights include the domed (old) *cathedral,* the pilgrimage *church of San Francesco di Paola* and the Gothic *Palazzo dei Giudici.* The *new cathedral,* which replaces the old, was built during this century.

An agricultural and industrial center, Milazzo is also the departure point for the Aeolian Islands. Hydrofoils and ferries leave at frequent intervals for most islands all summer and on reduced schedules in winter, sometimes curtailed by high seas. Day trips around the near islands can also be arranged.

Aeolian Islands (Lipari Islands)

See map on page 275.

*Lipari. This island group is famous for its superb natural setting, partly the result of the unique grotto and cave formations created by weathering of the soft volcanic rock. The islands closer to shore are the most developed for tourism; the farther islands have some facilities but are sought mainly by those who want to get away from it all to a beautiful, remote spot. This, the largest island, has been carved dramatically by wind and water, with angular slopes that rise high above the sea, quarries of

Lipari

pumice stone, and vineyards that produce Malvasia delle Lipari, a very good, moderately sweet wine, preferred with fruit or sweets. Swimming is fairly good on the island, as are water sports, especially sailing and undersea exploring. The *Museo Archeologico* contains important exhibits from Lipari's rich prehistorical past as well as artifacts from the Greek and Roman eras.

*Vulcano is the island closest to the mainland. Its rugged beauty and hot springs attract masses of tourists, and so it is best explored in spring and fall. In mythology this island was the birthplace of Aeolus, the god of the winds. Crevasses along the jagged coast hide sources of the hot springs, which turn the air into a sauna amid the caves. Natural mud baths find a host of people relaxing in the volcanic mud, whose ability to relieve aches, at least temporarily,

is affirmed by many bathers. Swimming beaches are tucked away in picturesque nooks between the rocks. Underwater sports are popular here, as they are throughout the islands. Interesting sights include the 391-meter- (1,282-foot-) *Gran Cratere;* the *Allume Grottoes,* from which alum is mined; the natural fumarole area (jets of steam and mud) around *Baia di Levante;* and the *Grotta del Cavallo.*

Strange rock formations arise from the sea between the islands of Lipari and Vulcano, giving the entire seascape an otherworldly look.

*Stromboli consists almost entirely of the active volcano that makes the island's nightlife mainly one of watching the cone for a spectacular show of fireworks, which can be brilliant red and dramatic during the frequent small eruptions. The cone should be approached with caution, and usually there are guides to make sure you do. The soil produces a

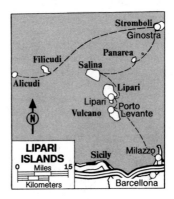

strong wine, somewhat similar to Lipari's. The houses and hotels are located mainly in two small villages, both of which have begun to develop for tourism by building swimming pools and other popular amenities.

The tiny nearby islet of **Strombolicchio* looks like a fantastic Medieval fortress. A staircase of 200 steps cut into the basalt rock leads to an *overlook* that shows you Stromboli in all its glory, as well as the Calabrese coast and the other islands.

Panarea is one of the most beautiful islands, and one that seeks to keep its exclusivity. Electricity is minimal and hotels are few, but the scenery is exquisite, the rock formations enchanting along a clear sea. Prehistoric ruins dot the land, and there is a thermal spring near the village of *San Pietro.* In the south half of Panarea, Bronze Age villages can be seen.

Salina, just 4 km. (2.5 miles) northwest of Lipari, was called Didyme by its ancient settlers. The little port of *Rinella* has a small hotel, but facilities are limited. The island is one of the most beautiful, for itself and its views.

Filicudi, the ancient Phoenicoessa, takes its name from the lush fern growth, or *felci,* that covers parts of the island. Its sights include the *Grotta del Bue Marino,* the towering *cliff of Canna,* and *Capo Graziano,* where Bronze Age relics have been found.

Alicudi, farther west, was called Ericusa in ancient times after the heather, or *erici,* that carpets its cliffs. The western edge of the island drops precipitously to the sea; on the eastern slopes, terraces are dotted with small houses, some of which take in overnight guests. Take a boat trip around the island if possible. The light here makes the sea and the island grottoes exquisitely beautiful.

Return to Route S 113 and continue southwest to a side road (follow signs) that runs south to **Castroreale,** which may have an ancient Siculi past. During the 12th century the Norman King Roger II took charge here. Frederick II of Aragon built the castle (now ruins) in 1324 and often lived in Castroreale. Many of its churches merit a visit, especially the little *church of Sant'Agata,* where a 16th century *Annunciation* by Antonello Gagini—whose work, with that of other members of the Gagini family, appears throughout Sicily—is displayed. *Castroreale Terme,* on the coast, is a noted spa, whose waters are reputed to cure a variety of ills.

Return to Route S 113, which crosses the *Fiumara Termini,* on whose banks in 269 B.C. an army from Syracuse led by Hieron II (see page 299) defeated the Mamertines.

To the south, Route S 185 leads over the scenic Mandrazzi Pass (1,125 meters; 3,700 feet), to **Taormina* (see page 291).

Continue west on Route S 113

to ***Tindari,** located at the site of the ancient city of Tyndaris, which was founded in 396 B.C. by Greek colonists from Syracuse. During the ninth century Arab invaders destroyed it. The *Greek theater* is well preserved and occupies a fine site, overlooking the sea and islands. Plays sometimes are performed here in summer. Also worth a visit are the ancient *basilica* and residential districts where foundations and floors are visible. The 16th-century *Santuario della Madonna Nera* (Sanctuary of the Black Madonna) stands at the highest point of **Capo Tindari,* where the panoramas of the Aeolian Islands are striking. The statue is venerated among local people and is the destination of pilgrimages from all over Sicily.

Follow Route S 113 past attractive beaches to the road (follow

Tindari

signposts) that branches north to **Capo d'Orlando,** where there is a resort of the same name with a pretty waterfront, a beach between steep cliffs, and uniquely shaped rock formations. In the summer, hydrofoils leave for the Aeolian Islands from here.

Return to Route S 113. Roads branch off south from here into the nearby *Monti Nebrodi* where towns still preserve the feeling of Medieval Sicily. Among the nearby towns you can visit are *San Marco d'Alunzio,* where Robert Guiscard, brother of Count Roger, built the first Norman castle in Sicily in 1061 (five years before the Battle of Hastings), *Alcara li Fusi,* where a mountain path leads to the Stone Age *Grotta del Lauro* in the town of *Longi;* and *San Fratello,* which was founded during the 11th century by Lombards.

On the now somewhat monotonous stretch of coast lie the seaside resorts of *Rocca di Caprileone, Torrenova, Sant'Agata Militello, Acquedolci, Marina di Caronia, Torre del Lauro,* and *Santo Stefano di Camastra,* renowned for the manufacture of ceramics, the best-known of Sicilian handicrafts. The surrounding hills provide very good clay, and the main street is filled with shops that display and sell ceramicware.

Shortly before you come to *Castel di Tusa,* a small road climbs south to ***Tusa,** a town with a Medieval tang. The remains of the Greek city of Halaesa, dating from the fifth century B.C., are being excavated, and thus far massive walls, an acropolis, and the agora with the base of a Hellenic temple have been recovered. Its site, shortly after the turn-off to Tusa, provides a splendid panorama.

Continue on Route S 113 to the small seaside resort of *Castel di Tusa,* where ancient and Medieval ruins have been uncovered.

**Cefalù (195 km.; 121 miles from Messina) is one of the oldest cities in Sicily, nestled in one of the most scenic locations, at the foot of an enormous cliff and looking out to sea and a graceful harbor. Sailors, swimmers and photographers love the town, which has one of the finest Norman cathedrals and some of the most beautiful mosaics in the world. Many streets have the white modular look of Arab villages.

The **Duomo is a grand monument to art and to spirituality. It was begun by King Roger II in 1131 in fulfillment of a vow made during a storm at sea. Since he sur-

vived, he built this masterpiece as a thanksgiving. It also was used as a fortress at one time, as the battlements on the roof show. The severe architecture, relieved by Arab lightness, makes it one of the finest of cathedrals, especially from the sides and back. The interior contains 12th-century **mosaics in Byzantine style, showing Christ as the all-powerful Pantocrator, but here Christ is gentle in his power and has an expression that is unlike any other of its kind. The lovely statue of the *Madonna* by Antonello Gagini (1533) is in the north transept.

The **Museo Mandralisca,* in Via Mandralisca, contains a masterpiece by Antonello da Messina, the *Portrait of an Unknown Man.* The collection also contains some interesting objects of antiquity, Arab vases, and seashells.

Nearby is the 13th-century **church of San Biagio,* one of several interesting churches of that era, including *San Domenico* and *San Francesco.* Other Medieval curios are the *public laundry* (*lavatoio medioevale*), with basins cut from the rock; and the *Osteria Magno,* part of a palace where Roger II lived when in Cefalù. The *Rocca* high above contains remnants of a fortress from the 13th century.

Cefalù has excellent tourist facilities, especially east of the city along the coast, where small resort hotels combine comfort and views. During the summer, festivals, fishing competitions, and sailboat regattas (and crowds) are

Cefalù

plentiful. The only problem is the traffic on this narrow, virtually inescapable main road from Palermo, which backs up for miles in good weather. To the west of Cefalù, walks or drives into the mountains to see the grottoes are fascinating. At Via del Piletto take the street to the left for *Gratteri* (at 657 meters; 2,155 feet) and *Lascari*, an area rich in grottoes to explore.

Continue west on Route S 113 to the ruins of the ancient Greek colony of ***Himera,** now called *Imera*. The city, which was founded in 648 B.C., is the site of a *Doric temple*. The Greek lyric poet Stesichorus lived here and wrote ballads that incorporate Sicilian folk legends. In 480 B.C. a decisive battle took place near Himera, in which the Greeks of Syracuse defeated the Carthaginians, killing 150,000 of Carthage's warriors. Those who survived were used as slave labor to build the city. Later Hannibal took revenge by razing the city and slaying the entire population.

Continue to **Termini Imerese,** which has been a thermal spa since antiquity. In the *Museo Civico* you will see elements of Roman life. An interesting excursion (12 km.; 7 miles from Termini Imerese) by way of S 285 south leads to the small town of *Caccamo*, whose panorama, at 500 meters (1,650 feet) is stunning. The **Castello* dating from about the seventh century, is among the best preserved—turrets, merlons and all.

Rejoin S 113 and continue through the resort of *Trabia* and the sandy beach of *Vetrana*, surrounded by groves of oranges and lemons. Past the seaside resort of *Santa Flavia* are the ruins of the Phoenician city of ***Solunto,** or Soluntum, but ruins that still command a magnificent view of a wide expanse of land and sea. Founded about 400 B.C., Soluntum became Roman after the First Punic War. The city was destroyed by the Saracens, who were establishing colonies for themselves in the west. Excavations have revealed paved streets, mosaic decorations, and houses with painted tiles depicting Leda and the Swan. The adjoining *museum* exhibits some of the small objects found at the site.

Stop at the harbor of picturesque *Porticello,* a favorite summer place for Palermitani.

*Bagheria, just to the south, is a dusty town that was once a princely domain. Prince Branciforte created the city, erecting his own villa and welcoming villas of his friends. Most interesting of these is the *Villa Palagonia,* where dwarfs and strange creatures in stone stand on the garden walls, and inside the villa a distorted mirrored ballroom, now in ruins, can be visited (near Piazza Garibaldi). More conservative are the nearby *Villa Villarosa* and the *Villa Valguarnera,* a beauty in its own park, also near Piazza Garibaldi. Baghería has some fine, sophisticated restaurants despite its unkempt appearance.

Continuing west you will reach Palermo.

***Palermo

See map on page 281.

The capital city of Sicily and the principal port of the island, Palermo is particularly rich in art treasures and historical relics.

The city's origins predate the Phoenicians, who settled there during the eighth century B.C. After the First Punic War the city became Roman. But it was in the sixth century A.D. that the city received its most significant influence, when Arabs colonized Sicily and made Palermo the beloved capital of the emirate, building more than a hundred mosques and palaces, fountains and orange groves that beautified the city as jasmine and roses perfumed the air. The Normans who succeeded them were so entranced that they retained many of the Arab ways, and King Roger was singularly successful in maintaining peace during the 30 years (1072–1202) it took the Normans to conquer Sicily. Each small town that the Arabs had created was invaded and destroyed, but, especially in Palermo, the Arab delicacies in form were preserved, and Roger's court was a center of interchange between Islam and Christendom. As a child of four, Frederick II Hohenstaufen was crowned King of Sicily. He was raised in the royal palace in Palermo in accordance with Western and Arabic rules (when there were any rules at all) and his love of Arab sumptuousness continued throughout his life. He spoke and wrote Arabic, kept a harem when he travelled, and decorated his castles in elaborate luxury.

When the pope crowned the French King Charles of Anjou as King of Southern Italy and Sicily in 1266, several popular revolts followed, culminating in the bloody Sicilian Vespers that began in Palermo, in which all Frenchmen on the island were slaughtered, so despised was the oppressive Anjou government. Then came the Spanish, whose love of splendor helped to create beautiful Baroque palaces and churches for themselves but did little for the average Sicilian.

When Goethe visited Palermo in 1787, he wrote, "Here I passed the most enjoyable hours in peace and quiet: This is the most wonderful place in the world. Italy without Sicily does not leave an impression on the soul; this is the key to everything."

In 1860 Garibaldi entered the city with his Thousand, and the Bourbons capitulated. Sicily had seen enough of foreign rule and became annexed to the new kingdom of Italy.

Between the two piazzas named for Sicilian patriots of 1848 (another revolt) and graced by their statues—*Piazza Castelnuovo* (1) and *Piazza Ruggero Settimo* (2)—lies Viale della Libertà, one of the most expensive streets of the city, and the site of the *Giardino Inglese* (3), the fragrant English garden. On Via Ruggero Settimo, which runs south from the double piazzas, are mansions of past glory, and finally the *Teatro Massimo* (1875–1897), on *Piazza Giuseppe Verdi* (4), one of the largest theaters in Europe and a major work of Basile, a master of Art Nouveau. The neighborhood here is busy with stores and bumper-to-bumper cars, so driving is impossible. On Via Sant'Agostino is the

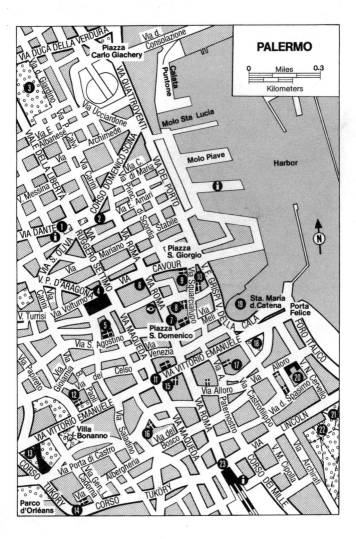

church of that name (5), with a lovely Gothic portal and some good statuary. The choir, the work of the great architect Giacomo Amato, is particularly fine.

From Piazza Giuseppe Verdi, Via Bara leads to *Piazza dell'Olivella* and the splendid Neoclassical *Oratorio di San Filippo Neri* (1769), and the *Chiesa dell'Olivella* (1598; restored).

An adjacent former 17th-century convent houses the ***Museo Archeologico Regionale*** (6). This museum contains one of the most important collections of antiquities in Italy, in its vastness and its beauty. The prize pieces are the *metopes* (fifth century B.C.) from atop the temple columns at Selinunte, a city on the southern coast. Mosaics, ceramics, and coins (always something to see in Sicily, where the gold coins of the Greeks were exquisite) are among the collections. On the ground floor, to the right of the *Chiostro Minore* (small cloister) is the *room of undersea archaeology,* filled with objects retrieved from the floor of the Mediterranean. The *Chiostro Grande* leads to the *Salone di Selinunte,* where the magnificent metopes can be found. The three *metopes of the temple C* are the ones most prized. A particularly impressive piece is the *Quadriga di Helios.* Look also for the *four metopes of the temple E* and the Etruscan collection, which comes from central Italy. In the *Sala dei Grandi Bronzi,* look for the Ariete, or ram, from the Greek colony at Syracuse, where

it adorned the Castello Maniace (see page 299). On the third floor look for the reproduction of the Paleolithic cave drawings found at Addaura on Monte Pellegrino, which is visible from Palermo.

From the east side of the museum, Via Roma leads to the ***church of San Domenico** (7), the largest church in the city and burial place for many prominent Sicilians—it is nicknamed "The Sicilian Hall of Fame." Behind San Domenico is the **Oratorio del Rosario di San Domenico* (8) with rich Baroque decoration and the altar painting *Madonna of the Rosary with St. Dominic and Other Saints* (1628) by Van Dyck.

Nearby is the *church of Santa Zita* (9) (rebuilt in 1586), whose **oratory,* like San Domenico's, has elaborate and beautiful stucco work by Serpotta, a master of the art. The 16th-century *church of San Giorgio dei Genovesi* (10) is farther along Via Squarcialupo.

From *Piazza Giuseppe Verdi* (4), Via Maqueda leads to the center of the old city, ****Quattro Canti** (11), the Four Corners that mark the intersection of Via Maqueda and Corso Vittorio Emanuele. The four corners are rounded off concavely, with four monuments that represent kings and saints and seasons. Turn right on Corso Vittorio Emanuele to the ***Duomo,** Santa Rosalia (12). It was begun in 1185 in Arab-Norman style and was repeatedly enlarged and altered. The cupola was added in 1781–1801 by the Florentine architect Ferdinando

Fuga. The original style is evident at the back. The *Gothic façade* facing Via Matteo Bonello has an impressive central portal built in 1352 and a battle-crowned arcaded gallery. The gallery is connected to the belltower by pointed-arch arcades, repeated on the *south façade,* which faces the Corso. A series of battlements in Moorish style and a portico in Catalan-Gothic (1465) prepare the visitor for the second richly decorated portal. The interior seems stark by contrast. The first and second chapels of the right side aisle contain the simple **Royal tombs* of red porphyry and white marble, in which two of Sicily's most illustrious kings are buried: Roger II and Frederick II Hohenstaufen, the emperor who was more feared than loved and always considered himself a Sicilian. The Emperor Henry IV and Constance of Aragon (the brilliant wife of Frederick and daughter of Roger) are also buried here. In the choir the stalls built in 1466 are notable; the bishop's throne composed of mosaics was created during the 12th century. At the right of the choir the chapel holds the silver shrine that contains the relics of Santa Rosalia, Palermo's patron saint. (Her shrine is located on Monte Pellegrino, the site of hundreds of pilgrimages each month.) Note the *Madonna della Scala* by Antonello Gagini nearby, in the *Nuova Sagrestia.*

Next to the belltower of the cathedral is the *Palazzo Arcivescovile* (Palace of the Archbishop),

built in 1460 and now containing a museum.

Through the park of *Villa Bonanno* and past the *memorial to Philip V* of Spain we reach the ****Palazzo dei Normanni** (13), now the seat of the Sicilian government. The palace foundations were built during the ninth century by Saracens on the ruins of a Roman fortress, then enlarged by the Normans in the 12th century and transformed into a royal palace. The **Torre Pisana to the right of the façade dates from the 16th century; once it served as the treasury, but now it houses an astronomical observatory. The beautiful courtyard, which you may be able to see, was built during the 17th century. Follow the signs to the Cappella Palatina, since the entrance is often from outside the palace.

The ****Cappella Palatina* (1132) is the most exquisite work in Sicily and vies with other masterpieces of Italian art in its awe-inspiring beauty. The experience of this jewellike chapel as a whole, and each individual aspect, is astonishing. On a gold background mosaic biblical scenes are developed with great skill; the effect is only slightly disturbed by the sometimes unfortunate restorations. The nave crossing is crowned with a cupola in Byzantine style, and the vault of wooden carved "stalactites" is a splendid Arab addition. The Arab paintings, influenced by the Persians, are among the finest in existence.

In the 12th-century *Sala di Re*

Ruggero, on the third floor of the palace, are wonderful mosaic hunting scenes in the Persian style, with animals, flowers, and a world of nature to act as backdrop for the king's court, at rest.

On the west side of the palace stands the *Porta Nuova,* a triumphal arch built for Charles V, in a style that is transitional between Baroque and Renaissance.

The **church of San Giovanni degli Eremiti** (14), delightfully eastern in its red domes against palm trees is to the south along *Via dei Benedettini.* In the garden are the remains of an Arab well from the mosque that was the church's base and a lovely *cloister* from the 13th century.

A second tour through Palermo begins at **Quattro Canti** (11). Around the corner is *Piazza Pretoria* (15), site of the city hall and the *church of Santa Caterina,* dazzlingly Baroque within. At the center of the piazza is the *Fontana Pretoria,* informally called the "Fountain of Shame" because of the nude figures. It was built for a northern Italian villa during the 16th century, with 37 figures representing Roman gods and goddesses, nereids and tritons, as well as other mythological figures. The nearby **Piazza Bellini** is one of Palermo's oldest and most attractive piazzas. Its beauty lies in the **church of the Martorana** and the *chapel of San Cataldo,* which stand together across the piazza. The Martorana, properly called Santa Maria dell'Ammiraglio, was built in 1143 in Arab-Norman

style and rebuilt several times. The belltower has escaped renovation, but much of the church has been redone in Baroque style, generally admitted to be a mistake here. Inside are fine mosaics of King Roger being crowned by Christ; his admiral, for whom the church is named, is at the Madonna's feet. San Cataldo preserves its fine Norman interior, but the picturesque red domes are what attract photographers. The Martorana is a favorite wedding church in Palermo.

A bit to the south is the oldest Jesuit church in Sicily, the *Chiesa del Gesù* (16), which was built in the 16th century. Its interior is exuberantly Baroque.

Another lovely church, this time a Gothic one, is *San Francesco d'Assisi* (17), east across Via Roma, with a gracious portal still remaining after extensive war damage. The interior contains some fine works, should you find it open (usually only during Mass). An arch by Laurana and statues by Serpotta, two artists of note whose works are often seen in Sicily, are among the treasures.

Near the church is the **Oratorio di San Lorenzo,** with powerful stucco reliefs and portrait busts by Serpotta. To the east is the *Piazza Marina* with the *Giardino Garibaldi* (18), where huge magnolia trees add a sultry note. Among the piazza buildings are the *Palazzo Chiaramonte,* the 14th-century residence of the Spanish viceroys; the *Palazzo delle Finanze* (1578); and the interesting Renaissance *Fontana del Garaffo*. The *Cala* nearby, the *old port* (19) with its fishing boats, has great charm. Alongside it stands the *church of Santa Maria della Catena*, built during the 15th century in a transitional Gothic-Renaissance style. The name comes from the chain, or *catena*, that was once drawn across the harbor here. The loggia, atop a high outside staircase, is especially attractive.

In back of it is the *Museo Internazionale delle Marionette,* where you may catch one of the puppet shows that are part of Sicily's folk tradition. Turning south, look for *Via Allora,* which will lead west to the *Palazzo Abbatellis* (20), where a restored convent now houses the **Galleria Regionale di Sicilia,* the home of one of the finest of Renaissance paintings, the *Annunciation* by Antonello da

Portal, Palazzo Abbatellis

Messina. A *bust of Eleanor of Aragon* is another of the museum's treasures.

Off the courtyard in the former chapel is the fresco *Triumph of Death*, a ghastly reminder of the plague years, by an unknown artist.

Farther east is the *church of the Madonna della Pietà,* with a superb Baroque façade, a masterpiece by Giacomo Amato. The *Foro Italico* promenade along the harbor will lead you to the *Villa Giulia,* or La Flora (21), designed in 1777, a lush garden of exotic plants, with intersecting paths and small ponds. To Goethe it was the most beautiful "garden of wonders," and today it still has charm. Across the garden is the *Botanical Garden* (22), planted in 1785 with a rich collection of tropical plants—date palms, sago palms, bamboo, and a giant magnolia. *Via Lincoln,* which runs alongside the garden, leads west to *Piazza Giulio Cesare,* where the main *railroad station* (23) is located. Via Roma, one of the main shopping streets in Palermo, leads back to the center of the city.

On *Corso Calatafimi,* at the western edge of Palermo, is the former Norman palace of *La Cuba,* which looks little like the elegant, Arab-style dwelling it was when King William II was around. The nearby *Palazzo della Ziza,* however, begun in 1160, has been splendidly restored to show some of this enchanted age, when the Norman court was among the most luxurious in the world. A short distance away stands the macabre *Convento dei Cappuccini,* where during the 17th and 18th centuries catacombs served as a bizarre burial place, with naturally mummified corpses sitting or hanging from pegs, still clothed as they were at their funerals.

In the south part of the city, the *church of Santo Spirito,* or "dei Vespri," is located in the cemetery of Sant'Orsola. It was here that the first incident of the Sicilian Vespers (1282) occurred, when a French soldier insulted a Sicilian bride at vespers, an act that ignited the already fiery Palermitani against the Angevins, whose detested rule came to an end after a virtual slaughter of the French in Sicily.

Several interesting side trips are possible from Palermo:
Monte Pellegrino (13 km.; 8 miles from Palermo) at 606 meters (2,000 feet), north of Palermo on the bay, can be reached by way of the port street, Via del Porto, following Via Monte Pellegrino, or by bus number 12. At the base of the mountain, the *Parco della Favorita* is a 19th-century park that was once the residence of the Spanish Bourbons. Its glamorous past is recalled by the *Palazzina Cinese,* a summer pavilion much favored by the queen, which unfortunately is not open to the public. Alongside it is the *Museo Etnografico Siciliano Pitrè,* with displays of Sicilian culture that include costumes, carts, and everyday objects. The *San-tuario di Santa Rosalia* on the mountain is an important shrine, dedicated to the patron saint of Palermo, who was a niece of the Norman King William II. Near the shrine, the road mounts to give fine ****views of the coast. Monte Pellegrino became famous during the First Punic War when the Carthaginian general Hamilcar lay siege to the Roman city of Panormus (Palermo), using the mountain as his base camp.

The Grottoes of *Addaura,* on the northern slope of Monte Pellegrino, are the site of the Ice Age cave drawings that can be seen in a model in the archaeological museum in Palermo. Apply at the Soprintendenza Archeologica, next to the museum to see the caves themselves.

Another possible side trip is to ***Mondello** (11 km.; 7 miles from Palermo) a popular resort (and very crowded in summer), that is a wonderful place to go to enjoy seafood at any of the trattorias that have sprung up here. Ice cream is another lure, and Palermo residents often drive out after dinner just to enjoy a *gelato* at the town's central piazza.

Ustica Island (57 km.; 35 miles from Palermo) has beaches and seafood and a protected natural area for undersea exploration. Ferries (2½ hours) and hydrofoils (1¾ hours) connect Palermo to the island, which is mobbed in summer but a pleasant respite from the city at other times.
***Monreale (8 km.; 5 miles southwest of Palermo on Route S

186, or take bus number 9) high above the once-splendid plain called the *Conca d'Oro* (Golden Conch Shell)—a sweep of land often praised in Arab poetry for its orange orchards and palaces by the sea—is now packed with houses to accommodate the country Sicilians who have come to seek work in the big city. Yet the sight is glorious still, with its panorama of the curving coast and sea. The highlight at Monreale is the ***Duomo*, whose **mosaics* of gold covering 6,300 square meters (67,800 square feet) in the vast interior are impressive. Here the Christ as Pantocrator is all-powerful, not tinged with the mercy found in Cefalù's cathedral mosaics (see page 278). Architecturally, the Duomo is most attractive from the rear, where the *apses* show great Norman strength. The cathedral was created by William II in 1172–1176. Its 12th-century *doors* are notable, but the most charming part is the ***Cloisters* that adjoin part of an old Benedictine monastery. A masterpiece of Medieval art, they are delicately patterned, with stone arches and columns richly decorated with mosaics and topped with capitals of intricate and fascinating designs.

For the continuation of Travel Route 19 from Palermo, take Route S 186 to *Bivio di Cristina*, turn right to *Particino*, where you rejoin Route S 113 to **Alcamo** a town dominated by a massive fortress and churches from the 14th–

Cloister, Monreale

17th centuries. *Sant'Oliva, Santa Chiara*, and the *Badia Nuova* are among the most beautiful; the frescoes in the *Assunta* are notable, and the Gothic arches of its interior date from the 13th century.

Just south of Alcamo the Autostrada forks, the southern route, A 29, crossing the mountains by way of Salemi to Marsala; the western route, A 29 dir., comes to the coast near Trapani and then turns south to Marsala. The A 29 goes south for 26 km. (16 miles) to Route S 188 to *Salemi*, an ancient city of the Elymni, who inhabited this part of Sicily prior to and during the Greek colonization period. One of Frederick II's many castles stands here, and an Early Christian basilica.

You may instead go west on Route S 113 from Alcamo to ****Segesta** (331 km.; 205 miles from Messina). Here the most romantic Greek temple in Sicily stands in fields of flowers with lovely views. The city was founded by the Elymni in prehistoric times; they frequently went to war during the sixth century B.C. with Selinunte, a Greek city on the southern coast. Eventually they sought the aid of Athens, and they later were allied with Carthage, in modern Tunisia. The city's decline began under the Romans, and in 1000 it was destroyed by Saracens who were colonizing Sicily.

The ruins of the ancient city lie on the hill of *Monte Barbaro,* from which the majestic **Temple looks out over flowering hills. The Doric columns were prepared for fluting (the vertical cuts) but were not finished. The cella—the sacred area at the center, which was common to such temples— was never built. Nearby the ancient **theater also occupies a splendid site, with views of the gorges as far as the Gulf of Castellamare in the distance.

Continue along Route S 113 to **Trapani** (369 km.; 229 miles from Messina), a major port and departure point for the Egadi Islands and Tunisia. Wine and salt, along with other products, are shipped from the ancient dock area that Phoenician ships once considered a port of call. The old city still has some attractive buildings. The chapel of Mary in the *Santuario dell'Annunziata* is lovely, and the *church of Santa Maria del Gesù* has an enameled terra-cotta *Madonna* by Andrea della Robbia. The *Museo Nazionale Pepoli,* set in a former convent, houses a splendid collection of intricate coral figures made during the 17th century, when coral was a major product. Some fine statues, portraits, and archaeological memorabilia make the visit well worth-while.

From Trapani there is a splendid side trip to ****Erice** (14 km.; 9 miles, from Trapani). A good, very curving mountain road leaves the eastern part of Trapani at Raganzili and ascends to *Erice,* which is also accessible by bus from Palermo and by a local bus or cable car from Trapani. The city's height (751 meters, 2,464 feet) places it above the clouds, which circle dreamily below the peaks. Erice is enchanting, the most beautiful town in Sicily after Taormina. It is well adapted to tourism, and its little Medieval streets are dotted with restaurants and cafés.

According to legend, the city was founded in devotion to the goddess Eryx (Astarte), whose followers were found throughout the Mediterranean. It was a cult of fertility, celebrating spring with ritual orgies. Greeks later worshiped her as Aphrodite, and the Romans called her Venus Erycina. The temple sanctuary is now the **Giardino Balio* (Balio gardens). Here, on a cliff high above the plateau of Trapani and in sight of

Tunisia on a clear day is her shrine, in the 12th–13th century ****Castello de Venere,** where only a well now remains, thought by some to be a sacrificial pit for virgins after the ritual. The mighty *walls* of the town date from the fifth-century B.C. in the lower part and are Norman in the upper part.

The restored **Chiesa Matrice* has a fine 15th-century portal, a beautiful rose window, and a splendid square campanile built as a lookout tower by the Aragonese; within, there is a 15th-century *Madonna* attributed to Francesco Laurana. The *Museo Comunale Cordici* shows some of the archaeological finds of the area. Almond pastries are the thing here, and you will be hard put to resist them. The pottery of Erice is dark, with earth tones, unlike Palermo's dazzling traditional ware.

Car ferries leave Trapani daily for the ***Egadi Islands** and **Pantelleria** (15–30 km.; 9–19 miles from Trapani). *Favignana,* the largest and closest, is a commercial tuna-fishing center, and is the best equipped for tourism. *Maréttimo* has archaeological sites and interesting grottoes, such as the Presepe and Cammello. *Levanzo* is the smallest island, very beautiful with its grottoes, views and lack of mass tourism. Levanzo is one of the most ancient of Sicily's inhabited islands, with cave paintings and drawings from prehistoric times which can be seen in the **Grotta Genovese.*

Boats for *Pantelleria* leave Trapani frequently, and there are planes from Trapani and Palermo (110 km.; 68 miles from Sicily; 70 km.; 43 miles from Tunisia). It's a stark landscape of novel forms common to volcanic islands. Grottoes at the water line can be explored by boat, and therapeutic springs relax muscles that have explored the cliffs and valleys and walked through the vineyards typical of the island. Capers are another crop of note. The natural setting, austere and dramatic, has its stalwart devotees, who return frequently, and its detractors, who see only a rock.

To continue Travel Route 19, drive south from Trapani on Route S 115 or the smaller but more scenic coastal road (unnumbered) through a fertile plain and past salt pans. On the way is the small island of ***Mozia,** ancient Motya, which was once a flourishing Phoenician port. Relics of that era can be seen in the *museum.* Boats travel the short distance across the *Stagnone channel.* Watch for signs to the *Station of Ragattisi,* where a road leads south to the narrow turnoff to the landing site and the boatman.

*Marsala (399 km.; 247 miles from Messina) is known internationally for its dessert wine, although today's crop of grapes turns out a varied and excellent cellar, including very good dry whites. The traditional Marsala vineyards can be visited; usually directions are posted by signs to Florio or Rallo wineries, among others. The city was founded by

Carthaginians in 397 B.C., and they called it Lilybaeum. The name Marsala came later, from the Arab settlers' words, Marsah-al Allah, the Harbor of God. Archaeological remains include a third-century A.D. Roman villa with thermal baths with colored mosaic floors. The *cathedral*, dedicated to St. Thomas of Canterbury, contains noteworthy statuary by Gagini and magnificent Flemish wall tapestries. *San Pietro* (16th century) has a gabled tower decorated with tiles. There is a *pinacoteca* of modern paintings and a *Garibaldi Museum*, a reminder that it was here he landed in 1860 with the Thousand, starting the war of independence. The shore promenade winds out to *Capo Boeo*, where the *Lilibeo foothills* open to fine seascapes.

TRAVEL ROUTE 20: *Messina–***Taormina–*Catania–(**Enna–*Caltanissetta)–***Syracuse (160 km.; 99 miles)

See map on pages 272–273.

This travel route follows the east coast of Sicily. Those with little time can take the Autostrada A 18, but the trip along the coast on Route S 114 is far more interesting. Along the way you'll visit Sicily's second largest city and tour the fertile lands that abut Mount Etna, the highest active volcano in Europe. The Travel Route terminates in the ancient Greek city of Syracuse.

Leave Messina (see page 271) on the lively shopping street Viale San Martino. The road winds past small towns and ports tucked away in rocky inlets, with umbrella pines and agaves, and orange, lemon, and tangerine groves adding tropical color.

To the right, good mountain roads lead to villages in the *Monti Peloritani*. To the east across the Strait of Messina is the Calabrian coast, dominated by the mountains of the Aspromonte. Continue to the scenic *Cape of Sant'Alessio*. There, on a rocky peak 429 meters (1,400 feet) high, the remarkable,

romantic town of *Forza d'Agro*, starkly Sicilian of past ages, overlooks the world. Continue south until you see the astonishing sight of Taormina's slopes and cliffs come into view. Ascending the high, hilly road is a thrilling experience, for the town and its site are among the world's most beautiful. From the top of the hill, the snow-capped peak of Etna, the very blue sea, tropical plants, and Medieval houses will enchant you, as they have generations of artists, writers, kings and queens. Less enchanting is the town's serious parking problem; car parks on the periphery are probably your best bet.

***Taormina** (53 km.; 33 miles from Messina) is situated on a 206-meter- (675-foot-), terraced cliff. Its unique setting has made it one of Europe's most coveted vacation resorts. Founded by Greeks during the early fifth century B.C., Taormina soon fell to Rome. In 902 it was conquered by Arabs, and in 1079 by Normans. The city was prosperous during the Middle Ages, serving as the seat of the Sicilian Parliament. Its sights are fascinating and varied: most of the principal buildings date from the Middle Ages. The **Palazzo Corvaia* is a 14th-century palace whose crenellated walls are built from lava; its court, garden, and tower tell of the strong Arab influence in Sicily. The *Palazzo del Duca di Santo Stefano* was built in Gothic style, with twin-arched windows, during the same period.

The *Badia Vecchia* (Old Abbey) consists of a high colonnaded hall with battlements; its façade was decorated with wide pointed-arch windows joined by clusters of columns. The black-and-white stone friezes between the arches are made from lava and pumice.

The Duomo, *San Nicola,* dates from the 13th century and was later rebuilt. Its external severity is softened by the lovely works of art inside. Its three aisles are separated by antique columns of pink marble. The fountain in front is a pleasant place to sit and enjoy the piazza, with its marvelous views over the surrounding hills. Behind the *church of Santa Caterina,* built during the 16th century, is the *Naumachia,* a long wall with niches dating from the late Roman period, when it supported a cistern, and the ruins of the *Odeon,* a building used for musical performances in imperial times.

Near here is the justifiably famous *Teatro Greco,* a tribute to the Greeks' ingenuity in finding the most beautiful spots for their theaters. The view from the center of the *cavea,* or seating area, is stunning: Mt. Etna, the sea, the cliffs, and the shore create an incomparable sight. Go there in the early morning, if necessary, to avoid crowds. Sunset here is spectacular, and the theater frequently is used for concerts and festivals.

Next to the theater is a small museum of antiquities. The old monastery of San Domenico has been made into a luxury hotel, the *San Domenico Palace.* Enjoying dinner or a drink on its terrace is a special experience because of the view.

Many hotels and pensions offer fine views; the *Jolly Diodoro,* next to the public gardens, has one of the best at more moderate prices, and little pensions that line the hills often have terraces with splendid sights all around.

On top of *Monte Tauro* at a height of 390 meters (1,280 feet) is a **castle* built on the foundation walls of the Greek acropolis. From here the panorama is superb, with the town, the volcano, and the Mediterranean all in view. Other splendid views can be had from the *Belvedere* and from the *Giardino Pubblico,* which is filled with fragrant herbs and exotic plants, flowers and pines.

Taormina's swimming beaches are down at the foot of the hill, especially at *Mazzarò, Spisione, *Isola Bella,* and *Naxos.* A cable car connects Mazzarò's little beach to the town, and a bus goes to Naxos, where there are white sand beaches. Most hotels have swimming privileges at private beaches, and they often have their own pools.

Continue south on Route S 114 to *Giardini Naxos,* a large resort which is also the site of **Naxos,** the very first Greek settlement in Sicily, founded during the eighth century B.C. and named for the Ionian island of Naxos. Artifacts from the ancient town and from the area are in the *Museo Archeologico,* in whose garden are remains of the ancient city wall. The excavations are to the south (follow signposts) in a beautiful orchard.

Route S 114 passes along the eastern slope of Mt. Etna (see page 295) and continues along the coast of the Ionian Sea. This stretch of coast is often called the Coast of the Cyclopes because of the huge volcanic rocks (*ciclopi*) in the sea, said to be those thrown by the blinded Cyclops of Mt. Etna at Ulysses' sailors.

*Acireale, perched 161 meters (530 feet) up on a hill, is an active, heavily built-up resort surrounded by groves of lemon, orange, and almond trees. Some fine Baroque buildings, such as the *Duomo* and the churches of *San Sebastiano* and *Santi Pietro e Paolo,* can be visited, and the town is well equipped with sulfur springs for therapeutic treatments or just relaxing. **Santa Maria la Scala,** the beach below Acireale, has an attractive port from which boats may be hired to go out to see the ciclopi rocks. **Aci Castello,** farther south, is dominated by a Norman fortress built on a cliff 70 meters (230 feet) above the sea. It offers a fine view of the coast beyond.

Past Ognina's bay we see the hurly-burly of city life that means Catania (101 km.; 61 miles from Messina) is near.

*Catania

See map on page 294.

Catania, at the foot of Mt. Etna, is Sicily's second largest city and is a major industrial and commercial port. Its Baroque streets are lined with fine palaces and churches, almost all in need of cleaning and restoration.

Catania was founded in 729 B.C. by Ionian Greeks from Naxos and was for centuries at war with the Doric Greeks of Syracuse. In 263 B.C. it was captured by Roman forces, and in 121 B.C. Mt. Etna erupted and flattened the city. Control passed through the hands of all of Sicily's invaders, who sought to control the Strait of Messina to the north and the southern waterway to Africa and the East. Under the Spanish it was a strong cultural center, but in 1669 Etna intervened in its destiny again. What Etna did not destroy, an earthquake in 1693 soon did. Reconstruction began during the 18th century according to the plans of the brilliant Giovanni Battista Vaccarini (1702–1768), who widened the streets and constructed Baroque palaces.

Among the points of interest are the ***Piazza del Duomo** (1), where Vaccarini's *Elephant Fountain* carries a grand obelisk from Egypt, similar to Bernini's in Rome. The *Palazzo del Municipio* (2) is another of his designs on the piazza, but his masterpiece is the ***Duomo** (3). The cathedral was originally built under the Normans, but the earthquake necessitated complete restoration. Besides works of art from the Middle Ages and the Renaissance, the Duomo contains the tomb of the composer Vincenzo Bellini, born in Catania in 1801; and tombs of the House of Aragon, which are found in *Sant'Agata's chapel,* a much venerated place where the patron saint of Catania is buried. Other interesting features of the cathedral include 16th-century choir stalls, Romanesque columns and the **Treasury,* which includes a gold crown of Richard the Lionhearted of England.

Just north of the cathedral is the Baroque *church of Sant'Agata* (4), crowned by a cupola, another work of Vaccarini.

Catania: Castello Ursino

Between the cathedral and the *Porto Vecchio* (5) lies *Villa Pacini* (6), whose small garden opens to a view of the harbor.

Slightly southwest of the center is the ***Castello Ursino** (7), the former fortress of Frederick II. This 13th-century castle is a fine example of a fortified construction of this period, and its four round towers have become the symbol of the city. Inside it is the **Museo Civico,* with a collection of weapons, oriental antiquities, and numerous artworks. Of particular interest are the Greek, Etruscan, and Roman ***bronzes, **vases,* and **sculpture.* Via Auteri leads from the castle to **Piazza Mazzini* (8), which is surrounded by an arcade containing 32 marble columns from a Roman basilica.

Crossing Via Vittorio Emanuele we come to the Baroque *church of San Francesco d'Assisi* (9) (on the right) and the house

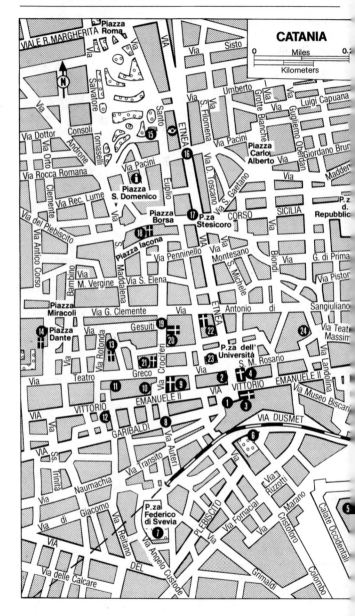

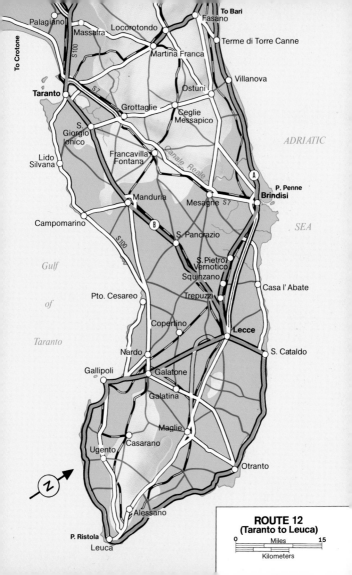

ROUTE 12
(Taranto to Leuca)

Dramatic ruins, such as the temple dedicated to Castor and Pollux, bear witness to the rich history of Agrigento.

A boar is the symbol of Florence's busy Porcellino market.

ROUTE 12
(Barletta to Bari)

0   Miles   15

Kilometers

The 14th-century Torre del Mangia towers above Siena's beautiful Piazza del Campo.

Cypress trees and umbrella pines enhance the timeless beauty of the Tuscan landscape.

The Palazzo Ducale in Venice, whose splendid apartments are open to the public, incorporates elements of Gothic and Renaissance design.

The magnificent Grand Canal, lined with 200 palaces, is Venice's main thoroughfare.

Trulli, round stone houses with conical roofs, are found only in the region of Apulia.

Some old traditions continue in the quiet serenity of Sardinia's countryside.

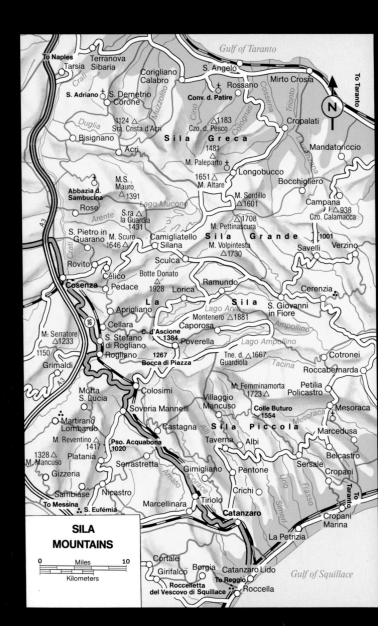

SILA MOUNTAINS

0 ——— Miles ——— 10

Kilometers

where Bellini was born (on the left) (10), which is now a museum of memorabilia of the great composer of *Norma* and *I Puritani*. Behind it, on Via del Teatro Greco, is the ***Roman theater,** built over a Greek base. The rows of seats rise in a semicircle from the slope of a hill. Next to the theater stands the **Odeon,* the scene of ancient concerts. Not far from here are other archaeological excavations, including the *Terme dell'Indirizzo* (12), remains of Roman thermal baths.

Slightly to the north is the *church of Santa Maria della Rotonda* (13), built from a round Roman building. Just to the west, steps lead to *Piazza Dante* where, next to a Benedictine monastery, the *church of San Nicolò* (14) can be visited. Built in Baroque style between 1693–1721, though never finished, it is one of the largest churches in Sicily. Inside, the sumptuous choir and the altar paintings in the semicircular side chapel are worth seeing. A stair leads to the cupola, 62 meters (200 feet) high, from which, if it is open, a fine view can be enjoyed— a premium for fitness.

The **Villa Bellini* (15), in the northern part of Catania has a garden with palm trees, flowers, and hedges arranged in the design of a clock; busts of Bellini and other composers add to the charm. To the east of the park is a well-preserved *Roman tomb* (16).

Via Etnea, a bustling shopping street, runs north to the *botanical garden* at the *university* and on to Etna itself, passing a *Roman amphitheater.* Just to the west of it is the *church of Santo Carcere* (18), named for the prison that was once on this site, where Sant'Agata was imprisoned for her faith and martyred.

*Via Crociferi (19), the Baroque showcase of Catania, is theatrically lined with Vaccarini flourishes. (It runs north and south, almost parallel to Via Etnea.) **San Giuliano* (20) (1738–1760), with a richly appointed interior, contains frescoes by Giuseppe Rapisardi and has an impressive nuns' choir. On the other side are the churches of *San Benedetto* and the *Gesuiti* (21) and a bit farther east is the *Collegiata* (22), a Jesuit college with four courtyards and a splendid Baroque façade. South of the Collegiata extends *Piazza dell'Università,* also sprinkled with Vaccarini contributions, and the university (23), which was founded there in 1444. The present building dates from 1790–1806. To the east stands the *Teatro Massino Bellini* (24), where opera performances are held in winter.

Catania is the ideal point of departure to visit **Mt. Etna** (68 km.; 42 miles from Catania) although you could also go from Taormina with an organized tour. It is possible to climb the volcano, or take a bus or Jeep to the crater, depending on how the volcano has been behaving. It also is possible to travel around the base to see the surrounding towns, most of which have particular appeal. The train called the *Circumetnea* makes the trip.

Mt. Etna is the highest active volcano in Europe, with a peak that is usually snow-capped. The Arabs called it *Mongibello* (from *monte* and the Arabic word *jebel,* or mountain). Its early eruptions were described by Pindar, and it has continued to erupt to the present, although fortunately no longer on a grand scale. The black lava is fascinating to climb, for you pass through stages of vegetation, from vineyards to orange trees, and chestnut trees that make a fine sight when they flower.

Leave Catania on *Via Etnea* going north. At the area of the lava flow, grapes and citrus groves can be seen. Continue to *Gravina di Catania* with two craters, 400 meters (1,300 feet) high. Stop at *Nicolosi* at 700 meters (2,300 feet), a popular summer resort, before reaching the *Monti Rossi,* with many craters formed in the eruption of 1669. The road continues its circuitous ascent, and there is a turn-off to the Grand Albergo Etna, a hotel from which there are superb views. To reach the crater you must hike or rent a Jeep, at *Rifugio Sapienza;* the cable car, because of seismic activity near the cone, is rarely working. At the crater's edge you are 3,340 meters, or 10,960 feet, above sea level, and the climb can be made only with a guide.

Return to Catania by way of *Zafferana Etnea,* a summer resort nestled high in the green hills, and *Trecastagni,* which has a lovely church in Renaissance style, a masterpiece of Antonello Gagini's.

It is also possible to make a **round-trip tour around Etna** (140 km.; 87 miles from Catania). Although there is only one main road, you must watch for signs to specific villages when the road forks. From *Trecastagni* (see above) go north to *Fornazzo,* where a road branches off to the *Citelli refuge* (may be closed) at 1,700 meters (5,575 feet) in the forest. From *Fornazzo* the road continues to *Linguaglossa,* a point of departure for guided tours of the Etna area. Here the panoramic road called *Mareneve* (sea and snow) climbs through pine forests to the *Rifugio-Albergo Mareneve* at 1,425 meters (4,675 feet), and *Rifugio Sucai* above.

From Linguaglossa drive west on Route S 120 along the northern slope to ***Randazzo.** Many houses here date from the 14th–16th centuries. Particularly inter-

Zafferana Etnea

esting is *Via degli Archi,* the street of the arcades, with Gothic houses. Other sites include the *cathedral of Santa Maria,* the *church of San Nicolò,* with a statue of the saint by Antonello Gagini, the *Palazzo Finocchiaro,* and the *Museo Vagliasindi.*

Turn south on Route S 284 and continue along the western edge of the volcano, by way of Maletto and Bronte, to Adrano.

Maletto, at 950 meters (3,100 feet), is the highest town in the area. A short excursion (6 km.; 4 miles) leads to *Santa Maria di Maniace.* This fortresslike abbey on the other side of Route S 120, also called the Castello Maniace, was given by King Ferdinand III in 1799 to the British admiral Nelson, who received the title "Duke of Bronte" at the same time. (Bronte is a nearby town.)

*Adrano, perched on a lava plateau, looks out on the Salso and Simeto river valleys. The town is surrounded by olive trees, orange groves and vineyards. It is built at the site of the ancient Adranon, founded in 400 B.C. and famous for its Temple to Adranos, a god of war and fire.

The 11th-century Norman *castle* is now a museum containing artifacts from the Stone and Bronze Ages. The *church of Maria Assunta* has ancient granite columns, and includes the former cloister of *Santa Lucia,* built in 1150 and restored in 1600.

Continue past *Biancavilla* and *Santa Maria di Licodia* to ***Paternò,** surrounded by lemon groves, an important exporter of citrus fruit. The **Norman castle,* built in 1073, was restored during the 15th century and again in 1958. Its rooms shelter the *Municipal Museum.* The *palace of Queen Eleanora* was converted into a Franciscan monastery in 1346. The town has several interesting churches.

Near Paternò are the ruins of the walls of *Hybla,* a city founded in the ninth century B.C. by the Siculi. Ancient Hybla was famous for the Temple to the Goddess Hyblaia and her oracle.

Cross the ridge of *Monte Territi* on Route S 121 to **Misterbianco,** located in the middle of a lava flow. As a result, the soil is fertile and suitable for growing olives, grapes, figs, and other fruits. About 3 km. (2 miles) west lies the scenic little town of *Motta Sant'Anastasia,* with a castle from the Norman era.

Return to ***Catania** (see page 292).

Catania is also a good point of departure for an inland excursion to ****Enna** and ***Caltanissetta,** since it is the railroad hub and major bus terminal of the eastern side of the island. Planning trips with Catania as a base is easy for visitors without a car, though the city's noise and confusion do not make it the most pleasant base. Much can be done on day trips from Taormina, but less conveniently. Enna and Caltanissetta can be reached by bus or by Autostrada A 19.

**Enna (75 km.; 47 miles from Catania) is called the Belvedere of Sicily, or, less romantically, the "navel" because of its situation near the center of the island. At an elevation of 950 meters (3,100 feet) it is the highest city in Sicily. It was founded by the Siculi, who were so receptive to Greek legends that the region was the center of the cult of Demeter, and the rape of Persephone was said to have taken place at nearby Lake Pergusa. In 664 B.C. the city was settled by Greeks, and later by Romans. Under Byzantium it gained great importance, but then attracted the Saracens and after them the Normans, Hohenstaufens, and the court of Aragon.

From the 13th-century ***Castello di Lombardia the entire island may be seen spread out like a relief map. The coasts, except the west coast, are barely 100 km. (60 miles) away. Across the mountains Mt. Etna towers majestically. The *Duomo has remarkable Gothic apses but was later rebuilt in Baroque style. The curved Spanish grilles in front of the windows show the Catalan influence.

In the municipal park there is an octagonal *tower, which also offers a good view.

Just 10 km. (6 miles) south on the road to Piazza Armerina is ****Lago di Pergusa,** which in ancient legend was the place where Persephone descended in winter and emerged in spring from the netherworld below. Now, in modern times, it is a racecourse, and the speeding cars excite the crowds' cheers but not their mythological fantasies.

*Piazza Armerina (34 km.; 20 miles from Enna) is built on terrac ⌐ at three levels. At the top is the *Duomo, a 17th-century work with an earlier Gothic belltower. The church of San Pietro has a charming interior, and San Giovanni dei Rodi, built during the 13th century, is a plain chapel that was used by the Knights of St. John.

Five km. (3 miles) farther south is the third-century A.D. ****Villa Romana del Casale,** which was probably a country retreat of the Emperor Maximian. Its **mosaic floors are exquisite, with geometric designs and figures depicting scenes of daily life, legends, and wild animals. As such they are of great importance historically, as well as for their beauty.

From Enna take Autostrada A 19 or Route S 117 bis and then S 122 to ***Caltanissetta,** (34 km.; 20 miles from Enna). The most modern city in the Sicilian interior, it is located in a major sulfur-mining area and is an important commercial center. The week before Easter is a good time to visit, for, like many Sicilian towns, it has dramatic processions and festivities before and on Easter Monday. Here the "procession of the mysteries" is held the Thursday before Easter.

Sights of interest include the Baroque cathedral and the churches of San Sebastiano and San Domenico, with unusual façades, the ruins of the Castello *di Pietrarossa,* and the *Museo Civico,* where the statues that are carried in the ceremonies at Easter are kept during the rest of the year.

The area of Caltanissetta has small Medieval towns with interesting feudal fortresses, and recent excavations have uncovered prehistoric settlements nearby.

To continue on Travel Route 24 take Route S 114, south from Catania. The road follows the *Golfo di Catania* and the *Golfo di Augusta,* both of which have beaches. The area around **Augusta** is heavily industrialized. In the city the sights include a Norman *castle,* with additions by Frederick II Hohenstaufen (now a prison); the *cloister* built in 1219 next to the *church of San Domenico;* and the 17th-century *cathedral.*

Continue on Route S 114 to Syracuse (160 km.; 99 miles from Catania).

***Syracuse

See map on page 301.

Syracuse (Siracusa), bordered on three sides by the Ionian Sea, is an important agricultural, commercial, and maritime center. From its port, direct shipping lines provide connections to Malta, Egypt, and many North African ports. Although the modern city is not particularly exciting, the old quarter on the island of *Ortygia* (connected by two bridges) and the *Archaeological Zone* are especially interesting. There are unique buildings from most eras of Sicilian history, although earthquakes have flattened much of the city through the centuries, and wars have been devastating. A splendid promenade along the harbor is invigorating; there are fine beaches to the south, and the cliffside is dotted with caves. A disco has been built on the ground floor of a splendid noble palace, for a bit of contrast; a Greek Theater Festival takes place in the theater where Euripides' plays were first produced; and, finally, the food is exquisite. Because of its sheltered location, the climate is the best in Sicily, the sun shines here all year, with a few exceptions in the winter.

Syracuse was founded in 734 B.C. by Greeks from Corinth. In 485 B.C. Gelon, the tyrant of Gela, a city nearby, conquered the city. Under his successors Syracuse grew into the largest and most beautiful of Greek colonial cities, rivaling Athens itself.

Dionysius I, who ruled the city in the fourth century B.C., saved it from a Carthaginian attack. Because of his war against the Carthaginians some 80 years later, Agathocles became the hero of countless legends. Under King Pyrrhus of Epirus, who temporarily drove both Romans and Carthaginians out of Sicily and maintained a strong army with elephants, Syracuse was considered unbeatable. Peace returned to Syracuse only under Hieron II (269–215 B.C.), who maintained friendly relations with Rome and the Egyptian Ptolemy. Science and poetry again flourished under his reign; Archimedes and Theocritus worked at his court.

In 212 B.C. Syracuse was conquered by Rome. Later it fell to Gothic, Byzantine, Saracen, and Norman forces. The city declined and didn't revive until the Aragon period, which saw a flowering of the Baroque in Sicily during the 18th century.

The fascinating old quarter of *Ortygia* is located on its own island, connected to the mainland by the *Ponte Nuovo*. On *Piazza Emanuele Pancali* are the ruins of the ***Temple of Apollo** (1), probably the oldest temple in Sicily. In 1938 it was uncovered from all the additions that had accrued over time, and excavation is still going on at the site.

Behind the temple, *Corso Matteotti* leads to *Piazza Archimede* with the *Fontana di Artemide* (2). At the corner of Via Montalto is the 14th-century **Palazzo Montalto,* with a Gothic façade.

Follow *Via Roma* past several public buildings to *Via Minerva* and turn right to the *Piazza Duomo* and the cathedral. The ****Duomo,** *Santa Maria del Piliero* (3), is built on the remains of a fifth-century B.C. Greek temple, which had been constructed over an earlier shrine. The Greek columns and parts of the building were integrated into the new cathedral, which was reconstructed in fine Baroque fashion after an earthquake leveled Ortygia in the 17th century. The interior, too, is almost a cultural

museum, with artistic treasures in painting and sculpture, fine grill-work, and a Norman baptismal font. In the *chapel of the Crucifix* (18th century) there is a painting attributed to Antonello da Messina (if it's been returned from safekeeping after a theft and recovery), and on the north aisle is a fine statue of the Sicilian Saint Lucy, whose feast day, December 13, is celebrated throughout the island with festivals of light. The *Palazzo Arcivescovile* (17th–18th centuries) and the *Biblioteca Alagoniana* stand next to the cathedral, and opposite them are Baroque palaces: the **Beneventano del Bosco* (with a disco below and a complaining noble family still in residence above) and the *Palazzo Verme.*

Follow the street at the far side of the Piazza south to *Via Capodieci,* a short walk away. Just to the left after a few buildings is the ***Museo Regionale d'Arte Medioevale e Moderna* in the *Palazzo Bellomo* (4). This 13th-century Swabian palace with 15th-century Catalan-style alterations now houses a delightful museum in which the picture gallery has the damaged masterpiece of the *Annunciation* by Antonello da Messina (1474) and Caravaggio's *Burial of Saint Lucy.* The folk collection is also interesting.

Continue south along the Lungomare to the **Castello Maniace* (5) at the tip of the island. The castle was named for a Byzantine general who took the city from the Arabs; it was erected by

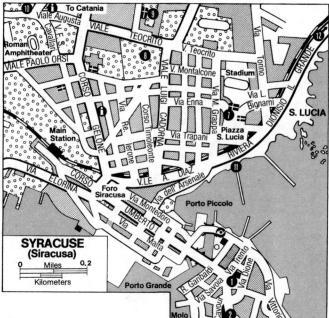

Frederick II Hohenstaufen. The tower and portal are remarkable.

Return through *Via Castello Maniace* to the ***Fonte Aretusa** (6), a freshwater spring named for the nymph Arethusa who, according to legend, leaped into the sea in Greece to escape the river god Alpheus and was changed by the goddess Artemis into a fountain. She flowed undersea to Syracuse, with Alpheus pursuing, and here they lie forever, she a fountain, and he the salt sea at the fountain's edge. Pindar, Virgil, and modern poets have praised the fountain, but more for its legendary origin than for its beauty. It is a basin with papyrus and other plants, and has a melancholy romantic look.

Follow the waterfront promenade, which leads past *Porto Grande* to *Porta Marina,* a Catalan gate that was the only entry into the city under Spanish rule.

The churches of importance include the 12th-century **Santa*

Lucia (7), at the far end of town to the north, erected at the site where she died a martyr in 303. ****Catacombs** run beneath the church, but they are usually closed. (See San Giovanni, below.)

The **Santuario della Madonnina delle Lacrime* (8) on Piazza della Vittoria is an unusual modern shrine, erected to honor the miraculous statue of the "Weeping Madonna" within, who answered the prayers of a dying Syracusan woman, it is believed, and is now appealed to by thousands of pilgrims. To the northwest stands the ****Basilica di San Giovanni alle Catacombe** (9), built in Byzantine and Norman style. Destroyed by the earthquake of 1693, it was later restored to its original form. The arches of the portico date from the 1102 Norman church. From the church, a passage leads to the ***Catacombs,* where there are many galleries and frescoed funeral chapels. These catacombs are natural grottoes which, as early as 300 B.C., were used as tombs; they were developed and enlarged by the Christians from the third to the fifth centuries A.D. Of special importance is the ***Crypt of St. Marciano,* believed by historians to be the first Christian church in Sicily. St. Paul (in The Acts of the Apostles) says that he stopped in Syracuse, and it would have been here that he preached to the Early Christians, at the altar in the chapel. A few blocks from the basilica is the park of *Villa Landolina,* now the site of the new ***Museo Archeologico Regionale,* which recently was moved from Ortygia to the new building on *Viale Teocrito.* Artifacts from prehistoric times to the second century B.C. are displayed in an exceptional, expanded collection. The Classical statuary is much praised, particularly the ***Venus Anadyomene,* probably a Roman copy of a Greek work. The **coin collection* is superb—coins produced here were among the most beautiful of their time. The ***Sarcophagus of Valerius and Adelphia* is another of the treasures.

Heading west on Viale Teocrito you'll reach the ancient quarter of *Neapolis,* with its ****Parco Monumentale della Neapolis* [10], which lies in the midst of lush vegetation. It is crossed by the panoramic ***Viale Rizzo,* which provides a splendid view of Syracuse and the sea. Many quarries (*latomie*) can be seen here, whose steep walls rise 30 meters (65–100 feet) into calcareous rock. The stone for the construction of the city was mined here. The most famous is the ***Latomia del Paradiso,* in which a gigantic cave is shaped like an earlobe, the *****Orecchio di Dionisio,** atop which the tyrant Dionysius was reputed to have eavesdropped on his slaves, thanks to the fine acoustics. (Clap your hands and see.) The surrounding gardens are brilliant and fragrant for most of the year.

More caves and grottoes lie northwest of this one, and in some

Orecchio di Dionisio

of them stone was quarried long after the Greeks left. Opposite is the entrance to the ***Greek theater,** cut out of the hillside during the fifth century B.C. and considered to be one of the largest and best-maintained theaters in the world. With a diameter of 134 meters (440 feet) and concentric wedge-shaped rows of seats carved from the rock, the theater resembles a gigantic fan. Its acoustics are extraordinary. In the presence of Hieron II, the tragedies of Aeschylus (whose *Persians* premiered here in 472 B.C.), Sophocles, and Euripides were performed on this stage. Since 1914 classical Greek tragedies have been performed here (in Italian) in even-numbered years.

Diagonally across from the entrance to the theater are the ruins of the monumental third-century B.C. ****Altar of Hieron II,* partially cut into the rock, in honor of Jupiter Liberator. Originally 200 meters (650 feet) long, it was the largest sacrificial altar known. Little remains of the colossal structure on which hundreds of oxen were sacrificed.

Nearby is the small **church of San Nicolò,* built during the 11th century in Norman style. Nearby, an antique reservoir leads to the ****Roman amphitheater* (probably first century A.D.), which was once flooded for mock naval battles, and also used for fights between gladiators and animals. It is the largest in Italy, next to Verona's amphitheater. Farther north is the **Via delle Necropoli Grotticelle,* an ancient street dating from Roman-Byzantine times and consisting of walls with niches in which funeral urns were placed.

For travellers with enough time, three short excursions can be made from Syracuse. Check first with the tourist office to see if the Catacombs of the Capuchins are open, and if so, head north along the *Riviera Dionisio il Grande* through the district of *Santa Lucia* to the former **Capuchin monastery* and the adjoining catacombs, the ****Latomia dei Cappuccini** (12). The ancient quarry, now covered with lush vegetation thanks to industrious monks, was used as a prison in 414 B.C. and still shows traces of the chisels wielded more than 2,000 years ago by Greek slaves and soldiers captured during the war with Athens.

About 9 km. (6 miles) north-west of the center of Syracuse, in the *Epipolae* or upper city, is the ****Castello Eurialo,** built during the 5th century B.C. under Dionysius I. Its grandiose combination of trenches, towers, ramparts, and walls makes it one of the principal surviving examples of Greek fortified architecture. When the Romans attacked the city in 212 B.C., Archimedes arranged mirrors and lenses on the Castello, and, by focusing the sun's rays on the sails of the Roman fleet, set the ships on fire.

Slightly south of the city is the *Fonte Ciane,* the source of the Ciane River. The upper river is bordered with papyrus plants and reeds. According to Greek legend the nymph Cyane, wife of the river god Anapos (another river's name, nearby), tried to stop Pluto from abducting Persephone, and

when she couldn't she was transformed into a spring, to weep forever.

Not far from the right bank are the remains of the *Olympeion,* a Doric temple erected in 500 B.C. to Zeus.

A slightly longer side trip to *Sortino* (35 km.; 22 miles northwest from Syracuse) is also worthwhile. Perched 440 meters (1,450 feet) above sea level, it is a village of attractive churches and a monastery. It is on the way to the necropolis of *Pantalica,* across the Anapo River, a strange, vast graveyard of the Siculi in deserted countryside, in use between the 13th and 8th centuries B.C. Many of the more than 5,000 cells were the tombs of entire families. Objects found in them are exhibited in the archaeological museum in Syracuse (see page 302).

TRAVEL ROUTE 21: ***Syracuse–*Ragusa–*Gela–***Agrigento–***Selinunte–*Marsala (395 km.; 245 miles)

See map on pages 272–273.

This travel route follows the south coast of Sicily. Route S 115 is a panoramic road, and between Syracuse and Marsala it passes through some of the most beautiful landscapes on the island, including Agrigento, a favorite among the Classical authors, and numerous seaside resorts. Side roads lead to beaches to the south. Some stretches can be covered on the Autostrada A 29.

The first leg of Travel Route 21 goes from Syracuse to Ragusa. There are two routes to choose from, through Palazzolo Acreide or through Noto (see page 305).

For the route by way of Palazzolo Acreide, leave *Syracuse* (see page 299) on Route S 124. Cross the Anapo River to reach *Floridia,* an agricultural center.

The road ascends through rugged mountains to **Palazzolo Acreide** (43 km.; 27 miles from Syracuse), a town in the *Monti Iblei,* 700 meters (2,300 feet) above sea level. Rebuilt in Baroque style after the earthquake of 1693, it has beautiful buildings from the 18th century. Close at hand are the ruins of an ancient city, Acree (Akrai), founded in the seventh century B.C. A small Greek theater, an agora, and an odeon dating from the third century B.C., and *latomie* (quarries) are part of a later development. Nearby, in a valley east of the hill, there are primitive rock statues called *santoni;* they are shown by the custodian in charge.

Leave the town and turn south on Route S 194 to *Giarratana* and follow the Irminio River to ***Ragusa** (81 km.; 50 miles from Syracuse), on a high plateau cut by deep gorges. It consists of an older city, *Ragusa Ibla,* and modern Ragusa. Ibla is the one to see, the site of ancient Hybla Heraea, a settlement of the Siculi. A fortress here dominates the valley of the Irminio. The Siculi settlement eventually became Greek, for they wiped out most of the Siculi settlements they found, and it was then ruled by Gela. After it was razed in the earthquake of 1693, Ragusa Ibla was rebuilt in Baroque style. The city expanded to the higher plateau, where it was laid out in modern fashion.

The Baroque look of Ragusa Ibla is accentuated by the *church of San Giorgio* (18th century), a Baroque structure to which a Classical dome was added, the work of the great Baroque architect Rosario Gagliardi. Other places to visit are the *church of San Giuseppe* and a collection of palaces, the most interesting of which is *Donnafugata,* where a museum has been established (special permission is needed to visit).

In upper Ragusa, the *Museo Archeologico* has some interesting relics of the area, from the Neolithic period to the Byzantine.

Major deposits of asphalt and oil near Ragusa account for its commercial significance.

If you wish to take the route to Ragusa through Noto, leave *Syracuse* (see page 299) by way of the *Porto Grande* and *Via Elorina* to Route S 115.

Avola is the center of an almond-growing region, and its beaches are much sought after. ****Noto** (32 km.; 20 miles from Syracuse) is perched on a hill in the midst of orchards. This enchanting Baroque city was rebuilt after the earthquake of 1693, several miles south of the original site. Its overall planning is astonishing to architects and city planners, who come here to study its subtle scenic effects. The principal buildings from the 18th century, often the work of Gagliardi, are located on or near the central street, Corso Vittorio Emanuele. They include the church and former convent of **San Domenico,* beautifully positioned next to the **church of Santissimo Salvatore;* the **Palazzo Ducezio* (now the city hall); the *church of San Francesco d'Assisi;* the *Bishop's Palace;* the *Duomo;* and the splendid **Via Nicolaci,** a street which leads dramatically along the sumptuous balconies of carved griffons and mermaids of the *Palazzo Nicolaci (Villadorata).* Statues in the *church of the Crocifisso* are superb, especially the Madonna in the right transept by Laurana. Significant archaeological artifacts can be seen in the *Museo Comunale.* The hot month of August is cooled by an ice-cream festival each year, and a summer concert series is held regularly. The ruins of *Noto Antica* lie about 8 km. (5 miles) north of the present town. The damage caused by the quake can be seen clearly.

The hermitage *San Corrado fuori le Mura,* also north of Noto, is the destination of many pilgrimages and a festival honoring the saint. About 7 km. (4 miles) southeast of Noto, very near the coast, are the ruins of *Eloro* (Helorus), a town founded in the 7th century B.C. *Noto Marino's* pretty beach and resort are nearby.

Continue on Route S 115 through *Rosolini* to **Ispica** where the *church of Santa Maria Maggiore* houses some of the major paintings of Vito d'Ana, a principal Sicilian painter of the 18th century. The town is situated on a ledge over the estuary of the **Cava d'Ispica,** 10 km. (6 miles) long, a gorge cut by mountain run-off. Its many caves were used as both homes and tombs between the Stone Age and the fifth century A.D.

For a side trip to **Pachino** and **Pozzallo** (33 km.; 20 miles from Ispica) take the road from *Ispica* southeast to *Pachino,* near *Marzamemi* and *Portopalo di Capo Passero,* popular seaside resorts. *Capo Correnti* is the southernmost point in Sicily. Another road leads from Ispica to *Pozzallo,* 10 km. (6 miles) to the southwest, one of the most popular beaches in this part of Sicily. By taking the coast road from here, you can visit a string of other beaches to the west.

From Ispica continue on Route S 115 to *Modica,* located at the foot of a promontory, where two valleys meet. The old city was destroyed by the 1693 earthquake, and the new city has an 18th-century appearance. Its outstanding features are the *cathedral of San Pietro* and the *church of San Giorgio,* at the top of a flight of 250 steps. Other sights include the ruined *church of Santa Maria di Gesù,* with a lovely doorway, and the small *church of San Giacomo fuori le Mura,* built in the 14th century.

Scicli, south of Modica by a scenic road that follows the *Fiumara di Modica,* makes a pleasant side trip. The town retains an 18th-century appearance. Its beautiful palaces include the *Palazzo Beneventano,* and it has several fine Baroque churches. Halfway between Modica and Scicli is the pilgrimage *church of Santa Maria delle Milizie.*

Route S 115 continues across the Irminio River to *Ragusa* (87 km.; 54 miles from Syracuse; see page 305).

From Ragusa, Route S 115 drops downhill to **Comiso,** with an interesting 14th-century castle and the churches of *Santissima Annunziata* and *San Francesco* from the same era. In the immediate vicinity, Siculi, Greek, and Roman necropoles have been found.

Vittoria is an attractive town on a high plateau, named in 1607 in honor of Vittoria Colonna, daughter of Spanish Viceroy Marcantonio Colonna. Sights include the Baroque *Duomo* and the Classical *theater*. The *park* offers a fine view of the Ippari River, the Hipparis praised by Pindar. The seaside resort of *Scoglitti* is 13 km. (8 miles) from Vittoria.

*Gela (145 km.; 90 miles from Syracuse) is one of the oldest cities in Italy. The site was inhabited by Sicani during the second millennium B.C. In 689 B.C., settlers from Crete and Rhodes arrived. In turn, some of Gela's Greek inhabitants founded Agrigento.

Gela quickly became one of the most powerful cities in Sicily. Aeschylus, the Athenian writer of tragedies, lived here. The decline came only after the tyrant Gelon moved his seat of power to Syracuse in 480 B.C. Gela was conquered in 405 B.C. by Carthage and sacked. It was settled again in 280 B.C. but later was completely destroyed by Agrigento.

The city was not resettled until 1233 under Frederick II Hohenstaufen, who called it Terranova, a name that was used until 1928. Now Gela is a seaside resort and important economically because of its petrochemical complex.

West of the city lies an ****archaeological zone** on the shore, where well-preserved Greek fortified walls have been excavated. They date from the sixth and fifth centuries B.C. and are evidence of Gela's strategic significance in antiquity. A second ****archaeological zone** lies to the east, in the *Parco delle Rimembranze.* The ****Archaeological Museum** contains interesting relics of the area, including a fifth-century horse head in terra-cotta, painted Attic vases, and ancient coins. Remains of an Archaic acropolis lie behind the museum, including ruins of two Doric temples and Greek houses from the ancient site.

*Lago Biviere is east of the industrial zone, surrounded by sand dunes. The dam of *Disueri,* 20 km. (12 miles) north of Gela has created an artificial lake. *Butera,* 14 km. (9 miles) northwest of Gela is the site of large prehistoric necropolises and a Norman castle. Route S 115 continues mainly along the coast to ***Falconara** where a fortress of the same name houses a rich collection of ceramics. A wide beach extends on both sides of the old fortress, near a grove of palm trees. **Licata** is a resort, with a castle and a museum of antiquity to explore. *Marina di Palma* has a good beach. About 28 km. (17 miles) beyond Marina di Palma is Agrigento (224 km.; 139 miles from Syracuse).

***Agrigento

See map below.

The spectacular *Valley of the Temples* is the first part of Agrigento to come into view, a sight and a city that has been praised since antiquity by authors such as Pindar, Virgil, and, more recently, Pirandello.

Agrigento was founded in 582 B.C. Called Akragas by the Greeks, it once housed more than 200,000 people. It flourished under the rule of the tyrants, was later destroyed by Carthage, was rebuilt, and then fell under Roman

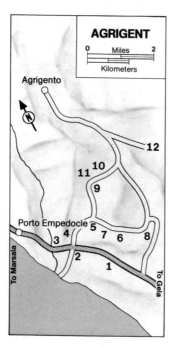

rule in 210 B.C., an unfortunate occupation that ended the city's grandeur and world renown. Arabs and Normans followed as colonial invaders, but the city never recovered. Agrigento is the hometown of the Greek philosopher Empedocles (ca. 500–ca. 430 B.C.) and the playwright Luigi Pirandello (1867–1936).

The ***Valle dei Templi** begins at the intersection of Routes S 115 and S 118. From here the *Strada Panoramica* bisects the valley and continues to the foot of the modern city, built on the hills above. At the seaward side of the highway is the **Tempio di Esculapio** (1) in which part of the cella (interior shrine room) remains, and two columns and a small staircase. **Tomba di Terone** (2) is 9 meters (30 feet) high and stands just outside the ancient walls near the Strada Panoramica. It's decorated with fluted Ionic columns and contains Doric elements; a Roman mausoleum of the first century B.C. Of the fifth-century ***Tempio dei Dioscuri** (3), only four Doric columns remain, a romantic fragment that is the most photographed Greek element in Sicily. Originally there were 34 fluted columns. The ****Tempio di Giove** (4) was erected after the Greek victory over the Carthaginians in 480 B.C. At 101 meters (331 feet) long and 53 meters (74 feet) wide, it was the largest temple in Sicily, though never finished. From perches about halfway up the columns on all sides, gigantic figures with raised arms supported the entablature.

One of these figures, the *Sleeping Giant,* lies here on the ground, a reconstruction of the original that can be found in the museum (see below). The **Tempio di Ercole** (5), probably destroyed by an earthquake in the Post-Classical period, is supposedly the oldest of the group and was built about 500 B.C. The building was 76 meters (250 feet) long and 28 meters (90 feet) wide. Inside, a large bronze statue of Hercules stood near the portico. Eight columns of the temple were excavated in 1923 and raised into their present position.

The fifth-century **Tempio della Concordia** (6), one of the best-preserved Doric temples in the world, stands alone at the top of the hill, elegant and powerful. It is 42 meters (140 feet) long and 19.7 meters (65 feet) wide; the 34 columns are fluted with 20 longitudinal grooves. We don't know to which deity it was originally dedicated; its present name comes from an inscription found near the temple. In the sixth century A.D., Saint Gregory, bishop of Agrigento, converted the temple into a church dedicated to Saints Peter and Paul. The walls of the cella were opened with arches, and the interior was divided into three aisles. The temple was restored in 1748 to its original form. The **Museum of Villa Aurea** (7) houses works in marble, terracotta and mosaic from the ancient site and is itself attractively located in a tropical garden on the grounds. The **Tempio di Juno Lacinia** (8), a Doric structure like all the others, dates from the fifth

century B.C. Its site, with a view of the hills, valley, and sea, is superb, and rewards those who walk up to it. Nearby are the sacrificial altar and cistern.

The **Case Romane** (9) is an area of Roman excavation at the foot of the modern city of Agrigento, farther west on the Strada Panoramica. Across the street from it is the *Museo Regionale Archeologico,* a fine small collection with a carefully arranged model of the *Tempio di Giove* and the Colossus. The Greek vases and sarcophagi are exceptional. Near the museum, behind the Medieval *church of San Nicola* (10), with its Norman portal, is the *Oratorium of Phalaris* (11), a Roman tomb of the first century B.C. Its columns on Attic bases have Doric capitals. The small *church of San Biagio* (12) was erected in Norman style in the 12th century. It was built on the foundations of a fifth-century B.C. temple dedicated to Demeter, who was worshiped enthusiastically here. Located high above the temples on the hill, it can also be reached through the town.

A "modern city" in Sicily is a relative designation. Agrigento's so-called modern city dates from the Medieval era, although it is surrounded by an unattractive urban sprawl of recent origin. It can be reached along Route S 118 and Via Crispi. The *Museo Civico* on Piazza Municipio has a picture gallery, but may now be closed. Other sights include the 13th-century Gothic *convent of Santo Spirito* and the *church of Santa Maria dei Greci,* built during the 14th century on the foundations of the Temple of Athena.

The *cathedral* was constructed on the ruins of a *Temple of Jupiter* and was later rebuilt, once recently after a landslide destroyed it. Many of its artworks are displayed in the **Cathedral Museum.* Of particular interest are Greek sculptures and **sarcophagi.* The unfinished *belltower* dates from the 15th century. Among places to stop on this main street, *Via Atena,* are the pastry shops—the rich sweets here are exceptional.

Return to Route S 115 and continue to **Porto Empedocle.** The ancient port area has little for tourists, though some of the seafood restaurants are good. Its industrialization was a boon to Sicily's economy but not to its beauty.

Continue west on Route S 115 from Porto Empedocle. The road curves inland to *Monteallegro,* and shortly afterward a side road turns south to *Capo Bianco* and the ruins of **Eraclea Minoa.** Ancient Herakleia Minoa was a colony of Selinunte (see below). The ruins of the Greek theater by the sea are impressive, and the beaches along here are lovely. The seaside resort of ***Sciacca** was founded in the seventh century B.C. by Selinunte's inhabitants. Today it is a well-known spa where people go to ease the pains of arthritis and skin diseases. Besides its thermal spa, Sciacca has some lovely palaces and churches from the Middle Ages and Renaissance. Statues by the

Gaginis enliven the *Duomo,* and the *church of Santa Margherita* has a fine portal sculpted by Laurana. The Renaissance **Palazzo Steripinto* and the *Casa Arone* and *Castello Luna* (in ruins), are part of Sciacca's charm, but its true beauty is in the sweep of the *sea promenade.* Look for some of the city's pretty ceramics.

From Sciacca there are two brief side trips which are of interest. *Caltabellotta* (20 km.; 12 miles northeast) can be seen high above Sciacca, a white city by day and a sparkling fantasy at night. It rises 760 meters (2,500 feet) above sea level and is fun to explore. King Roger managed to put a Norman castle here, perhaps because of the view—which is spectacular—as well as for defense. Closer to Sciacca is *San Calogero* (8 km.; 5 miles), an ancient thermal spa that can be visited in the mountains.

At *Menfi* (315 km.; 195 miles from Syracuse) another scenic stretch begins. Shortly after crossing the *Belice River* you'll see the access road to *****Selinunte** (336 km.; 208 miles from Syracuse). On a spacious, lonely landscape by the sea, the bare ruins of Selinunte are poignantly evocative of their Greek past. Selinunte was founded by Doric settlers around 650 B.C. Its *Zona Monumentale* is one of the major archaeological sites of Sicily, although no temple is well preserved, because of war, earthquake, and the Spaniards—who took the stones to build their palaces. The structures on the east side have been partially restored and are perhaps the most beautiful columns and bases here. The metopes that lined the column tops are in the archaeological museum in Palermo.

Selinunte was destroyed around 409 B.C. during the war with Carthage. The temple ruins are marked with letters because none of the names are known. Among the most impressive are the gigantic *Temple D* on the east hill (550–480 B.C.), *Temple C* from the same period, and the later *Temple E*, with 38 columns; they are all partially reconstructed. The metopes from *Temple E* are among those in the Palermo museum. In the nearby quarry of *Cusa* you can see the stages involved in stone cutting and the columns that were being cut when the invasion came. *Marinella di Selinunte*, a small resort, is nearby and usually welcome, for the Selinunte site is large and the weather usually hot.

From Selinunte, take S 115 north to ***Castelvetrano.** Founded in the 11th century, it is the center of a wine- and olive-oil–producing region. Sights include remarkable stucco work by Ferraro and Serpotta, the great masters of stucco design. The *church of San Giovanni* has a marble statue by Antonello Gagini of John the Baptist. Attractive stucco design can also be seen at the *church of San Domenico.*

In the *Museum* on Piazza Garibaldi is the sixth-century ****Ephebus of Selinunte,** a fine ancient Sicilian work. (Stolen but recovered; supposed to be returned.)

About 5 km. (3 miles) west of Castelvetrano is the artificial *Lago della Trinità* and the **church of the Santissima Trinità di Delia,* a beautifully restored Arab-Byzantine chapel. (Ask around for the custodian to open it.)

From *Campobello di Mazara,* off Route S 115, an 8-km.- (5-mile-) road leads through a plain covered with vineyards to the long beach of Tre Fontane.

*Mazara del Vallo lies at the estuary of the Mazaro River, where there has been a settlement since Phoenician times. The city gained importance during the ninth century under the Arabs and later the Normans. Sights include the *cathedral,* which has a sculpture of the Norman Count Roger on horseback above the west door and some fine statues inside. The town still has an Arab flavor, owing to its past and to its new inhabitants from North Africa, who live in the ancient Casbah.

The church of *Santa Caterina* has a good statue of the saint by Antonello Gagini. Go toward the harbor, where the shore is lined with public gardens. The *Palace of the Knights of Malta* houses the *City Museum,* with collections of early civilizations. Outside the city is the Norman church of *San Nicolò Regale* and the *Madonna dell'Alto,* both interesting to visit. This port is one of Italy's major fishing ports, and you can take a boat trip through the canals to visit it. Route S 115 leads on to ***Marsala** (395 km.; 245 miles from Syracuse; see page 289).

Sardinia

Sardinia, the second largest island in the Mediterranean, has historical monuments, art treasures, and natural attractions in equal measure.

Those who know the island well describe it as a small continent on its own, with an indigenous history that goes back to prehistoric times.

Away from the hotels of Alghero, the Costa Smeralda, the capital Cagliari, and the island's other modern tourist resorts, you'll feel that you've travelled back in time. Country roads frequented by old ox carts cross a landscape of primitive towns with huts of unfired bricks and tiny outdoor wall ovens, high granite rocks, and fields of asphodel lilies. Natives of this rocky island say that God made it on the sixth day—with leftover rocks.

In the Gulf of Orosei (on the east coast), in Poetto near Cagliari, near Santa Margherita di Pula, in Marina di Arbus and Turri Manna are particularly beautiful and sandy beaches. The nicest, however, is at Piscinas, south of Oristano, where a 2-km.- (1.2-mile-) wide band of sand dunes, reminiscent of the Sahara, borders the sea. Until well into October, the temperature of the water is over 70°F. The following three routes can be combined into one tour.

TRAVEL ROUTE 22: *Olbia–**Costa Smeralda–Santa Teresa di Gallura–*Porto Torres–*Sassari–**Alghero (167 km.; 104 miles)

See map on page 313.

This Travel Route takes you north along the Sardinian coast from the port of Olbia, which connects by boat to the mainland, and the spectacular Emerald Coast to Alghero, the island's most popular resort town.

The busiest port in Sardinia is ***Olbia,** where passenger ships arrive daily from Civitavecchia on the Italian mainland. (There is also ferry service from Genova and Livorno.) The city, founded by the Phoenicians, has been for centuries a center of the cork trade, a major natural resource of Sardinia. Delicious mussels are harvested in the gulf. The sandy bays around the city are popular, and tourist facilities are good.

The main sights of Olbia include the *Punic necropolises* with trench graves, located between Via Brigata Sassari, Via Mameli and Via La Marmora; and, on a hill near the train station, the Pisan-Romanesque **church of San Simplicio* (11th century). Its triple-aisled interior has Roman columns and Romanesque arches and contains a collection of inscriptions, urns, and milestones. The fjordlike harbor offers

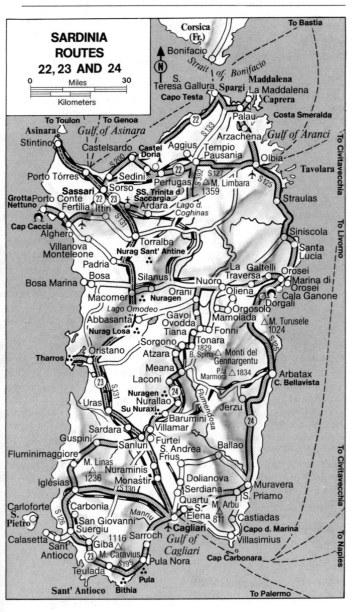

**SARDINIA
ROUTES
22, 23 AND 24**

0   Miles   30

Kilometers

a beautiful view of the craggy *Gulf of Olbia* and the rocky islands of *Tavolara* and *Molara*.

Two roads lead to Sassari: the long coast via the Costa Smeralda and Castelsardo, and Route S 127, which cuts inland (see page 317). If you choose the coast road, leave Olbia going north on Corso Umberto. Just outside the city, turn east onto Route S 127 and continue along the rocky, scenic coast to **Golfo Aranci.** This fishing village, located on the gulf of the same name, is a ferry harbor and a vacation resort. It has a fine beach and facilities for scuba diving. Leaving Golfo Arancio on Route S 127, take the right-hand road at the fork where S 127 turns left. After about 6 km. (4 miles) a side road on the right goes north to *Porto Rotondo,* a picturesquely located beach resort.

**Costa Smeralda (*Emerald Coast*) is the area north from the Golfo degli Aranci, past the gulfs of *Marinella, Cugnana* and *Pero,* to the *Golfo di Arzachena*—a beautiful coastline of cliffs, grottoes, and sandy beaches.

Costa Smeralda

The Aga Khan was instrumental in turning this once desolate peninsula into a rather exclusive resort area and the principal international attraction of the island. Scuba and skin divers find the waters in the area especially appealing because of the many reefs.

Baia Sardinia, at the northeastern point of the Gulf of Arzachena, has one of the most beautiful sandy and rocky beaches in Sardinia and is a popular resort.

Arzachena (76 km.; 47 miles from Olbia) is an ancient town, beautifully located on the southern slope of *Punta Martino* (336 meters; 1,100 feet). From here you can easily reach *Cannigione* to the northeast (8 km.; 5 miles), which has an attractive beach.

Route S 125 from Arzachena to *Palau* traverses rocky plateaus and lonely valleys with bizarre granite formations—a constantly enchanting countryside. Palau itself is a small fishing village with pleasant, uncrowded beaches.

From Palau you can take a ferry to ***La Maddalena,** the largest of the seven main islands in the Arcipelago della Maddalena. Until the 19th century this was a refuge for pirates; now it is a resort with wonderful beaches and facilities for scuba and skin-diving. In 1803 and 1804 the island served as Lord Nelson's headquarters, and the parish church in the town of La Maddalena has a chandelier given by Nelson and officially deeded to the town in his handwriting. The entire archipelago was fortified by the Italian government for quartering its fleet, but those fortifications were razed after World War II.

You can follow the panoramic road around La Maddalena and, on a swinging bridge, cross the Strait of Passo della Moneta to **Caprera,** where Garibaldi spent his last years. His house is now a museum, and his tomb is in the olive grove near the house. The house and tomb are visited by many Italians, especially on June 2, the anniversary of his death.

From *Palau,* continue on Route S 133 and S 133 bis to *Porto Pozzo,* a pretty bay with unusual granite formations, over a pass (90 meters; 300 feet) that offers a good view toward **Santa Teresa Gallura** (115 km.; 71 miles from Olbia), a town with wide, sandy beaches and, farther on, a rocky coast. Near its fjordlike harbor are the ruins of a Graeco-Roman structure from which you can see Corsica, only ten nautical miles to the north.

You can enjoy an even more beautiful view from nearby *Capo Testa,* which also has Roman ruins and sandy beaches between high cliffs.

The coast road continues southwest through a desolate part of the island, where bare, craggy rocks plunge into the water. You'll find attractive beaches, however, at *Vignola Mare* and *Portobello di Gallura.*

About 2 km. (1.2 miles) before crossing the Coghinas River, near the village of *Codaruina,* a side road on the left at *Badesi* leads southeast on a side trip to **Terme di Castel Doria,** on *Lago di Castel Doria.* Its sulfurous hot springs were frequented by the Romans; now there are modern therapeutic facilities for bathing and drinking treatments, and mud packs. On a nearby hill lie the ruins of a Genovese castle.

Continue on Route S 200 to **Nostra Signora de Tergu,* a 12th-century church. Past the remarkable *Elephant Rocks*—actually caves used during the Stone Age—is ***Castelsardo.** This enormous fortress, built in the 12th century, is perched on a cape and surrounded by water on three sides, providing magnificent panoramic views from its terraces. Under the Genovese it was rebuilt and is now called *Castel Genovese.* In the late Gothic *cathedral* (from about 1500) are paintings by local artists and a splendid 15th century Madonna.

The narrow streets of Castelsardo, accessible only by foot, are very picturesque. In many places they are interrupted by arches and stairways.

Continue along the coast road. Side roads diverge to prehistoric *nuraghi,* fortified dwellings shaped like cones and built without mortar.

About 14 km. (9 miles) after Castelsardo, Route S 200 turns inland through *Sorso,* an olive- and grape-growing center, to Sassari (page 316). Continuing along the coast road, you'll come first to *Marina di Sorso,* a resort with high sand dunes, then *Platamona Lido,* a fine beach, and finally to ***Porto Torres** (222 km.; 138

miles from Olbia), an important port from which ferries leave frequently for Genoa, Civitavecchia, Bastia, Nice and Toulon. There are extensive Roman ruins in the city, and many of the artifacts discovered here are displayed in the *Antiquarium*. In the eastern section of Porto Torres is the *church of San Gavino*, dating from the 11th century. In the crypt is the tomb of the saint. The interior columns are Romanesque. There are ornamental arches along the sides and twin doors from the 15th century in the Catalan-Gothic style.

At the beginning of the 19th century the *"marker column"* was erected to mark the end of the road from Cagliari to Porto Torres. It was taken from a Roman temple and decorated with Classical elements. Near the harbor is a fortified *tower* from the 14th century. West of the harbor a *Roman bridge* with seven arches spans the Turritano River. Near the bridge is the *Palazzo di Re Barbaro*, in fact, a Roman bath facility.

Stintino, on the western side of the *Golfo dell'Asinara*, makes an attractive side trip (29 km.; 18 miles) from Porto Torres. Located between a saltwater lagoon and an attractive beach, the waters are perfect for diving. Off Capo del Falcone lie the small island of *Piana* and the larger island of *Asinara*. Asinara has the remains of a fortress built by Chaireddin Barbarossa, the notorious Algerian pirate, and is now a penal colony.

If you turn inland from Porto Torres on Route S 131, you'll pass by *Monte d'Accodi*, which has the remains of a Stone Age altar and two menhirs—vertical stones with prehistoric inscriptions—and finally reach ***Sassari** (241 km.; 149 miles from Olbia), the second largest city in Sardinia, located amid gardens and olive groves. The old quarter, once surrounded by walls, still has winding, narrow Medieval streets lined with old houses, surrounding the **Duomo di San Nicola*, with its Spanish Baroque façade (the interior is restored). Behind the cathedral on Via Santa Catarina is the *Palazzo del Duca*, now the city hall and a museum of folklore. The *Museo G. A. Samna* houses important collections in the fields of archaeology, art and ethnography, including many Stone Age finds.

West of the cathedral in the large Piazza Santa Maria is the *church of Santa Maria di Betlem*, rebuilt but still preserving its Romanesque façade. Inside are wonderfully carved Baroque altars, and the cloister is graced by a 14th-century fountain.

Apart from its churches and some houses, Sassari is largely a modern town, and its new apartment buildings surrounded by large green areas give the city a pleasant, relaxed air. Despite its modernity, Sassari is known for its numerous religious and folk festivals, during which the participants wear magnificent costumes and bring to life the ancient traditions of Sardinia. During Holy Week there are many processions, and particularly impressive is the Procession of the Dead Savior on

Traditional Sardinian dress

Good Friday. The Cavalcata Sarda (Sardinian Cavalcade), with horsemen, traditional costumes and dances, celebrates Ascension Day in May; and the Processione dei Candelieri (Procession of the Candlesticks), a parade of tradesmen and farmers, occurs on Ferragosto (August 14).

The second route from Olbia to Sassari is through *Tempio Pausania*. Leave Olbia going west on Route S 127 and drive uphill through a desolate mountain landscape with macchia, olive and cork oak groves past *Telti*, with the remains of a Roman military camp, to *Calangianus*, where cork bark is processed. In the vicinity are *nuraghi* (fortified cone-shaped dwellings), dolmens (prehistoric tomb chambers of thick stone slabs or blocks), and a megalithic grave.

A side trip to the *Lago di Liscia* (17 km.; 10 miles from Calangianus) on Route S 427 leads through forests of cork oaks to the artificial lake of Liscia. North of here is an area with several *nuraghi*.

Continue to **Tempio Pausania,** where the main industry is also cork. This popular town is in a beautiful location and is a good starting point for trips into the surrounding mountains. Interesting sights include the 15th-century cathedral and, across from it, the *church of San Pietro*, which was built in the Romanesque style and has a later Baroque façade.

You can take a very pleasant walk through *Viale Fonte Nuova* and the splendid *Aggius Valley* to the hot springs of *Fonte Rinaggiu*, which produce therapeutic water with a high mineral content. There are attractive side trips from Tempio Pausania to the *Limbara mountains* and to ***Lago del Coghinas** (17–25 km.; 11–16 miles). South of Tempio Pausania a panoramic road turns east from Route S 392 in the Limbara range and leads to *Monte Balistreri*, a distance of 17 km. (11 miles). The road climbs to 1,300 meters (4,250 feet), and from its highest point it offers a complete view of northern Sardinia.

Route S 392 crosses the pass of *La Variante* (676 meters; 2,218 feet) to the **Lago del Coghinas* (25 km.; 16 miles). A 350-meter- (1,150-foot-) bridge spans one arm of this gigantic artificial lake. There is a good view of the ruins of the old *Castello Acuto* on your left. Soon after crossing the bridge, you'll arrive in *Oschiri*, which, with its domed parish church, lies about midway between Olbia and

Sassari. A small road off of Route S 597 leads to the eastern shore of the lake, site of the *church of Nostra Signora di Castro* (14th century) and the ruins of a Medieval fortress. There are also remains of *nuraghi* and buildings from Roman times.

Leave Tempio Pausania (see page 317) on Route S 127 going west and cross the island's main river, the Coghinas. Two roads continue to Sassari. Because of the magnificent landscapes, you should take the northern road, which winds through Perfugas, Nulvi, and Osilo. **Perfugas** lies on the Altana River, which empties three miles further north into the *Lago di Castel Doria* (see page 315). The Catalan-Gothic *church of San Giorgio* (15th century) contains a polyptych by a 16th-century Sardinian master. From Perfugas you may wish to make a side trip (16 km.; 10 miles), to ***Sedini.** Route S 134 leads to the Pisan-Romanesque **church of San Pietro delle Immagine* (11th–13th centuries), the town of *Bulzi,* and to **Sedini,* perched on a steep slope. In the town are the Catalan-Gothic *church of Sant'Andrea* (1517) and the ancient *rock tombs* (domus de janas), which later were transformed into cave dwellings.
A 40-minute hike leads to the ruins of a Benedictine church in the Lombard style, **San Nicola di Silanis* (12th century). Dolmens (see page 317) and *nuraghi* (see page 315) are nearby.

Route S 127 continues on from

Perfugas to *Laerru,* where *nuraghi* and limestone caves with stalactites can be seen. The next town, **Martis** (87 km.; 54 miles from Olbia), has a good Gothic *parish church.* A walk of about 30 minutes leads from here to a petrified forest of strangely shaped rocks and limestone formations. From *Nulvi* footpaths lead to several *nuraghi.* The Orria *nuraghe,* 3 km. (2 miles) southeast of town, provides a wide view of the surrounding countryside. The winding road continues to **Osilo,** with the ruins of a **fortress* from the 13th century, whose towers also offer a splendid view. Continue through the fertile vineyards and olive groves to ***Sassari** (129 km.; 80 miles from Olbia; see page 316).

From Sassari take Route S 127 bis southwest, toward the coast. The road crosses the railroad tracks and the Mannu River. Remains of *nuraghi,* and vineyards, orchards, and fields of flowers line the road.

**Alghero (167 km.; 104 miles from Olbia) is the most popular resort in Sardinia. The city, surrounded by olive groves and pine forests, has an important fishing port, a 5-km. (3-mile) beach, scenic cliffs along the shore, and excellent tourist facilities. Dark coral from the *Gulf of Alghero* is worked into precious jewelry in the city; accordingly, the coast is called the Coral Riviera.

Alghero reveals Sardinia's Spanish heritage in many of its most impressive structures. The bastions and the city walls, which still surround the old quarter, were erected by Genovese and Catalan builders in the 12th–14th centuries. The Catalans, who occupied the city in 1355, left their mark in the architecture of many of the houses, the appearance of the promenades (called *ramblas*), and the language of the local people.

Try to visit the old gate, *Porta a Mare,* an entrance to the old quarter; the 14th-century *cathedral; Casa Doria* from the 16th century, with a beautiful Renaissance portal, in the Medieval *Via Principe Umberto;* the *church of San Francesco* (14th–15th centuries), with a two-story, 16th-century cloister; and, on a piazza of the same name on the waterfront, **Torre Sulis,* the remains of the Genovese fortifications from the 13th century. The shore promenade, *Lungomare Dante,* begins here—it is a wonderful place to watch the sunset.

A marvelous boat excursion (about 40 minutes) leads to *Capo Caccia* (13 km.; 8 miles from Alghero). This red limestone cliff rises 170 meters (555 feet) above the water and encloses the ***Gulf of Porto Conte,* which has been praised for its beauty since antiq-uity. The gulf has a wonderful beach, a pine forest offering delicious shade, hotels, water-sport facilities and other tourist attractions. The ***Grotta di Nettuno* (Neptune Grotto), carved by the sea, has an inner lake and fantastic stalactite formations. It can be reached by boat or by descending 620 steps cut into the rock.

Between Alghero and *Porto Conte* is the modern resort of *Fertilia.*

Short excursions from Alghero include the underground prehistoric necropolises in ***Anghelu Ruiu* (13 km.; 8 miles north on the road to Porto Torres), with rock engravings from the early Bronze Age; the beautiful pilgrimage church of *Valverde* (8 km.; 5 miles east); on Route S 292, the mountainous area of *Scala Piccada* and, by way of the **Su Pischinale Pass* (681 meters; 2,234 feet)—a wonderful view in itself—to *Villanova Monteleone* (25 km.; 16 miles). Farther on, the romantic mountain village of **Monteleone Rocca Doria* is particularly lovely. It has a Genovese fortress from the 15th century and a late Romanesque church.

TRAVEL ROUTE 23: *Sassari–Macomer–*Oristano– Iglesias–*Cagliari (219 km.; 136 miles)

See map on page 313.

This Travel Route takes you south from Sassari through parts of Sardinia's spectacular interior and to sections of the coast. En route you'll marvel at the Phoenician ruins, Medieval fortresses, mountain passes, and seaside villages before entering Cagliari, the capital of Sardinia.

Leave *Sassari* (see page 316) going south on Route S 131. In 15 km. (9 miles), Route S 597 branches off to the monastery of ****Santissima Trinità di Saccargia,** built in the 12th century in Pisan-Romanesque style. The walls of the church, the abbey, and the bell tower are striped with alternating limestone and black basalt. Inside, frescoes date to the 13th century.

A little farther (3 km.; 2 miles) on the same road are the old country *church of San Michele di Salvenero* (12th century, Pisan-Romanesque) and *Sant'Antonio di Salvenero* (13th century). About 13 km. (8 miles) farther, on the right, is *Ardara,* site of the Lombard-Romanesque **church of Santa Maria del Regno* (1170) on a hill. This church has a beautiful late Gothic altar painting. About 6 km. (3.5 miles) farther on S 597 is the turnoff, on the left, for the **cathedral of Sant'Antioco di Bisarcio,* built in 1150 on the ruins of a small church that burned

Santissima Trinità di Saccargia

down in 1090. It has a triple-arched front portal with ornamental motifs, monolithic columns with highly decorated capitals, and a round-arch frieze at the eaves.

Torralba (39 km.; 24 miles from Sassari) is the point of departure for trips to the Pisan-Romanesque **church of San Pietro di Sorres* (12th century), near the town of *Borutta,* and to the ****Nuraghe palace of Sant'Antine,** built in the tenth or ninth century B.C. This is the largest, best-preserved, and highest (16 meters; 52 feet) prehistoric building on the island. In the central tower is a spiral staircase leading to the upper floor. The towers at the corners have battlements with embrasures. Many small *nuraghi* are found in the immediate area.

Just south of Sant'Antine a road branches east from Route S 131 to *Bonorva,* known for its horses and cattle-breeding and for its Catalan-Gothic parish church. About 9 km. (5.5 miles) farther east are the ****Grotte di Sant'Andria Priu,** with the largest *domus de janas* on the island. The 20 funeral chambers cut into the rock—from approximately 2400–1800 B.C.—are similar to the Etruscan tombs found in central Italy. Later these tombs were transformed into dwellings.

Continue south on Route S 131 to **Macomer** (75 km.; 47 miles from Sassari). This magnificently situated town was an important relay station in Roman times, and in the Middle Ages it became a military outpost. Now it is an intersection for several rail lines and highways. It is also a cheese-making center. Stone Age *nuraghi* are found throughout the surrounding area. From Macomer there is a pleasant side trip to *Bosa* (29 km.; 18 miles), west on Route S 129. Dominated by the Medieval *Castello di Serravalle,* the town also boasts the **church of San Pietro,* from the 11th century. It is the oldest Romanesque church in Sardinia. A 2-km.- (1.2-mile-) path leads to San Pietro from the castle. *Bosa Marina* is a small fishing village with a good beach. A jetty leads to *Isola Rossa,* with a lighthouse and a 16th-century watchtower.

Another side trip follows Route S 129 east from Macomer to **Silanus,* with its pre-Romanesque church, *Santa Sabina; San Lorenzo,* a Romanesque church built in the 12th century; and a two-story *nuraghe.* You may wish to continue through other small towns, some with beautiful Medieval churches, to *Nuoro* (see page 326). From here you may then follow Route S 131 dir. southwest to *Abbasanta.* You will pass **Lago Omodeo,* one of the largest artificial lakes in Europe. Just west of the junction of Routes S 131 dir. and S 131 is the three-story *nuraghe *Losa,* with corridors, rooms and cupolas.

Continue on Route S 131. When you reach *Tramatza,* drive 6 km. (4 miles) northwest to *Milis,* a small town surrounded by orange and lemon groves. Its Roman-

esque church, *San Paolo,* dates to the 12th–13th centuries. The surrounding villages all have Romanesque churches and *nuraghi.*

The next city is ***Oristano** (125 km.; 78 miles from Sassari), a busy commercial and agricultural center. Sights here include the *Torre di San Cristoforo* (13th century); remains of Medieval walls; the *Duomo,* which was built in the 13th century and altered and enlarged in the 18th century—its campanile dates from the 14th century; the *Antiquarium Arborense* at Via Vittorio Emanuele 8, which displays artifacts from the *nuraghi* era, Punic and Roman weapons, pitchers, and jewelry; the Classical *church of San Francesco* in Via Sant'Antonio, with Gothic ruins and art treasures inside; the *Palazzo Eleonora d'Arborea* at Via Parpaglia 4, built in the 14th century, with early Renaissance windows and a memorial to Eleonora of Arborea, a 14th-century *giudice* (judge), ruler of the giudicato of Arborea, who was famous for her wise influence on the future of Sardinia.

Marina di Torre Grande, the best beach near Oristano, has a round, fortified Spanish tower. It is 8 km. (5 miles) away.

Other excursions include the nearby lagoon of *Stagno di Cabras,* with its rich fishing grounds; the fishing village of *Cabras,* with its Medieval fortress; and the peninsula of *Sinis,* with its Early Christian **church of San Salvatore,* which has a crypt containing late antique frescoes and a Roman spring, and, farther on, *San Giovanni di Sinis,* a church that includes the remains of a Byzantine structure from the fifth century.

At the southern tip of the peninsula are the **Ruins of *Tharros,** a Phoenician settlement that later fell to Carthage and then to Rome. Excavations have revealed remains of a Phoenician temple, foundations of Roman houses, baths, temples and theaters, the remains of water mains, and a Phoenician necropolis with Roman tombs from the fifth to second centuries B.C.

Leaving Oristano going south, you soon come to *Santa Giusta* (11th–12th centuries), high on a hill. It is a good example of Sardinian Romanesque architecture, which was influenced by Pisa. Following Route S 131 will take you through a fertile wheat- and grape-growing region to *Uras,* where the road starts to climb between hills and *nuraghi.*

Sardara is worth a short stop for its church in the Romanesque and Gothic styles, *San Gregorio* (14th century). There are also *nuraghi* from the ninth century B.C. Byzantine elements are visible in the small *church of Sant'Anastasia.*

The *Terme di Sardara,* west of the town, were famous in antiquity for their hot springs. The water is reputed to treat rheumatism, arthritis, kidney stones, and other ailments. To the south stands the Medieval *fortress of Monreale,* built on a hill. In 1478 Sardinian fighters heroically resisted the

Santa Giusta

Aragonese, who stormed the fortress. Continue on Route S 131 to **Sanluri,** which is dominated by a 14th-century castle that now houses a weapons museum. At *Serrenti,* a side road leads 6 km. (4 miles) west to *Samassi,* known for its Nasco wine, which is similar to Spanish sherry. The town has a parish church with a Gothic campanile and a Romanesque-Gothic church, *San Gemiliano* (13th century), with a beautiful Renaissance tomb.

Route 131 continues to wind south, past *Nuraminis* and *Monastir* (197 km.; 122 miles) and through the fertile Campidano region to ***Cagliari** (see page 324).

Detour through Guspini and Iglesias by taking the road west from the Terme di Sardara (see above) or Route S 197 west from Sanluri (see above) to Guspini, where there is a 15th-century Aragonese-Gothic *church of San Nicola di Mira.* Pick up Route S

126, a scenic mountain road that winds through passes and rocky gorges and offers wonderful views of the sea at every turn.

Continue on Route S 126 to **Iglesias** (77 km.; 48 miles from Sanluri). Since the Middle Ages this city has been the center of lead, zinc, and silver mining in Sardinia. The pretty *old quarter,* with towers and the remains of walls, is perched on the slope of Monte Altare. *Castello di Salvaterra,* a 13th-century fortress located above the city, was renovated in 1325 by the Aragonese. The city has many Medieval churches, some built in the Pisan-Romanesque style, some in the Catalan-Gothic style. Among the most interesting are *San Francesco* (16th century) and *Nostra Signora di Valverde* (13th–14th centuries). The single-aisle Romanesque *cathedral of Santa Chiara* (1288) was later redone in the Gothic manner.

The *Museo di Mineralogia,* at the Istituto Tecnico Minerario, has fine collections of rocks and semiprecious stones as well as ancient artifacts.

The *church of Nostra Signora del Buon Cammino,* 300 meters (1,000 feet) above the city, offers wonderful views.

In this area, and especially around nearby *Monteponi,* mines have been worked for over 2,000 years. The excavation of millions of cubic meters of rock has formed craters and funnel-shaped pits over 100 meters (330 feet) deep. The crater walls glitter in yellow, brown, or reddish hues, depending on the type of stone. The oldest rock strata in Italy are found here. From Iglesias, take Route S 130 east to *Domusnovas.* Just 3 km. (2 miles) to the northwest is the 20-meter (65-foot) high *Grotta di San Giovanni.* A brook and a road just passable by car run through it.

Route S 130 continues past *Siliqua* and *Villaspeciosa*—where a side road south leads to *Uta,* which has a Romanesque church, *Santa Maria*—and the Elmas airport to ***Cagliari** (58 km.; 36 miles from Iglesias; see page 324). From Iglesias, you can detour through the southern tip of Sardinia by going south on Route S 126 to *San Giovanni Suergiu.* From there, drive over a dam to the island of **Sant'Antioco* (ancient Sulcis, first a Punic settlement, then a Roman one), which has fine beaches and a coast popular with divers. The catacombs of the *church of Sant'Antioco,* built in 1102 over the tomb of the saint and his mother, Saint Rosa, have Punic, Roman, and Byzantine columns, altars, and tombs. There is a ferry from *Calasetta* on Sant'Antioco to the island of **San Pietro* and the resort of *Carloforte* and interesting caves in the steep cliffs.

Return to the Sardinian mainland and follow Route S 195 around the scenic southern tip. Side roads lead to beaches, lagoons, *nuraghi* and archaeological sites. At **Capo Teulada,* the southernmost point of Sardinia, the cliffs drop 22 meters (72 feet) into the sea. To the northeast is the resort **Santa Margherita di Pula,* a popular and comfortable place to vacation. From Pula, where there is a 16th-century Spanish watchtower, a road leads to the ruins of **Nora.* Originally a Phoenician settlement, Nora was conquered by the Carthaginians and then the Romans in the third century B.C. There, on a panoramic site, you can see a labyrinth of streets and alleys with covered water ducts and mains, ruins of houses, temples, and baths.

Route S 195 continues north to *Sarroch,* where you can see the *nuraghe *Domu' es'Orcu* from the 16th century B.C. The road continues through orange, lemon, almond and olive groves and vineyards to Cagliari.

*Cagliari

The capital of Sardinia, founded by the Phoenicians and a major port in antiquity, is set against steep mountains on the Golfo di Cagliari. The old quarter, called the *Castello,* is built against the hills, while the new quarter extends along the coast. By the harbor on Via Roma is the modern, but Gothic-style, *city hall,* and running northeast from there, the wide *Largo Carlo Felice* goes up to the *Piazza Yenne.* The piazza is named for the viceroy Yenne, who began construction of the Carlo Felice road between Cagliari and Sassari.

The *Passeggiata Coperta,* a flight of marble steps, leads to the *Terrazza Umberto I,* which is laid out on the partially preserved Medieval bastion of San Remy. There are beautiful views from the terrace, and still more impressive views from the *Bastione Santa Caterina,* higher still. Via Università leads from here to the recently founded university and to the massive 14th-century *Torre dell'Elefante.*

The ***Cathedral of Santa Cecilia** was built by Pisans in 1312. Inside are the two halves of a pulpit from the Pisa cathedral, given to Cagliari when the cathedral was built here. It is a masterpiece of 12th-century Pisan sculpture. The cathedral houses the tomb of Martin II of Aragon and a crypt with the tombs of princes of the House of Savoy and relics of Early Christian martyrs. The rich church treasury may be seen in the **Cathedral Museum.*

Via Martiri leads from the cathedral to the nearby ***Museo Archeologico,** which holds more than 400 bronze statues from the eighth to fifth centuries B.C., a rich collection of Punic artifacts, and many Roman and Greek sculptures. There is also a picture gallery with works by Spanish and Sardinian masters.

The fortified tower of *San Pancrazio,* built in 1304, is close by. Through the *Porta Cristina* (19th century) continue to *Viale Buon Cammino,* a promenade with a fine view of the Pisan, Spanish and Piedmontese ramparts and bastions.

Turn left to the imposing third-century ***Roman amphithe-**

ater, cut into the rock. This is the principal Roman structure on Sardinia. During the summer, operas are performed here. The *botanical garden* is across from the amphitheater. Near the garden on Via Ospedale is the Baroque *church of San Michele,* which has rich ornaments in stucco and marble.

Via Tigellio leads from the botanical garden to the **Casa di Tigellio*—the well-preserved remains of three Roman houses. **Punic-Roman necropolises* lie on a hill north of the botanical garden, with ancient funeral chambers cut into the rock.

The *cave tomb of Attilia Pomptilla,* located on Viale Sant'Avendrace, offers a fascinating look into the Roman world.

On a small hill in the southern part of the city is the *Santuario di Bonaria,* a pilgrimage church dedicated to the patron saint of the city and to seafarers. At its side is the cemetery, and nearby is the **basilica of San Saturnino* (also known as Santi Cosma e Damiano), an Early Christian church from the fifth century, whose eastern wing, in the early Romanesque style, dates from the 11th century. Farther north is the early

Cagliari

Gothic *church of San Domenico,* with a Catalan-Gothic cloister.

Several excursions can be made from Cagliari. *Cala Mosca,* 4 km. (2.5 miles) away, lies on a scenic, rocky inlet with a small beach. The fashionable suburb of *Poetto* (6 km.; 4 miles) has a gently sloping beach. Inland on Route S 125, *San Gregorio* and *Campu Omu* (22 km.; 14 miles) are on the slope of *Monte degli Sette Fratelli* at an elevation of 1,023 meters (3,350 feet).

East of Cagliari, the **coast of Villasimius* extends for 50 km. (30 miles). It has scenic cliffs and beaches and fine hotels.

TRAVEL ROUTE 24: **Cagliari–*Barumini–Sorgono–*Nuoro–*Olbia (339 km.; 210 miles)

See map on page 313.

Travel Route 24 takes you north from Cagliari to Olbia with a choice of two different routes. The inland route heads north through Nuoro where many of Sardinia's old customs have been preserved. The route along the island's picturesque east coast allows you to explore lagoons, grottoes, and enjoy a swim at any of the many beautiful beaches.

Leave *Cagliari (see page 324) going north on Route S 131 to *Monastir* (22 km.; 14 miles), an oriental-looking town in the hilly *Trexenta*, a wheat-growing region. Nuraminis is the site of a 16th-century cathedral. At *Villasanta* (42 km.; 26 miles from Cagliari), turn north on Route S 197, which runs through olive groves, wheat fields and vineyards to **Villamar.** Its tiny Romanesque church, *San Pietro* (13th century), and beautiful late Gothic parish church are worth visiting.

*Barumini (63 km.; 9 miles from Cagliari) is one of the most important archaeological sites in Sardinia. It is dominated by an enormous **nuraghe fortress*, one of the best examples of megalithic culture in the Mediterranean basin, surrounded by the largest nuraghic village on the island. The complex, called Nuraghe Su Nuraxi, dates from the 13th to eighth centuries B.C. The new town lies to the east of this site.

Northwest of Barumini is the volcanic table mountain called *Giara di Gesturi*. Rare birds nest around small crater lakes; there are also many *nuraghi* ruins on the slopes of the mountain.

Continue past *Nuragus* to *Nurallao*, and turn north on Route S 128 toward the Gennargentu mountain range. The two peaks to the northeast are called *Bruncu Spina* (1,829 meters; 6,000 feet)

and *Punta La Marmora* (1,834 meters; 6,017 feet).

Continue past *Laconi*, a summer resort with the ruins of a Medieval fortress, to the plateau of *Pranu Guttutorgio*. You can take mountain hikes from the small farming and sheepherding hamlets at *Sorgono*.

The next stretch of Route S 128 is particularly beautiful, with spectacular views out across the countryside. Take Route S 389 dir. through *Fonni*, a ski resort, north to Nuoro. Or follow Route S 128 through *Gavoi*, a summer resort in the woods, and visit its parish *church of San Gavino*, built in the 16th century. Route S 128 then passes through *Orani* and *Oniferi*, with *nuraghi* and megalithic tombs; turn east on S 129 to the provincial capital of ***Nuoro** (205 km.; 127 miles from Cagliari), picturesquely situated on a hillside, between limestone hills to the south and the peak of *Ortobene* (995 meters; 3,264 feet) to the east. More than the other cities on the island, Nuoro has preserved many of the old customs and traditions of Sardinia.

From the 19th-century *Duomo*, *Viale Sant'Onofrio* leads south to the panoramic hill of the same name, which has a park and the *Museo Regionale del Costume*, a folklore museum. In the old quarter of *San Pietro* is the house where the writer Grazia Deledda was born; he won the Nobel Prize for literature in 1926. A 15-minute walk leads through *Viale Ciusa* to *Nostra Signora della Solitudine,* a country chapel built in 1625 and transformed in 1959 into the Pantheon of Nuoro to hold Deledda's remains. From here a road leads 8 km. (5 miles) through woods and past granite cliffs to ***Monte Ortobene,** with spectacular views and where you'll find mountain inns and summer houses.

Twelve km. (7 miles) southeast of Nuoro, at the foot of a dolomite mountain, lies **Oliena,** known both for its wine and for its rich traditional costumes. A wild and romantic gorge runs from the sheer drop of the dolomite wall, *Sopramonte* (1,463 meters; 4,800 feet) to the town. The surrounding mountains shelter the largest caves on the island.

North of Nuoro extends a dolomite landscape strewn with rocks. The architecture of the villages reflects the rugged lifestyle of the Sardinian shepherds, especially the steep and narrow streets of the mountain village of *Orune, where the houses are mainly made of large rocks.

Route S 129 leads from Nuoro to *Orosei*. At *La Traversa* (225 km.; 140 miles) a road on the right leads to a *nuraghi* village 2.5 km. (1.5 miles) away, ****Serra Orrios,** where some 70 round structures are gathered in groups around piazzas with wells.

Other *nuraghi* settlements in the area are now being excavated.

Galtelli was a bishop's seat in the Middle Ages, and the town has several fine Medieval churches. There are *nuraghi* settlements in the vicinity, as well as prehistoric cave tombs. Route S 129 continues to the port town of **Orosei,** the center of a rich agricultural region, with several interesting churches and houses of the nobility, dating from the 15th to 18th centuries. A road leads from the town to *Marina di Orosei,* where a beach extends along the northern edge of the Gulf of Orosei.

You also can travel from *Cagliari (see page 324) to Orosei on Route S 125, which follows, in part, the east coast of the island. The road leads through *Muravera,* surrounded by orange and almond groves, and *Villaputzu,* a village that looks as if it might be located in Africa, with its white houses made of loam and limestone, to *Tortoli,* from which a side road leads 5 km. (3 miles) east

Nuraghi

to ***Arbatax** (145 km.; 90 miles, from Cagliari). The port of this large fishing village is surrounded by red rocks rising directly out of the sea. It has become a popular resort largely because of its beautiful location, its long, white sandy beach, and the fine scuba and skin diving. The nearby picturesque cape of *Bellavista* has interesting rock formations and grottoes. Driving north again on Route S 125, you will have splendid views out over the wild rocky landscape and the sea.

*Dorgali (65 km.; 40 miles, north of Arbatax) was originally a Saracen settlement. The clothing style of the women—black skirt, black veil and red bodice—is Arabic in origin. The town lies among limestone mountains in a dolomite landscape of great archaeological importance. There are several *nuraghi* villages in the nearby *Lanaitto valley.* Along the road to La Traversa (see page 327) is the

Sardinian handiwork

large *nuraghe* of *Oveni.* Dorgali is also famous for its crafts, which include ceramics, filigree, leather and rugs.

Backtracking a bit on Route S 125, turn east through a steep coast intersected by many grottoes and caves, for 9 km. (6 miles) to **Cala Gonone,** a picturesque village with a beautiful and quite popular beach. Excursion boats make trips to the numerous grottoes along the coast, the most famous of which is the **Grotta del Bue Marino,* about 5 km. (3 miles) south, or 30 minutes by boat. Its underground galleries, 5 km. (3 miles) long, are laced with stalactites and stalagmites.

The nearby resort of *Cala Luna* is also quite pretty and has a sandy beach beneath cliffs.

Orosei (see page 327) is 21 km. (13 miles) north of Dorgali. Here Routes S 125 and S 129 meet.

Route S 125 continues up the coast through *Santa Lucia* where there is a scenic road inland to *Siniscola.* On the coast you can visit the grotto *Cane Cortoe* and the remains of the *nuraghi* village of *Lututai. La Caletta,* the port of Siniscola, has a pretty, sandy beach.

From Siniscola, the road hugs the coast, with turnoffs to good swimming beaches. The road passes the salt pond of *San Teodoro* and has views of the island of *Molara* and the long rocky island of *Tavolara* (564 meters; 1,850 feet high), and finally comes to ***Olbia** (339 km.; 210 miles from Cagliari; see page 312).

Practical Information

This chapter is divided into two sections. The first, **General Trip Planning,** offers information you'll need for planning and researching your trip, as well as tips on transportation to and around Italy and other items of interest. (See listing in *Contents* for full range of subjects covered.)

The second section, **Town-by-Town,** is organized alphabetically by town and provides information that will be helpful on site, such as local tourist offices, hotels, and transportation.

General Trip Planning

Choosing When to Go. Travelling in Italy can be marvelous in every season; at any given time of the year there is a section of the country particularly suitable for vacationing. Major cities should be avoided in the second half of August at the time of the Ferragosto holidays (Assumption of the Virgin), when most Italians take their vacations and many shops and restaurants close.

Winter is the time to enjoy skiing on the majestic slopes of Italy's Alps, in resorts ranging from the chic Val d'Aosta to the picturesque Trentino-Alto Aldige region. The end of winter also heralds the raucous and joyful *Carnevale* festivities in Venice. This annual celebration prefaces the religious observance of Lent. For the culturally oriented, the first signs of winter are invariably associated with the December opening of the opera season in Milan. In the renowned La Scala opera house, you can thrill to awe-inspiring performances in magnificent surroundings.

With the exception of Easter, when tourists throng the cities and Italians jam the resorts, spring is considered one of the most pleasant times to travel here. And festivals of every kind (Medieval archery, music, religious processions, opera, and film) distinguish the season. Of particular note is the Festival of Saint Efisio in Cagliari, Sardinia (May 1–4), when thousands of pilgrims in 17th–century costume walk in a procession through the streets.

During the summer months, coastal and hill resorts are very popular ways to cool off. As in the spring, the summer is alive with Medieval tournaments, sports exhibitions, and religious ceremonies. One of the most talked-about festivals is the Palio, held in Siena each July, which culminates in an exciting and dangerous horse race around the city's main square.

Fall ushers in another round of near-perfect weather for travel. One of the highlights is the Truffle Fair held in Alba in the Piedmont in September. This is the harvesting season, and the fields appear timeless in their beauty.

Italy's off-peak season lasts from November through April. Hotels reduce their prices by as much as 30 percent, with the exception of winter resorts.

It is advisable to pack clothes you can layer to compensate for Italy's variable climates. Be sure to include a warm sweater, for evenings can get cool even during the summer. You should try to wear low-heeled, comfortable shoes (even running shoes) whenever possible—walking down cobblestone streets can become painful otherwise. A raincoat and an umbrella are musts for the winter. Also remember to bring something to cover bare arms and shoulders when visiting museums and churches. Do not wear shorts when sightseeing, as you may be denied entrance to certain places.

Average Temperature and Climate. Italy's climate is diverse, due to its variegated topography. Except along the coasts, northern Italy has hot summers and cold winters, typical of the European continent. As you move farther south, the climate is moderated by the sea, especially in places like Sicily and Sardinia. The mountainous regions, even in central and southern Italy, experience brisk winds in the late fall and heavy snowfall in the winter. Summers tend to be dry, with high temperatures and little humidity, and winters are usually wet, with rain falling most heavily from October through December.

The temperature in Italy is measured in degrees centigrade. Below is a listing of average daily temperatures in centigrade and Fahrenheit by month for several major cities:

	January		February		March	
	$C°$	$F°$	$C°$	$F°$	$C°$	$F°$
Florence	7	45	8	47	10	50
Milan	2	36	4	40	10	50
Naples	10	50	12	54	14	58
Palermo	11	52	13	56	16	60
Rome	9	49	11	52	14	57

	April		May		June	
	$C°$	$F°$	$C°$	$F°$	$C°$	$F°$
Florence	16	60	19	67	24	75
Milan	14	58	19	66	22	72
Naples	17	63	21	70	24	75
Palermo	18	64	22	72	26	79
Rome	17	62	21	70	25	77

	July		August		September	
	C°	F°	C°	F°	C°	F°
Florence	25	77	21	70	18	64
Milan	24	75	23	74	19	67
Naples	28	83	26	79	23	74
Palermo	29	84	27	80	24	75
Rome	28	82	26	78	23	73

	October		November		December	
	C°	F°	C°	F°	C°	F°
Florence	17	63	13	55	8	46
Milan	13	56	7	45	4	39
Naples	19	66	16	60	11	52
Palermo	20	68	16	60	12	53
Rome	18	65	13	56	8	47

National Holidays. Listed below are the national holidays in Italy. Specific dates for some holidays vary from year to year.

New Year's Day (January 1)
Epiphany (January 6)
Liberation Day of 1945 (April 25)
Easter Monday
Labor Day (May 1)
Ferragosto (Assumption of the Virgin, August 15)
All Saints' Day (November 1)
Feast of the Immaculate Conception (December 8)
Christmas Day (December 25)
Santo Stefano (December 26)

The holidays of the Proclamation of the Republic and National Unity Day are celebrated on the second Saturday in June and November, respectively. All offices, shops, and banks also close on feast days that honor their town's patron saint:

April 25 Saint Mark—Venice
June 24 Saint John the Baptist—Genoa, Turin, and Florence
June 29 Saint Peter and St. Paul—Rome
September 19 San Gennaro—Naples
October 4 Saint Petronio—Bologna
October 30 Saint Saturino—Cagliari
November 3 Saint Guisto—Trieste
December 6 Saint Nicola—Bari
December 7 Saint Ambrose—Milan

Virtually everything closes during these times. If you intend to drive, make certain that your gas tank is full, because gas stations probably will not be open.

Time Zones. Rome is on Central European Time (one hour ahead of Greenwich Mean Time and six hours ahead of Eastern Standard Time). Therefore, if it is noon in New York or Toronto, Canada, it is 6:00 P.M. in Rome; and when it is noon in London, it is 1:00 P.M. in Rome. There is a 14-hour time difference between Sydney, Australia, and Rome. When it is noon in Sydney, it is 2:00 A.M. the following day in Rome.

Italy observes Daylight Savings Time (Central European Time plus one hour) from early April until late September.

Remember that the Italians use a 24-hour clock rather than differentiating between A.M. and P.M. Midnight is expressed as 24:00; 1:00 A.M. as 1:00; noon as 12:00; 1:00 P.M. as 13:00, etc.

Passport and Visa Requirements. All visitors to Italy must carry a valid passport to enter the country. Visas are required only for stays longer than three months, and can be obtained from the Italian consulate before your trip. If you're in Italy and you decide to go to another country that requires a visa, these forms can be obtained through that country's consulate in Italy.

Customs Entering Italy. Items used personally for professional or private purposes (jewelry, watches, portable typewriters, etc.) do not have to be declared upon arrival in Italy. Non-EEC members may bring in two still cameras with ten rolls of film, a transistor radio, 400 cigarettes, 500 grams of tobacco, two bottles of wine, and one bottle of liquor. EEC members may import 300 cigarettes, one bottle of wine, and one bottle of liquor. Up to 500,000 lire may be brought into Italy; there is no limit on the amount of traveller's checks or foreign currency that you may import.

Customs Returning Home from Italy. To simplify passage through customs, travellers who have nothing to declare are now commonly given a green card in the plane travelling home. Travellers with goods to declare must follow the red signs as indicated in the airport.

If you travel with items from home that were manufactured abroad (e.g. cameras), carry all receipts with you so that you will not have to pay duty.

U.S. residents may bring back $400 worth of foreign goods duty-free. (Exempt merchandise includes books, no more than one liter of liquor, 200 cigarettes, 100 cigars, and one bottle of perfume.) A 10 percent duty is levied on the retail value on the next $1,000 worth of merchandise. Beyond $1,400 worth of merchandise, the rate of duty is decided by the customs officer.

You may ship goods duty-free to the U.S. if you mail them to a residence other than your own. Packages must be marked "Unsolicited Gift-Value Under $50." If you wish to export modern objets d'art and antiques from Italy, you must receive permission from the Office for the Protection of Arts and Antiquities.

U.S. citizens may find it helpful to obtain "Know Before You Go," a publication written by the U.S. Customs Service, which lists all goods you are prohibited from importing, including endangered or extinct species, fur coats, tortoise-shell products, etc. Contact: U.S. Customs Service, Customs Information, Room 201, 6 World Trade Center, New York, N.Y. 10048; tel. (212) 466-5550.

Canadian residents may return duty-free with $150 worth of foreign purchases, or $300 if they have been out of the country for seven days or more. Canadians may also return with 40 ounces of alcohol, 50 cigars, 200 cigarettes, and two pounds of tobacco. Packages can be sent duty-free, marked "Unsolicited Gift-Value Under $40."

Australians over the age of 18 may return with $400 worth of foreign articles, one liter of alcohol, and 250 grams of tobacco products.

Residents of Great Britain over age 17 may return with 200 cigarettes, 50 cigars, one liter of alcohol, and 50 grams of perfume.

Embassies and Consulates in Italy.

American Embassy
Via Vittorio Veneto 121
I-00187 Rome
tel. (06) 46 741

U.S. Consulates:
Lungarno Amerigo Vespucci 46
I-50123 Florence
tel. (055) 29 82 76

Banca d'America e d'Italia Building
Piazza Portello 6
I-16134 Genoa
tel. (010) 28 27 41

Via Principe Amadeo
I-20121 Milan
tel. (02) 65 28 41

Piazza della Repubblica
I-80122 Naples
tel. (081) 66 09 66

Via Vaccarini 1
I-90143 Palermo
tel. (091) 29 15 32

Via Piomba 23
I-10123 Turin
tel. (011) 51 74 37

British Embassy
Via XX Settembre 80A
I-00187 Rome
tel. (06) 47 55 44

British Consulates:
Via San Lucifero 87
I-09100 Cagliari
tel. (070) 66 27 55

Palazzo Castelbarco
Lungarno Corsini 2
I-50123 Florence
tel. (055) 21 25 94

Via XII Ottobre 2
I-16121 Genoa
tel. (010) 56 48 33

Via San Paolo 7
I-20121 Milan
tel. (02) 80 34 42

British Consulates:
Via Francesco Crispi 122
I-08122 Naples
tel. (081) 20 92 27

Via Marchese di Villabianca 9
I-90143 Palermo
tel. (091) 25 33 64

Via Rossini 2
I-34132 Trieste
tel. (040) 69 13 50

Corso M. d'Azeglio 60
I-10126 Turin
tel. (011) 68 78 32

Accademia 1051
I-30100 Venice
tel. (041) 27 20 70

Canadian Embassy
Via G.B. de Rossi
I-00161 Rome
tel. (06) 84 53 41

Canadian Consulate:
Via Vittor Pisani 19
I-20124 Milan
tel. (02) 66 97 45

Australian Embassy
Via Alessandria 215
I-00198 Rome
tel. (06) 83 27 21

Italian Embassies and Consulates.

In the U.S.:

320 Park Avenue
New York, N.Y. 10021
tel. (212) 737-9100

500 North Michigan Avenue
Chicago, IL 60611
tel. (312) 467-1550

11661 San Vincente Blvd., Suite 911
Los Angeles, Calif. 90049
tel. (213) 820-0622

Italian consulates are also located in Boston, Detroit, Houston, New Orleans, Philadelphia, San Francisco, and Washington, D.C.

In the U.K.:

14 Three Kings Yard
London SW1
tel. (01) 628-8200

In Canada:

275 Slater Street, 11th Floor
Ottawa, Ontario K1P 5H9
tel. (613) 232-2401

Australia:

12 Grey Street-Deakin
ACP 2000 Canberra
GPOB 360
tel. (02) 733-333

Getting to Italy by Air. *From the U.S.:* The major air carriers flying from both coasts of the United States include Alitalia, Pan Am, and Trans World Airlines. *From the U.K.:* The major air carriers that fly from Great Britain to Italy include Alitalia, British Airways, and British Caledonian. *From Canada:* The major air carriers that fly nonstop from Canada to Italy are Canadian Airlines and Alitalia. Air Canada flies to London, where you can change airlines to complete your journey. *From Australia:* Australian Airlines, Continental, United Airlines, and Quantas all fly to the west coast of the United States, where you can switch to another airline.

There are a bewildering variety of ever-changing special fares, hotel packages, fly/drive, and other deals that depend on the travel season, the amount of time you can spend, the number of places you wish to visit, etc. Keep an eye on the advertisements in your newspaper's travel section and make your travel arrangements through a reliable agent or tour operator to get the best fares and packages.

Note: Always confirm both your departing and return flights at least 72 hours before your scheduled departure. Especially during the summer, many airlines flying to Europe overbook their flights and can be ruthless about bumping passengers off the reserved list.

Getting to Italy by Boat. The only transatlantic passenger ship that sails from the United States to Italy is Cunard Lines' *Queen Elizabeth II*, which sails from April to December between New York and various ports in Great Britain, France, and Italy. Although expensive, an ocean cruise is a sumptuous, relaxing way to travel. For more detailed information, contact your travel agency or:

Cunard Lines
555 Fifth Avenue
New York, N.Y. 10017
tel. (212) 880-7500
Nationwide reservations: 1-800-5-Cunard

You also can sail the Atlantic on Polish Ocean Lines. Its ship, the *Stefan Batory,* is not as grand as the *QE 2,* but it is still a wonderful way to travel. For more detailed information, contact:

McLean Kennedy Passenger Services
410 St. Nicolas Street
Montreal, Québec H24 2P5
Canada
tel. (514) 849-6111

Getting to Italy by Train/Bus from the U.K.: You have many transportation options when travelling from other European countries to Italy. From Great Britain, you can take a ferry from the Channel ports or combine a rail trip with a hovercraft ride, sojourn briefly in France, and continue by rail. If you prefer to travel by bus, Europlines offers bus service from London to major cities in Italy.

Hotels and Other Accommodations. Accommodations in Italy range from opulent hotels to simple but friendly *pensioni*. You can also relax in a good motel right near the road or rent an entire villa for a week in the country.

Free information concerning accommodations can be obtained before leaving home from any Italian Government Tourist Office. In this guide, hotels have been classified according to five categories: 🏠🏠🏠 *Luxury;* 🏠🏠🏠 *First Class;* 🏠🏠🏠 *Second Class;* 🏠🏠 *Third Class;* and 🏠 *Fourth Class.* These ratings correspond to the Italian Government Tourist Office's classifications. Luxury, First Class, and Second Class are delineated by three houses, a designation that indicates the quality of service and accommodations. The higher prices for Luxury and First Class hotels reflect the amenities they offer.

It is always advisable to book rooms in advance, especially during the high season—and especially in Florence and Venice. The peak travel season extends from April to December, when the rates are highest and the hotels are the most crowded. December, January, and February are the peak months at ski resorts. Off-season is November through March in most cities and resort areas. Off-peak at ski resorts is April to May and September to November.

When requesting rates, ask for the all-inclusive price (*tutto incluso*), which includes an 18% service charge at first-tier hotels (9% for all other hotels), a 22% tax, and a visitor's fee.

Pensioni. These are essentially smaller hotels that include the price of one or two meals a day in the cost of the room. Pensioni are friendly places to stay where you can enjoy conversation with other guests and your Italian hosts.

Guesthouses. These inns offer the convenience of a simple room in the country. They are peaceful, relatively inexpensive places to stay.

Motels. Located along major highways, motels in Italy are clean and accessible. Among their advantages are their good regional food and their telex and telephone facilities. These three motel chains are well known for their quality: ACI Motels (Automobile Club of Italy); AGIP Motels (Azienda Generale Italiana Petroli, a gas company); and Pavesi Motels.

Villas and Apartments. If you anticipate a long stay in one area, you might find it useful to rent a villa for a month. Below is a listing of information sources for accommodations:

At Home Abroad
405 East 56th Street
New York, N.Y. 10022
tel. (212) 421-9165

Four Star Living
964 Third Avenue
New York, N.Y. 10022
tel. (212) 891-8199

Vacanze in Italia
153 West 13th Street
New York, N.Y. 10011
tel. (212) 242-2145

Villas International
71 West 23rd Street
New York, N.Y. 10010
tel. (212) 929-7585
(800) 221-2600

Currency Regulations. The Italian unit of currency (which also is used in San Marino and Vatican City) is the lira. Banknotes are available in denominations of 500, 1,000, 2,000, 5,000, 10,000, 20,000, 50,000, and 100,000 lire. Coins of 5, 10, 50, 100, 200, and 500 lire are in circulation. Smaller coin denominations are rare, so don't be surprised if you receive your change in candy! The Italian government is currently upgrading this system so that one new lira will be the equivalent of 1,000 old lire; doublecheck rates before you embark on your travels.

Your national currency, as well as traveller's checks, may be exchanged at most banks or at the airport. Try not to exchange currency at hotels or restaurants, as they usually offer less favorable rates and add a surcharge. To obtain the best rate of exchange before leaving home, first track currency fluctuations in the newspaper, and then change your money at a bank.

Credit cards are used in Italy; the most widely accepted cards are American Express and Visa.

Business Hours and Closings. The siesta period is still widely observed in businesses throughout Italy. Banks are usually open Monday through Friday from 8:30 A.M. to 1:30 P.M. and from 3:00 to 4:00 P.M. Banks close at 11:30 A.M. on August 14, December 24, and December 31 as a partial holiday.

Government offices and businesses are open from 9:00 A.M. to 1:00 P.M. and from 3:00 to 7:00 P.M. Department stores are open from 9:00 A.M. to 12:30 P.M. and from 4:00 to 7:30 P.M. The exception is in larger cities, where department stores may have extended hours.

Museums generally are open from 9:30 A.M. to 4:30 P.M. Tuesday through Friday or Saturday, 9:00 A.M. to 2:00 P.M. for state-owned museums, and from 9:30 A.M. to 1:00 P.M. on the weekends. However, hours for museums and galleries vary from region to region and are subject to frequent change. Check the museum before embarking on a long day's journey. Churches usually are open from 9:00 A.M. to noon and 3:00 to 7:00 P.M.

By law, restaurants must close one day a week. Restaurants in each area alternate days of closing; every establishment posts a sign stating its schedule. In northern Italy, hours are usually noon to 2:00 P.M., and 8:00 to 10:00 P.M. In central Italy and in the south, restaurants serve from 1:00 P.M. to 3:00 P.M., and from 9:00 to 11:00 P.M. These hours are flexible depending upon the establishment, and may open earlier and close later.

Postage. Post offices are open Monday through Friday from 8:30 A.M. to 2:00 P.M. and on Saturdays from 8:30 A.M. to noon. In larger cities, some stay open from 9:00 A.M. to 7:00 or 8:00 P.M. On the last day of every month, post offices close at noon. Stamps can also be purchased at many tobacco shops.

Air mail not exceeding 20 grams sent to an EEC country costs 560 lire; to all other destinations it costs 650 lire. All postcards cost 450 lire.

Telephones. There are two types of public telephones in Italy. Older phones require 100 or 200 lire coins or special tokens called *gettoni,* which can be obtained from tobacco shops and newsstands. To activate these phones, insert the coin or token, wait for the tone, then dial and wait for your party to respond. Newer phones accept gettoni, coins, or magnetic cards. These cards can be purchased at local SIT (Società Italiana per l'Esercizio Telefonico) offices, and they have a value of 6,000 or 9,000 lire. They are more convenient to use for long-distance calls. You also can obtain assistance for international calls at local SIT offices or ASST (Azienda di Stato per i Servizi Telefonici), which are open Monday through Friday, 7:00 A.M. to 10:00 P.M.

General Telephone Information. The following numbers are useful for information purposes. In most provinces, this number will be preceded by a local prefix.

Emergency, police	113
Immediate Action Service	112
(ambulance, police)	
International operator	15
within EEC (English-speaking)	
Intercontinental operator	170
Cables, telegrams	186
Time	161
Traffic Information	194
Local Information	12
ACI (Automobile Club Italiano)	116

Travelling in Italy. From the modern superhighways to the accessibility of Rome's Metropolitana (subway) system, Italy offers a profusion of transportation alternatives. Depending upon your objective, you can drive through hushed, ancient villages of extraordinary beauty, take a speedy train ride, or sail the coastal waters aboard a ferry.

Taxis. Most taxi rides from the major airports to cities should run between 20,000 and 40,000 lire. Agree upon a fixed price before you enter the cab to avoid being overcharged. Fares run approximately 500 lire per kilometer during the day, and prices start at 2,500 to 4,000 lire, depending on what city you're in. There is a 3,000 lire supplement during evening hours (10:00 P.M. to 7:00 A.M.) and 1,000 lire on Sunday and public holidays. Luggage costs an extra 500 lire per bag. Tip the taxi driver 15 percent of the bill.

Subway system. Some of Italy's major cities, including Milan, Naples, and Rome, have a subway system dubbed the Metropolitana. Rome's system, for example, has two lines: Line A runs east–west between the Vatican area and Ottaviano; Line B runs north–south from Stazione Termini to Laurentino. Fares are 700 lire, and books of ten tickets cost 6,000 lire. Tickets are available from subway stations, tobacco shops, and newsstands.

Air Travel. Alitalia and ATI (Aero Transporti Italiani), Aliguila and Transavio, offer frequent service between Italy's major cities. Discounts are available if you fly at night, on the weekend, or as a family group.

Ferries. A number of major ferry lines travel between the mainland and the larger and smaller islands. They also travel international routes. The Tirrenia line runs between Genoa–Cagliari, Civitavecchia–Cagliari, Genoa–Palermo, Livorno–Sardinia, and Naples–Palermo. The Grandi Traghetti lines connect Genoa–Sardinia. The Siremar ferry lines tour the Aeolian (Lipari) Islands, while the Toremar lines cruise the Tuscan Islands, including Elba. The Caremar lines skirt Capri and the other Naples Gulf Islands, and the Pontine Islands. Alimar lines (jumbo hydrofoil) connect Naples and Palermo. Adriatica ferries offer passage between Italy and Greece, Yugoslavia, Albania, and Egypt.

Buses. Italy has an excellent network of city and touring buses. Schedules are available from tourist agencies and automobile clubs throughout the country. Numerous bus lines organize day trips at reasonable prices from large cities and tourist resorts. You can purchase tickets from tobacco shops and newsstands. One-way fares are 700 lire, or you can purchase a half-day ticket for 1,000 lire, which gives you unlimited travel.

Driving in Italy. The Italian road system includes over 5,900 kilometers of extremely well-maintained superhighways. Roads are designated as follows: *autostrade* (superhighways, usually toll roads); *strade statali* (state highways), *strade provinciali* (secondary roads); and *strade comunali* (local roads).

Documentation. All drivers must carry an international driver's license, or their own national driver's license (with a translation), and national car registration papers if driving their own vehicle. If you are renting a vehicle, you must have an International Driver's License, available at any ACI (Automobile Club Italiano) office or any AAA office in the U.S. Their main address is at Via C. Colombo 261, I-00185 Rome, tel. (06) 51 060.

You also must carry an International Insurance Certificate (Green Card, *Carta Verde*) in your vehicle. It is available through the ACI, for periods of 15, 30, or 45 days. It is wise to take out temporary insurance through an Italian company in case of an accident.

Car Rentals. Car-rental agencies can be found throughout the country's major cities and at the airports. Major companies such as Avis, Budget, Europcar, Hertz, InterRent, and Maggiore have local branches almost everywhere.

Road Warning Signs. You should familiarize yourself with the following words that appear on road signs:

Alt	Stop
Attenzione	Caution
Caduta massi	Falling rocks
Dare la precedenza	Yield
Deviazione	Detour
Divieto di Sosta	No parking
Divieto di Sorpasso	No passing
Pagamento Pedaggio	Toll
Pericolo	Danger
Rallentare	Reduce speed
Sbarrato	Road closed
Senso unico	One-way street
Svolta pericolosa	Dangerous bend
Tenere la destra (la sinistra)	Keep to the right (left)

Driving Regulations. In Italy, driving is on the right-hand side of the road. The general rule is that at an intersection the car on the right has the right of way. Drivers are notoriously aggressive in Italy, so be prepared—especially in congested areas.

Passing. You may pass on the left. If the vehicle in the left lane has signaled a left-hand turn, you may pass on the right.

Parking on the road is allowed outside cities and towns. Any difficulties with a vehicle must be signaled by a triangular danger sign issued by the ACI. You can also park in restricted zones, Zona Disco, with the purchase of a disc at any gas station. To park in historic areas you will need a special pass which can be obtained from your hotel.

Gasoline is expensive. Discount coupons are available through the local ACI, if you are driving your own car. Hours at gas stations run approximately from 7:00 A.M. to 7:00 P.M., with a three-hour break from 12:30 to 3:30 P.M. Many gas stations are closed on weekends and holidays, except for 24-hour stations on major highways. Gasoline is available by the liter in either super, regular (*normale*), or diesel.

Safety belts. It is compulsory for the driver and the front-seat passenger to use seat belts in the car.

Tolls on autostradas are calculated by the distance travelled and the size of your car (i.e. you must pay a higher toll if you drive a large car). Payment is collected when you exit the toll district.

Speed limits. Limits depend on the size of the car. Subcompacts (up to 600 cc.) can go 80 km. on roads and highways, and 90 km. on autostradas; compacts (up to 900 cc.) can go 90 km. on roads and 110 km. on autostradas; standards (up to 1,300 cc.) can go 100 km. on roads and 130 km. on autostradas; and larger cars (over 1,300 cc.) can go 110 km. on roads and 140 km. on autostradas.

Traffic Accidents and Road Assistance. In the case of a traffic misdemeanor, you can pay your fine on the spot to the police officer issuing the ticket at approximately one-third of the cost. For serious accidents you will need to collect information about what happened, insurance policy numbers, license plate numbers, and any witnesses.

Assistance and towing services are extremely well organized in Italy. The ACI (Automobile Club Italiano) is open 24 hours a day. Emergency call boxes are placed on autostradas and other roads. In the case of a breakdown, dial 116 for assistance, which is free. Autostradas are peppered with SOS call boxes, which are designated by a button with a monkey-wrench symbol, or a button with a red cross in case of a medical emergency. Police are constantly on patrol along the highways, and they can always assist you.

Trains. Train travel is a delightful way to introduce yourself to Italy's astoundingly beautiful countryside, and a train trip permits you to absorb these vistas without having to concentrate on driving.

The track network of the Italian State Railways (Ferrovie dello Stato, FS) extends approximately 16,000 km. (10,000 miles). State-owned trains can be divided into the following categories: TEE, Intercity, *rapidi, espressi, diretti,* and *locali. Rapidi* (express trains) connect major cities. TEEs and Intercity trains come under the heading of *rapidi* trains. The TEE (Trans Europe Express) was the most efficient train network in Europe until France surpassed it with the TGV trains. TEEs provide international service. They offer first-class seating only, and you must make reservations in advance. Intercity trains are a recent addition to the Italian system; they are essentially older TEE trains with second-class cars added to lessen the expense. *Espressi* are long-distance trains that make stops at major stations. *Diretti* trains make more stops, and *locali* stop at all stations and continue into rural areas. With the exception of *locali* and *diretti* trains, which offer only second-class seating, many trains carry both first- and second-class cars. A supplement is charged for all tickets on the TEEs, the *rapidi,* and the Intercity trains except for passengers holding Eurail or BTLC passes. Brochures and information on schedules are available at major train stations. *Il Treno,* the Italian State Railways' timetable, can be purchased at train stations and at newsstands. You also can obtain information from the following Italian State Railways offices:

In the U.S.:
500 North Michigan Avenue
Chicago, IL 60611
tel. (312) 644-6651

666 Fifth Avenue
New York, N.Y. 10103
tel. (212) 397-2667

6033 West Century Boulevard,
Suite 1090
Los Angeles, CA 90045
tel. (213) 338-8620

In Australia:
123 Clarence Street
Sydney, NSW 200

In Canada:
111 Avenue Road
Toronto, Ontario MFR 3J8
tel. (416) 927-7712

2055 Peel Street
Montreal, Québec H3A 1V4
tel. (514) 845-9101

In the U.K.:
Marco Polo Hall
3–5 Lansdowne Road
Croydon CR9 1LL

50–51 Conduit Street
London W1R 9FB

Different kinds of passes are offered for train travel, with a variety of discounts, depending on your individual schedule. Some passes eliminate the supplemental fee that is normally added on Intercity, *rapidi,* and TEE trains.

All tickets may be purchased at the railroad station or at travel agencies in Italy or in the United States. Tickets also can be bought from the Italian State Railways' travel agency, the Compagnia Italiana Turismo (CIT), which has offices throughout Italy and in many other European cities. It is advisable to buy your ticket before your train departs, as there is a 20% surcharge added to the regular cost if you board without it. First-class tickets cost approximately 20% more than second-class tickets. You can also guarantee your seat (in first or second class) by making a reservation, which is required for all TEE and Intercity trains.

Sleeping Accommodations. Intercity and TEE trains have sleeping accommodations. You can choose between a sleeping car (*vettura-letto*), which has one to three beds; tourist compartments, which are second-class compartments that accommodate two to three people; or couchettes (*cuccette*), which are first- or second-class seats converted to berths.

Reduced Fares. There are also a number of reduced-fare programs available:

Italian Tourist Ticket. This ticket may be purchased only by non-Italian residents. Referred to as the BTLC (Biglietto Turistico de Libera Circolazione), this ticket is good for travel within Italy for periods of 8, 15, 21, or 30 days. It gives you unlimited mileage in first or second class, and children travel at half-price.

Italian Kilometric Ticket. This *"Chilometrico"* pass gives you unlimited travel up to 3,000 km. (1,860 miles) within a two-month period. You may make up to 20 trips, and you are required to pay any supplements.

Family Card. A Family Card (*Carta Famiglia*) entitles a group of three or more to a 30% discount on all trains.

Silver Card. The Silver Card (*Carta d'Argento*) entitles a traveller above the age of 65 to a 30% discount on all trains. The Rail Europe Senior (RES) card entitles women over 60 and men over 65 to discounts on international travel.

Eurail Pass. This pass allows the traveller unlimited first-class travel on rail networks through 16 European countries. Passes are valid for 15 days, 21 days, or one, two, or three months, and entitle travellers to a variety of special discounts. The *Eurail Youthpass* for travellers under 26 years of age allows unlimited second-class rail travel on passes valid for one or two months. The *Eurail Saverpass* offers unlimited first-class travel to three or more people travelling together. The pass is valid for 15 days. All passes must be used within six months of purchase.

Eurail Flexipass. This pass also allows unlimited first-class travel to 16 European countries, but passes must be used within 21 days of purchase.

Restaurants. In Italy, breakfast (usually just a cup of cappuccino and perhaps a *cornetto*, or croissant) is a meal of little consequence. Lunch is normally several courses. Italian restaurants begin serving at noon, though most Italians, especially in Rome and in the south, lunch much later. Dinner is rarely eaten before 7:00 P.M., and in the cities, some restaurants remain open until late in the evening. In better establishments, diners are expected to choose from a set menu, or at least to order an appetizer and an entree. A small cover charge (*coperto*) includes the bread. Pasta dishes are eaten only as a first course (*primo*), and usually preceded by an antipasto. The second course (*secondo*) normally consists of a meat or fish dish, and is followed by a salad. Fruit or sweets round out the meal. At cafés and bars, waiter service at a table costs considerably more than stand-up service at the bar. For bar service, it is customary to pay the cashier first and then hand the receipt to the barman with your order. Trattorias, pizzerias, grills, and cafeterias (*tavola calda*) serve snacks and lighter meals.

Tipping. If the check at a restaurant does not indicate that a service charge is included, a tip of 15 percent is expected. General guidelines for tipping are as follows: Bellhops should receive 1,500 lire per bag; chambermaids should receive 1,000 lire a day; a concierge should receive 15 percent of your total hotel bill; doormen should be tipped 1,500 lire for calling a cab; the room service waiter should be given 1,000 lire; theater ushers should receive 500 lire per person; taxi drivers should receive 15 percent of the charge; tour guides should receive 1,500 lire per person for half-day tours, and 2,500 lire for full-day tours. In cafés and bars, 15 percent is expected unless you are standing at the bar—tip 200 lire if you are just drinking coffee, or 1,000 if you are drinking cocktails or eating sandwiches.

Electricity. The voltage in cities and towns is either 125 or 220. You should bring an adapter for all electrical appliances and verify your hotel's voltage capacity before use.

Sports and Recreation. Italy offers the sports lover a wonderful assortment of activities in every season. From water-skiing, swimming, and fishing, to horseback riding and tennis, Italy is a perfect place to practice your favorite sport or acquire a taste for a new one.

Skiing. Italians generally ski in the Apennines, especially on runs in the outskirts of Bologna, the Ancona area, Calabria, on the slopes of Mount Etna, and in the mountains of Sardinia. Internationally famous winter resorts are Courmayeur and Breuil-Cervinia in the western Alps, the Livigno sports region tucked up next to Switzerland north of Brescia, and the Dolomiti Superski sports facility in the eastern Alps. For more information, contact the Federazione Italiana Sport Invernali at Via Piranesi 44B, I-20137 Milan, tel. (02) 73 81 12.

Water sports. Most coastal and lake resorts are suitable for swimming, sailing, and waterskiing. In general, beaches are sandy or rocky. White sand beaches are found on the Riviera di Ponente and the Riviera di Levante along the Ligurian Sea, the Tyrrhenian Sea south of Rome, all around Sardinia except for the north coast, near Palermo, and on the south coast of Sicily. Lakes Garda, Maggiore, Como, Iseo, and Bolsena are all excellent for swimming. For further information on waterskiing, contact the Federazione Italiana Sci Nautico at Via Piranesi 44B, I-20137 Milan, tel. (02) 73 81 12. For information on swimming, contact the Federazione Italiana Nuoto at Viale Tiziano 70, I-00196 Rome, tel. (06) 36 851.

Fishing. A license is required to fish in all inland waters. It is issued to foreigners for three months by local authorities. You do not need a license to fish in the Mediterranean or Adriatic, except in some harbors where permission from the local authorities is needed. The lakes in northern Italy and the rivers of the Val d'Aosta are stocked with trout, sturgeon, and carp. Mountain rivers are full of salmon, trout, and grayling. For more information, contact the Federazione Italiana Pesca Sportiva at Viale Tiziano 70, I-00196 Rome, tel. (06) 39 47 54.

Scuba diving and fishing. Underwater fishing and spearfishing are popular on the rocky shore of the Ligurian coast and the Tremiti Islands, the Tuscan Islands, Elba, Sardinia, the Aeolian (Lipari) Islands, the rocky shores of Sicily, and southern Italy. The use of scuba diving equipment for professional and sport fishing underwater is no longer allowed, and fishing nets are not permitted. Contact the Federazione Italiana Pesca Sportiva for further information.

Golf. Italy is not a nation of golfers, but there are excellent 9-, 18-, and 27-hole golf courses around the country. There are 27-hole courses in Fiano (near Turin), Monza (outside Rome), and in Rome. There are 18-hole courses in Almenno, San Bartolomeo, the Lido in Venice, Carimate Parco, Cernobbio, and Menaggio (in the province of Como). For more information, contact the Federazione Italiana Golf at Via Flaminia 388, I-00196 Rome, tel. (06) 39 46 41.

Tennis. Tennis courts are available in larger cities and resorts. In the summer, many resorts and towns organize tennis classes for young people. For additional information, contact the Federazione Italiana Tennis at Viale Tiziano 70, I-00196 Rome, tel. (06) 36 851.

Horseback riding. Riding is very popular in Italy and riding schools are located on the mainland and Sardinia, Sicily, and Elba. Riding excursions are organized frequently throughout the countryside; there are also bridle trails in resorts and larger towns. For more information, contact the Federazione Italiana Sport Equestri at Viale Tiziano 70, I-00196 Rome, tel. (06) 39 02 28.

Casinos. For those who view gambling as a sport, Italy has fine casinos in which to indulge. San Remo, on the Riviera, and Campione, on Lake Lugano, are open all year. The Palazzo-Vendramin in Venice is open from October 1 to March 31, and the Venice Lido is open from April 1 to September 30. You must be 18 or older and have your passport to be admitted to the casinos.

Shopping. Italy is well-known as one of the foremost producers of high fashion. Its talented designers make clothing that rivals the French fashion industry. Italy is also famous for a profusion of high-quality goods including glassware, faience, and leather products. Almost anywhere you go, you'll find things you want to bring home with you. Below is a listing of some areas and their specialties:

You can find superb art galleries in *Bologna,* as well as high-quality clothing ranging from the trendy to the classic. *Deruta* offers beautiful traditional pottery, and faience pottery, which is also the main offering in *Faenza,* where this delicate craft was invented. *Florence,* one of the most-visited cities in Italy, offers filigree jewelry, handsome leather goods, exquisite lingerie, and a wide selection of shoes and clothing. Rare wines can be found in *Genoa,* as well as beautiful crystal and ceramics. The *Lombardy* region is renowned for its production of wrought-iron and embossed copper products, as well as finely crafted furniture, antiques, and silk. *Milan,* its largest city, also is a center for high fashion with such designers as Giorgio Armani, Laura Biagiotti, Gucci, Krizia, Missoni, and Valentino. In *Naples,* you can find lovely cameo jewelry and delicate necklaces and earrings made of coral. Fine books stand out in *Palermo,* which is also famous for its leather products and antiques. *Rome,* like Milan, is a city of haute couture; its collections of shoes, hats, jackets, and gloves are enough to turn anyone's head and keep it permanently glued to shop windows. *Siena* is well known for its wonderfully crafted paper products for desk and office, modeled after the 17th-century design of marbled paper. Its fabrics are also worth a second and third look. *Turin's* main shopping attraction is its extraordinary lingerie and its fine antique porcelain. *Venice* is synonymous with intricate glassware, fragile lace, and Carnevale masks, which are sold all year. You can find marvelous ceramics in *Vietri; Verona* sells good perfume and children's clothes; and *Volterra* offers a selection of fine alabaster.

VAT Refund. In larger shops and stores, you may be able to apply for the Value Added Tax Refund (VAT) if you have spent 250,000 lire or more (the figure is slightly higher for residents of EEC countries). Since Italy is not as devoted to this practice as other EEC countries, many shops may not wish to return the 18% tax. If they do, however, the money will be transferred in lire to your bank account at home after both you and the store have filled out the special accompanying forms.

Clothing Sizes. Listed below are standard clothing-size equivalents for the U.S., Great Britain, and Europe:

		U.S.	U.K.	Europe
Chest	*Small*	34	34	87
	Medium	36	36	91
		38	38	97
	Large	40	40	102
		42	42	107
	Extra Large	44	44	112
		46	46	117
Collar		14	14	36
		14½	14½	37
		15	15	38
		15½	15½	39
		16	16	41
		16½	16½	42
		17	17	43
Waist		24	24	61
		26	26	66
		28	28	71
		30	30	76
		32	32	80
		34	34	87
		36	36	91
		38	38	97

	U.S.	U.K.	Europe
Men's Suits	34	34	44
	35	35	46
	36	36	48
	37	37	49½
	38	38	51
	39	39	52½
	40	40	54
	41	41	55½
	42	42	57
Men's Shoes	7	6	39½
	8	7	41
	9	8	42
	10	9	43
	11	10	44½
	12	11	46
	13	12	47
Men's Hats	6¾	6⅝	54
	6⅞	6¾	55
	7	6⅞	56
	7⅛	7	57
	7¼	7⅛	58
	7½	7⅜	60
Women's Dresses	6	8	36
	8	10	38
	10	12	40
	12	14	42
	14	16	44
	16	18	46
	18	20	48
Women's Blouses and Sweaters	8	10	38
	10	12	40
	12	14	42
	14	16	44
	16	18	46
	18	20	48
Women's Shoes	4½	3	35½
	5	3½	36
	5½	4	36½
	6	4½	37
	6½	5	37½
	7	5½	38
	7½	6	38½
	8	6½	39
	8½	7	39½
	9	7½	40

	U.S.	**U.K.**	**Europe**
Children's Clothing	2	16	92
(*One size larger for knitwear*)	3	18	98
	4	20	104
	5	22	110
	6	24	116
	6X	26	122
Children's Shoes	8	7	24
	9	8	25
	10	9	27
	11	10	28
	12	11	29
	13	12	30
	1	13	32
	2	1	33
	3	2	34
	4¹/₂	3	36
	5¹/₂	4	37
	6¹/₂	5¹/₂	38¹/₂

General Sources of Information. The Italian Government Tourist Office, known as E.N.I.T. (Ente Nazionale Italiano per il Turismo), can help with inquiries and is a useful source of information. Below are the addresses of its offices in the U.S., Canada, and Great Britain:

In the U.S.:

630 Fifth Avenue, Suite 1565
New York, N.Y. 10111
tel. (212) 245-4822

500 North Michigan Avenue,
Suite 1046
Chicago, IL 60611
tel. (312) 644-0990

360 Post Street, Suite 801
San Francisco, Calif. 94108
tel. (415) 392-5266

In Canada:

3 Place Ville Marie, Suite 2414
Montreal, Québec H3B 3M9
tel. (514) 866-7667

In the U.K.:
1 Princes Street
London W1R 8AY
tel. (01) 408-1254

201 Regent Street
London W1R 8AY
tel. (01) 439-2311

There is no Italian Government Tourist Office in Australia.

Tourist offices in Italy are divided into three basic types: local tourist offices, which provide information for specific towns; regional tourist offices, which are helpful for inquiries concerning larger regions; and provincial tourist offices, which have information regarding individual cities and their adjacent provinces.

Regional tourist offices are known as Assessorato Regionale per il Turismo, and are located in every regional capital. They are a particularly good source for travel information; hours are from 8:00 A.M. to 12:30 P.M., and from 2:00 to 6:00 P.M., Monday through Friday. They are located in the regional areas of Abruzzo, Basilicata, Calabria, Campania, Emilia-Romagna, Friuli-Venezia Giulia, Lazio, Liguria, Lombardia, Marche, Molise, Piedmonte, Puglia, Sardegna, Sicilia, Toscana, Trentino, Umbria, Valle d'Aosta, and Veneto. These offices carry regional and city maps, provide extensive hotel listings, and can even make reservations in advance.

Metric/U.S. Weight, Measure, Temperature Equivalents.

Throughout the text, metric weights and measures are followed by U.S. equivalents in parentheses: likewise, Fahrenheit degrees are provided for centigrade temperatures. The following table is a quick reference for U.S. and metric equivalents.

Metric Unit	U.S. Equivalent	U.S. Unit	Metric Equivalent
Length		**Length**	
1 kilometer	0.6 miles	1 mile	1.6 kilometers
1 meter	1.09 yards	1 yard	0.9 meters
1 decimeter	0.3 feet	1 foot	3.04 decimeters
1 centimeter	0.39 inches	1 inch	2.5 centimeters
Weight		**Weight**	
1 kilogram	2.2 pounds	1 pound	0.45 kilograms
1 gram	0.03 ounces	1 ounce	28.3 grams
Liquid Capacity		**Liquid Capacity**	
1 dekaliter	2.38 gallons	1 gallon	0.37 dekaliters
1 liter	1.05 quarts	1 quart	0.9 liters
1 liter	2.1 pints	1 pint	0.47 liters

(*Note: there are 5 British Imperial gallons to 6 U.S. gallons.*)

Dry Measure		Dry Measure	
1 liter	0.9 quarts	1 quart	1.1 liters
1 liter	1.8 pints	1 pint	0.55 liters

To convert centigrade (C°) to Fahrenheit (F°):
$C° \times 9 \div 5 + 32 = F°$.

To convert Fahrenheit to centigrade:
$F° - 32 \times 5 \div 9 = C°$.

Town-by-Town

Included under each town listing are population and region, as well as information on local tourist offices, hotels, and transportation such as airports, train stations, and ferry connections. Some towns do not maintain tourist information offices; however, you usually can get information at the local city hall or train station. Hotels are classified according to our rating system and the one used by the Italian Government Tourist Office (for a full explanation, see page 336).

Abano Terme (Population 14,400; Veneto)
   Information: Via Pietro d'Abano 18. **Transportation:** Train station.
Accommodations: 🏨🏨🏨 (*Luxury*) Grand Hotel Royal Orologio. 🏨🏨🏨 (*1st class*) Hotel President (Italhotel); La Residence. 🏨🏨 Europa Terme; Universal. 🏨 Firenze.

Acireale (Population 50,000; Sicily)
   Information: Corso Umberto 179. **Transportation:** Airport and train station, Catania. **Accommodations:** 🏨🏨🏨 (*2nd class*) Maugeri; Aloha d'Oro. 🏨🏨 Pattis.

Aeolian (Lipari) Islands (Population: 13,500; Sicily)
   Information: *Lipari,* Corso Vittorio Emanuele 239. **Transportation:** Ferry: Messina, Naples, Milazzo, Capo Orlando, Cefalù, Palermo, and others. **Accommodations:** 🏨🏨🏨 (*1st class*) Carasco, *Lipari.* (*2nd class*) Giardino sul Mare, Gattopardo, *Lipari;* La Sciara Residence, *Stromboli;* Garden Vulcano, Eolian, Archipelago, *Vulcano.* 🏨🏨 Villa Diana, *Lipari;* Lisca Bianca, *Panarea;* Punta Scario, *Salina;* Scari, *Stromboli.*

Agrigento (Population: 50,000; Sicily)
   Information: Viale della Vittoria 255. **Transportation:** Train station. **Accommodations:** 🏨🏨🏨 (*1st class*) Jolly dei Templi; Tre Torri. 🏨🏨🏨 (*2nd class*) Della Valle; Colleverde; Pirandello. 🏨🏨 Bella Napoli; Paris.

Alassio (Population: 14,000; Liguria)
   Information: Viale Gibb 26. **Transportation:** Train station. **Accommodations:** 🏨🏨🏨 (*1st class*) Spiaggia; Mediterranée; Diana Grand. 🏨🏨🏨 (*2nd class*) Corso; Beau Sejour; Majestic. 🏨🏨 Bavaria; Bristol; Eden; Rio; Beau Rivage. 🏨 Ada; Lux; Rodi.

Albenga (Population: 20,000; Luguria)
   Information: Viale Martiri della Libertà 17. **Transportation:** Train station. **Accommodations:** 🏨🏨 Giardino; Italia. 🏨 Torino; Ancora d'Oro; Marisa.

Alberobello (Population: 11,000; Apulia)
   Transportation: Train station: Bari. **Accommodations:** 🏨🏨🏨 (*1st class*) Dei Trulli. 🏨🏨🏨 (*2nd class*) Astoria. 🏨 Lanzilotta.

Alessandria (Population: 102,000; Piedmont)
Information: Via Savona 26. **Transportation:** Train station. **Accommodations:** 🏨 (*2nd class*) Alli due buoi Rossi; Astoria. 🏨 Royal; Parigi. 🏨 Napoleon; Croce Bianca; Italia; Falcone.

Alghero (Population: 29,500; Sardinia)
Information: Piazza Porta Terra. **Transportation:** Airport, Fertilia (6.5 km., 4 miles, from town); Sassari. **Accommodations:** 🏨 (*1st class*) Calabona; Carlos V; El Faro (Italhotel). 🏨 (*2nd class*) Continental; Dei Pini.

Amalfi (Population: 7,400; Campania)
Information: Corso delle Repubbliche Marinare 25. **Transportation:** Ferry: Ischia, Capri, Salerno, Positano, Naples. Train station, Vietri sul Mare. **Accommodations:** 🏨 (*1st class*) Excelsior Grand Hotel; Luna; Santa Caterina. 🏨 (*2nd class*) Aurora; Dei Cavalieri; Residence; Miramalfi. 🏨 Sant' Andrea; Lidomare.

Ancona (Population: 108,000; Marches)
Information: Via Thaon de Revel; Stazione Ferrovie Stato. **Transportation:** Ferry: Brindisi, Corfu; Train station. **Accommodations:** 🏨 (*1st class*) Grand Hotel Palace; Jolly; Grand Hotel Passetto. 🏨 (*2nd class*) Fortuna, Roma e Pace. 🏨 (*Motel*) MotelAgip, Palombina Nuova.

Anzio (Population: 25,000; Latium)
Information: Via Pollastrini 3. **Transportation:** Ferry, Ponti Islands and Formia; Train station, Rome. **Accommodations:** 🏨 (*2nd class*) Dei Cesari; Lido Garda; Succi (Lavinio). 🏨 Riviera; La Bussola; La Tavernetta. 🏨 La Sirenetta (Lavinio).

Aosta (Population: 39,000; Valle d'Aosta)
Information: Piazza Emilio Chanoux 3 and Piazza Narbonne. **Transportation:** Train station. **Accommodations:** 🏨 (*1st class*) Valle d'Aosta. 🏨 (*2nd class*) Europe; Roma; Norden. 🏨 Joli; Gran Paradiso. 🏨 Les Geraniums; Gallina; Monte Emilius.

Arenzano (Population: 6,000; Liguria)
Information: Via Pierino Negrotto Cambiasi 2. **Transportation:** Train station. **Accommodations:** 🏨 (*1st class*) Grand Hotel Arenzano. 🏨 (*2nd class*) Miramare; Ena. 🏨 Piccolo; Vittoria. 🏨 Massa.

Arezzo (Population: 84,000; Tuscany)
Information: Piazza Risorgimento 116. **Transportation:** Train station. **Accommodations:** 🏨 (*1st class*) Drago; Minerva. 🏨 (*2nd class*) Continentale; Graverini; Europa. 🏨 Da Cecco. 🏨 Roma.

Arona (Population: 11,500; Valle d'Aosta)
Information: Piazza Stazione. **Transportation:** Train station. **Accommodations:** 🏨🏨🏨 (*1st class*) Antares; Atlantic. 🏨🏨 Clipper; Florida; Giardino; Cristallo. 🏨 Splendor dal Bimbo; San Carlo.

Ascoli Piceno (Population: 55,000; Marches)
Information: Via Trivio 1; Corso Mazzini 229. **Transportation:** Train station. **Accommodations:** 🏨🏨🏨 (*2nd class*) Marche; Gioli; Pennile. 🏨🏨 Piceno. 🏨 Nuovo Picchio.

Assisi (Population: 25,000; Umbria)
Information: Piazza del Comune 12. **Transportation:** Train station. **Accommodations:** 🏨🏨🏨 (*1st class*) Subasio; Giotto. 🏨🏨🏨 (*2nd class*) Umbra; Dei Priori; San Francesco. 🏨🏨 San Pietro; Sole.

Bardolino (Population: 4,300; Veneto)
Information: Piazza Matteotti 53. **Transportation:** Train station, Verona. **Accommodations:** 🏨🏨🏨 (*2nd class*) Kriss; San Pietro. 🏨🏨 Bologna; Speranza.

Bari (Population: 350,000; Apulia)
Information: Via Melo 253; Corso Vittorio Emanuele 68. **Transportation:** Airport Palese (9 km.; 5.5 miles); Ferry, Ancona, Brindisi; Train station. **Accommodations:** (*Luxury*) Ambasciatori; Palace. 🏨🏨🏨 (*1st class*) Grand Hotel e d'Oriente. 🏨🏨🏨 (*2nd class*) Victor; Leon d'Oro; Boston; 7 Mari; Plaza; Majesty.

Barletta (Population: 67,000; Apulia)
Information: Piazza Aldo Moro. **Transportation:** Train station. **Accommodations:** 🏨🏨🏨 (*2nd class*) Artù; Helios Residence; Royal. 🏨🏨 Il Focolare; La Terrazza; Centrale. 🏨 Longano.

Battaglia Terme (Population: 3,000; Venetia)
Information: Traversa Terme 23 a. **Transportation:** Train station, Padua. **Accommodations:** 🏨🏨 Terme Euganee; Nuovo Regina. 🏨 Primavera; Al Sole.

Baveno (Population: 3,500; Valle d'Aosta)
Information: Piazza Dante 15. **Transportation:** Train station. **Accommodations:** 🏨🏨🏨 (*1st class*) Splendid. 🏨🏨🏨 (*2nd class*) Romagna; Beau Rivage. 🏨🏨 Elvezia; Ankara Touring; Florida. 🏨 Gardenia; Ortensie; La Ripa.

Bellagio (Population: 3,500; Lombardy)
Information: Lungolago A. Manzoni 1. **Transportation:** Train station, Como. **Accommodations:** 🏨🏨🏨 (*Luxury*) Grand Hotel Serbelloni. 🏨🏨🏨 (*2nd class*) Belvedere; Du Lac; Florence. 🏨🏨 Fioroni; Pergola; Silvio. 🏨 Giardinetto; Roma; Suisse.

Belluno (Population: 34,000; Veneto)
Information: Via Psaro 21; Piazza Martiri 27. **Transportation:** Airport; Train station, San Pinetto in Campo (7 km., 4.5 miles). **Accommodations:** 🏨🏨 (*2nd class*) Europa; Villa Carpenada. 🏨 Astor; Dolomiti; Centrale; Sole. 🏠 Taverna; Bel Sit. *Nevegal:* 🏨🏨 (*2nd class*) Pineta. 🏨 Olivier; Nevegal.

Benevento (Population: 60,000; Campania)
Information: Via Nicola Sala, Parco de Santis. **Transportation:** Train station. **Accommodations:** 🏨🏨🏨 (*1st class*) President. 🏨🏨 (*2nd class*) Italiano. 🏨 La Cittadella. 🏠 Sole.

Bergamo (Population: 130,000; Lombardy)
Information: Viale V. Emanuele; Via Tasso 2. **Transportation:** Train station. **Accommodations:** 🏨🏨🏨 (*1st class*) Excelsior San Marco. 🏨🏨 (*2nd class*) Arli; Città dei Mille; Cappello d'Oro. 🏨 Del Moro; Agnello d'Oro; Commercio; Piemontese. 🏠 San Giorgio; Sole.

Bologna (Population: 493,000; Emilia-Romagna)
Information: Via Leopardi 1; Piazza Nettuno 1; Main train station. **Transportation:** Airport (7 km.; 4.5 miles); Borgo Panigale Train station. **Accommodations:** 🏨🏨🏨 (*Luxury*) Royal Hotel Carlton. 🏨🏨🏨 (*1st class*) Jolly, Piazza XX Settembre; Elite (Italhotel), Via A. Saffi 36. 🏨🏨🏨 (*2nd class*) Alexander, Viale Pietramellara 47; Cristallo, Via S. Giuseppe 5. 🏨 Tre Vecchi, Via Indipendenza 47; Astor, Via Fioravanti 42. 🏠 Eliseo, Via Testoni 3. *Bologna-Borgo Panigale:* 🏨🏨🏨 (*Motel*) Motel Agip, Via E. Lepido 203/4.

Bolsena (Population: 4,800; Latium)
Transportation: Train station, Orvieto. **Accommodations:** 🏨🏨🏨 (*2nd class*) Columbus Hotel del Lago. 🏨 Lido; Le Naiadi; Moderno. 🏠 Eden; Nazionale.

Bolzano (Population: 105,000; Trentino–Alto Adige)
Information: Parrocchia 11–12. **Transportation:** Airport, San Giacomo (5 km.; 3 miles); Train station. **Accommodations:** 🏨🏨🏨 (*1st class*) Parkhotel Laurin, Laurinstraße 4; Grifone, Waltherplatz 7. 🏨🏨 (*2nd class*) Città di Bolzano; Waltherplatz 21; Lewald, Via Maso della Pieve 17; Pircher, Meraner Str. 52. 🏨 Flora, Fagenstr. 27; Adria, Perathonerstraße 17; Ariston, Romstr. 82. 🏠 Bel Sit, Romstr. 9.

Bordighera (Population: 12,000; Liguria)
Information: Via Roberto 1. **Transportation:** Train station. **Accommodations:** 🏨🏨🏨 (*1st class*) Grand Hotel del Mare; Ampelio (Italhotel). 🏨🏨🏨 (*2nd class*) Centro; Della Punta; Britannique et Jolie; Astoria; Excelsior. 🏨 Sirena; Parigi; Michelin; Aurora; Mirelia.

Brescia (Population: 206,000; Lombardy)

Information: Corso Zanardelli 38. **Transportation:** Train station. **Accommodations:** 🏨🏨🏨 (*1st class*) Ambasciatori, Via Crocifissa di Rosa 92; Master, Via Apollonio 72. 🏨🏨🏨 (*2nd class*) Capri, Viale S. Eufemia 37. 🏨🏨 Cristallo, Viale Stazione 12; Astron, Via Togni 14. 🏨🏨 (*Motel*) MotelAgip, Viale Bornata 42.

Bressanone (Population: 15,000; Trentino–Alto Adige)

Information: Via Stazione 9. **Transportation:** Train station. **Accommodations:** 🏨🏨🏨 (*1st class*) Dominik; Elefant. 🏨🏨🏨 (*2nd class*) Gasser; Jarolim; Temlhof. 🏨🏨 Goldene Traube; Burgstall. 🏨 Kreuztal, Trametsch.

Brindisi (Population: 82,000; Apulia)

Information: Via Bastioni Carlo V. **Transportation:** Airport, Casale (5 km.; 3 miles); Ferry, Ancona, Corfu, Piräus and others; Train station. **Accommodations:** 🏨🏨🏨 (*1st class*) Majestic, Corso Umberto 151. 🏨🏨🏨 (*2nd class*) Corso, Corso Roma 83; L'Approdo, Via del Mare. 🏨🏨 Bologna, Via Cavour 41; Torino, Via Martinez 19. 🏨 La Rosetta, Via San Dioniso 2.

Cagliari (Population: 250,000; Sardinia)

Information: Piazza Matteotti 9. **Transportation:** Airport, Elmas (8 km.; 5 miles); Ferry, Genoa, Naples, Palermo; Train station. **Accommodations:** 🏨🏨🏨 (*2nd class*) Mediterraneo, Lungomare Colombo 46; Moderno, Via Roma 159; Italia, Via Sardegna 27; Panorama, Viale Armando Diaz 231. 🏨🏨 Solemar, Viale Diaz 146. 🏨 Fiora, Via Sassari 43. 🏨🏨 (*Motel*) MotelAgip, Circonvallazione Nuova.

Canazei (Population: 1,600; Trentino–Alto Adige)

Information: Via Roma 24. **Transportation:** Train station, Bolzano. **Accommodations:** 🏨🏨🏨 (*2nd class*) Diana; Tyrol; Faloria; Croce Bianca; Rosa. 🏨🏨 Italia; Chalet Pineta.

Capri, Isle of (Population: 13,000; Campania)

Information: Piazza Umberto 19. **Transportation:** Ferries from Marina Grande to Naples, Ischia, Sorrento, Massalubrense, Amalfi, and others. **Accommodations:** 🏨🏨🏨 (*Luxury*) Quisisana & Grand. 🏨🏨🏨 (*1st class*) Luna; Regina Cristina; La Scalinatella. 🏨🏨🏨 (*2nd class*) Gatto Bianco; La Pineta; Flora; La Vega; Villa Sarah. 🏨🏨 Canasta; Tirrenia e Robert's; Florida. *Marina Grande:* 🏨🏨🏨 (*2nd class*) Excelsior Parco. 🏨🏨 Belvedere e Tre Re; Maresca. 🏨 Bristol; Svizzero. *Marina Piccola:* 🏨🏨🏨 (*2nd class*) Carlton. 🏨 Quattro Stagioni. *Anacapri:* 🏨🏨🏨 (*1st class*) Caesar Augustus; Europa Palace. 🏨🏨🏨 (*2nd class*) Villa Patrizia; San Michele. 🏨🏨 Bellavista; Biancamaria.

Caserta (Population: 70,000; Campania)
Information: Corso Trieste 39. **Transportation:** Train station. **Accommodations:** 🏨 (*2nd class*) Centrale; Europa. 🏨 Vittoria; Tre Re. 🏨 Royal.

Catania (Population: 400,000; Sicily)
Information: Largo Paisiello 5. **Transportation:** Airport, Fontanarossa (5 km.; 3 miles); Ferry, Palermo, Siracusa and others; Train station. **Accommodations:** 🏨 (*1st class*) Jolly, Piazza Trento 13; Excelsior, Piazza Verga. 🏨 (*2nd class*) Central Palace, Via Etnea 218. 🏨 Nettuno, Viale Lauria. 🏨 Italia, Via Etnea; Moderno, Via Alessi 9.

Catanzaro (Population: 76,000; Calabria)
Information: Via F. Spasari; Piazza Stocco 5; Piazza Rossi. **Transportation:** Train station. **Accommodations:** 🏨 (*2nd class*) Grand Hotel, Piazza Matteotti 8; Guglielmo, Via Tedeschi 1. 🏨 Casalbergo, Via Plutino. 🏨 Alla Stazione, Viale Stazione. *Catanzaro/Lido:* 🏨 (*2nd class*) Lido; Niagara.

Cattolica (Population: 17,000; Marches)
Information: Piazza Nettuno 1. **Transportation:** Train station. **Accommodations:** 🏨 (*1st class*) Caravelle. 🏨 (*2nd class*) Victoria Palace; Negresco; Royal Madison; Savoia. 🏨 Europa Monetti; San Marco; Vienna. 🏨 Serenissima.

Cernobbio (Population: 8,500; Lombardy)
Information: Via Regina 33. **Transportation:** Train station, Como. **Accommodations:** 🏨 (*Luxury*) Villa d'Este. 🏨 (*1st class*) Regina Olga Reine du Lac. 🏨 (*2nd class*) Miralago; 🏨 Centrale; Terzo Crotto. 🏨 Giardino.

Cesenatico (Population: 18,000; Emilia–Romagna)
Information: Viale Roma 112. **Transportation:** Train station. **Accommodations:** 🏨 (*2nd class*) Esplanada; Britannia. 🏨 San Pietro; Des Bains; Roxy. 🏨 Duse; Tiboni; Ori; Leonardo.

Chieti (Population: 53,000; Abruzzi)
Information: Via B. Spaventa 29. **Transportation:** Train station: Chieti-Scalo. **Accommodations:** 🏨 (*2nd class*) Grande Albergo Abruzzo; Sole; Dangio. 🏨 Marrucino; Garibaldi. *Chieti-Scalo:* 🏨 Nuovo. 🏨 Degli Amici.

Chioggia Sottomarina (Population: 47,000; Veneto)
Information: Lungomare Adriatico Centro. **Transportation:** Train station. **Accommodations:** 🏨 (*2nd class*) Ritz; Anzoletti; Bristol; Vittoria Palace. 🏨 Florida; Capinera; Park Hotel; Stella d'Italia.

Chiusa (Klausen) (Population: 5,000; Tuscany)
Transportation: Train station. **Accommodations:** 🏨🏨 (*2nd class*) Sylvanerhof; Post. 🏨 Grauer Bär; Sonne. 🏨 Gamp; Zum Hirschen.

Civitavecchia (Population: 44,000; Latium)
Information: Viale Garibaldi 42. **Transportation:** Train station. **Accommodations:** 🏨🏨🏨 (*1st class*) Sunbay Park Hotel. 🏨🏨🏨 (*2nd class*) Mediterraneo-Suisse. 🏨🏨 Traghetto; Miramare. 🏨 Roma Nord; La Medusa.

Como (Population: 98,000; Lombardy)
Information: Piazza Cavour 16. **Transportation:** Train station. **Accommodations:** 🏨🏨🏨 (*1st class*) Metropole e Suisse; Barchetta Excelsior; Villa Flori; Como. 🏨🏨🏨 (*2nd class*) Park Hotel; Plinius. 🏨🏨 Tre Re; Engadina.

Cortina d'Ampezzo (Population: 8,000; Veneto)
Information: Piazzetta S. Francesco; Piazza Roma 1. **Transportation:** Train station, Calazo, Pieve di Cadore. **Accommodations:** 🏨🏨🏨 (*Luxury*) Miramonti Majestic. 🏨🏨🏨 (*1st class*) Savoia (Italhotel). 🏨🏨🏨 (*2nd class*) Majoni; Ancora; Serena. 🏨🏨 Pocol; Nord; Columbia; Panda. 🏨🏨 (*Motel*) MotelAgip, Via Roma 70.

Cosenza (Population: 75,000; Calabria)
Information: Via Pasquale Rossi. **Transportation:** Train station. **Accommodations:** 🏨🏨🏨 (*2nd class*) Imperiale, Viale Trieste; Centrale, Via del Tigrai. 🏨🏨 Alexander, Via Monte S. Michele 3; Principe, Via Monte S. Michele; Mondial, Via Molinella 24. 🏨 Bruno, Corso Mazzini 27. (*Motel*) MotelAgip, S 19.

Courmayeur (Population: 1,400; Valle d'Aosta)
Information: Piazzale Monte Bianco. **Transportation:** Train station, Pré Saint Didier. **Accommodations:** 🏨🏨🏨 (*1st class*) Royal (Italhotel). 🏨🏨🏨 (*2nd class*) Courmayeur; Centrale; Croux. 🏨🏨 Berthod; Svizzero; Vittoria. 🏨 Ferrato; Roma. *Entrèves:* 🏨🏨🏨 (*1st class*) Des Alpes. 🏨🏨🏨 (*2nd class*) La Brenva; La Grange; Pilier d'Angle. 🏨🏨 Aiguille Noire. 🏨 Chalet Chanton.

Cremona (Population: 70,000; Lombardy)
Information: Piazza del Comune 8. **Transportation:** Train station. **Accommodations:** 🏨🏨🏨 (*2nd class*) Este; Astoria; Continental. 🏨 San Marco; Bologna. 🏨🏨 (*Motel*) MotelAgip, north exit.

Crotone (Population: 47,000; Calabria)
Information: Via XXV Aprile 83. **Transportation:** Harbor; Train station. **Accommodations:** 🏨🏨🏨 (*2nd class*) Bologna; Casarossa. 🏨🏨 Italia; Jorno. 🏨 Pale; Europa.

Desenzano (Population: 12,000; Lombardy)
Information: Piazza Matteotti 27. **Transportation:** Train station.
Accommodations: 🏨🏨🏨 (*1st class*) Park Hotel. 🏨🏨🏨 (*2nd class*) La Vela;
Mayer e Splendid; Europa; Benaco; Nazionale. 🏨🏨 Vittorio.

Diano Marina (Population: 4,000; Liguria)
Information: Corso Garibaldi 60. **Transportation:** Train station.
Accommodations: 🏨🏨🏨 (*1st class*) Diana Majestic. 🏨🏨🏨 (*2nd class*)
Bellevue-Méditerranée; Sasso; Caravelle; Golfo e Palme; Tiziana; Palace. 🏨🏨 Metropol; Caprice; Piccolo Hotel.

Egadi Islands (Isole Egadi) (Population: 6,000; Sicily)
Information: *Trapani,* Piazza Saturno. **Transportation:** Ferry, Trapani. **Accommodations:** 🏨🏨🏨 (*2nd class*) L'Approdo di Ulisse, *Favignana.* 🏨 Egadi, *Favignana;* Paradiso, *Levanzo.*

Enna (Population: 28,000; Sicily)
Information: Piazza N. Colaianni. **Transportation:** Train station.
Accommodations: 🏨🏨🏨 (*2nd class*) Belvedere; Grande Albergo Sicilia:
🏨🏨 Riviera; La Giara (both in Enna-Pergusa).

Fano (Population: 53,000; Marches)
Information: Via C. Battisti 10. **Transportation:** Train station.
Accommodations: 🏨🏨🏨 (*1st class*) Elisabeth; 🏨🏨🏨 (*2nd class*) Continental; Plaza; Excelsior. 🏨🏨 Astoria; Europa; Corallo; Marina. 🏨 Metauro.

Ferrara (Population: 158,000; Emilia-Romagna)
Information: Largo Castello 22. **Transportation:** Train station.
Accommodations: 🏨🏨🏨 (*1st class*) Astra, Viale Cavour 55. 🏨🏨🏨 (*2nd class*) Europa, Corso Giovecca 49; Astra, Viale Cavour 55; Touring, Viale Cavour 11. 🏨🏨 Nord-Ovest; Viale Po 52; Santo Stefano, Viale S. Stefano 21. 🏨 Annunziata, Piazza della Repubblica 5; Nazionale, C. S. Porta Reno 32; Alfonsa, Via Padiglioni 5. *Lido degli Estensi:* 🏨🏨🏨 (*2nd class*) Tropicana; Conca del Lido; Logonovo. 🏨🏨 Corallo; Moderno. 🏨 Villa Azzurra. *Lido delle Nazioni:* 🏨🏨🏨 (*2nd class*) Delle Nazioni. 🏨🏨 Quadrifoglio; Europa. *Lido degli Scacchi:* 🏨🏨🏨 (*2nd class*) Alfiere. 🏨🏨 Eden. *Lido di Pomposa:* 🏨🏨🏨 (*2nd class*) Park. 🏨🏨 Lido. 🏨 Donatella. *Lido di Spina:* 🏨🏨 Gallia; Continental. 🏨 Caravel. *Porto Garibaldi:* 🏨🏨 Canoa. 🏨 Ariston.

Finale Ligure (Population: 13,000; Liguria)
Information: Via S. Pietro 14. **Transportation:** Train station.
Accommodations: 🏨🏨🏨 (*1st class*) Moroni; Residenza Punta Est. 🏨🏨🏨 (*2nd class*) Miramare. 🏨🏨 Colibri; Internazionale. 🏨🏨 Bel Sit; Principe; Park Hotel Castello. 🏨 Azzurra, Ferrero; Riviera.

Fiuggi (Population: 6,000; Latium)

Information: Piazza G. Frascara 4. **Transportation:** Train station, Rome, Anagni. **Accommodations:** 🏨🏨 (*Luxury*) Vallombrosa e Majestic. 🏨🏨 (*1st class*) Silva Hotel Splendid. 🏨🏨 (*2nd class*) Astoria; Alfieri; San Giorgio; Tripoli; Michelangelo; Sforza. 🏨 Mirage; Polaris; Sporting; Edison.

Florence (Firenze) (Population 458,000; Tuscany)

Information: Via Manzoni 16 and Via Tornabuoni 15. **Transportation:** Airport, Peretola (5 km.; 3 miles); Train station. **Accommodations:** 🏨🏨 (*Luxury*) Excelsior, Piazza Ognissanti 3. 🏨🏨 (*1st class*) Jolly Carlton, Piazza V. Veneto 4; De la Ville, Piazza Antinori 1; Kraft, Via Solferino 2. 🏨🏨 (*2nd class*) Balestri, Piazza Mentana 7; Hermitage, Vicolo Marzio 1; De la Pace, Via Lamarmora 28. 🏨 Alfa, Via Alfieri 9; Boboli, Via Romana 63. 🏨🏨 (*Motel*) MotelAgip, Firenza-North exit. *Fiesole:* 🏨🏨 (*1st class*) Villa San Michele. 🏨🏨 (*2nd class*) Aurora. 🏨 Villa Bonelli.

Foggia (Population: 157,000; Apulia)

Information: Via Senatore E. Perrone 17. **Transportation:** Airport, Rome; Train station. **Accommodations:** 🏨🏨 (*1st class*) Cicolella, Viale XXIV Maggio 60. 🏨🏨 (*2nd class*) Palace Hotel Sarti, Viale XXIV Maggio 48; President, Via degli Aviatori 80. 🏨 (*Motel*) Motel Salice, S 16.

Forlì (Population: 110,000; Emilia-Romagna)

Information: Corso della Repubblica 23. **Transportation:** Airport 4 km. (2.5 miles) from town; Train station. **Accommodations:** 🏨🏨 (*1st class*) Della Città, Via Fortis 8; Principe, S 9. 🏨🏨 (*2nd class*) Masini, Corso Garibaldi 28; Air Hotel, Via Morandi 7. 🏨 Astoria, Piazza Ordelaffi; Vittorino, Via Baratti 4; Lory, Via Lazzarini 20.

Formia (Population: 16,400, Latium)

Information: Viale Unitá d'Italia 30/34. **Transportation:** Train station. **Accommodations:** 🏨🏨 (*1st class*) Grande Albergo Miramare. 🏨🏨 (*2nd class*) Ariston, Romantic. 🏨 Del Golfo; Marino. 🏨 Villa Ida; Europa; Little Garden.

Forte Dei Marmi (Population: 10,000; Tuscany)

Information: Piazza Marconi. **Transportation:** Train station. **Accommodations:** 🏨🏨 (*Luxury*) Augustus. 🏨🏨 (*1st class*) Atlantico; Raffaelli Park; Ritz; Byron. 🏨🏨 (*2nd class*) Bandinelli; Belvedere; Tirreno; Le Pleiadi. 🏨 Pigalle; Olimpia; La Pace.

Francavilla al Mare (Population: 6,500; Abruzzi)

Information: Piazzale Sirena. **Transportation:** Train station. **Accommodations:** 🏨🏨 (*2nd class*) Punta de l'Est. 🏨 Mare Blu; Royal. 🏨 Vittoria; Principe; Renato.

Gaeta (Population: 22,000; Latium)
Information: Piazza XIX Maggio. **Transportation:** Train station.
Accommodations: ⌂⌂⌂ (*2nd class*) Aenaea's Landing; Flamingo. ⌂
Rock Garden. *San Vito:* ⌂⌂⌂ (*2nd class*) Il Ninfeo; Le Rocce. *Serapo:* ⌂⌂⌂
(*2nd class*) Mirasole; Serapo. ⌂⌂ Sabbia d'Oro.

Gallipoli (Population: 22,000; Apulia)
Transportation: Train station, Lecce. **Accommodations:** ⌂⌂⌂ (*1st
class*) Costa Brada. ⌂⌂ Rivabella; Cristina. ⌂⌂ (*Motel*) Motel di Mattina,
Torre Pizzo.

Garda (Population: 2,900; Veneto)
Information: Lungolago Regina Adelaide. **Transportation:** Train
station, Peschiera. **Accommodations:** ⌂⌂⌂ (*1st class*) Regina Adelaide.
⌂⌂⌂ (*2nd class*) Flora; Terminus e Garda; Cortina. ⌂⌂ Conca d'Oro; Tre
Corone; San Marco.

Gardone (Population: 2,800; Lombardy)
Information: Viale Roma 8. **Transportation:** Train station,
Desenzano. **Accommodations:** ⌂⌂⌂ (*1st class*) Grand Hotel (Italhotel).
⌂⌂⌂ (*2nd class*) Fiordaliso; Monte Baldo; Il Riccio. ⌂⌂ Bellevue; Villa
Capri. ⌂ Nord; Garda & Suisse.

Gela (Population: 56,000; Sicily)
Information: Via Palazzi 66. **Transportation:** Train station. **Accommodations:** ⌂⌂⌂ (*2nd class*) Caposoprano. ⌂⌂ Excelsior; Sole.

Genoa (Genova) (Population: 780,000; Liguria)
Information: Via Porta degli Archi 10/5, Via Roma 11, and at the
airport and train station. **Transportation:** Airport Sestri Ponente (6 km.;
3.5 miles); Ferries: Naples, Corsica, Sicily, North Africa and the Continent; Train station. **Accommodations:** ⌂⌂⌂ (*Luxury*) Colombia. ⌂⌂⌂ (*1st
class*) Savoia-Majestic (Italhotel), Via Arsenale di Terra 5. ⌂⌂⌂ (*2nd
class*) Aquila & Reale, Piazza Acquaverde 1; Crespi, Via A. Doria 10;
Vittoria Orlandini, Via Balbi 45. ⌂⌂ Bertola, Via Colombo 1/4; Fiume,
Via Fiume 9r; Torinese, Via A. Gramsci 291r. ⌂ Rex, Via De Gasperi 9;
San Marco, Via A. Doria 4A; Lausanne, Via Balbi 33A. *Nervi:* Information: Piazza Pittaluga 4R. ⌂⌂⌂ (*1st class*) Astor Residence. ⌂⌂⌂ (*2nd
class*) Esperia; Nervi. ⌂⌂ Panoramica; Riposo. ⌂ Piccolo Eden. *Pegli:*
⌂⌂⌂ (*2nd class*) Mediterranée. ⌂⌂ Dei Gerani. ⌂ Miranda.

Grosseto (Population 70,000; Tuscany)
Information: Via Monterosa 206. **Transportation:** Train station.
Accommodations: ⌂⌂⌂ (*2nd class*) Lorena; Nalesso. ⌂⌂ Maremma; Tir-
reno; Quattro Strade; Leon d'Oro. ⌂ Vittoria; Il Giappone.

Gubbio (Population: 32,000; Umbria)
   Information: Piazza Oderisi 6. **Transportation:** Train station, Fossato di Vico. **Accommodations:** 🏨🏨 (*2nd class*) Bosone; San Marco; Pinolo. 🏨 Oderisi; Padule; Gattapone.

Imola (Population: 55,500; Emilia-Romagna)
   Transportation: Train station. **Accommodations:** 🏨🏨🏨 (*1st class*) Olimpia; Imola. 🏨🏨 (*2nd class*) Molino Rosso. 🏨 Del Turismo; Campana.

Imperia (Population: 40,000; Liguria)
   Information: Viale Matteotti 22. **Transportation:** Train station. **Accommodations:** 🏨🏨 (*2nd class*) Kristina; Corallo; Croce di Malta; Centro. 🏨 Ariston; Concordia. 🏨 Adria; Costa; Ambra.

Ischia (Population 37,000; Campania)
   Information: Naples, Via Vittorio Emanuele 32; Porto d'Ischia, Via Fornaci 10 and Scalo Portosalvo; Lacco Ameno, Corso Angelo Rizzoli 2; Via Iasolina. **Transportation:** Airport, helicopter service; Ferries: Naples, Capri, and others. **Accommodations:** *Porto d'Ischia:* 🏨🏨🏨 (*Luxury*) Jolly; Excelsior; Punta Molino. 🏨🏨🏨 (*1st class*) Aragona Palace Terme; Alexander; Continental Terme. 🏨🏨 (*2nd class*) Nuovo Lido; Central Park Terme; Mare Blu; Bristol Palace; Bellevue; Hermitage e Park Terme; Regina Palace. 🏨 Villa Diana. *Casamicciola Terme:* 🏨🏨🏨 (*1st class*) Cristallo Palace; La Madonnina; Manzi. 🏨🏨 (*2nd class*) Gran Paradiso; Elma; Stefania. 🏨 Carmen; Candia. 🏨 Magnolia; Ouisisana; Piccolo Paradiso. *Forio:* 🏨🏨 (*2nd class*) Parco Maria; Zaro; Splendid. 🏨 Villa Teresa; Tritone; Il Gattopardo. 🏨 Hibiscus. *Monterone:* 🏨🏨 (*2nd class*) Villa Thomas Terme. 🏨 Castaldi. *Lacco Ameno:* 🏨🏨🏨 (*Luxury*) Regina Isabella. 🏨🏨🏨 (*1st class*) San Montano. 🏨🏨 (*2nd class*) Antares; Il Fungo. 🏨 Bristol; La Pace; Principe. 🏨 Terme Marina; Villa Angelica. *Barano d'Ischia–Maronti:* 🏨🏨🏨 (*1st class*) Parco Smeraldo. 🏨🏨 (*2nd class*) Helios; Villa San Giorgio. 🏨 La Mandorla; Da Franceschina; Maronti; Villa al Mare. *Serrara Fontana–Sant'Angelo:* 🏨🏨 (*2nd class*) Vulcano; San Michele; La Palma. 🏨 Casa Rosa; Loreley; Romantica. 🏨 Margherita; Villa Franz; Del Sole.

Laigueglia (Population: 1,800; Liguria)
   Information: Via Milano 33. **Transportation:** Train station. **Accommodations:** 🏨🏨🏨 (*1st class*) Laigueglia; Splendid. 🏨🏨 (*2nd class*) Bristol; Dalia; Windsor. 🏨 Mediterraneo; Beau Séjour. 🏨 Castello; Armida; La Quiete; Olivella.

L'Aquila (Population: 65,000; Abruzzi)
   Information: Via XX Settembre 8. **Transportation:** Train station. **Accommodations:** 🏨🏨🏨 (*1st class*) Grand Hotel. 🏨🏨 (*2nd class*) Duca

degli Abruzzi; Le Cannelle; Castello. 🏨 Italia. 🛏 Aurora; Centrale; Leon d'Oro; Milani.

La Spezia (Population: 124,000; Liguria)

Information: Via Mazzini 47. **Transportation:** Ferry: Portovenere, Lerici, and others; Train station. **Accommodations:** 🏨🏨🏨 (*1st class*) Jolly; Residence. 🏨🏨🏨 (*2nd class*) Tirreno; Astoria; Genova. 🏨 Astra; Corallo; Diana; Firenze e Continental. 🛏 Stefania; Birillo; Bellavista. 🏨 (*Motel*) MotelAgip, in Sarzana, on the by-pass road to Via Aurelia.

Latina (Population: 93,000; Latium)

Information: Via Duca del Mare 19. **Transportation:** Train station, Latina Scalo. **Accommodations:** 🏨🏨🏨 (*1st class*) Garden. 🏨🏨🏨 (*2nd class*) De la Ville; Park; Miramare; Tirreno (both in Lido di Capo Portiere); Europa. 🏨 Fogliano (in Lido di Capo Portiere); Caty (in Lido di Foce Verde). 🛏 Giusi; Centrale.

Lecce (Population: 92,000; Apulia)

Information: Piazza Sant'Oronzo. **Transportation:** Airport; Train station. **Accommodations:** 🏨🏨🏨 (*1st class*) President, Via Salandra 6. 🏨🏨🏨 (*2nd class*) Delle Palme, Via Leuca 90; Risorgimento, Via Imperatore Augusto 19. 🏨 Patria-Touring, Piazzetta G. Riccardi, 13.

Lecco (Population: 54,000; Lombardy)

Information: Via Nazario Sauro 6. **Transportation:** Train station. **Accommodations:** 🏨🏨🏨 (*2nd class*) Don Abbondio; Giordano. 🏨 Caviate; Croce di Malta. 🛏 Du Torri.

Leghorn (Livorno) (Population: 175,000; Tuscany)

Information: Piazza Cavour 6. **Transportation:** Harbor; Train station. **Accommodations:** 🏨🏨🏨 (*2nd class*) Gran Duca; Boston; Touring; Giappone; Universal. 🛏 Giardino. 🏨🏨🏨 (*Motel*) MotelAgip, (8 km.; 5 miles) north on Via Nazionale 1, in Stagno.

Lerici (Population:14,500; Liguria)

Information: Via Roma 47. **Transportation:** Ferry: La Spezia, Portovenere; Train station, La Spezia. **Accommodations:** 🏨🏨🏨 (*2nd class*) Europa; Venere Azzurra; Shelley. 🏨 Italia; Florida; Miramare.

Lido di Ostia (Population: 4,400; Latium)

Information: Rom, Via Parigi 11. **Transportation:** Train station, Rome. **Accommodations:** 🏨🏨🏨 (*1st class*) Satellite Palace. 🏨🏨🏨 (*2nd class*) Ping-Pong; Lido. 🏨 Sirenetta; La Scaletta. 🛏 Tirrenia; Bellavista.

Limone sul Garda (Population: 1,000; Lombardy)

Information: Via Comboni 15. **Transportation:** Train station, Desenzano. **Accommodations:** 🏨🏨🏨 (*1st class*) Ideal; Leonardo da

Vinci. 🏨🏨🏨 (*2nd class*) Lido; San Giorgio. 🏨🏨 Splendid; Europa; Garden; Mignon. 🏨 Mercedes.

Lipari Islands (See Aeolian Islands)

Loreto (Population: 10,000; Marches)
Information: Via G. Solari 3. **Transportation:** Train station. **Accommodations:** 🏨🏨🏨 (*2nd class*) Bellevue & Marchigiano; Giardinetto. 🏨🏨 Pellegrino e Pace; Santuario; Casa San Francesco. 🏨 Vecchia Fattoria.

Lucca (Population: 91,000; Tuscany)
Information: Piazza Guidiccioni 2; Via Vittorio Veneto 40. **Transportation:** Train station. **Accommodations:** 🏨🏨🏨 (*1st class*) Napoleon, Viale Europa 1. 🏨🏨🏨 (*2nd class*) Universo, Piazza Puccini 1. 🏨🏨 La Luna, Corte Compagni 12; Ilaria, Via del Fosso 20; Rex, Piazza Stazione 2; Moderno, Via Civitali 9. 🏨 La Pace, Corte Portici 2.

Maderno-Toscolano (Population: 2,100; Lombardy)
Information: Lungolago Zanardelli 18. **Transportation:** Train station, Desenzano. **Accommodations:** 🏨🏨🏨 (*2nd class*) Benaco; Maderno; Milano. 🏨🏨 Splendid; Eden; Garden. 🏨 La Fiorita; Diana; Garda.

Malcesine (Population: 3,000; Veneto)
Information: Via Capitanato del Porto 1. **Transportation:** Train station, Peschiera, Rovereto. **Accommodations:** 🏨🏨🏨 (*2nd class*) Olivi; Maximilian; Vega. 🏨🏨 Diana; Sirena; Piccolo Hotel. 🏨 Al Marinaio; Campagnola.

Manfredonia (Population: 53,000; Apulia)
Information: Corso Manfredi 26. **Transportation:** Harbor; Train station. **Accommodations:** 🏨🏨🏨 (*2nd class*) Gargano. 🏨🏨 Azzurro. 🏨 San Michele. *Manfredonia–Siponto:* 🏨🏨🏨 (*2nd class*) Cicolella; Apulia. 🏨 Ninfa Marina.

Mantua (Population: 61,000; Lombardy)
Information: Piazza Andrea Mantegna 6. **Transportation:** Train station. **Accommodations:** 🏨🏨🏨 (*1st class*) Rechigi. 🏨🏨🏨 (*2nd class*) Dante; Mantegna; Apollo; Cristallo.

Marsala (Population: 86,000; Sicily)
Information: Via Mario Rapisardi 8. **Transportation:** Harbor; Train station. **Accommodations:** 🏨🏨🏨 (*2nd class*) Stella d'Italia; Cap 3000. 🏨🏨🏨 (*Motel*) MotelAgip, exit Mazara del Vallo.

Matera (Population: 41,800; Basilicata)
Information: Piazza Vittorio Veneto 19. **Transportation:** Train station. **Accommodations:** 🏨🏨🏨 (*2nd class*) President; De Nicola. 🏨🏨 Italia. 🏨 Moderno; Roma.

Menaggio (Population: 4,000; Lombardy)
   Information: Via Lusardi 8; Piazza Garibaldi 7. **Transportation:** Train station; Como. **Accommodations:** 🏨🏨🏨 (*1st class*) Grand Hotel Victoria. 🏨🏨🏨 (*2nd class*) Bellavista. 🏨🏨 Loveno; Miralago; Corona. 🏨 Meneghet; Vapore.

Merano (Population: 34,000; Trentino–Alto Adige)
   Information: Corso Libertà 47. **Transportation:** Train station, Bolzano. **Accommodations:** 🏨🏨🏨 (*Luxury*) Palace. 🏨🏨🏨 (*1st class*) Grand Hotel Bristol; Meranerhof. 🏨🏨🏨 (*2nd class*) Eurotel; Baviera. 🏨🏨 Iris; Lux; Kofler. 🏨 Hedy; Alba; Salut.

Messina (Population: 270,000; Sicily)
   Information: Piazza Caivoli 45, Via Giordano Bruno 121. **Transportation:** Ferry: Villa San Giovanni, Reggio di Calabria and others; Train station. **Accommodations:** 🏨🏨🏨 (*1st class*) Jolly, Via Garibaldi 126; Royal Palace, Via Tommaso Canizzaro. 🏨🏨🏨 (*2nd class*) Venezia, Piazza Cairoli 4; Paradis, Via Pompea 441; Europa on Highway 114 in Pistunina. 🏨🏨 Moderno Terminus, Via I. Settembre 15; Panoramic in Colle San Rizzo.

Milan (Milano) (Population: 1.8 million; Lombardy)
   Information: Via Marconi 1, main train station. **Transportation:** Airport, Linate (7 km.; 4 miles) and Malpensa (16 km.; 9.5 miles); Train station. **Accommodations:** 🏨🏨🏨 (*Luxury*) Palace, Piazza della Repubblica; Principe e Savoia, Piazza della Repubblica 17. 🏨🏨🏨 (*1st class*) Executive, Viale Luigi Sturzo 45; Jolly Touring, Via Tarchetti 2. 🏨🏨🏨 (*2nd class*) Auriga, Via Pirelli 7; Manin, Via Manin 7; Ariosto, Via Ariosto 22; Florida, Via Lepetit 33; Star, Via dei Bossi 5; Mediterraneo, Via Muratori 14; Astoria, Viale Murillo 9. 🏨🏨 Garden, Via Rutilia 6; Cervo, Piazzale Principessa Clotilde; Gala, Viale Zara 89. 🏨🏨🏨 (*Motel*) MotelAgip, on the south exit of the highway in San Donato; MotelAgip in west Milan on the Autostrada Tangenziale.

Milazzo (Population: 30,000; Sicily)
   Transportation: Ferry to Aeolian Islands; Train station. **Accommodations:** 🏨🏨🏨 (*1st class*) Residenzial; Eolian Inn Park; Silvanetta Palace. 🏨🏨🏨 (*2nd class*) Saverly. 🏨🏨 Mignon Riviera; Flora.

Modena (Population: 180,000; Emilia-Romagna)
   Information: Corso Canalgrande 1A. **Transportation:** Train station. **Accommodations:** 🏨🏨🏨 (*1st class*) Fini Hotel (Italhotel), Via Emilia Est; Canalgrande, Corso Canal Grande 6. 🏨🏨🏨 (*2nd class*) Eden, Via Emilia Ovest 666; Donatello, Via Giardini 402. 🏨🏨 Estense, Viale Berengario 11; Libertà, Via Blasia 10. 🏨 La Torre, Via Cervetta 5. 🏨🏨🏨 (*Motel*) MotelAgip, northern entrance.

Modica (Population: 47,000; Sicily)
Transportation: Train station. **Accommodations:** 🏨 (*Motel*) Motel di Modica. 🏨 Minerva.

Monreale (Population: 24,000; Sicily)
Information: see Palermo. **Transportation:** Train station, Palermo. **Accommodations:** 🏨 (*2nd class*) Carrubella. 🏨 Il Ragno. 🏠 Savoia.

Montecatini Terme (Population: 21,000; Tuscany)
Information: Viale Verdi 66. **Transportation:** Train station. **Accommodations:** 🏨 (*Luxury*) Grand Hotel & la Pace. 🏨 (*1st class*) Croce di Malta. 🏨 (*2nd class*) Astoria. 🏨 Torretta; Biondi; Reale. 🏠 Giusti; Umbria; Palo Alto.

Montegrotto Terme (Population: 1,500; Veneto)
Information: Viale Stazione 56. **Transportation:** Train station, Padua. **Accommodations:** 🏨 (*Luxury*) International Bertha. 🏨 (*1st class*) Augustus Terme; Garden Terme; Terme Neroniane. 🏨 (*2nd class*) Continental; Terme Cristallo; Vulcania. 🏨 Eliseo; Luna; Mondial. 🏠 San Marino; Antiche Terme.

Montepulciano (Population: 14,000; Tuscany)
Transportation: Train station. **Accommodations:** 🏨 (*2nd class*) Tre Stelle. 🏨 Panoramic; Marzocco. 🏠 Tiziana; Ambra.

Naples (Napoli) (Population: 1.3 million; Compania)
Information: Palazzo Reale; Via Partenope 10a; Via San Carlo 15; Stazione Centrale; Stazione Mergellina; Stazione Marittima; Stazione Circumvesuviana; Aeroporto Capodichino. **Transportation:** Airport, Capodichino (5 km.; 3 miles); Ferry: Capri, Procida, Ischia, Sorrento, Cagliari, Palermo, Catania, Messina, Aeolian Islands, and others; Train station. **Accommodations:** 🏨 (*Luxury*) Excelsior, Via Partenope 48. 🏨 (*1st class*) Vesuvio (Italhotel), Via Partenope 45. 🏨 (*2nd class*) Royal, Via Partenope 38; Jolly, Via Medina 70; San Germano, Via Beccadelli 41; Palace Hotel, Piazza Garibaldi; Rex, Via Palepoli 12; Serius, Viale Augusto 74. 🏨 Cristal, Via Torino 108; Eden, Corso Novara 9; Sayonara, Piazza Garibaldi 60; Miramare, Via Nazario Sauro 24; Splendid, Via Manzoni 96; Domitiana, Viale Kennedy 143. 🏠 Astoria, Via Santa Lucia 90; Colibri, Via Caracciolo 10; Del Sole, Via Santa Lucia 76. 🏨 (*Motel*) MotelAgip, in Secondigliano, on Via Nazionale (8 km.; 5 miles) from city center.

Noli (Population: 2,500; Liguria)
Information: Corso Italia 8. **Transportation:** Train station. **Accommodations:** 🏨 (*2nd class*) Capo Noli; Miramare. 🏨 Diana; Miramare. 🏠 Pontevecchio; L'Ancora.

Nuoro (Population: 35,000; Sardinia)
Information: Piazza Italia 9. **Transportation:** Train station. **Accommodations:** 🏨🏨🏨 (*1st class*) Sandalia. 🏨🏨🏨 (*2nd class*) Grazia Deledda; Grillo; Moderno. 🏨🏨🏨 (*Motel*) MotelAgip, Via Trieste. *Monte Ortobene*: 🏨🏨 Fratelli Sacchi.

Olbia (Population: 30,000; Sardinia)
Information: Via Catello Piro 1. **Transportation:** Ferry: Genoa, Civitavecchia and others; Train station, Civitavecchia; Airport, Olbia. **Accommodations:** 🏨🏨🏨 (*1st class*) President. 🏨🏨🏨 (*2nd class*) De Plam. 🏨🏨 Gallura; Mastino; Minerva. *Olbia-Porto Rotondo:* 🏨🏨🏨 (*1st class*) Relais Sporting, San Marco. *Olbia-San Pantaleo:* 🏨🏨🏨 (*2nd class*) Rocce Sarde. *Olbia-Pittulongu:* 🏨🏨🏨 (*2nd class*) Pozzo Sacro. *Costa Corallina:* 🏨🏨🏨 (*2nd class*) La Capanna.

Orta San Giulio (Population: 1,200; Valle d'Aosta)
Information: Piazza M. Motta. **Transportation:** Train station. **Accommodations:** 🏨🏨🏨 (*1st class*) San Rocco. 🏨🏨 Orta; La Bussola.

Ortisei (Sankt Ulrich) (Population: 5,000; Trento–Alto Adige)
Information: Piazza Stetteneck. **Transportation:** Train station, Ponte Gardena. **Accommodations:** 🏨🏨🏨 (*1st class*) Aquila; Hell. 🏨🏨🏨 (*2nd class*) Gardena; Engel. 🏨🏨 Astoria; Digon; Ladinia; Murit; Somont.

Orvieto (Population: 30,000; Umbria)
Information: Piazza del Duomo 24. **Transportation:** Train station. **Accommodations:** 🏨🏨🏨 (*2nd class*) Maitani; Aquila Bianca; Italia; La Badia. 🏨🏨 Virgilio; Europa; Kristall; Orvieto Residence. 🏨 Corso.

Ospedaletti (Population: 4,000; Lombardy)
Information: Corso Regina Margherita 1. **Transportation:** Train station. **Accommodations:** 🏨🏨🏨 (*1st class*) Le Rocce del Capo. 🏨🏨🏨 (*2nd class*) Petit Royal; Floreal; Firenze. 🏨🏨 Lia; Savoia; Marisida. 🏨 Italia.

Otranto (Population: 5,000; Apulia)
Information: Via Garibaldi 9. **Transportation:** Train station, Lecce. **Accommodations:** 🏨🏨🏨 (*2nd class*) Miramare. 🏨 Bellavista.

Padua (Padova) (Population: 240,000; Veneto)
Information: Piazzetta Pedrocchi 18; Atrio Stazione Ferroviaria. **Transportation:** Train station. **Accommodations:** 🏨🏨🏨 (*1st class*) Plaza, Corso Milano 40. 🏨🏨🏨 (*2nd class*) Grande Italia, Corso del Popolo 81. 🏨🏨 Igea, Via Ospedale Civile 87; Mignon, Via Luca Belludi 22. 🏨 Piccola Vienna, Via Beato Pellegrino 133; Al Camin, Via Cavalotti 44.

Paestum–Capaccio (Population: 6,000; Campania)
Information: Via Aquilia. **Transportation:** Train station, Salerno.

Accommodations: 🏨 (*2nd class*) Calypso; Park Motel; Schuhmann; Taverna dei Re; Mec; Ariston. 🏨 Olimpia; Villa Rita. 🏨 (*Motel*) Paestum. 🏨 Clorinda; La Sorgente. 🏨 (*Motel*) Autostello ACI; Park Motel.

Palermo (Population:701,000; Sicily)
   Information: Piazza Castelnuovo 34–35; Vialla Igiea; Piazza S. Sepolcro; also in the train station and airport, and at the harbor. **Transportation:** Airport, Punta Rarsi (30 km.; 18 miles); Ferry: Naples, Cagliari, Tunis, Tripoli, and others; Train station. **Accommodations:** 🏨 (*Luxury*) Villa Igiea Grand Hotel, Salita Belmonte 1. 🏨 (*1st class*) Jolly, Foro Italico; Europa, Via Agrigento 3; Mediterraneo, Via Rosolino Pilo 44. 🏨 (*2nd class*) Centrale, Corso Vittorio Emanuele 327; Sole, Corso Vittorio Emanuele 291. 🏨 Bristol, Via Maqueda 437; Touring, Via M. Stabile 136; Moderno, Via Roma 276. 🏨 Firenze, Via Candelai 68; Orientale, Via Maqueda 26. (*Motel*) MotelAgip, Viale della Regione Siciliana.

Palestrina (Population: 13,000; Latium)
   Transportation: Train station. **Accommodations:** 🏨 Stella.

Pallanza–Verbania (Population: 10,500; Piedmont)
   Information: Corso Zanitello 6. **Transportation:** Train station. **Accommodations:** 🏨 (*1st class*) Majestic. 🏨 (*2nd class*) Astor; Belvedere; San Gottardo; Miralago in Intra. 🏨 Sant'Anna; Italia. 🏨 Touring in Intra.

Palmi (Population: 22,000; Calabria)
   Information: Piazza I. Maggio 4. **Transportation:** Train station. **Accommodations:** 🏨 (*2nd class*) Arcobaleno. 🏨 Oscar. 🏨 La Quiete. *Palmi-Lido:* 🏨 Miami. *Palmi-Pietrenere:* 🏨 South Paradise.

Pantelleria (Population: 10,000; Sicily)
   Transportation: Ferry: Trapani, Palermo, Egadi Islands. **Accommodations:** 🏨 (*2nd class*) Del Porto; Punta Tre Pietre. 🏨 Turistico Residenziale.

Parma (Population: 175,000; Emilia-Romagna)
   Information: Piazza Duomo 5. **Transportation:** Train station. **Accommodations:** 🏨 (*1st class*) Park Hotel Toscanini, Viale A. Toscanini 4; Park Hotel Stendhal, Via Bodoni 3; Palace Hotel Maria Luigia, Viale Mentana 140. 🏨 Daniel, Via Gramsci 16; Savoy, Via 20 Settembre 3; Button, Strada San Vitale 7. 🏨 Principe, Via Emilia Est 46.

Paterno (Population: 40,000; Sicily)
   Transportation: Train station. **Accommodations:** 🏨 Sicilia. *Paterno-Serra La Nava:* 🏨 Grande Albergo Etna.

Pavia (Population: 85,000; Lombardy)
   Information: Corso Garibaldi 1. **Transportation:** Train station. **Accommodations:** 🏨 (*2nd class*) Ariston; Palace; Rosengarten. 🏨 Excelsior; Splendid. 🏠 Regisole; Bella Napoli.

Perugia (Population: 142,000; Umbria)
   Information: Corso Vannucci (Palazzo Donnini) 94/a. **Transportation:** Train station. **Accommodations:** 🏨 (*1st class*) Perugia Plaza, Via Palermo 88; La Rosetta, Piazza Italia 19; Park Hotel in Ponte San Giovanni. 🏨 Grifone, Via Silvio Pellico 1; Barone, Via Tuderte 20/P; Tevere in Ponte San Giovanni.

Pesaro (Population: 93,000; Marches)
   Information: Piazza Libertà and Via Rossini 41. **Transportation:** Train station. **Accommodations:** 🏨 (*1st class*) Vittoria. 🏨 (*2nd class*) Excelsior; Baltic; Vesuvio. 🏨 Capitol; Adriana; Vienna. 🏠 K 2; Fabbri.

Pescara (Population: 137,000; Abruzzi)
   Information: Via Nicola Fabrizi 171; Corso Umberto 65. **Transportation:** Airport; Train station. **Accommodations:** 🏨 (*1st class*) Carlton, Viale Riviera 35; Singleton, Piazza Duca d'Aosta. 🏨 (*2nd class*) Maja, Viale Riviera 201. 🏨 Igea, Via Milano 81; Alba, Via Forti 14; Adria, Via Firenze 141. 🏠 Marisa, Viale Regina Margherita 39; Stella, Piazza Garibaldi 43. 🏨 (*Motel*) MotelAgip, northern entrance of the autostrada, in Montesilvano Marina.

Peschiera del Garda (Population: 8,000; Veneto)
   Information: Piazzale Betteloni 15. **Transportation:** Train station. **Accommodations:** 🏨 Laura; Milano; Peschiera; Bel Sito; La Perla. 🏠 Piccolo Hotel; San Marco; Dolci Colli; Fortuna.

Piacenza (Population: 107,000; Emilia-Romagna)
   Information: Via San Siro 17; Piazzetta dei Mercanti 10. **Transportation:** Train station. **Accommodations:** 🏨 (*1st class*) Grande Albergo Roma. 🏨 (*2nd class*) Del Capello; Florida; Nazionale. 🏨 Milano; Stella. 🏠 Cavalletto.

Piazza Armerina (Population: 21,000; Sicily)
   Information: Piazza Garibaldi. **Transportation:** Train station, Enna. **Accommodations:** 🏨 (*1st class*) Jolly. 🏨 (*2nd class*) Selene; Park Hotel Paradiso.

Pietra Ligure (Population: 10,000; Liguria)
   Information: Piazza Martiri della Libertà 31. **Transportation:** Train station. **Accommodations:** 🏨 (*1st class*) Royal. 🏨 (*2nd class*) Paco; Mediterranée; Sartore. 🏨 Geppi; Azucena. 🏠 Rosengarten; Rio; Villa Serena.

Piombino (Population: 40,000; Tuscany)
  Information: Piazza Premuda. **Transportation:** Ferry, Elba; Train station. **Accommodations:** 🏨🏨🏨 (*2nd class*) Centrale. 🏨🏨 Esperia; Colledi; Tuscania. 🏨 Italia; Moderno.

Pisa (Population: 103,000; Tuscany)
  Information: Lungarno Mediceo 42; Piazza Duomo. **Transportation:** Airport, San Giusto (3 km.; 1.5 miles); Train station. **Accommodations:** 🏨🏨🏨 (*1st class*) Grand Hotel Duomo (Italhotel), Via Santa Maria 94; D'Azeglio, Piazza Vittorio Emanuele II; Cavalieri, Piazza Stazione. 🏨🏨 Terminus, Via Colombo 45; Arno, Piazza della Repubblica. 🏨 Ariston, Via Maffi 42. *Marina di Pisa:* Information: Piazza Sardegna. 🏨 Manzi; Milena. *Pisa-Tirrenia:* Information: Largo Belvedere. 🏨🏨🏨 (*1st class*) Continental. 🏨🏨🏨 (*2nd class*) Bristol. 🏨🏨 Vittoria; Tirrenia Villa Laura. 🏨 Mediterraneo; Pensione Medusa.

Pistoia (Population: 94,000; Tuscany)
  Information: Piazza del Duomo (Palazzo Vescovi). **Transportation:** Train station. **Accommodations:** 🏨🏨🏨 (*2nd class*) Milano; Patria; Le Rose; Residence Il Convento. 🏨🏨 Appennino; Leon Bianco. 🏨 Giappone; Autisti; Firenze.

Pompeii (Population: 23,000; Campania)
  Information: Via Sacra 1. **Transportation:** Train station, Naples. **Accommodations:** 🏨🏨🏨 (*2nd class*) Bristol; Del Santuario; Villa Laura. 🏨🏨 Palma; Diomede; Europa; Fauno. 🏨 Da Amitrano; Amleto; Degli Amici; Del Santuario. 🏨 (*Motel*) Villa dei Misteri; Pompeii Scai.

Ponza Islands (Population: 6,000; Latium)
  Transportation: Ferry: Naples, Anzio, Formia, Terracina. **Accommodations:** 🏨🏨🏨 (*1st class*) Chiaia di Luna. 🏨🏨🏨 (*2nd class*) Bellavista; La Baia; Cernia. 🏨🏨 Mari; Del Capitano. 🏨 Silvia (in Santa Maria).

Porto Azzurro (Elba) (Population: 3,500; Tuscany)
  Information: see Portoferraio. **Transportation:** Train station, Piombino. **Accommodations:** 🏨🏨🏨 (*2nd class*) Plaza; Cala di Mola. 🏨🏨 Due Torri; Rocco; Belmare. 🏨 Lido (Pension); Barbarossa (Pension).

Portoferraio (Elba) (Population: 11,000; Tuscany)
  Information: Calata Italia 26. **Transportation:** Harbor; Train station, Piombino. **Accommodations:** 🏨🏨🏨 (*1st class*) Fabricia. 🏨🏨🏨 (*2nd class*) Picchiaie Residence; Massimo. 🏨🏨 Nuova Padulella; Touring. 🏨 Il Faro; Santo Stefano.

Portofino (Population: 1,200; Liguria)
  Information: Via Roma 35. **Transportation:** Ferry: Santa Margherita, San Fruttuoso, Chiavari, and others; Train station, Santa Mar-

gherita Ligure. **Accommodations:** 🏨🏨🏨 (*Luxury*) Splendido. 🏨🏨🏨 (*1st class*) Nazionale. 🏨🏨🏨 (*2nd class*) Piccolo; San Giorgio. 🏨 Eden; Puny.

Porto Torres (Population: 21,000; Sardinia)
Information: Corso V. Emanuele 9. **Transportation:** Ferry, Genoa, Civitavecchia; Train station. **Accommodations:** 🏨🏨🏨 (*2nd class*) Torres, La Casa. 🏨🏨 Da Elisa; Motel Libissonis. 🏨 Royal.

Portovenere (Population: 6,000; Liguria)
Information: see La Spezia. **Transportation:** Ferry: La Spezia, Lerici; Train station: La Spezia. **Accommodations:** 🏨🏨🏨 (*1st class*) Royal Sporting. 🏨🏨🏨 (*2nd class*) Belvedere; San Pietro. 🏨🏨 Paradiso; Le Grazie (Ortsteil Le Grazie). 🏨 Genio.

Positano (Population: 3,500; Campania)
Information: Via del Saracino 4. **Transportation:** Harbor; Train station, Naples, Salerno. **Accommodations:** 🏨🏨🏨 (*1st class*) Le Sirenuse; Miramare; Royal; San Pietro. 🏨🏨🏨 (*2nd class*) Le Sirenuse; Buca di Bacco; Casa Albertina; Covo dei Saraceni; Montemare; Poseidon; Savoia. 🏨🏨 Casa Maresca; Vittoria; Santa Caterina. 🏨 Casa Guadagno; Pupetto; Maria Luisa.

Potenza (Population: 50,000; Basilicata)
Information: Via Alianelli. **Transportation:** Train station. **Accommodations:** 🏨🏨🏨 (*2nd class*) Park; Tourist. 🏨🏨 Miramonti; Casa del Sacro Cuore. 🏨 Monticchio; Galgano.

Pozzuoli (Population: 64,000; Campania)
Information: Via Campi Flegrei 3. **Transportation:** Naples. **Accommodations:** 🏨🏨🏨 (*2nd class*) Tennis Hotel: Solfatara. 🏨🏨 San Giuseppe; Mini Hotel; Villaverde. 🏨 Flegreo. *Arco Felice–Lucrino:* 🏨🏨 Alba; Belvedere delle Rose; Villa Verde.

Prato (Population: 160,000; Tuscany)
Information: Via Luigi Muzzi 51; Via Cairoli 48. **Transportation:** Train station. **Accommodations:** 🏨🏨🏨 (*1st class*) Palace; President. 🏨🏨🏨 (*2nd class*) Moderno; Flora. 🏨🏨 Giardino; San Marco. 🏨 Centrale.

Procchio (Elba) (Population: 1,000; Tuscany)
Information: see Portoferraio. **Transportation:** Harbor; Train station, Piombino. **Accommodations:** 🏨🏨🏨 (*1st class*) Del Golfo; Desirée. 🏨🏨🏨 (*2nd class*) La Perla; Brigantino. 🏨🏨 Delfino. 🏨 L'Edera; La Pergola.

Procida, Isle of (Population: 11,600; Campania)
Transportation: Ferry: Naples, Ischia. **Accommodations:** 🏨🏨 Arcate; Riviera.

Ragusa (Population: 64,000; Sicily)
Information: Via Natalelli 131; Palazzo Camera di Commercio.
Transportation: Train station. **Accommodations:** 🏨 (*2nd class*)
Jonio; Montreal. 🏨 Tivoli; Miramare. 🏚 Belvedere.

Rapallo (Population: 20,000; Liguria)
Information: Via Diaz 9. **Transportation:** Train station. **Accommodations:** 🏨 (*Luxury*) Grand Hotel Bristol. 🏨 (*1st class*) Grande
Italia e Lido; Eurotel. 🏨 (*2nd class*) Astoria; Miramare; Giulio Cesare;
Riviera; Rosa Bianca. 🏨 Claridge; Canali; Rapallo. 🏚 L'Oblo; Astor;
Duomo.

Ravello (Population: 2,600; Campania)
Information: Piazza Duomo 10. **Transportation:** Train station,
Vietri sul Mare/Amalfi. **Accommodations:** 🏨 (*1st class*) Palumbo.
🏨 (*2nd class*) Caruso; Villa Cimbrone; Rufolo. 🏨 Giordano; Parsifal;
Toro; Villa Amore. 🏚 La Rosa dei Venti.

Ravenna (Population: 138,000; Emilia–Romagna)
Information. Piazza San Francesco; Via Salara 8. **Transportation:**
Train station. **Accommodations:** 🏨 (*1st class*) Jolly, Piazza Mameli 1;
Bisanzio (Italhotel), Via Salara 30. 🏨 Diana, Via G. Rossi 49; Cappello,
Via IV Novembre 41; Argentario, Via Roma 45; Trieste, Via Trieste 11.
🏚 Piccolo, Via Baiona 54; Teodorico, Via delle Industrie 36. *Casal Borsetti:* 🏨 Turismo Europa. 🏚 Cantuccio; Bella Romagna (Pension). *Lido
di Savio:* Information: Viale Romagna 168. 🏨 (*2nd class*) Casacci;
Cosmopol. 🏨 Rex; Venus. 🏚 Il Bisarte. *Lido di Classe:* 🏨 (*2nd class*)
Adler. 🏨 Astor; Brasilia. *Marina di Ravenna:* Information: Viale delle
Nazioni 159. 🏨 (*1st class*) Park Hotel. 🏨 (*2nd class*) Marepineta. 🏨
Serena; Alba; Internazionale; Rivaverde; Belvedere; Bristol. 🏚 Stella
Azzurra; Luna; Bermuda; Da Zama. *Marina Romea:* Information: Viale
Italia 112. 🏨 (*2nd class*) Corallo; Solaria. 🏨 Royal Columbia; Eden. 🏚
Ondina (Pension); Millipini (Pension). *Punta Marina:* Information: Via
della Fontana 4. 🏨 Elite; Clipper; Otello; 🏚 Adria; Dafne; Medusa.

Reggio di Calabria (Population: 165,000; Calabria)
Information: Via Demetrio Tripepi 72; Corso Garibaldi 329;
Stazione Centrale. **Transportation:** Airport; Harbor, Messina; Train station. **Accommodations:** 🏨 (*1st class*) Excelsior, Piazza Indipendenza.
🏨 (*2nd class*) Miramare, Via Fata Morgana 1; Primavera, Via Pentimele 177; Palace Hotel Masoanri's, Via Vittorio Veneto 95. 🏨 Eremo,
Via Eremo Botte; Esperia, Via Palamolla; Moderno, Via Torrione 67. 🏚
Abruzzo, Via Caprera 5; Noel, Via G. Zerbi; Saturnia, Via Capera 5.

Riccione (Population: 32,000; Emilia–Romagna)
Information: Piazzale Ceccarini 10, Palazzo del Turismo. **Transportation:** Train station. **Accommodations:** 🏨 (*1st class*) Savioli; Atlan-

tic; Abner's; Augustus. 🏛🏛🏛 (*2nd class*) Adlon; Baltic; Lungomare; Ambasciatori. 🏛🏛 Daniel's; Poker; Roma; Sporting. 🏛 Regen; Karina; Gardenia; Niagara.

Rieti (Population: 43,000; Latium)
   Information: Via Cintia 87; Portici del Comune. **Transportation:** Train station. **Accommodations:** 🏛🏛🏛 (*2nd class*) Quattro Stagioni; Miramonti. 🏛🏛 Europa; Serena. 🏛 Meli; Stella. *Terminillo Pian de Valli:* 🏛🏛🏛 (*1st class*) Togo Palace. 🏛🏛🏛 (*2nd class*) Cristallo. 🏛🏛 Cavallino Bianco; Belsito. 🏛 Fusacchia (Pension).

Rimini (Population: 115,000; Emilia–Romagna)
   Information: Piazzale Indipendenza. **Transportation:** Airport, Miramare (5 km.; 3 miles); Harbor; Train station. **Accommodations:** 🏛🏛🏛 (*Luxury*) Grand Hotel, Piazzale Indipendenza. 🏛🏛🏛 (*1st class*) Bellevue, Piazzale Kennedy 12; Ambasciatori, Viale A. Vespucci 22. 🏛🏛🏛 (*2nd class*) National, Viale Vespucci 42; Waldorf, Viale Vespucci 28; Club House, Viale Vespucci 52. 🏛🏛 Lotus, Via Rovani 3; Aristeo, Viale Regina Elena 106; Diplomat, Viale Regina 17; Sporting, Viale Vespucci 20; Eurogarden, Via Lettimi 3. 🏛 Nancy, Viale Leopardi 11; Atlas, Viale Regina Elena 74. *Rivazzurra di Rimini:* 🏛🏛 Christian, Viale Lecce 4; Grand Meeting, Viale Regina Margherita 46; De France, Viale Regina Margherita 48. *Miramare di Rimini:* 🏛🏛🏛 (*2nd class*) Touring, Viale Regina Margherita 82. 🏛🏛 Coronado Airport, Via Flaminia 390; Ascot, Viale Principe di Piemonte 38. 🏛 Kadett, Via Marconi 30; Giannini, Viale Principe di Piemonte 10; Belvedere, Viale Regina Margherita 80. *Rimini–Viserba:* 🏛🏛 Byron; Sirio; Albatros. 🏛 Bologna; Aurora; Costa Azzurra; Viserba. *Rimini–Viserbella:* 🏛🏛 Albatros; Sirio; Diana; Palos; Biagini. *Torre Pedrera:* 🏛🏛🏛 (*1st class*) Punta Nord. 🏛🏛🏛 (*2nd class*) El Cid; Doge; Du Lac. 🏛🏛 Acapulco; Arabesco; Ideal; Graziella. 🏛 Milanese; Ben Hur; Conti; Angeli.

Riva del Garda (Population: 13,000; Trentino–Alto Adige)
   Information: Palazzo dei Congressi. **Transportation:** Train station, Rovereto. **Accommodations:** 🏛🏛🏛 (*1st class*) Du Lac et du Parc. 🏛🏛🏛 (*2nd class*) Astoria. 🏛🏛 Diana; Brione. 🏛 Alpino.

Rome (Roma) (Population: 2.9 million; Latium)
   Information: ENIT, Via Marghera 2, also at Stazione Termini, Via Parigi 5, Leonardo da Vinci Airport (Fiumicino) and at entrances to Autostradas A1 and A2. **Transportation:** Leonardo da Vinci Airport, Fiumicino (30 km.; 18 miles); Train station. **Accommodations:** 🏛🏛🏛 (*Luxury*) Ambasciatori Palace, Via Vittorio Veneto 70; Eden, Via Ludovisi 49 (Italhotel). 🏛🏛🏛 (*1st class*) Jolly, Corso d'Italia 1; Victoria, Via Campania 41. 🏛🏛🏛 (*2nd class*) Madison, Via Marsala 60; Milani, Via Magenta 12; Aretusa, Via Gaeta 14. 🏛🏛 Stazione, Via Gioberti 36; Aris-

ton, Via Filippo Turati 16. ⌂ Pantheon, Via dei Pastini 131; Salut, Piazza Indipendenza 13. ⌂⌂ (*Motel*) MotelAgip, on Via Nazionale 1 (8 km.; 5 miles), Via Aurelia.

Rovigo (Population: 52,000; Venetia)
Information: Via H. Dunant 10; Corso del Popolo 78. **Transportation:** Train station. **Accommodations:** ⌂⌂⌂ (*1st class*) Europa Palace. ⌂⌂⌂ (*2nd class*) Corona Ferrea. ⌂⌂ Bologna. ⌂ Belvedere.

Saint Vincent (Population: 4,700; Valle d'Aosta)
Information: Via Roma 50. **Transportation:** Train station. **Accommodations:** ⌂⌂⌂ (*1st class*) Billia. ⌂⌂⌂ (*2nd class*) Elena. ⌂⌂ Corallo; Delle Rose; Dina; Henry. ⌂ Mentino; Etoile de Neige; Suisse.

Salerno (Population: 160,000; Campania)
Information: Via Velia 2; Piazza Amendola 7; Piazza Ferrovia. **Transportation:** Harbor; Train station. **Accommodations:** ⌂⌂⌂ (*1st class*) Jolly, Lungomare Trieste 1. ⌂⌂⌂ (*2nd class*) Elea, Via Trento 98; Fiorenza, Via Trento 145; Montestella, Corso Vittorio Emanuele 156. ⌂⌂ Salerno, Via G. Vicinanza 42; Suisse, Via G. B. Amendola 62; Tirreno, Corso Garibaldi 124. ⌂ La Nina, Via Trento 193; Italia, Corso Vittorio Emanuele 84; Santa Rosa, Corso Vittorio Emanuele 14; Toscana, Lungomare G. Marconi 33.

Salo (Population: 9,000; Lombardy)
Information: Lungolago Zanardelli 39. **Transportation:** Train station, Desenzano. **Accommodations:** ⌂⌂⌂ (*1st class*) Duomo. ⌂⌂⌂ (*2nd class*) Ideal; Benaco; Vigna. ⌂ Eden; Conca d'Oro; Gambero.

Salsomaggiore Terme (Population: 18,600; Emilia–Romagna)
Information: Viale Romagnosi 7. **Transportation:** Train station. **Accommodations:** ⌂⌂⌂ (*Luxury*) Grand Hotel Milano. ⌂⌂⌂ (*1st class*) Centrale Bagni; Porro. ⌂⌂⌂ (*2nd class*) Valentini; Cavour-Bolognese. ⌂⌂ Cristallo; Excelsior; Suisse. ⌂ Panda; Brescia.

San Felice Circeo (Population: 5,500; Latium)
Information: Piazza Luigi Lanzuisi. **Transportation:** Train station, Terracina. **Accommodations:** ⌂⌂⌂ (*1st class*) Maga Circe. ⌂⌂⌂ (*2nd class*) Le Pleiadi; Circeo; Neanderthal; Punta Rossa. ⌂⌂ Golfo Sereno; Da Alfonso al Faro. ⌂ Mastropeppe.

San Gimignano (Population: 9,000; Tuscany)
Information: Piazza del Duomo 1. **Transportation:** Train station, Poggibonsi. **Accommodations:** ⌂⌂⌂ (*2nd class*) La Cisterna; Bel Soggiorno; Pescille; Leon Bianco.

San Giovanni Rotondo (Population: 22,000; Apulia)
Information: Piazza Europa 104. **Transportation:** Train station,

Foggia. **Accommodations:** 🏨 (*2nd class*) Gaggiano; Parco delle Rose; Suore San Giuseppe. 🏨 Vittorio; San Pietro; Santoro; Santa Maria delle Grazie. 🏠 Bianco; Sollievo.

Santa Cristina Valgardena (Population: 1,500; Trentino–Alto Adige)

Information: Via Chemun 25b. **Transportation:** Train station, Ponte Gardena. **Accommodations:** 🏨 (*1st class*) Diamant; Monte Pana. 🏨 (*2nd class*) Post; Cristallo. 🏨 Gardena; Max. 🏠 Tannenheim; Geier.

San Remo (Population: 62,000; Liguria)

Information: Largo Nuvoloni 1. **Transportation:** Train station. **Accommodations:** 🏨 (*Luxury*) Royal (Italhotel). 🏨 (*1st class*) Gran Hotel Londra. 🏨 (*2nd class*) Miramare; Des Etrangers; Villa Maria. 🏨 Morandi; Nizza; Nike. 🏠 Eletto; Polonia.

Santa Margherita Ligure (Population: 12,000; Liguria)

Information: Corso Rainusso 2, Via XXV Aprile 2/b. **Transportation:** Ferry, Portofino; Train station. **Accommodations:** 🏨 (*Luxury*) Imperial Palace; Grand Hotel Miramare (Italhotel). 🏨 (*1st class*) Lido Palace; Metropole. 🏨 (*2nd class*) Minerva; Helios; La Vela; Mediterraneo. 🏨 Jolanda; Europa; Conte Verde; Terminus; Lombardia & Bristol. 🏠 Rosy; San Giorgio.

Santa Maria Capua Vetere (Population: 32,000; Campania)

Transportation: Train station. **Accommodations:** 🏨 (*2nd class*) Milano. 🏠 (*Motel*) Motel delle Mostre.

Santa Marinella (Population: 8,000; Latium)

Information: Via Aurelia 363. **Transportation:** Train station, Rome. **Accommodations:** 🏨 (*2nd class*) Cavalluccio Marino; Le Naiadi. 🏨 Del Sole.

Sant'Antioco, Isle of (Population: 11,000; Sardinia)

Information: Piazza De Gasperi. **Transportation:** Harbor; Train station. **Accommodations:** 🏨 Moderno. 🏠 Mercury; Sant'Antiaco. *Capo Sperone:* 🏨 La Fazenda.

Santa Teresa di Gallura (Population: 3,500; Sardinia)

Information: Piazza Vittorio Emanuele 1. **Transportation:** Train station, Palau. **Accommodations:** 🏨 (*2nd class*) Shardana (by the Capo Testa). 🏨 Corallaro; Li Nibbari. 🏠 Marinario; Esit-Miramare; Bacchus; Belvedere.

Sapri (Population: 7,500; Campania)

Transportation: Train station. **Accommodations:** 🏨 Santa Caterina; Tirreno; Vittoria. 🏠 Riviera; Traiano.

Sassari (Population: 100,000; Sardinia)
Information: Piazza d'Italia 19. **Transportation:** Airport, Fertilia (35 km.; 21 miles); Harbor, Porto Torres (19 km.; 12 miles); Train station. **Accommodations:** 🏛🏛🏛 (*1st class*) Jolly Grazia Deledda, Viale Dante 47. 🏛🏛 Frankhotel, Via Armando Diaz 20; Marini in Ottava. 🏛 Giusy, Piazza Sant'Antonio 22; Paradiso (pension), Via Cavour 55; Famiglia (pension), Viale Umberto 65. 🏛🏛🏛 (*Motel*) MotelAgip, in Serra Secca (2 km.; 1 mile, from city center). *Sassari–Stintino:* 🏛🏛🏛 (*2nd class*) Grand Hotel Rocca Ruja, Capo Falcone. 🏛🏛 Lina; Silvestrino.

Savona (Population: 80,000; Liguria)
Information: Via Paleocapa 9 and 59. **Transportation:** Harbor; Train station. **Accommodations:** 🏛🏛🏛 (*2nd class*) Astoria; Riviera Suisse. 🏛🏛 Acqui; Italia; Pessano; San Marco. 🏛 Ghione. 🏛🏛🏛 (*Motel*) MotelAgip, in Zinola, Via Nizza 62.

Scanno (Population: 2,800; Abruzzi)
Information: Piazza Santa Maria della Valle 12. **Accommodations:** 🏛🏛🏛 (*2nd class*) Mille Pini; Miramonti; Park Hotel; Del Lago. 🏛🏛 Belvedere; Vittoria; Seggiovia. 🏛 Eden.

Sciacca (Population: 36,000; Sicily)
Information: Corso Vittorio Emanuele 84. **Transportation:** Harbor; Train station. **Accommodations:** 🏛🏛🏛 (*1st class*) Delle Terme. *Sciacca–San Calogero:* 🏛🏛 Monte Kronio.

Senigallia (Population: 40,000; Marches)
Information: Piazza Morandi 2. **Transportation:** Train station. **Accommodations:** 🏛🏛🏛 (*1st class*) Excelsior. 🏛🏛🏛 (*2nd class*) City; Cristallo; Baltic; Italia. 🏛🏛 Mareblu; Olimpia. 🏛 Trieste; Garden.

Serra San Bruno (Population: 3,000; Calabria)
Transportation: Train station, Chiaravalle. **Accommodations:** 🏛🏛 Certosa. 🏛 Centrale.

Sestriere (Population: 800; Piedmont)
Information: Piazza Agnelli 11. **Transportation:** Train station, Turino. **Accommodations:** 🏛🏛🏛 (*2nd class*) Grand Hotel Sestriere; Cristallo. 🏛🏛 Belvedere; Miramonti. 🏛 Olimpic; Sud-Ovest.

Siena (Population: 64,000; Tuscany)
Information: Via di Città 5; Banchi di Sotto 20; Piazza del Campo. **Transportation:** Train station. **Accommodations:** 🏛🏛🏛 (*Luxury*) Park Hotel, Via di Marciano 16. 🏛🏛🏛 (*1st class*) Certosa di Maggiano, Strada di Certosa 82; Villa Scacciapensieri (Italhotel), Via di Scacciapensieri 24. 🏛🏛🏛 (*2nd class*) Castagneto, Via dei Cappuccini 55; Garden, Via Custoza 2; Minerva, Via Garibaldi 72. 🏛🏛 Lea; Viale 24 Maggio 10.

Sirmione (Population: 2,300; Lombardy)
Information: Località Colombare; Viale Marconi 2. **Transportation:** Train station, Desenzano. **Accommodations:** 🏨🏨🏨 (*Luxury*) Grand Hotel Terme. 🏨🏨🏨 (*2nd class*) Catullo; Riel. 🏨🏨 Benaco; Mauro. 🏨 Pace; Speranza.

Siusi (Population: 700; Trento–Alto Adige)
Transportation: Train station, Bolzano. **Accommodations:** 🏨🏨🏨 (*1st class*) Edelweiss. 🏨🏨🏨 (*2nd class*) Siusi and Villa Hermes; Enzian; Bad Ratzes. 🏨🏨 Ortler; Plunger. 🏨 Florian; Dolomitenhof; Waldrast. *Alpe die Siusi:* 🏨🏨🏨 (*1st class*) Eurotel Siciliar. 🏨🏨🏨 (*2nd class*) Steger-Dellai. 🏨🏨 Paradiso; Santer. 🏨 Monte Piz; Icaro; Zorzi.

Sorrento (Population: 13,500; Campania)
Information: Via Luigi de Maio 35; Via Correale 7. **Transportation:** Ferry: Naples, Capri, Ischia; Train station, Naples. **Accommodations:** 🏨🏨🏨 (*1st class*) Vesuvio; Aminta; Belair; Carlton; Cesare Augusto; Continental; Europa Palace; Excelsior–Vittoria; Imperial-Tramontano; Parco dei Principi; President; Bristol; Royal. 🏨🏨🏨 (*2nd class*) Atlantic; Bellevue; Central; Claridge; Continental; Eden; La Solara; Plaza; Ascot; Bellevue Syrene. 🏨🏨 Astoria; Britannia; Del Mare; Desiree; Girasole; Santa Lucia; Villa Igea; Tourist. 🏨 Faro; Il Pozzo; Apollo; Schweizerhof; Rivoli; Del Corso.

Sperlonga (Population: 5,000; Latium)
Transportation: Train station. **Accommodations:** 🏨🏨🏨 (*2nd class*) Grand Hotel La Playa; Parkhotel Fiorelle; Miralago. 🏨🏨 Amyclae; La Sirenella; Major; Aurora. 🏨 Saloon; Corallo.

Spoleto (Population: 40,000; Umbria)
Information: Piazza della Libertà 7. **Transportation:** Train station. **Accommodations:** 🏨🏨🏨 (*2nd class*) Dei Duchi. 🏨🏨 Manni; Europa. 🏨 Clarici; Nuovo Clitunno.

Spotorno (Population: 2,800; Liguria)
Information: Via Aurelia 43. **Transportation:** Train station. **Accommodations:** 🏨🏨🏨 (*2nd class*) Royal. 🏨🏨 Ligure; La Pineta; Tirreno; Roma; Aurora. 🏨 Zunino; Vallega; L'Inglese.

Stresa (Population: 6,000; Piedmont)
Information: Piazzale Europa 1. **Transportation:** Train station. **Accommodations:** 🏨🏨🏨 (*Luxury*) Grand Hotel et des Iles Borromées. 🏨🏨🏨 (*1st class*) Regina Palace. 🏨🏨🏨 (*2nd class*) Milan au Lac; Astoria. 🏨🏨 Speranza du Lac; Della Torre; Royal; La Fontana. 🏨 Primavera; Meeting; Italie e Suisse. *Isola Bella:* 🏨 Elvezia. *Isola dei Pescatori:* 🏨🏨🏨 (*2nd class*) Verbano. 🏨 Belvedere.

Stromboli (See Aeolian Islands)

Subiaco (Population: 9,100; Latium)
Information: Via Cadorna 59. **Transportation:** Train station, Rome.
Accommodations: 🏨 Belvedere; Roma. *Subiaco–Monte Livata:* 🏨🏨🏨
(*2nd Class*) Livata. 🏨 Italia. 🏨 La Genziana. *Subiaco–Campo
dell'Osso:* 🏨🏨🏨 (*2nd class*) Europa.

Sulmona (Population: 24,000; Abruzzi)
Information: Piazza Garibaldi 63; Corso Ovidio 286. **Transporta-
tion:** Train station. **Accommodations:** 🏨🏨🏨 (*2nd class*) Artu; Traffico.
🏨 Salvador; Armando. 🏨 Stella.

Susa (Population: 8,000; Piedmont)
Transportation: Train station. **Accommodations:** 🏨🏨🏨 (*2nd class*)
Napoleon. 🏨 Meana. 🏨 Stazione; Sole; Tre Corone.

Syracuse (Siracusa) (Population: 116,000; Sicily)
Information: Via Maestanza 33; Main train station. **Transportation:**
Ferry: Catania, Messina, Naples, Malta and others; Train station.
Accommodations: 🏨🏨🏨 (*1st class*) Jolly, Corso Gelone 45. 🏨🏨🏨 (*2nd
class*) Panorama, Via Necropoli Grotticelle 33; Villa Politi, Via Politi 2;
Park, Via Filisto 80. 🏨 Scala Greca, Via Avola 7; Riviera, Via Eucleida
9; Aretusa, Via F. Cripsi 75. 🏨 Centrale, Corso Umberto 141; Milano,
Corso Umberto 10. 🏨🏨🏨 (*Motel*) MotelAgip, Viale Teracati 30/32. *Sir-
acusa–Priolo:* 🏨 Royal.

Taggia-Arma di Taggia (Population: 14,000; Liguria)
Information: Via P. Boselli. **Transportation:** Train station. **Accommodations:** 🏨🏨🏨 (*1st class*) Vittoria-Grattacielo. 🏨🏨🏨 (*2nd class*) Miramare; Arma. 🏨 Europa; Svizzera. 🏨 Milano; Giuan; Roma.

Tagliacozzo (Population: 5,000; Abruzzi)
Information: Piazza Andrea Argoli. **Transportation:** Train station.
Accommodations: 🏨🏨🏨 (*1st class*) Garden. 🏨🏨🏨 (*2nd class*) Bocconcino;
Nuovo Marina. 🏨 Gatto d'Oro. 🏨 Stella.

Taormina (Population: 9,000; Sicily)
Information: Largo Santa Caterina; Corso Umberto 144. **Transpor-
tation:** Airport, Catania; Train station, Giardini–Taormina. **Accommodations:** 🏨🏨🏨 (*Luxury*) San Domenico Palace. 🏨🏨🏨 (*1st class*) Jolly
Hotel Diodoro; Excelsior Palace. 🏨🏨🏨 (*2nd class*) Timeo; Vello d'Oro;
Bristol Park Hotel; Méditerranée; Villa Riis; Villa Paradiso; Continental; Sole-Castello; San Michele. 🏨 Condor; La Campanella; Belsog-
giorno. *Taormina–Mazzarò:* 🏨🏨🏨 (*Luxury*) Mazzarò Sea Palace
(Italhotel). 🏨🏨🏨 (*1st class*) Atlantis Bay. 🏨🏨🏨 (*2nd class*) Baia Azzurra;
Isola Bella. 🏨 Ionic Hotel Mazzarò. 🏨 Villa Amenta (pension); Raneri
(pension). *Giardini-Naxos:* 🏨🏨🏨 (*2nd class*) Arathena Rocks; Kalos;
Nike; Sporting Baja. 🏨 Costa Azzurra; Panoramic. 🏨 La Riva (pension); Del Sole (pension).

Taranto (Population: 240,000; Apulia)
Information: Corso Umberto 113. **Transportation:** Airport, Grottaglie (20 km.; 12 miles); Harbor; Train station. **Accommodations:** ☗☗☗ (*1st class*) Mar Grande Park Hotel, Viale Virgilio 90; Palace, Viale Virgilio 10. ☗☗☗ (*2nd class*) President, Via Campania 136; Plaza, Via d'Aquino 46. ☗☗ Imperiale, Via Pitagora 94; Miramare, Via Roma 4; Aquila 'Oro, Via Margherita 8. ☗ Dandolo, Piazza Fontana 3. *Taranto–Lido Azzurro:* ☗☗☗ (*2nd class*) Tritone. *Riva dei Tessali:* ☗☗☗ (*1st class*) Residence Club.

Tarquinia–Lido di Tarquinia (Population: 13,300; Latium)
Information: Piazza Cavour 1. **Transportation:** Train station. **Accommodations:** ☗☗☗ (*2nd class*) G. H. Helios. ☗☗ Tarconte. ☗ Velca Mare; Miramare.

Tempio Pausania (Population: 15,000; Sardinia)
Information: Piazza Gallura. **Transportation:** Train station, Sassari. **Accommodations:** ☗☗☗ (*2nd class*) Petit Hotel. ☗☗ Delle Sorgenti; San Giuseppe; San Carlo. *Monte Limbara:* ☗☗☗ (*2nd class*) Valliciola.

Teramo (Population: 50,000; Abruzzi)
Information: Via del Castello. **Transportation:** Train station. **Accommodations:** ☗☗☗ (*2nd class*) Abruzzi; Garden; Gran Sasso. ☗ Vittoria; Touring.

Terlano (Terlan) (Population: 1,700; Trentino–Alto Adige)
Transportation: Train station. **Accommodations:** ☗☗☗ (*2nd class*) Moarhof; Weingarten. ☗☗ Greifenstein; Platzer. ☗ Hubertus; Seebacher.

Termini Imerese (Population: 25,000; Sicily)
Information: Via Municipio 1. **Transportation:** Airport; Harbor. **Accommodations:** ☗ Elena.

Terni (Population: 112,000; Umbria)
Information: Via Cesare Battisti 7/A. **Transportation:** Train station. **Accommodations:** ☗☗☗ (*1st class*) Valentino; Garden. ☗☗☗ (*2nd class*) De Paris; Allegretti. ☗☗ Brenta; Motel Tiffany.

Terracina (Population: 36,000; Latium)
Information: Via Lungo Linea 156. **Transportation:** Train station. **Accommodations:** ☗☗☗ (*2nd class*) L'Approdo Grand Hotel; River; Riva Gaia. ☗☗ Meson Feliz; Piccolo Hotel; Torino. ☗ Astoria; Lido; Hegelberger; Villa Selma.

Tivoli (Population: 46,000; Latium)
Information: Vicolo Missione 3; Piazzale Nazioni Unite. **Transportation:** Train station, Rome. **Accommodations:** ☗☗☗ (*2nd class*) Motel River. ☗☗ Padovano. ☗ Monte Ripoli; Eden Sirene. *Bagni di Tivoli:* ☗☗☗ (*2nd class*) Delle Terme. ☗ Delle Rose; Grottino.

Todi (Population: 19,000; Umbria)

Information: Piazza del Popolo. **Transportation:** Train station. **Accommodations:** 🏨 (*1st class*) Bramante. 🏨 (*2nd class*) Villaluisa. 🏨 Zodiaco.

Torbole (Population: 2,200; Trentino–Alto Adige)

Information: Via Lungolago Verona. **Transportation:** Train station, Rovereto. **Accommodations:** 🏨 (*2nd class*) Piccolo Mondo. 🏨 Ifigenia; Paradiso; Villabella. 🏨 Monte Baldo; Santa Lucia; Goethe.

Torino (Turin) (Population: 1.2 million; Piedmont)

Information: Via Roma 222; Stazione Porta Nuova. **Transportation:** Airport; Train station. **Accommodations:** 🏨 (*Luxury*) Jolly Hotel Principi di Piemonte. Via P. Gobetti 15. 🏨 (*1st class*) Turin Palace Hotel (Italhotel), Via Sacchi 8. 🏨 (*2nd class*) Jolly Hotel Ambasciatori, Corso Vittorio Emanuele 104; Concord, Via Lagrange 47; City, Via Juvara 25; Royal, Via Regina Margherita 249. 🏨 Patria, Via Cernaia 42; Alexandra, Lungo Dora Napoli 14; Genio, Corso Vittorio Emanuele 47; Victoria, Via Nino Costa 4. 🏨 Eden, Via Donizetti 22; Cristallo, Corso Traiano 28/9; Giada, Via Gasparo Barbera 6. 🏨 (*Motel*) MotelAgip, Settimo Torinese (Autostrada, northern exit).

Torre del Lago Puccini (Population: 1,800; Tuscany)

Information: Viale Marconi 209. **Transportation:** Train station, Viareggio. **Accommodations:** 🏨 (*2nd class*) National Park. 🏨 Da Antonio. 🏨 Da Pina; Butterfly (pension); Giuly (pension).

Toscolano–Maderno (See Maderno)

Trani (Population: 44,000; Apulia)

Information: Corso Cavour 83. **Transportation:** Train station. **Accommodations:** 🏨 (*2nd class*) Holiday; Trani. 🏨 Capirro; Riviera. 🏨 Italia; Romagna.

Trapani (Population: 70,000; Sicily)

Information: Corso Italia 10; Piazzetta Saturno. **Transportation:** Airport, Birgi (14 km.; 8 miles); Ferry, Egadi Islands; Train station. **Accommodations:** 🏨 (*2nd class*) Astoria Park Hotel. 🏨 Cavallino Bianco. 🏨 Vittoria.

Tremezzo (Population: 1,800; Lombardy)

Information: Via Regina 3. **Transportation:** Train station, Como. **Accommodations:** 🏨 (*1st class*) Grand Hotel Tremezzo. 🏨 (*2nd class*) Bazzoni & Du Lac. 🏨 Rusall; Azalea; Villa Edy.

Tremiti Islands (Apulia)

San Domino (Population: 4,000): **Transportation:** Ferry: Manfredonia, Vieste, Rodi Garganico, Termoli, Vasto, Ortona, and others. **Accommodations:** 🏨 (*2nd class*) Kyrie. 🏨 San Domino. 🏨 Gabbiano.

Trento (Trient) (Population: 99,000; Trentino–Alto Aidge)
Information: Via Alfieri 4; Piazza Dante 1. **Transportation:** Train station. **Accommodations:** 🏨🏨 (*2nd class*) Grand Hotel Trento. 🏨 America; Alessandro Vittoria. 🏨 Ancora; Monaco; Roma.

Trevi (Population: 8,000; Umbria)
Information: Piazza Mazzini 6. **Transportation:** Train station. **Accommodations:** 🏨🏨🏨 (*1st class*) Della Torre. 🏨 Il Cochetto.

Treviso (Population: 89,000; Veneto)
Information: Via Toniolo 41. **Transportation:** Airport; Train station. **Accommodations:** 🏨🏨🏨 (*1st class*) Continental. 🏨🏨🏨 (*2nd class*) Carlton; Al Foghèr; Cà del Galletto. 🏨 Campeol; Al Cuor.

Trieste (Population: 300,000; Friuli–Venezia Giulia)
Information: Via G. Rossini 6/I; Piazza dell'Unità d'Italia 4; Main train station. **Transportation:** Airport, Ronchi (3 km.; 1.5 miles); Train station. **Accommodations:** 🏨🏨🏨 (*1st class*) Jolly, Corso Cavour 7; Grand Hotel Duchi d'Aosta, Unità d'Italia 2. 🏨🏨🏨 (*2nd class*) Colombia, Via della Geppa 18; San Giusto, Via Belli 3; Continentale, Via San Nicolò 25. 🏨 Abbazia, Via della Geppa 20; Brioni, Via Ginnastica 2; Istria, Via Timeus 5. 🏨 Al Collio, Piazza Venezia 4; Fiore, Via Zonta 4. 🏨🏨🏨 (*Motel*) MotelAgip, Autostrada Duino-south. *Sistiana:* 🏨🏨🏨 (*1st class*) Europa. 🏨🏨🏨 (*2nd class*) Posta. 🏨 Alla Pineta; Belvedere; Dolina. 🏨 Alabarda; Al Centro. *Opicina:* 🏨🏨🏨 (*1st class*) Park Hotel Obelisco. 🏨 Daneu. 🏨 Malalan; Diana; Valeria. *Grignano:* 🏨🏨🏨 (*Luxury*) Adriatico Palace. 🏨🏨🏨 (*2nd class*) Riviera. 🏨 Mignon.

Tropea (Population: 9,000; Calabria)
Transportation: Train station. **Accommodations:** 🏨🏨🏨 (*2nd class*) La Pineta; Park Hotel. 🏨 Virgilio; Costa Azzurra; Punta Faro.

Urbino (Population: 17,000; Marches)
Information: Via Puccinotti 35. **Transportation:** Train station. **Accommodations:** 🏨🏨🏨 (*2nd class*) Montefeltro. 🏨 Due Querce; Italia. 🏨 Panoramic.

Ustica, Island of (Population: 1,500; Sicily)
Information: Piazza Vito Longo 7. **Transportation:** Ferry, Palermo. **Accommodations:** 🏨🏨🏨 (*2nd class*) Grotta Azzurra. 🏨 Cottage; Patrice; Stella Marina. 🏨 Clelia.

Varazze (Population: 15,000; Liguria)
Information: Viale Nazioni Unite. **Transportation:** Train station. **Accommodations:** 🏨🏨🏨 (*2nd class*) Cristallo; Eden; Aristo; Savoy; El Chico. 🏨 Ideale; Europa.

Vasto (Population: 30,000; Abruzzi)
Information: Piazza del Popolo 18–20. **Transportation:** Train station. **Accommodations:** 🏨🏨🏨 (*2nd class*) Panoramic; Total. 🏨 Palizzi; Nuova Italia. *Marina di Vasto:* Information: Rotonda del Lungomare Dalmazia. 🏨🏨🏨 (*2nd class*) Royal; Baiocco; Adriatico. 🏨 (*Motel*) Perrozzi. 🏨 Bristol; Europa; Lido. *Vasto–Punta Penna:* 🏨 Faro; La Vela.

Venice (Venezia) (Population: 368,000; Venetia)
Information: Castello 4421; San Marco 71 c; Piazzale Roma; Stazione Santa Lucia. **Transportation:** Airport, Tessera (8 km.; 5 miles); Train station. **Accommodations:** 🏨🏨🏨 (*Luxury*) Bauer-Grunwald. 🏨🏨🏨 (*1st class*) Monaco e Grand Canal, San Marco 1325 (Italhotel); Park, Giardino Papadopol (Italhotel). 🏨🏨🏨 (*2nd class*) Capri, Santa Croce 595; Boston, San Marco 848. 🏨 Atlantico, Castello 4416; San Fantin, San Marco 1930A. 🏨 San Giorgio, San Marco 3781. *Venezia–Lido:* 🏨🏨🏨 (*Luxury*) Excelsior. 🏨🏨🏨 (*1st class*) Des Bains. 🏨🏨🏨 (*2nd class*) Cappelli; Rigel. 🏨 Sorriso; Cristallo; Reiter. 🏨 Giardinetto.

Ventimiglia (Population: 27,000; Liguria)
Information: Via Cavour 61. **Accommodations:** 🏨🏨🏨 (*2nd class*) Bel Soggiorno; Francia. 🏨 Sole e Mare; Calipso. 🏨 Lido; XX Settembre.

Vercelli (Population: 53,000; Piedmont)
Information: Viale Garibaldi 90. **Transportation:** Train station. **Accommodations:** 🏨🏨🏨 (*2nd class*) Viotti; Modo; Europa. 🏨 Cerruti; Brusasca. 🏨 Valsesia; Sport.

Verona (Population: 266,000; Veneto)
Information: Piazza Bra 10. **Transportation:** Airport, Verona-Villafranca; Train station. **Accommodations:** 🏨🏨🏨 (*Luxury*) Due Torri, Piazza Sant'Anastasia 4 (Italhotel). 🏨🏨🏨 (*1st class*) Colomba d'Oro, Via C. Cattaneo 10. Accademia, Via Scala 12; Victoria, Via Adua 8. 🏨🏨🏨 (*2nd class*) Italia; Via G. Mameli 64. 🏨 Piccolo, Via Camuzzoni 3. 🏨🏨🏨 (*Motel*) MotelAgip, Via Unità d'Italia, Via Nazionale, east entrance.

Viareggio (Population: 60,000; Tuscany)
Information: Viale G. Carducci 10. **Transportation:** Train station. **Accommodations:** 🏨🏨🏨 (*1st class*) Astor & Residence (Italhotel). 🏨🏨🏨 (*2nd class*) Miramare; Liberty. 🏨 Metropol; Lupori. 🏨 Baghino; Dal Fattore; Carrara (pension).

Vibo Valentia (Population: 27,000; Calabria)
Information: Piazza Dïaz 8. **Transportation:** Train station. **Accommodations:** 🏨🏨🏨 (*1st class*) 501 Hotel. 🏨 Risorgimento. 🏨 Il Terrazzino; Miramonti. *Vibo Valentia Marina:* 🏨 S. Venere; Miramare; La Capannina.

Vicenza (Population: 120,000; Veneto)

Information: Piazza Duomo 5; Piazza Matteotti. **Transportation:** Train station. **Accommodations:** 🏨 (*2nd class*) Europa, Viale San Lazzaro. 🏨 Cristina, Corso SS. Felice e Fortunato 32; Continental, Viale Trissino 89; Alfa Hotel, Via dell'Oreficeria 50. 🏨 Castello, Piazza Castello 26; Trieste, Viale Trieste 81. 🏨 (*Motel*) MotelAgip, Via degli Scaligeri, Zona Fiera.

Vietri sul Mare (Population: 8,000; Campania)

Transportation: Train station. **Accommodations:** 🏨 (*2nd class*) Raito (in Raito). 🏨 La Lucertola; Bristol. 🏨 Vietri. *Vietri–Marina:* 🏨 Ancora. *Vietri–Raito:* 🏨 (*1st class*) Raito.

Villa San Giovanni (Population: 14,500; Calabria)

Information: Main train station. **Transportation:** Ferry, Messina; Train station. **Accommodations:** 🏨 (*2nd class*) Piccolo. 🏨 Cotroneo. 🏨 Moderno; Orientale. *Cannitello:* 🏨 (*2nd class*) Castello di Alta Fiumara; Santa Trada Residence; Home. 🏨 (*Motel*) Autostello ACI.

Vipiteno (Sterzing) (Population: 5,000; Trentino–Alto Adige)

Information: Piazza Città 3. **Transportation:** Train station for the Brenner Line: Munich, Innsbruck, Brenner, Bressanone, Bolzano, Trento, Verona, Venice, and others. **Accommodations:** 🏨 (*2nd class*) Schwarzer Adler. 🏨 Goldenes Kreuz; Fugger; Hubertushof; Wipptaler Hof; Lamm. 🏨 Sterzinger Hof; Goldene Krone; Elisabeth; Nestl; Helene.

Viterbo (Population: 58,000; Latium)

Information: Piazzale dei Caduti 14; Piazza Verdi 4 a. **Transportation:** Train station. **Accommodations:** 🏨 (*2nd class*) Mini Palace; Balletti Park (in San Martino al Cimino). 🏨 Leon d'Oro; Oasi (on Route S2). 🏨 Tuscia.

Voghera (Population: 42,000; Lombardy)

Transportation: Train station. **Accommodations:** 🏨 (*2nd class*) Domus; Rallye; Reale d'Italia; Zenit.

Volterra (Population: 18,000; Tuscany)

Information: Via Turazza 2. **Transportation:** Train station. **Accommodations:** 🏨 (*2nd class*) San Lino. 🏨 Nazionale; Etruria.

Index

(If more than one page number appears next to the name of a site, the number in boldface indicates the page where the detailed description appears in the text.)